Alchemies of the Mind
Rationality and the Emotions

JON ELSTER

CAMBRIDGE
UNIVERSITY PRESS

PUBLISHED BY THE PRESS SYNDICATE OF THE UNIVERSITY OF CAMBRIDGE
The Pitt Building, Trumpington Street, Cambridge CB2 1RP, United Kingdom

CAMBRIDGE UNIVERSITY PRESS
The Edinburgh Building, Cambridge CB2 2RU, UK   http://www.cup.cam.ac.uk
40 West 20th Street, New York, NY 10011-4211, USA   http://www.cup.org
10 Stamford Road, Oakleigh, Melbourne 3166, Australia

© Jon Elster 1999

First published 1999

Printed in the United States of America

Typeset in Palatino 10/12 pt. in LATEX 2$_\varepsilon$ [TB]

A catalog record for this book is available from the British Library

Library of Congress Cataloging-in-Publication Data
Elster, Jon, 1940–
Alchemies of the mind : rationality and the emotions / Jon Elster.
p.   cm.
Includes bibliographical references and index.
ISBN 0-521-64279-5 (hardcover). – ISBN 0-521-64487-9 (pbk.)
1. Emotions.   2. Emotions – Social aspects.   3. Emotions in
literature.   I. Title.
BF531.E   1999
152.4 – dc21   98-24493
                                                           CIP

ISBN 0 521 64279 5 hardback
ISBN 0 521 64487 9 paperback

Alchemies of the Mind

Jon Elster has written a comprehensive, wide-ranging book on the emotions in which he considers a large variety of theoretical approaches.

Drawing on history, literature, philosophy, and psychology, Elster presents a full account of the role of the emotions in human behavior. While acknowledging the importance of neurophysiology and laboratory experiment for the study of emotions, Elster argues that the serious student of the emotions can learn more from the great thinkers and writers of the past, from Aristotle to Jane Austen. He attaches particular importance to the work of the French moralists, notably La Rochefoucauld, who demonstrated the way the need for esteem and self-esteem shapes human motivation. The book also maintains a running dialogue with economists and rational-choice theorists.

Combining methodological and theoretical arguments with empirical case studies and written with Elster's customary verve and economy, this book will have a broad appeal to students and scholars in philosophy, psychology, economics, and political science, as well as literary studies, history, and sociology.

"Elster draws instructively on sources as varied as social psychology, history, game theory, neuroscience, fiction, and the philosophy of science. The book is exceptionally insightful, and it achieves a remarkable synthesis of divergent bodies of literature that perhaps no one else could have accomplished."

Alfred Mele, Davidson College

"This book will undoubtedly find a wide readership, not only among the fans of Elster's previous work, but among the growing number of specialists in various fields who have become captivated by the theory of emotion."

Ronald de Sousa, University of Toronto

Jon Elster is Robert K. Merton Professor of Social Science at Columbia University and author of twelve previous books, of which nine have been published by Cambridge University Press.

For C. F.

Contents

Contents

Preface and Acknowledgments

In this book I return to some of the themes I discussed in *Sour Grapes* (1983). An equivalent of sour grapes is "sweet lemons," the transmutation of bitterness into sweetness, analogous to that of base metals into gold. The mental alchemies that I discussed in that earlier book, notably in the title chapter, had a limited range. In particular, they did not have any place for the *emotions* as fuel, raw material, and final product of these processes. The purpose of the present book is to say something about the role of the emotions in mental life and in the generation of behavior.

In Chapter I I propose an account of explanation in the social sciences that, although less ambitious than nomological explanation, goes beyond mere narrative or description, however "thick." The central idea is that of a *mechanism*, a recurring and intelligible causal pattern. The emotional reactions, mental alchemies, and other forms of psychic causality that I discuss elsewhere in the book are instances of mechanisms in this sense.

In Chapter II I discuss some prescientific or, better, extrascientific sources for the study of the emotions. I first consider Aristotle, whose account of emotions in the *Rhetoric* remains utterly fresh and insightful. Next, I consider the treatment of emotions by the French moralists, from Montaigne to La Bruyère. Finally, I discuss what we can learn about the emotions from a handful of novelists and playwrights: Shakespeare, Racine, Mme de Lafayette, Jane Austen, Stendhal, and George Eliot.

In Chapter III I discuss a subset of the emotions in their social and historical context. I first consider shame, in its relation to social norms and to other "self-conscious emotions," notably guilt. Next I consider envy and related emotions, and I conclude by discussing the emotions involved in the pursuit of honor. A running theme in this chapter is the distinction between the social emotions that are based on comparison, such as envy, and those that are based on interaction, such as anger.

Chapters II and III serve two functions. On the one hand they discuss texts and behavioral patterns that I believe to be intrinsically interesting in their own right. On the other hand, they provide numerous examples of specific emotional reactions and mechanisms on which I draw in Chapter IV, in which I move closer to a general account of the emotions. Here, I first try to summarize current psychological views of the emotions. I then consider whether emotions enhance or undermine rational choice, and whether the emotions themselves can be assessed by standards of rationality.

In Chapter V, drawing on the discussion of the French moralists in Chapter II and on the discussion of irrational emotions in Chapter IV, I discuss the causes and reasons that make people hide their motivations from themselves and from others. On the one hand, there is the phenomenon of unconscious transmutation of one motive into another. On the other hand, there is the phenomenon of conscious misrepresentation of one's motives in front of an audience. Whereas earlier chapters address themselves mainly to philosophers, psychologists, and historians, this chapter is more oriented toward economics, political science, and law. I believe in fact that the relevance of emotion ranges across all the social sciences, the humanities, and legal studies. I hope the book can help making that relevance better appreciated.

Nancy Cartwright, G. A. Cohen, Robyn Dawes, Dagfinn Føllesdal, Peter Hedström, George Loewenstein, Richard Posner, Nils Roll-Hansen, Bernt Stigum, and the late Amos Tversky commented on an earlier version of Chapter I. I also benefited from comments by the participants in a conference on mechanisms in Stockholm in June 1996, and from discussions with John Ferejohn, Bernard Manin, Pasquale Pasquino, Adam Przeworksi, and Susan Stokes. Bernard Manin, Amélie Rorty, and Bernard Williams gave critical and constructive comments on my discussion of Aristotle in Chapter II. Chapter III relies heavily on two previous papers on envy and revenge, the first published in a *Festschrift* for Thomas Schelling edited by Richard Zeckhauser (1991), and the second in *Ethics* (1990). I thank William Miller for his helpful comments on my discussion of his work in an earlier draft. Chapter IV grew out of a course I taught at Columbia University in 1995. I am grateful to my students for their contributions, and to John Alcorn, Akeel Bilgrami, Russell Hardin, and Roger

Petersen for taking the time to talk to us about their work. Earlier versions of Chapter V were presented at talks at the University of California at Irvine in February 1995, at a conference on ethics and economics in Oslo, December 1995, and at a conference on rationality and cognition at Georgetown Law Center in November 1996. I am grateful to John Ferejohn and Mike Seidman for their comments at the latter meeting, and to Siri Gullestad and Sissel Reichelt for comments on that chapter. I also want to acknowledge useful comments by Louis-André Gerard-Varet, A. Leroux, Pierre Livet, and Alain Wolfelsperger at a colloquium in Marseille in June 1997.

Atul Kohli read Chapters I and V of an earlier draft. Avner Ben-Ze'ev, David Cohen, Joseph Frank, David Laitin, Robert Merton, and Roger Petersen read the entire draft. I benefited greatly from their comments. I am particularly indebted to Robert Merton for urging me to write the Coda. Finally, I want to thank Aida Llalaby for her invariably friendly and competent assistance, my research assistant Joshua Rosenstein, as well as Cheryl Seleski and the marvelously efficient library staff at the Russell Sage Foundation, which provided me with a fellowship to finish this book.

Chapter I

A Plea for Mechanisms

I.1. INTRODUCTION

Are there lawlike generalizations in the social sciences? If not, are we thrown back on mere description and narrative? In my opinion, the answer to both questions is no. The main task of this chapter is to explain and illustrate the idea of a *mechanism* as intermediate between laws and descriptions. Roughly speaking, mechanisms are *frequently occurring and easily recognizable causal patterns that are triggered under generally unknown conditions or with indeterminate consequences*. They allow us to explain, but not to predict. An example from George Vaillant gives a flavor of the idea: "Perhaps for every child who becomes alcoholic in response to an alcoholic environment, another eschews alcohol in response to the same environment."[1] Both reactions embody mechanisms: doing what your parents do and doing the opposite of what they do. We cannot tell ahead of time what will become of the child of an alcoholic, but if he or she turns out either a teetotaler or an alcoholic we may suspect we know why.

Over the years, I have increasingly come to view the ideal of lawlike explanation ("covering-law explanation") in history and the social sciences as implausible and fragile. Early on, I was struck by Paul Veyne's discussion of the idea of providing a nomological explanation of Louis XIV's unpopularity. Suppose we start from the generalization that "any king imposing excessive taxes becomes unpopular." To take care of counterexamples, we would soon have to modify the statement by introducing exceptions and qualifications, the cumulative effect of which would be to "reconstitute a chapter of the history of the reign of Louis XIV with the amusing feature of being written in the

---

1. Vaillant (1995), p. 65.

1

present and the plural" rather than in the past tense and the singular.[2] Later Raymond Boudon offered forceful arguments in the same vein.[3]

I was even more struck by the total lack of consensus among the best practitioners in the social sciences and by the numerous failures of prediction – both the failures to predict and the predictions that failed. My own studies of collective bargaining[4] and of the allocation of scarce goods[5] entrenched this generally skeptical attitude, bordering on explanatory nihilism. The downfall of Communism in Eastern Europe and its subsequent reemergence provide two stunning examples of massive social changes that were virtually unanticipated by the scientific community. The virulent civil war in the former Yugoslavia offers another. What pulled me back from the nihilist conclusion was the recognition that the idea of a mechanism could provide a measure of explanatory power.

As I reached this conclusion I discovered that it had been anticipated by Nancy Cartwright's claim that "the laws of physics lie." Hence the resort to explanation by mechanism in the social sciences may not be due to their less developed state or to the complexity of their subject matter, but to more general facts about human understanding or about the world. The following passage will convey some of the flavor of Cartwright's argument:

Last year I planted camellias in my garden. I know that camellias like rich soil, so I planted them in composted manure. On the other hand, the manure was still warm, and I also know camellia roots cannot take high temperatures. So I did not know what to expect. But when many of my camellias died, despite otherwise perfect care, I knew what went wrong. The camellias died because they were planted in hot soil. . . .

So we have an explanation for the death of my camellias. But it is not an explanation from any true covering law. There is no law that says that camellias just like mine, planted in soil which is both hot and rich, die. To the contrary, they do not all die. Some thrive; and probably those that do, do so *because* of the richness of the soil they were planted in. We may insist that there must be some differentiating factor which brings the case under a covering law: in soil which is rich and hot, camellias of one kind die; those of another thrive. I will not deny that there may be such a covering law. I merely repeat that our ability to give this humdrum explanation precedes our knowledge of that

2. Veyne (1971), p. 198.
3. Boudon (1984).
4. Elster (1989a).
5. Elster (1992).

law. On the Day of Judgment, when all laws are known, these may suffice to explain all phenomena. But in the meantime we do give explanations; and it is the job of science to tell us what kinds of explanations are admissible.[6]

Cartwright's example relies on what I call *type B mechanisms*. Briefly defined (see I.2 for a fuller discussion), they arise when we can predict the triggering of two causal chains that affect an independent variable in opposite directions, leaving the net effect indeterminate. I contrast them with *type A mechanisms*, which arise when the indeterminacy concerns which (if any) of several causal chains will be triggered. An example from the natural sciences of type A mechanisms can be taken from fear-elicited behavior in animals.[7] Environmental stimuli can trigger one of three mutually incompatible fear reactions: fight, flight, or freeze. We know something about the conditions that trigger these reactions. Thus, "in response to a painful shock, animals will typically show increased activity, run, jump, scream, hiss or attack a suitable target (e.g., another animal) in their vicinity; but, in response to a stimulus associated with shock, the animal will most likely freeze and remain silent. [The] brain mechanisms that mediate these two kinds of reactions are quite distinct."[8] But although we can identify the conditions that trigger freeze versus either fight or flight, we do not know which will trigger fight versus flight. "Rather than thinking in terms of two systems for reaction to different classes of punishment, it makes better sense to imagine a single fight/flight mechanism which receives information about all punishments and then issues commands *either* for fight *or* for flight depending on the total stimulus context in which punishment is received."[9] But to say that the independent variable is "the total stimulus context" is equivalent to saying that the two responses are triggered under "generally unknown conditions." Cartwright's example and the flight–fight example provide robust instances of mechanisms in the natural sciences.[10]

In developing the idea of a mechanism I proceed as follows. In I.2 I provide a somewhat more precise definition of the notion of a mechanism. In I.3, I discuss proverbs as a source of insight into

---

6. Cartwright (1983), pp. 51–2. The substance of Cartwright's book being concerned with quantum mechanics, this homely example obviously cannot convey more than "some of the flavor" of her argument.
7. I am indebted to Nils Roll-Hansen for suggesting this example.
8. Gray (1991), p. 244.
9. *Ibid.*, p. 255.
10. In IV.2 I give examples of type A and B mechanisms that are observed in the physiological expression of the emotions.

3

mechanisms. In I.4 and I.5 I discuss the privileged place of mechanism reasoning in Montaigne and Tocqueville. Sections I.3 through I.5 overlap to some extent with the more systematic sections, and some readers may find them confusing or redundant. I believe, however, that it is worthwhile showing that the idea of a mechanism, far from being a novel or radical innovation, has deep roots in common-sense psychology as well as in the writings of some of the greatest social thinkers.[11] In particular, because mechanisms are so central to Tocqueville's thinking and Tocqueville so central for the study of mechanisms, I draw on his work throughout this chapter. In I.6 I discuss some pairs of psychological mechanisms in more detail. In I.7 I indicate how these elementary mechanisms may form building blocks in constructing more complex explanations. In I.8 I discuss some conditions under which it may be possible to move beyond the ex post identification of mechanisms to predictive statements ex ante. Section I.9 offers a few conclusions.

I.2. EXPLAINING BY MECHANISMS

Let me begin by clearing up a terminological ambiguity. In *Explaining Technical Change*, I used the term "mechanism" in a sense that differs from the one adopted here.[12] In that work I advocated the *search for mechanisms* as more or less synonymous with the reductionist strategy in science. The explanation of cell biology in terms of chemistry and of chemistry in terms of physics are strikingly successful instances of the general strategy of explaining complex phenomena in terms of their individual components. In the social sciences this search for mechanisms (or for "microfoundations") is closely connected with the program of *methodological individualism* – the idea that all social phenomena can be explained in terms of individuals and their behavior.

In that earlier analysis, the antonym of a mechanism is a *black box*.[13] To invent an example at random, suppose somebody asserted that

---

11. My experience when finding the idea of a mechanism in these writers can itself be analyzed in terms of mechanisms. On the one hand, the discovery produced a "recognition effect" that made me feel good. As these great writers had the idea, there must be something to it. On the other hand, the discovery produced a "humiliation effect" that made me feel bad. As they thought of it first, I have less of which to be proud. I am not sure about the net effect, but I think it is positive.
12. Elster (1983a).
13. But see Suppes (1970), p. 91, for the point that "one man's mechanism is another man's black box"; along similar lines, see also King et al. (1994), p. 86.

unemployment causes wars of aggression and adduced evidence for a strong correlation between the two phenomena. We would hardly accept this as a lawlike generalization that could be used in explaining specific wars, unless we were provided with a glimpse inside the black box and told *how* unemployment causes wars. Is it because unemployment induces political leaders to seek new markets through wars? Or because they believe that unemployment creates social unrest that must be directed towards an external enemy, to prevent revolutionary movements at home? Or because they believe that the armament industry can absorb unemployment? Although many such stories are conceivable, some kind of story must be told for the explanation to be convincing, where by "story" I mean "lawlike generalization at a lower level of aggregation."

In the present analysis, the antonym of a mechanism is a scientific *law*. A law asserts that given certain initial conditions, an event of a given type (the cause) will *always* produce an event of some other type (the effect). An example: If we keep consumer incomes constant, an increase in the price of a good will cause less of it to be sold ("the law of demand"). Again, we may ask for a story to support the law. One story could be that consumers maximize utility. Gary Becker showed, however, that the law of demand could also be supported by other stories, such as that consumers follow tradition or even that they behave randomly.[14]

In more abstract terms, a law has the form "If conditions $C_1, C_2, \ldots$ C_n obtain, then always E." A covering-law explanation amounts to explaining an instance of E by demonstrating the presence of $C_1, C_2,$ $\ldots C_n$. At the same abstract level, a statement about mechanisms might be "If $C_1, C_2, \ldots C_n$ obtain, then sometimes E." For explanatory purposes, this may not seem very promising. It is true, for instance, that when there is an eclipse of the moon, it sometimes rains the next day, yet we would not adduce the former fact to explain the latter. But consider the idea that when people would like a certain proposition to be true, they sometimes end up believing it to be true. In this case, we often do cite the former fact to explain the latter, relying on the familiar mechanism of wishful thinking.

This is not a lawlike phenomenon. Most people hold some beliefs that they would like to be false. Ex ante, we cannot predict when they will engage in wishful thinking – but when they do, we can recognize it after the fact. Of course, the mere fact that a person adopts a

14. Becker (1962).

belief that he would like to be true does not show that he has fallen victim to wishful thinking. Even if the belief is false or (more relevantly) inconsistent with information available to him, we cannot infer that this mechanism is at work. He might, after all, just be making a mistake in reasoning that happens to lead to a conclusion that he would like to be true. To conclude that we are indeed dealing with wishful thinking, more analysis is needed. Is this a regular pattern in his behavior? Does he often stick to his beliefs even when evidence to the contrary becomes overwhelmingly strong? Does he seem to be strongly emotionally attached to his belief? Can other hypotheses be discarded? By standard procedures of this kind we can conclude, at least provisionally, that wishful thinking was indeed at work on this particular occasion. In doing so, we have offered an explanation of why the person came to hold the belief in question. The mechanism provides an explanation because it is *more general* than the phenomenon that it subsumes.

In my earlier terminology, going from a black-box regularity to a mechanism is to go from "if A, then always B" to "if A, then always C, D, and B." In this perspective, mechanisms are good because their finer grain enables us to provide better explanations. Understanding the details of the causal story reduces the risk of spurious explanations, that is, of mistaking correlation for causation. Also, knowing the fine grain is intrinsically more satisfactory for the mind.[15] On the view set out in the present chapter, the move from theory to mechanism is from "if A, then always B" to "if A, then sometimes B." In this perspective, mechanisms are good only because they enable us to explain when generalizations break down. They are not desirable in themselves, only *faute de mieux*. Because fine grain *is* desirable in itself, I also urge the further move to "if A, then sometimes C, D, and B."

Mechanisms often come in pairs. For instance, when people would like the world to be different from what it is, wishful thinking is not the only mechanism of adjustment. Sometimes, as in the story of the fox and the sour grapes, people adjust by changing their desires rather than their beliefs.[16] But we cannot make a lawlike statement to the effect that, "Whenever people are in a situation in which rational principles of belief formation would induce a belief that they would like to be false, they fall victim either to wishful thinking or to adaptive preference formation." To repeat, most people hold some beliefs that they

15. On both points, see Elster (1983a), Chapter I.
16. Elster (1983b).

would like to be false. Or take another pair of mechanisms: Adaptive preferences versus counteradaptive preferences (sour grapes versus forbidden fruit). Both phenomena are well known and easily recognizable: Some people prefer what they can have; others tend to want what they do not or cannot have. Yet it would be absurd to assert that all people fall in one of these two categories. Similarly, some people are conformists, some are anticonformists (they do the opposite of what others do), and some are neither.

When the paired mechanisms are mutually exclusive, they are what I call type A mechanisms. An explicit recognition of this phenomenon is found in a discussion of the gambler's fallacy and its nameless converse:

When in a game there is a 50% chance of winning, people expect that a small number of rounds will also reflect this even chance. This is only possible when runs of gains and losses are short: a run of six losses would upset the local representativeness. This mechanism may explain the well-known gamblers fallacy: the expectation that the probability of winning increases with the length of an ongoing run of losses. The representativeness heuristic predicts that players will increase their bet after a run of losses, and decrease it after a run of gains. This is indeed what about half the players at blackjack tables do.... But the other half show the reverse behaviour: they increase their bets after winning, and decrease them after losing, which is predicted by the availability heuristic. After a run of losses, losing becomes the better available outcome, which may cause an overestimation of the probability of losing. [The] repertoire of heuristics predicts both an increase and decrease of bet size after losing, and *without further indications about conditions that determine preferences for heuristics, the whole theoretical context will be destined to provide explanations on the basis of hindsight only.*[17]

Yet paired mechanisms can also operate together, with opposite effects on the dependent variable. Even when the triggering of these mechanisms is predictable, their net effect may not be. These are what I call type B mechanisms. For an example, consider the impact of taxes on the supply of labor:

A high marginal tax rate lowers the opportunity cost or "price" of leisure, and, as with any commodity whose price is reduced, thereby encourages people to consume more of it (and thus do less work). But, on the other hand, it also lowers people's incomes, and thereby may induce them to work harder so

---

17. Wagenaar (1988), p. 13; italics added.

and lost than never to have lost at all." I return to Tennyson's and Donne's dicta in I.6.

- *Don't put all your eggs in one basket.* This advice for portfolio diversification may be contrasted with the advice suggested by the phrase *Jack of all trades and master of none,* that is, that one should invest heavily in one line of activity rather than spread oneself thinly over many. In situations that are characterized both by risk aversion and increasing marginal returns, either advice might trigger the decision.[31]
- *Haste makes waste.* This dictum may be contrasted with *he who hesitates is lost.* As in the previous pair, one mechanism reflects the benefits of conservatism and the other the dangers of conservatism. The *Random House Dictionary* cites Robert Fulghum saying, "Place your bet somewhere between haste-makes-waste and he-who-hesitates-is-lost."[32] Whatever the value of this idea as a piece of advice, I conjecture that it is inadequate to explain actual choices. Because of the difficulty in determining the proper compromise between the two considerations, there may be a tendency to opt for one of the extremes.
- *To remember a misfortune is to renew it.* This proverb may be contrasted with *the remembrance of past perils is pleasant.*[33] The two ideas correspond to the endowment effect and the contrast effect respectively, further discussed in I.6.
- *Familiarity breeds contempt.* A rough contrast to this mechanism is what we may call the "Thaler endowment effect,"[34] to distinguish it from the "Tversky endowment effect" that I discuss in I.6. On the one hand, "My neighbour's domestic arrangements, his house and his horse, though equal to my own are better than my own, because they are not mine."[35] On the other hand, "People often demand much more to give up an object than they would be willing to pay to acquire it."[36]

---

31. On one conception of risk aversion, it *means* decreasing marginal returns. For the conception I have in mind here, see Bromiley and Curley (1992).
32. Titelman (1996), p. 131.
33. Both occur in the main collection of proverbial sayings from antiquity, the *Sentences* of Publilius Syrus (see Nisard 1869–78, vol. 6, pp. 797, 775). Syrus also includes the positive version of the second proverb, *past happiness augments present misery* (*ibid.*, p. 769).
34. Thaler (1980).
35. Montaigne (1991), p. 720; see also Shattuck (1996), p. 70.
36. Thaler, Kahneman, and Knetsch (1992), p. 63.

- *If you've got it, flaunt it.* The opposite idea is also listed, *if you've got it, hide it.* On the one hand, many people enjoy provoking and basking in the envy of others. On the other hand, envy may trigger destructive urges in the envious and thus induce the possessor of riches to hide them from the sight of others, including the tax collector. (See also III.3.)
- *Whoever is not a great enemy is not a great friend.* This proverb from Dournon's dictionary may be contrasted with another from the same source, *who is cruel to his enemies will be rude to his friends.* In I.6 I cite a similar pair of sayings from Plutarch about the relation between attitudes towards friends and towards enemies.
- *Necessity is the mother of invention.* This dictum may be contrasted with a Norwegian proverb, *it is expensive to be poor.* On the one hand, poverty enhances the motivation to innovate. On the other hand, it deprives one of the resources that may be necessary for innovation. I return to this desire–opportunity pair in I.6.
- *Nothing succeeds like success.* Against this proposition we may set the saying that *pride goes before a fall.* The two are related to the gambler's fallacy and its converse as discussed in the passage from Wagenaar cited above. Yet the two pairs also differ. In games of pure chance, positive or negative autocorrelations are figments of the gambler's imagination. They may help us explain how he places his bets, but not how the dice fall. In games of skill and similar activities, however, the correlations may actually help us explain the outcomes. On the one hand, success may breed confidence that breeds more success. On the other hand, success may breed overconfidence that breeds failure, either by making the person behave more carelessly or (thought the Greeks) by triggering divine punishment.[37]

I.4. MECHANISMS IN MONTAIGNE

Reading Tocqueville's *Democracy in America* helped me to formulate the idea of a mechanism. Later, reading Montaigne's *Essays* with this idea in mind helped me both to understand him better and to refine the concept. Here, I begin with Montaigne.[38]

37. Dodds (1951), p. 31.
38. All page references to Montaigne (1991).

this phenomenon under the heading of "reactance" (see I.2). In various experiments, he eliminated options from the choice set of subjects[47] and found that the options were valued more highly after the elimination than before.[48] He adds, however, that "a 'sour grapes' effect was noted in some of the results, which . . . presumably mitigated the reactance effects."[49]

On reflection, we need to distinguish among three different phenomena: People can align their preferences with what they do not have, with what they cannot have, and with what they are forbidden to have. The first is the sheer desire for novelty, which, if satisfied, immediately yields to a new desire. The second is the tendency to desire objects that are not merely absent or forbidden, but strictly unattainable: The grass is always greener on the other side of the fence. The third is forbidden fruit proper. The attraction of extramarital relationships, for instance, often owes a great deal to this mechanism.

These three mechanisms differ in their fine grain. Only the first is intrinsically dissonance-producing. A person who when in Chicago always wishes to be in New York and vice versa cannot durably alleviate his tension by acting to realize his desire. The second mechanism may have a more reasonable explanation. The desire for an unattainable object may not be a desire to possess it, only a desire that it be attainable. To do something because you cannot do otherwise is intrinsically unsatisfactory. Even if you like it and prefer it to anything else, you may still suspect that you like it *because* you cannot do otherwise. Your preference might just be sour grapes, and that's a souring thought. Montaigne tells an amusing story about Thales: When he "condemned preoccupations with thrift and money-making he was accused of sour grapes like the fox. It pleased him, for fun, to make a revealing experiment; for this purpose he debased his knowledge in the service of profit and gain, setting up a business which in one year brought in as much wealth as the most experienced in the trade were hard put to match in a lifetime."[50] Others might make

---

47. When the options were objects to be allocated at random rather than chosen by the subject, the eliminated options tended to decrease rather than increase in value (Brehm 1966, p. 27).
48. Noting that the effect may arise because knowledge that an object is unavailable suggests that it is popular and therefore worthwhile having, he tried to exclude this influence (*ibid.*, pp. 15, 24).
49. *Ibid.*, p. 37; see also n. 19 above.
50. Montaigne (1991), p. 153; see also Aristotle's *Politics* 1259ᵃ 7–20. Thus La Rochefoucauld did not get it quite right when he argued that "[t]he scorn for riches displayed by the philosophers was a secret desire to recompense their own merit for the

the same experiment to prove to themselves that the desire is their own and not shaped by necessity. Fasting is not like starving.[51] As for forbidden fruit proper, the satisfaction derived from overcoming the obstacles to possession may make the process worthwhile even if possession itself is quickly followed by satiation.

Is there a mechanism that is to forbidden fruit as wishful thinking is to sour grapes? In other words, does the phenomenon of counteradaptive preferences have an analogue in *counterwishful thinking*? To answer this question, we would need a better understanding of dissonance creation in general. Whereas dissonance reduction serves an obvious psychic function, it is not clear what need if any is served by dissonance creation. It could be that it serves no need at all, but simply reflects some kind of psychic malfunctioning, a "crossing of the wires in the pleasure machine," to use a phrase of Amos Tversky's (personal communication). It could also be, however, that even frustration of desires provides some benefits. Most of us at some time have enjoyed the pleasures of self-pity. To achieve them, we may either renounce material benefits or take a psychic short-cut by adjusting our desires or beliefs so that we can tell ourselves that the situation is hopeless. The reward from self-pity is a bit like the reward from scratching a sore.[52] If there is something to this idea, we can extend the earlier analysis to counteradaptive preferences and counterwishful thinking: Even though they satisfy the same short-term need, their long-term consequences may differ. I return to the issue of counterwishful thinking in Chapters II and IV.

SPILLOVER, COMPENSATION, AND CROWDING OUT

The compensation effect and the spillover effect were briefly mentioned in I.5. An example from Plutarch can be taken from his essay "How to Profit from One's Enemies." Here he first observes "that a man is farthest removed from envying the good fortune of his friends or the success of his relatives, if he has acquired the habit of commending his enemies, and feeling no pang and cherishing no grudge when they prosper."[53] This is the spillover effect: Envy of one's enemies

injustice of Fortune by scorning those very benefits she had denied them; it was a private way of remaining unsullied by poverty; a devious path towards the high respect they could not command by wealth." (Maxim 54).
51. Sen (1993), p. 40.
52. See Ainslie (1992) for an analysis of the latter phenomenon.
53. Plutarch, "How to profit from one's enemies," 91B

tends to induce envy of one's friends. A few pages later he notes that "since all human nature bears its crop of contention, jealousy and envy . . . , a man would profit in no moderate degree by venting these emotions upon his enemies, and turning the course of such discharges, so to speak, as far away from his associates and relatives."[54] This is the compensation effect: Envy of one's enemies immunizes against envy of one's friends.

More formally, the spillover effect is that if a person follows a certain pattern of behavior P in one sphere of his life, X, he will also follow P in sphere Y. The compensation effect is that if he does not follow P in X, he will do so in Y. To these we should add the *crowding-out effect*: If he does follow P in X, he will not do so in Y. If the compensation effect and the crowding-out effect obtain simultaneously, they yield a *zero-sum effect*.[55]

Tocqueville's analyses of American democracy rely heavily on these mechanisms and on their interaction. Rather than repeating what I have written elsewhere on this topic,[56] I give some examples from other subject matters and other writers. I begin with an example from discussions of participatory democracy. First, there is the thesis advocated by Carole Pateman: If people participate in decision making at the workplace, they will also become more predisposed to participate in politics.[57] This is the spillover effect. Second, there is what we may call the Oscar Wilde thesis: Even under socialism, Wilde observed, there will be only seven evenings in the week, implying that participation in one sphere will be at the expense of participation in other spheres. This is the crowding-out effect. Third, one might argue that people have a need to participate in joint decision-making processes, so that if they are denied, say, democracy at the workplace

---

54. *Ibid.*, 91F.
55. Claims that mental life in general is subject to a zero-sum law amounts to a theory – the "hydraulic theory of the mind" – rather than to a mechanism. It is, moreover, a false theory, as acutely noted by Tocqueville: "It would seem that civilized people, when restrained from political action, should turn with that much more interest to the literary pleasures. Yet nothing of the sort happens. Literature remains as insensitive and fruitless as politics. Those who believe that by making people withdraw from greater objects they will devote more energy to those activities that are still allowed to them treat the human mind along false and mechanical laws. In a steam engine or a hydraulic machine smaller wheels will turn smoother and quicker as power to them is diverted from the larger wheels. But such mechanical rules do not apply to the human spirit" (Tocqueville 1986, p. 168).
56. Elster (1993a), Chapter 4.
57. Pateman (1970).

there will be a strong demand for political democracy, and vice versa. This is the compensation effect.

In an article on the organization of leisure, Harold Wilensky traces what he calls "the compensatory leisure hypothesis" and "the spill-over leisure hypothesis" back to Engels's work *The Conditions of the Working-Class in England in 1844*.[58] The first states that the worker who is alienated at work compensates by active and energetic leisure activities; the second that "he develops a spillover leisure routine in which alienation from work becomes alienation from life; the mental stultification produced by his labour permeates his leisure." As in the case of the relation between religion and politics (I.5), we may ask whether a conjunction of the two mechanisms might not offer a more satisfactory account than either of them taken separately.

The question of whether people who act out their aggression on one occasion are more or less likely to behave aggressively on later occasions seems to be similarly undecided. For some, aggressive behavior serves as catharsis; for others, as a trigger of more aggression.[59] A similar question may be asked about the perennial debate over the effects of media violence on actual violence: catharsis or stimulation or both? This question does not apply only to the modern issue of the relation between violence on television and behavior. In a book on the history of dueling that I discuss at some length in III.4, François Billacois suggests that the relation between violence on the stage and revenge behavior in sixteenth-century England and France was governed by the compensation effect: "At a time when France was a prey to duels and collective revenge, its theatre gave only a minor place to the theme of revenge; in England, which escaped these convulsions of social sensibility, the theatre was dominated until 1620 by the theme of vengeance, by the Revenge Tragedy. Can this simply be coincidence?"[60]

In other parts of his book, Billacois notes the co-presence of the compensation and spillover effects. In his discussion of the relation between duel and warfare he observes that contemporaries argued in terms of both mechanisms: "Many observers thought that the Wars of Religion 'engendered these particular disorders,' or at least that 'it is

58. Wilensky (1960).
59. Krebs and Miller (1985), pp. 40–41.
60. Billacois (1990), p. 31. To explain the paucity of duels in Spain, he similarly argues that in Castillian society the duel and the bullfight "could be a substitute for one another" (*ibid.*, p. 38).

from the heart of our civil wars that our duels have taken their vigour, so well do these two evils go together.' But others judged it to be the end of the civil, and indeed international, hostilities under Henri IV that produced so large a number of quarrels, these being the only 'way by which young men believe that they can gain greater praise in times of peace.'"[61] A similarly dual relation obtained between dueling and competitive scholarly activities. For young aristocrats, "intellectual combats and mimed confrontations may have fulfilled a function of sublimation and diverted the aggression of young gentlemen away from bloody fights." For the children of the bourgeoisie, however, "this 'heroic ambience,' combined with the daily presence of gentlemen of the same age as themselves, was an effective school for diffuse propaganda in favour of dueling."[62]

So far I have considered spillover and compensation as intrapersonal mechanisms of attitude formation. The previous remarks suggest, however, that one may enlarge the perspective to consider how similar effects may be at work in interpersonal relations. When young aristocrats and young elite commoners are educated together, the compensation effect may dampen the dueling tendencies of the former while the spillover effect enhances those of the latter. Another example is provided by individual donations to charity. A spillover-like mechanism is that embodied in the *norm of fairness*: If others give more I should give more too.[63] A compensation-like mechanism arises from more outcome-oriented utilitarian reasoning: If others give more, my contribution matters less so that I can give less.[64] I return to this example below.

CONTRAST EFFECT VERSUS ENDOWMENT EFFECT

In the mid-1980s Amos Tversky suggested (personal communication) that past experience has a dual effect on present welfare. On the one hand, there is an endowment effect: A memory of a good experience is a good memory, the memory of a bad one a bad memory. Hence a good past tends to improve the present, a bad past to make it worse. On the other hand, there is a contrast effect: A good experience in

---

61. *Ibid.*, p. 79. His own view is that although foreign wars reduce the number of duels, civil wars stimulate them (*ibid.*, pp. 80–81).
62. *Ibid.*, p. 136.
63. Elster (1989b), p. 187 ff.; Sugden (1984).
64. Elster (1989b), p. 46 ff.; Margolis (1982).

the past tends to devalue less good experiences in the present, and a bad event in the past will similarly throw the present into favorable relief. A meal at a superlatively good French restaurant may cause one to enjoy later meals at French restaurants (and perhaps at other restaurants too) less than one would have otherwise have done. Conversely, there is nothing like recovery from illness to make you appreciate a normal state of health.[65]

Given the existence and regular operation of these two mechanisms, we can ask several questions. First, there is a mechanism of type B_2: If a positive or negative experience triggers a negative or positive contrast effect (and assuming no endowment effect), will the net effect be positive or negative? This question has been much discussed ever since Allen Parducci observed that "if the best can come only rarely, it is better not to include it in the range of experiences at all."[66] Second, there is a mechanism of type B_1: What is the net effect, mediated by contrast and endowment, of experiences at an earlier time on welfare at a later time? This was the question identified by Tversky. Third, combining the first two questions, we might ask about the net effect of the initial experience on welfare overall, either as discounted to the earlier time or without discounting. In a given case, the net effect on *later* welfare might be negative if the negative contrast effect is stronger than a positive endowment effect, and yet the net effect on *overall* welfare might be positive if the positive utility from the experience itself is greater than the negative net effect at the later times. Thus to reconcile the apparently different assessments by Tennyson and Donne cited in I.3, we may assume that Donne refers to what is best *today* and Tennyson to what is best *overall*. (In addition, of course, they refer to different types of past experience.) To my knowledge, nobody has studied the third and more important question.

In a study of the net effect, Amos Tversky and Dale Griffin assume that the contrast effect, unlike the endowment effect, requires

65. These phenomena should not be confused with the opponent-process mechanism (I.2). In that process, an initial positive experience generates a later negative experience independently of whatever other events may transpire. In the presently discussed case, the subsequent effects depend on later events. If all my later meals are taken in superlatively good French restaurants, the contrast effect will not operate.

66. Parducci (1968), p. 90. Conversely, he argues that "[t]he ideal lower end-point might be a strong electric shock, unbearable, but quickly over. The shock would have to be readministered occasionally, whenever it dropped from the context or whenever its memory ceased to be dreadful" (Parducci 1984, p. 16). Parducci (1995) provides a full account of the theory.

some similarity between the present and the past.[67] The superlative French meal will not, for instance, tend to devalue a meal in a Chinese restaurant. In this specific case, that assumption seems reasonable. If, however, we imagine a man in prison dwelling miserably on how it felt to be free or a recovering patient enjoying his improved health, we do not need to stipulate a contrast between specific types of experience. Given this assumption and the high susceptibility of judgments of similarity to framing effects, they note that "one should find ways to treat the positive experiences of the past as different from the present."[68] They also note, however, that people may not have much freedom of choice in the framing of hedonic events. I return to that issue in I.8.

The bulk of their study is devoted to an analysis of net effects in specific experimental situations. Although they assert that their predictions were confirmed, this turns out to mean mainly that if the past events were dissimilar from the present ones there was no contrast effect. In addition, they note that the principle of loss aversion suggest a prediction (which was confirmed) that the negative contrast effect following a high payoff will be larger than the positive contrast effect following a low payoff.[69] They do not, however, offer any prior reasons for believing that the contrast effect will dominate the endowment effect or vice versa when both operate. It turns out that in one of their two experiments the endowment effect was stronger, whereas in the other the two effects were of roughly equal strength. Although loss aversion is cited as an explanation for the difference between the two experiments, no explanation is given for the results obtained in any one of them. As is often the case in the social sciences, we may be able to explain the slope of a relationship but not its intercept.

Tversky and Griffin state that they "know of no explicit attempt to integrate [the endowment and contrast effects]."[70] We do, however, find exactly that in Hume's *Treatise of Human Nature*. He first notes that, "[i]n general we may observe that in all kinds of comparison an object makes us always receive from another, to which it is compar'd, a sensation contrary to what arises from itself in its direct and immediate survey."[71] He then proceeds to apply this distinction to the

67. Tversky and Griffin (1991).
68. *Ibid.*, p. 299.
69. *Ibid.*, p. 305.
70. *Ibid.*, p. 298.
71. Hume (1960), p. 375.

intrapersonal case just discussed as well as to interpersonal comparisons. In the latter, "[t]he direct survey of another's pleasure naturally gives us pleasure, and therefore produces pain when compar'd with our own. His pain, consider'd in itself, is painful to us, but augments the idea of our own happiness, and gives us pleasure."[72] In the former, "the prospect of past pain is agreeable, when we are satisfy'd with our present condition; as on the other hand our past pleasures give us uneasiness, when we enjoy nothing at present equal to them."[73] Although Hume does not here explicitly mention the endowment effect of the past, it is implicit in his more general category of "direct and immediate survey." He does not, however, in either of the two cases try to assess the net effect of this direct survey and the sensation that arises from comparison. Before him, as we saw, Montaigne also noted the interpersonal and intrapersonal endowment and contrast effects. Unlike Hume, he did try to assess their net effect in specific cases without, however, offering any general reason why the one or the other effect should dominate.

Later, George Loewenstein and I generalized Tversky's idea to a larger variety of experiences.[74] In addition to endowment and contrast effects that arise from one's own past experiences, we identified similar effects that arise from the anticipation of one's future experiences, from other people's experiences, and from merely imagined or counterfactual experiences. Because the term "endowment" does not fit these other contexts, we used "consumption effect" as the more general term. To some extent we also addressed the question of the net effect. We noted that in interpersonal comparisons there is a transition from a dominant consumption effect to a dominant contrast effect that occurs at the point of equality.[75] We also noted the absence of a contrast effect when the future is expected to be worse than the present. In other cases, however, the net effect remains indeterminate. It is an open question, for instance, whether the consumption effect of daydreaming can offset the contrast effect.[76] Also,

72. *Ibid.*, p. 376.
73. *Ibid.*
74. Elster and Loewenstein (1992).
75. This conclusion was drawn from Loewenstein, Thompson, and Bazerman (1989).
76. See Elster (in press a), Section III.2, for a discussion of daydreaming. Note that in daydreaming, any consumption effect comes first and any contrast effect that might be produced occurs later, upon return to reality. If people discount the future they might indulge in daydreaming, therefore, even if on balance it makes them worse off.

counterfactual speculations ("I was only one number away from winning the big prize in the lottery") may trigger both effects with indeterminate net result.[77]

Consumption and contrast effects are not the only results of interpersonal comparisons. Abraham Tesser compares the painful contrast effect (or envy) with a pleasurable "reflection effect," basking in the reflected glory of a superior individual.[78] Because both envy and reflected glory depend on our closeness to the other person, they will wax and wane together, the net effect being in general indeterminate.[79] In one of his experiments Tesser found that the two effects were of approximately equal magnitude, with zero net effect *as far as pleasure or pain goes.* Yet this finding does not imply that this condition is equivalent to one in which the subject and the comparison person are equal, in which case each effect would be zero. The latter condition would produce not only zero net pleasure or pain, but also zero arousal (see IV.2). Tesser found, however, that the subjects in the former condition did experience arousal, as evidenced in their enhanced ability to perform simple tasks and decreased ability to perform complex tasks.[80] I return to some methodological implications of this finding in I.9.

DESIRES AND OPPORTUNITIES

Actions are caused by desires and opportunities. But the explanation of behavior need not stop there. We may go one step further and inquire into the causes of the causes. In some cases, the desires are caused by the opportunities. In others, desires and opportunities have a common cause in an antecedent variable, as in Fig. I.1.

77. McMullen, Markman, and Gavanski (1995), p. 155.
78. Tesser (1991).
79. According to Ben-Ze'ev (1992, p. 568) "Achievements of those very close to us evoke pride *rather than* envy when these achievements are . . . connected with us in such a manner that we can share the credits they bestow" (my italics). Thus he asserts, in my terminology, that closeness is the triggering variable in a type A mechanism. Tesser, by contrast, asserts that closeness is part of a set of conditions that induce both pride and envy in a type B mechanism. A priori, one cannot tell who is right – or whether both might sometimes be.
80. Hume (1960, p. 278) was wrong, therefore, when he asserted that "[t]o excite any passion, and at the same time raise an equal share of its antagonist, is immediately to undo what was done, and must leave the mind at last perfectly calm and indifferent." The fallacy is to identify "calm" and "indifferent." The first refers to absence of arousal, the second to absence of net pleasure or pain.

I shall discuss both cases, with reference to the "Tocqueville effect" in the explanation of revolutionary behavior. In a dynamic version, the effect says that discontent with existing conditions increases when conditions improve. The static version is that discontent is greater when conditions are better. Although Tocqueville runs the dynamic and the static effects together,[81] they are clearly distinct; either might exist without the other.[82] I first discuss the dynamic and then the static effect.

The standard account of the dynamic Tocqueville effect is that when opportunities increase, aspiration levels increase even faster, making for more discontent. The idea lacks, I think, the compelling simplicity one would want to have in a mechanism.[83] More satisfactory is Tocqueville's idea that "the mere fact that certain abuses have been remedied draws attention to the others and they now appear more galling."[84] Also, economic progress makes for more occasions for abuse, by bringing more individuals into contact with the inefficient state administration.[85] Moreover, as suggested by Albert Hirschman and Michael Rothschild, economic progress that is not accompanied by ascent along other dimensions may create a frustrating state of status incongruence.[86]

The possibility of telling different fine-grained stories to support the dynamic Tocqueville effect illustrates the move from "if A, then sometimes B" to "if A, then sometimes C, D, and B" (see I.2). Whichever of the stories we prefer, it seems clear that the dynamic Tocqueville effect may but need not go together with a net increase in discontent. After all, economic satisfaction might offset the frustration caused by dealings with state bureaucrats or by status incongruence. Tocqueville does not offer a theory to the effect that economic progress invariably causes revolution, but an argument to the effect that it may do so. The status incongruence version shows this especially clearly. Although economic progress satisfies one desire, it creates another and leaves it unsatisfied. The net effect of an increase in opportunities on satisfaction and on the desire for further change can go either way.

---

81. Tocqueville (1955), p. 176.
82. See Elster (1989b), p. 68 for a similar distinction in the analysis of wage bargaining.
83. Hirschman and Rothschild (1973), p. 46.
84. Tocqueville (1955), p. 177.
85. *Ibid.*, pp. 178–79.
86. Hirschman and Rothschild (1973), p. 46.

Consider next the static effect – the relationship between hardship and change.[87] In I.3 I suggested that necessity may be not only the mother of invention but also an obstacle to invention. Although invention requires motivation, which is stimulated by necessity, it also requires resources that may be lacking in situations of hardship. A similar two-pronged argument applies to collective action, and more specifically to revolutionary behavior. Revolutions are rarely caused by extreme hardship, because people living at subsistence conditions have to spend all their time simply staying alive. They may have the desire for change, but no opportunities to effect it. Conversely, the well off may have the opportunities but not the desire. In between, there may be a range of incomes that have a positive net effect – mediated by desires and opportunities – on the propensity to engage in revolutionary behavior. Although the static Tocqueville effect cannot be monotonic throughout the whole income range, the tendency for middle peasants to be more revolutionary than landless peasants indicates that it may be monotonic in the lower part of the range. Even in that range, however, the sign of the net effect is in general indeterminate, although the sign of the first derivative is not.

The static and dynamic effects may obviously be combined. When people grow richer, their frustration may increase; at the same time, their increased wealth may give them the resources to do something about their dissatisfaction. I now proceed to a more general discussion of such cases.

I.7. MOLECULAR MECHANISMS

In this section I go beyond elementary or atomic mechanisms to molecular mechanisms, both at the intrapersonal and the interpersonal levels. The usefulness of the mechanism approach is, I believe, particularly apparent in the analysis of complex psychic and social phenomena. As in earlier sections, the purpose is to illustrate and stimulate the imagination rather than to argue for any specific thesis.

The idea of molecular intrapersonal mechanisms can be illustrated by the following example. Suppose you have been with a lover for a while, but that he or she decides to break off the relationship. Because of the contrast effect, there is an initial reaction of grief. You may then observe your mind play the following trick on you: To reduce the pain

87. The following draws on Elster (1985), pp. 352–53.

of separation, you redescribe your lover to yourself so that he or she appears much less attractive. This, obviously, is a case of sour grapes, or adaptive preference formation. You then notice, however, that the endowment effect is also affected. By degrading the other, you can no longer enjoy the memory of the good times you had together. In fact, you will feel like a fool thinking back on the relationship you had with an unworthy person. To restore the good memories you have to upvalue the other, but then of course the grief hits you again.

The exact course of events depends on the relative strength of the different mechanisms at work. Just as people "may vary in the degree to which their reactions are dominated by endowment or by contrast,"[88] they may also differ in their susceptibility to adaptive preference formation. A person dominated by the contrast effect and highly vulnerable to the sour-grapes mechanism will initially be very miserable and then quickly overcome the grief. A person dominated by the endowment effect will not suffer so much in the first place. Others may be miserable for a long time, and still others may experience cycles of misery and relief. If we add counteradaptive preference formation to the range of mechanisms, even more possibilities come into play. Such interplay of mechanisms is the stuff of novels and of everyday life. Perhaps it is time for the social sciences to consider them.

Tocqueville relies heavily on molecular interpersonal mechanisms. In *The Ancien Régime* he plays on both the compensation effect and the spillover effect in his explanation of the radical character of the French Revolution. Because of the lack of political freedom under the old regime, "the political ferment was canalized (*refoulé*) into literature, the result being that our writers now became the leaders of public opinion and played for a while the part which normally, in free countries, falls to the professional politician":[89] This is the compensation effect. Later, "when the time came for action, these literary propensities were imported into the political arena":[90] This is the spillover effect.

In *Democracy in America*, the analysis of the relation between public and private life involves an interaction of the compensation, spillover, and crowding-out effects. For an American, "[t]o take a hand in the government of society and to talk about it is his most important business and, so to say, the only pleasure he knows. . . . But if an American

88. Tversky and Griffin (1991), p. 298.
89. Tocqueville (1955), p. 142.
90. Tocqueville (1955), p. 147.

should be reduced to occupying himself with his own affairs, at that moment half his existence would be snatched away from him; he would feel it as a vast void in his life and would become incredibly unhappy" (p. 243). Public life fills a need left unsatisfied by commercial or domestic activities. This is the compensation effect. Next, the habit of association generated in political life is generalized to civil life: "[P]olitics spread a general habit and taste for association" (p. 521). This is the spillover effect. Finally, "civil associations ... far from directing public attention to public affairs, serve to turn men's mind away therefrom, and getting them more and more occupied with projects for which public tranquillity is essential, discourage thoughts of revolution" (p. 523). This is the crowding-out effect.

Earlier, I mentioned that people might have two opposite responses to the level of charitable contributions observed in others. Some might give more when others give more; others might give less when others give more. The same responses may be observed in situations that generate collective action problems, such as revolutions.[91] At low levels of participation in a revolutionary movement, some of those who have not yet joined may ask themselves why they should risk their lives or freedom when so few others are doing it, whereas others might decide to join the movement because their participation could really be crucial at this stage. At higher levels of participation the former might tell themselves, "It is only fair that I do my share rather than act as a free rider." The latter might use exactly the opposite reasoning: "Now that so many others have joined the movement, there is really no need for me to stay in." The exact course of the revolution and its ultimate success or failure may depend crucially on the number of individuals who respond according to the one or the other mechanism, and on the thresholds that will trigger their participation and nonparticipation.

A final example may be taken from a recent book by Timur Kuran subtitled "The Social Consequences of Preference Falsification."[92] Contrary to what is suggested by this phrase, the book does not deal only with *preference falsification*, that is, the overt or public expression of preferences that one does not hold in private. It also deals extensively with *preference change*, that is, the transformation of one set of privately held preferences into another.

---

91. The following draws on Elster (1989b), pp. 202–6 and especially on Elster (1993a), pp. 15–24.
92. Kuran (1995).

34

There are many situations in which people may want to misrepresent their preferences (V.3). Kuran focuses on preference falsification motivated by the fear of the social disapproval that one would incur by expressing the privately held view. Similarly, there are many mechanisms of preference change. In the case of the fox and the sour grapes, the cause of the preference change is motivational, namely the tension that arises when I want something that I cannot get. Tension may also arise when I discover that I hold a belief or a preference that differs from that of the members of some reference group. As a consequence, I may end up adjusting my belief to that of others. Despite his focus on conformism, Kuran does not study this motivational mechanism of preference change. Instead, his theory of conformist preference change appeals to a cognitive mechanism, namely people's reliance on what he calls *the heuristic of social proof*: "[I]f a great many people think in a particular way, they must know something that we do not."[93] Moreover, he explicitly argues against the motivational theory. He claims that whereas preference falsification is motivated, preference change is not. For reasons explained elsewhere,[94] I believe he is wrong. The evidence and arguments for motivated preference change remain overwhelmingly strong.

Preference falsification and preference change might interact in several ways. (i) When other people falsify their preferences, they might cause my preferences to change. I might come to believe, falsely, that a majority holds a certain view, which I then adopt. The mechanism might, as suggested, be either (ia) motivational or (ib) cognitive. I might, that is, conform to their views either because of a need for cognitive consonance or because of a belief that the majority is likely to be right. (ii) When I falsify the expression of my preferences in response to outside pressure, I might end up changing the preferences themselves. This could only be due to a motivational mechanism, that is, the tendency to reduce the dissonance caused by saying in public what I do not believe in private. As Kuran does not believe in motivated preference change, his theory has room only for (ib). Although he recognizes the impact of the majority view on private belief formation, it is mediated exclusively by a cognitive mechanism. And although he recognizes the aversiveness of a discrepancy between what one believes in private and what one asserts in public, the main

93. Kuran (1995), p. 163.
94. Elster (1996a).

causal role it plays in his theory is to affect what one asserts in public, not what one believes in private.

I.8. FROM MECHANISMS TO LAWS

Although it is difficult to establish laws in the social sciences, that goal will always, for better or for worse, continue to guide scholars. In this section I discuss some ways of going beyond mechanisms to lawlike statements.

ELIMINATING SPURIOUS MECHANISMS

In some cases, the presence of two opposed mechanisms may be an artifact of social perception. Consider again "like attracts like" versus "opposites attract each other." These apparently opposed statements may in fact turn out to be different versions of the same claim, analogous to the glass that is both half-full and half-empty. If people's curiosity and thirst for novelty is triggered by options that are neither very similar to nor very dissimilar from one's present state,[95] their marital choices might be uniquely guided by the search for an optimal difference between their spouse and themselves.[96] Depending on the perspective, that difference might be seen as closer to similarity or to dissimilarity, giving rise to the two opposed proverbs. I am not claiming that this is the correct explanation. Perhaps marital choices are actually bipolar rather than centered in the middle range. All I am claiming is that even if the latter is the case, we can understand why these choices have been *perceived* to be bipolar.

The point can also be put in a slightly different way. If attractiveness is an inversely U-shaped function of novelty or similarity, each of the two opposing mechanisms might simply describe different parts of the curve. "On the rising point of such a curve, increased liking is held to result from increases in the independent variable (e.g., unexpectedness, complexity). Ultimately, some optimal level is reached, whereafter increases in the independent variable are held to give rise

95. Middleton (1986).
96. Byrne and Kurmen (1988).

to reductions in liking. Thus, up to a point, 'the more the merrier,' after which, 'one can have too much of a good thing.'"[97] In III.4 I cite a similar example from Plutarch.

In some contexts the dual attractions of likes to likes and of opposites to opposites appear to be genuinely different phenomena that cannot be reduced to the same underlying causal structure. If the contraries are complementary to each other, their union may form the basis of organic solidarity in Durkheim's sense. (Conversely, mechanical solidarity is based on similarity.) Some people may seek spouses who are different from themselves because they sense that the other can provide something they need but do not have themselves. A mercurial person, for instance, may seek or welcome the stability provided by a more even-tempered partner. Others may seek the comforts of familiarity and the benefits of being able to take lots of things for granted. These mechanisms are very unlike the choice of a spouse who appears attractively mysterious because he or she is optimally different from oneself.

PREDICTING MECHANISMS FROM OUTCOMES

I have been assuming that mechanisms shape outcomes, but it may also be the other way around. Consider again donations to charity. Earlier, I identified two mechanisms that can be summarized as "give much when others give much" and "give little when others give much." An indeterminacy then arises if we are unable to predict which individuals in which situations will be subject to the one or the other reaction. We could, however, look at the problem the other way, and assume that although people would like to give as little as possible, they would also like to tell a story – that is, cite a mechanism – to others and to themselves that justifies small donations.[98] As I argue at greater length in V.2, they care about their self-image as well as about their self-interest. We can then predict that small donations by others will trigger the fairness mechanism and large donations the utilitarian mechanism. The outcome is the same in both cases, namely small donations. This identity obtains not because different motivations yield the same outcome (as in Becker's analysis of the

97. Ortony, Clore, and Collins (1988), p. 166.
98. For a different (but compatible) approach to self-serving reasons for not giving to charity, see Rabin (1995).

law of demand), but because people adopt the motivation that will yield the desired outcome.

This example is a bit awkward, because if donations are always going to be low it is not clear that there could ever be an occasion for releasing the utilitarian mechanism. In other examples that I now proceed to cite, this difficulty does not arise. Let me first cite a Jewish joke about anti-Semitism:

Ignace Paderewski, Poland's post–World War I premier, was discussing his country's problems with President Woodrow Wilson.
"If our demands are not met at the conference table," he said, "I can foresee serious trouble in my country. Why, my people will be so irritated that many of them will go out and massacre the Jews."
"And what will happen if your demands are granted?" asked President Wilson.
"Why, my people will be so happy that they will get drunk and go out and massacre the Jews."[99]

Similarly, studies of gambling have "found that, like ... winners, losers increased the riskiness of subsequent bets."[100] If you win you can afford to take bigger risks; if you lose, you increase the odds to recoup your losses. It is also significant that in the twenty questions developed by Gamblers Anonymous to help problem gamblers diagnose themselves, all the following appear:

7. After losing, do you feel you must return as soon as possible and win back your losses?
8. After you win, do you have a strong urge to return and win more?
18. Do arguments, disappointments, or frustrations create within you an urge to gamble?
19. Do you have an urge to celebrate any good fortune by a few hours of gambling?

Other addictive behaviors, such as smoking or drinking, have similar features: They are triggered by bad news or bad moods as well as by good news and by good moods. In either case, "this calls for a drink" or "this calls for a cigarette" is cited as the justification for indulging one's craving.

99. Telushkin (1992), p. 112.
100. Greenberg and Weiner (1966), cited in Cornish (1978), p. 17.

Amos Tversky and Eldar Shafir conducted a series of experiments that are relevant in this connection.[101] One of them, which is related to gambling, also finds that a majority of subjects assert that they will accept a second gamble if they won in a prior gamble *and* if they have lost in a prior gamble; however, only a minority say they will accept a second gamble if they do not know whether they have won or lost in the first. As they observe, this is a violation of the sure-thing principle, which states that if x is preferred to y knowing that event A obtained, and if x is preferred to y knowing that A did not obtain, then x should be preferred to y even when it is not known whether A obtained.

Their explanation for the observed violation of this principle is cognitive, not motivational. But at least in the gambling example – and assuming that the subjects like the thrill of gambling and do not only think in financial terms – a motivational explanation could also be possible. If one really wants to gamble but knows that it is not a good idea, one needs an excuse, a reason, a story to justify doing so. Winning will provide one story; losing will provide another; but ignorance does not. One cannot decide to accept the gamble by telling oneself that whatever happens in the first gamble one *will have* an excuse for continuing, because that is not how excuses work. They are not planned ahead of time; rather, one observes the situation when it arises and finds a reason in it to do what one wants to do. A similar "disjunction effect" may arise in the triggering of emotions, as we shall see in IV.2.

To the extent that mechanisms provide one with excuses for doing what one would like to do, we can predict which mechanism will in fact be triggered under which conditions. The effect is a little bit like "hedonic framing." The hypothesis of hedonic framing states that "people edit gambles in a way that would make the prospects appear most pleasant (or least unpleasant)."[102] In other words, hedonic framing involves a preference-based choice among different ways of describing the same situation. Similarly, the would-be minimizer of charitable donations compares the fairness mechanism and the utilitarian mechanism and settles for the one that allows him to donate as little as possible, consistent with his need to retain his self-respect. In both cases, the comparison and choice would have to take place unconsciously: One cannot *decide* to trick oneself in these ways. A difference between the two effects can be brought out by citing an

101. Tversky and Shafir (1992).
102. Thaler and Johnson (1990), p. 53.

objection to hedonic framing: "Imagine you had just received an un-expected gain of $50. This could be hedonically reframed into two gains of $25, but why stop there? Why not 50 gains of $1?"[103] By con-trast, the hedonic manipulation of mechanisms as excuses is limited by the small number of stories that are available.

A final example may be taken from Aristotle's *Rhetoric* (1372^b22 ff.), where he discusses "the kind of people to whom one does wrong." They include, among others, "those who have either never been or often been wronged before; in neither case will they take precau-tions; if they have never been wronged they think they never will, and if they have often been wronged they feel that surely it cannot happen again." The reasoning that Aristotle's wrongdoer imputes to his victims takes the form of the gambler's fallacy and its converse (I.2). A plausible (but not compelling) interpretation is that their de-sire to believe themselves invulnerable to aggression causes them to believe in a mechanism that will justify the belief that they are in fact invulnerable. Similarly, as we shall see in Chapter IV, beliefs may be induced by the emotions they justify.

IDENTIFYING THE TRIGGERS

Consider "absence makes the heart grow fonder" versus "out of sight, out of mind." La Rochefoucauld pointed to a possible trig-gering factor that would explain when the one or the other mecha-nism would be observed: "Absence lessens moderate passions and intensifies great ones, as the wind blows out a candle but fans up a fire" (Maxim 276). Here the generalizing strategy is to identify a particular aspect of the *situation* that allows us to predict which mechanism will be triggered.[104] Similarly, Tversky and Griffin show that the endowment effect dominates the contrast effect when the present event differs qualitatively from the past one. With regard to the opponent-process effect (I.2), Solomon argues that the main effect dominates in the initial episodes, and the opponent effect in later episodes. In addiction, for instance, euphoria initially domi-nates withdrawal, which then comes to dominate in later stages, as shown in Fig. I.2.

103. *Ibid.*, p. 56.
104. The French have a proverb, "un peu d'absence fait un grand bien" (Dournon 1993, p. 10) that suggests a different triggering feature: A brief absence stimulates love, while a longer one extinguishes it.

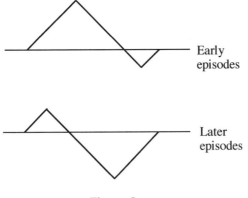

Early
episodes

Later
episodes

Figure I.2.

In other cases, we might be able to point to properties of the *individual* that allow us to predict the triggering of a particular mechanism.[105] As Tversky and Griffin also mention, some individuals may be more sensitive to the contrast effect than to the endowment effect, and perhaps we might be able to identify them on the basis of other properties.[106] Yet if Walter Mischel is right in his claim that there is little intrapersonal, cross-situational consistency, such differences might themselves be situation-specific.[107] Moreover, the behavior might not be rigidly fixed to a given type of situation. If Tocqueville is right in arguing that people have a need for a sphere in which they are independent and also for a sphere in which they are subject to authority, which sphere serves which need may be a somewhat arbitrary matter.

A more ambitious strategy for anchoring mechanisms in laws relies on catastrophe theory. When I gave a talk on this topic some years ago, I cited various pairs of opposed mechanisms – sour grapes versus forbidden fruits, the attraction of likes versus the attraction of

---

105. Regarding the choice of defense mechanism, for instance, Vaillant (1993, p. 107) argues that "[w]ith defense choice, as with creativity in general, it is the protagonist and not the situation that determines the mode of expression." I return to this issue in V.2.
106. In some cases we may invoke features of the situation *and* of the individual to predict the net effect. Thus when an emotional stimulus triggers opposite reactions in the sympathetic and the parasympathetic nervous systems (IV.2), the net effect may depend both on the intensity of the stimulus and on the location of the individual on an extravert–introvert scale (Geen 1983, cited after Hatfield et al. 1994, p. 136).
107. Mischel (1968).

opposites, conformism versus anticonformism. Normal Schofield then remarked in the discussion that this kind of *bifurcation* is exactly what one would expect in cusp catastrophe models. In these models, the surface describing the behavior of a dependent variable as a function of two independent variables folds in on itself in a cusp. Within a certain range, a given constellation of the independent variables is thus consistent with several values of the dependent variable. Moreover, these values tend to be far apart from each other, corresponding to the polarized nature of mechanisms.

More recently, Abraham Tesser and John Achee have developed an argument of this kind more systematically.[108] They observe that in many social situations the function relating the independent variables to the dependent variable is two-valued rather than one-valued, and hence the distribution of behaviors bimodal rather than unimodal. Brehm's theory of "reactance," for instance, is based on the premise that social pressure can decrease as well as increase conformity.[109] John Roemer's idea of the "psychology of tyranny" is also relevant here.[110] The tyrant induces fear in his subjects, but also hatred. The fear makes them less likely to rebel, the hatred more likely. Tesser and Achee argue, however, that the indeterminacy disappears once we go beyond state variables and introduce path dependence or hysteresis:

Dissonance theory provides a very nice psychological model for hysteresis. Assume that one's disposition is consonant with engaging in the behavior and that undergoing negative social pressure is dissonant with engaging in the behavior; one's disposition is dissonant with not engaging in the behavior, and the presence of negative social pressure is consonant with not engaging in the behavior. If one starts out high on the behavior in the face of strong social pressure, then as one's disposition decreases, dissonance increases. To reduce the dissonance, one will look for additional cognitions to support the behavior. Hence the behavior will tend to remain high even in the face of a decreasing disposition. On the other hand, starting with strong social pressure and low levels of behavior, increasing one's disposition will increase dissonance. To reduce the dissonance, one will look for additional cognitions to support not engaging in the behavior. Hence the behavior will remain low even though the disposition is increasing.[111]

108. Tesser and Achee (1994).
109. Brehm (1966), Chapter VI.
110. Roemer (1985a).
111. Tesser and Achee (1994), p. 104.

The model has several further implications. In the first case, as the disposition continues to decrease in the face of strong social pressure, there will come a point when the person switches from engaging in the behavior to not engaging in it. In the second case, as the disposition continues to increase, there will come a point when the person switches from not engaging in the behavior to engaging in it. Moreover, the level of disposition at which the first switch occurs is lower than the level at which the second occurs. A person who has adopted an unpopular opinion will need to see a lot of the evidence for it fritter away before he gives it up, whereas an uncommitted person will need a lot of evidence for it before adopting it. Finally, a given combination of social pressure and disposition can lead to high as well as low engagement in the behavior, depending on where the person initially started up.

Many of the arguments offered by Tesser and Achee are tantalizingly similar to the ideas I am developing here. It may indeed turn out to be the case that pairs of opposed mechanisms correspond to different parts of the cusp surface. In that case, we could use knowledge of the past behavior of the individual to go beyond mechanisms and predict what he or she will do. This would still fall short of the ideal of science, which is to predict and explain using state variables only. Appealing to past values of the variables in order to explain behavior in the present is intrinsically unsatisfactory.[112] Although we would prefer to explain in terms of the traces left by the past in the present rather than in terms of the past itself, this approach would at least provide a determinate explanation.

Yet unless I am mistaken the argument made by Tesser and Achee differs in an important respect from the one I am making here. Although they refer to Brehm's work about pressure to conform generating anticonformism,[113] their main interest is actually in conformism versus nonconformism. Elsewhere I have described these antonyms

112. Elster (1976a).
113. "J.W. Brehm suggested the presence of a motive to maintain one's freedom to behave as one wishes. This countermotive to conformity is termed *reactance*. There is now a substantial body of literature documenting the operation of this motive. In one study, for example, Heilman gave subjects on the streets of New York the opportunity to sign a petition for an issue they mildly endorsed. In the course of the interaction, some of the subjects learned that someone else believed that people should not be allowed to sign such petitions. This latter group was more likely to sign the petitions than were subjects who were not exposed to this social pressure. So, sometimes social pressure encourages contrary behavior" (Tesser and Achee 1994, pp. 103–104: references deleted).

of conformism as its external and internal negation respectively.[114] The person who stands up to pressure, and disregards what others think if he believes he is right, is autonomous. As La Bruyère observed in a passage quoted above, however, the person who always does the opposite of what others do or want him to do is as heteronomous – dependent on others – as the conformist is.[115] In the catastrophe model, the opposite of adaptive preference formation would presumably be the absence of any causal influence of the feasible set on the preferences. In my approach the antonym is counteradaptive preference formation. Although the catastrophe model may be capable of explaining when we do or don't bend to pressure, it does not seem capable of explaining why we sometimes bend over in the opposite direction.

I.9. A PLEA FOR DISAGGREGATION

When opposing explanation by mechanisms to explanation by laws I have assumed that the latter is invariably deterministic. Much social science, however, relies on statistical explanation. This procedure is notoriously plagued by many conceptual difficulties. In particular, statistical explanation can neither predict nor explain individual cases.[116] Although explanation by mechanisms cannot predict either, it can at least explain individual events after the fact. Statistical regularities have less explanatory power than the propensities embodied in mechanisms.

To see why statistical regularities are insufficient for prediction, consider the following inferences:

1a. If the barometer is falling, it will almost certainly rain.
2a. The barometer is falling.
3a. It almost certainly will rain.

1b. When there are red skies a night, it almost certainly won't rain.
1b. The sky is red tonight.
1c. It almost certainly won't rain.

114. Elster (1993a), Chapter 2.
115. See also Elster (1983b), pp. 23, 67.
116. The following draws heavily on Hempel (1965), as summarized in Elster (1983a), pp. 46–7.

Here all four premises may be true, and yet both conclusions cannot be true. To see why statistical explanation cannot even explain individual cases after the fact, consider the following example. Jones is recovering from illness after treatment by penicillin. Because most people treated for that illness by penicillin do recover, we could try to explain Jones's recovery by an inductive statistical explanation. It might be the case, however, that Jones belongs to the group of individuals who are immune to treatment by penicillin, and that he simply recovered spontaneously, as sometimes also happened in the prepenicillin era.

The mechanism approach provides yet another reason why statistical explanations tend to be weak and unreliable. Suppose that we set out to study the dependence of donations to charity on the amount of money donated (and known to be donated) by other people, and that there turns out to be very little correlation. It could be tempting to conclude that people do not really take into account how much others give when deciding how much to give themselves. An alternative explanation might be that the population consists of two roughly equal-sized groups, one motivated by the norm of fairness and one motivated by more utilitarian considerations. On this account, *everybody* would look to others before deciding how much to give, but differ in the way the decisions of others affect their own. To uncover the presence of these two opposed mechanisms (nonlawlike tendencies), one has to go to a lower level of aggregation and look inside the black box. Economists "tend to aggregate data even though they have been gathered from heterogeneous groups. The homogeneity assumptions are misplaced.... Individual differences do not cancel each other out; consistent, independent psychological variables are important aspects of improving predictions."[117]

This perspective suggests a reinterpretation of Mischel's findings. Contrary to what would be implied by a universal spillover effect, people who are altruistic, aggressive, or impulsive in one context (e.g., work) do not systematically behave the same way in other settings (e.g., the family). It does not follow, however, that there is no causal relationship operating across contexts. It might be the case

---

117. Lewis (1982), p. 32. Or as Diego Gambetta (1997, p. 112) says in an analysis of schooling decisions in the Piedmont, "it is often a risk of empirical analysis ... that one may conclude that there is no effect when there are opposite ones neutralizing each other. A mechanisms sensitive approach makes such conclusions less likely."

that what we observe is the net effect of spillover and compensation. Suppose, for instance, that we found a relatively weak correlation between individual rates of time discounting across different activities or for different goods. The explanation might be that for some individuals the habit of foresight spills over from one sphere to other spheres, whereas for others the demands of self-control are so strenuous that when they achieve it in one part of their life they have to give themselves a break elsewhere.[118]

Similarly, it has often been observed that human beings are subject to two very strong desires: The desire to be like others and the desire to differ from others, conformism and anticonformism. If some individuals are strongly dominated by the former desire and others by the latter, the aggregate effect might be very weak, supporting the idea that people are mostly autonomous rather than heteronomous. Theories of voting behavior, for instance, have identified both an underdog mechanism and a bandwagon mechanism.[119] Those subject to the former tend to vote for the candidate who is behind in preelection polls, whereas those subject to the latter vote for the front-runner. If the two types are evenly mixed, there might be no noticeable net effect, so that the polls would be good predictors of the actual vote. The lack of influence of polls on voting in the aggregate does not show, however, that individuals are unaffected by the polls. The neutral aggregate could mask a homogeneous population of unaffected individuals – or a heterogeneous population of individuals who are all strongly affected but in opposite directions.[120]

George Vaillant observes that in the aggregate, "there is no evidence that [various mediating factors] statistically increase the risk of alcohol abuse in children if they are not biologically related to the alcoholic family member."[121] Yet, as he goes on to say in the statement cited in the opening paragraph of this chapter, this weak aggregate effect could mask two strong, oppositely directed effects at a less aggregate level. If that is in fact the case, strategies of intervention might be justified that would be pointless if children were never or rarely driven to alcoholism because their parents drink. This is perhaps the most important implication of the argument. For research

---

118. See Nisan (1985) for a related idea.
119. Simon (1954).
120. In fact, as observed in Simon (1954), for any mix there exists a fixed-point prediction that, if published, will turn out to be exact. In general, however, this prediction does not correspond to the preelection poll.
121. Vaillant (1995), p. 65.

purposes as well as for purposes of public policy, identification of subgroups may be crucial.

The plea for disaggregation also has consequences for the intrapersonal case. In I.6 I discussed Tesser's findings that the conjunction of the contrast effect and the reflection effect may yield an emotional state that is neutral as far as pleasure and pain goes. To predict behavior, however, we may need to know the strength of each mechanism, not only their net effect. Type B mechanisms within individuals may neutralize each other, as may type A mechanisms across individuals, but that does not allow us to infer that they are absent. Nor can we assume that the net effect is all that matters for prediction or intervention.

Chapter II

Emotions Before Psychology

II.1. INTRODUCTION

The psychological analysis of the emotions is little more than a hundred years old. Darwin's *Expression of Emotion in Man and Animals* (1872) and William James's "What Is an Emotion" (1884) are the first studies of the emotions using scientific methodology. Over the past century, empirical and theoretical studies of the emotions have accumulated at an accelerating rate. In Chapter IV, I draw on these contributions to outline my understanding of what the emotions are and what they do.

In many ways, these modern studies go beyond anything that is found in writers from earlier centuries. The idea of "depressive realism" (IV.3), to cite just one example, was not anticipated in prescientific writings on the emotions. Yet many of the recent insights were already present, often in aphoristic and condensed form, in earlier writers. In II.2 I argue, for instance, that Aristotle anticipated the key elements of the modern theories and, moreover, had important insights that have not yet been rediscovered. I also believe that with respect to an important subset of the emotions we can learn more from moralists, novelists, and playwrights than from the cumulative findings of scientific psychology. These emotions include regret, relief, hope, disappointment, shame, guilt, pridefulness, pride, *hybris*, envy, jealousy, malice, pity, indignation, wrath,[1] hatred, contempt, joy, grief, and romantic love. By contrast, the scientific study of the emotions can teach us a great deal about anger, fear, disgust,

---

1. I follow Frijda (1994) in using "wrath" for revenge-seeking anger. Aristotle argued that all anger seeks revenge (II.2), a view that is neither obviously true nor obviously false. I return to his claim at several places below.

parental love, surprise, and sexual desire (if we count the last two as emotions).

There are two main reasons why the scientific study of the more complex emotions is so difficult. On the one hand, animal experiments cannot tell us much about them because the animals typically used for laboratory studies are thought to be incapable of having them. No one to my knowledge has suggested that rats are capable of feeling malice or regret. Experiments with primates hold out more promise. One has demonstrated, for instance, guilt (or shame?) in subordinate macaques, by giving them access to females and allowing them to copulate in the absence of the alpha male, and then observing that their behavior is more submissive than usual when he returns.[2] Apparently, they feel pangs of conscience induced by behavior that is unobserved by others.

Yet even primate studies cannot tell us anything about the interplay between emotion and cognition that is a crucial aspect of emotions in humans. One reason is that the range of beliefs that can be held by other animals is so limited. We can distinguish objects of beliefs along three dimensions. First, the objects may be observable or unobservable. Second, they may be physical or mental. Third, they may be real or imagined. As far as I know, animals can only form beliefs about real, physical objects. These need not be observable. We know from many studies that animals are capable of forming mental representations of physical objects that are absent from the present sensory field.[3] But there is no evidence that animals can form the more complex beliefs of which humans are capable, such as beliefs about mental states (beliefs, emotions, motivations) and counterfactual beliefs. I discuss these beliefs in IV.2. In particular, animals cannot form beliefs about their own emotions. Nor does there seem to be any evidence that animal beliefs can be distorted by emotion, in the ways that I discuss in II.3 and IV.3.

On the other hand, financial and ethical constraints limit the extent to which one can study the more complex emotions by laboratory experiments on humans. To determine the relative strength of self-interest and emotion, for instance, one might have to create a situation in which a large number of subjects were offered large sums of money to act in an emotionally abhorrent way. Unless one uses

2. De Waal (1996), p. 110.
3. Elster (1983a), pp. 132–33.

49

first-world research grants to study third-world subjects[4] – or unless one is willing to take the risk that subjects would refuse the money so that the sums never had to be paid – experiments of this sort are simply too expensive. To explore shame by giving people an opportunity to steal money and then letting them be discovered would violate ethical guidelines for research on human subjects. As a result of these limitations, laboratory experiments tend to involve somewhat trivial, low-stake issues. Also, the general tendency in psychological experiments to rely on self-reports rather than on behavioral evidence makes it hard to interpret many findings. Even when the reports are reliable, it may be hard to validate them, because of a systematic tendency to underestimate the subjective impact of past, future, or hypothetical visceral sensations.[5]

I believe, therefore, that prescientific insights into the emotions are not simply superseded by modern psychology in the way natural philosophy has been superseded by physics. Some men and women in the past have been superb students of human nature, with more wide-ranging personal experience, better powers of observation, and deeper intuitions than almost any psychologist I can think of. This is only what we should expect: There is no reason why one century out of twenty-five should have a privilege in wisdom and understanding. In the case of physics, this argument does not apply. Advances in mathematics and experimental techniques have made it possible to go far beyond what could be achieved in earlier centuries. There has been no similar revolution in psychology. Although the pages of psychological journals testify to a great deal of concern with methodology, even the most sophisticated statistical analysis cannot compensate for the intrinsic limitations of laboratory studies on humans.

Although many philosophers have discussed the emotions – Descartes, Spinoza, Hume, and Kant among them – I have found Aristotle to be the most insightful. By keeping very close to the phenomena, he avoids the implausible constructions that we find in Descartes or Hume. More than any other philosopher, he shows how emotions are rooted not only in individual psychology, but also in social interaction. His minutely detailed analyses of the antecedents of the various emotions have never, to my knowledge, been equaled. And whereas what Descartes, Spinoza, Hume, and Kant say about the

4. As in Cameron (1995).
5. Loewenstein (1996).

emotions tells us little about the social and political order in which they lived, Aristotle's discussion of the emotions is also a main source for our understanding of Athenian society and politics.

Although there is no clear boundary line between the moralists and the moral philosophers, the former may be identified by their less systematic, sometimes aphoristic, sometimes anecdotal approach. Also, their concern is with moral psychology rather than with morality as such. In classical antiquity, Plutarch and Seneca stand out. Here, I shall limit myself to four modern writers – Montaigne, Pascal, La Rochefoucauld, and La Bruyère. They all remain important because of their extreme psychological acuity and powers of formulation. As in the case of Aristotle, we can also draw on their work for insights on the role of the emotions in their own social world. Montaigne and La Rochefoucauld, in particular, were men of very wide experience. They had seen battle, so they knew about courage and how people simulate it. They had lived at the court, so they knew about courtly love and how people dissimulate it.

Novels and plays are another inexhaustible source of insights and hypotheses. Whereas many of the fictional examples used by philosophers to illustrate this or that theory of the emotions fail to convince because they are too obviously made up for that purpose, the words and actions of characters in a novel or play have an independent authority that allows us to use them as examples and counterexamples. The writers I have found useful as touchstones for theories of the emotions are Shakespeare, Racine, Mme. de Lafayette, Jane Austen, Stendhal, and George Eliot. This is a personal and idiosyncratic choice. I claim only that we can learn about the emotions from their writings, not that we cannot also learn, and perhaps learn more, from other writers.

Before I proceed, I should explain the place of the present chapter and the following in the book as a whole. On the one hand, I believe that the matters discussed in these chapters have considerable intrinsic interest. On the other hand, the discussion of writers who have thought deeply about the emotions as well as the historical case studies offered in Chapter III provide an indispensable basis for the more theoretical approach that I develop in Chapter IV. If I had tried to state the general argument in an abstract form or using brief examples only, I doubt that it would have carried much convincing power. By drawing on a larger repertoire of analyses and examples, I hope that the abstract propositions will gain not only in vividness but in plausibility. In addition, the discussion in II.3 of the French moralists lays the groundwork for the discussion of irrational emotions in IV.3. It also sets the stage for Chapter V – both by stating a basic division of motivations into reason, interest, and passion, and by explaining how the need for esteem and for self-esteem can transform one of these motivations into another.

II.2. ARISTOTLE ON THE EMOTIONS

Aristotle's analysis of the emotions in the *Rhetoric* is valuable both for the light it throws on the emotions in general and for what it says about the role of the emotions in Greek political life.[6] In Chapter III I occasionally draw on Aristotle to discuss the latter topic. Here, I want to consider his theory of the emotions taken by itself. Unless my reading of the literature is seriously skewed, it seems that the two relevant bodies of scholarship are entirely unaware of each other. Psychological studies of the emotions never refer to Aristotle or to Aristotelian scholarship. Conversely, commentators on the *Rhetoric* never cite empirical studies of the emotions, and only exceptionally do they refer to recent philosophical analyses. I shall try to show that Aristotle has things to say about the emotions that could usefully be incorporated in the modern psychological accounts, and conversely that some issues of Aristotelian scholarship may be illuminated by modern psychology. Given the complexities of Aristotelian interpretation and my ignorance of Greek, what I have to say on the latter topic is doomed to be tentative.

Although the *Rhetoric* is the only text in which Aristotle offers something like a systematic analysis of the emotions, it is not the only one. In addition to various references scattered throughout the corpus, there are extensive analyses in the *Nicomachean Ethics* and important references in the *Politics*. In trying to pull together these texts, I use a conceptual framework further developed in IV.2, in which I characterize the emotions in terms of six features: Bodily arousal, physiological expressions, cognitive antecedents, intentional objects, valence (pleasure–pain), and action tendencies. My first aim is to show that this characterization – which is intended to summarize modern thinking about the emotions – was already present in Aristotle.

6. References in the text are to the standard pagination of the Aristotelian corpus. I have mainly used the Revised Oxford Translation of Aristotle but sometimes relied on other translations of the cited works or on translations of individual passages in various commentaries.

(A seventh feature – that each emotion has a unique qualitative feel – is not found in Aristotle.) Next, I consider his analyses of specific emotions, notably anger, hatred, fear, envy (and its nameless converse), pity, indignation (and its nameless converse), shame, and contempt. In conclusion, I say a few words about the contemporary relevance of Aristotle's theory. I begin, however, with a brief remark or the *Rhetoric* itself.

THE RHETORIC

The work presents itself as a study of the art of persuasion through speech, and occasionally is a handbook of political manipulation. It is also, and perhaps above all, "the earliest systematic discussion of human psychology" in Western thought.[7] In this work, Aristotle distinguishes among three kinds of speech, and three means of persuasion. There is political speech, that is, deliberation in the assembly about "ways and means, war and peace, national defence, imports and exports, and legislation" ($1359^b20–21$). There is forensic speech, that is, speeches before the court by plaintiffs and defendants in a suit. Finally, there is epideictic speech, or speech in praise or censure of somebody. The means are *ethos*, *pathos*, and *logos*: "[T]he first kind depends on the personal character of the speaker; the second on putting the audience in a certain [emotional] frame of mind; the third on the proof, or apparent proof, provided by the words of the speech itself" ($1356^a2–4$).

As Aristotle observes, the third kind of speech and the first kind of means are closely related: "[T]he ways in which to make [our hearers] trust the goodness of other people are also the ways in which to make them trust our own" ($1366^a26–28$). (See III.4 for the importance of self-praise in Athenian legal oratory.) He also claims that the first kind of speech relies exclusively on the third kind of means: When the interests of the audience are at stake, "there is no need ... to prove anything except that the facts are what the supporter of a measure maintains they are" ($1354^b31–32$). Conversely, he suggests that the second kind of speech cannot rely on the first kind of means: "To conciliate the listener [e.g., by appeals to emotion] is what pays here" (*ibid.*). (But see III.3 for a passage from the *Politics* which points in a different direction.)

7. Editorial remark in Kennedy (1991, p. 122).

The passions occur in two different contexts in the *Rhetoric*. In book I they are treated as independent variables in order to explain behavior. Here, Aristotle considers three aspects of wrongdoing: the motives of wrongdoers, their states of mind, and to whom they do wrong. Among the motives, he cites anger as the cause of revenge (1369^b11–12). Among their states of mind, he cites their belief of being able to stave off a trial, or have it postponed, or corrupt the judges (1372^a33–34). To identify the kind of people to whom they do wrong, he mentions that "a man may wrong his enemies, because that is pleasant: He may equally wrong his friends, because that is easy" (1373^a3–5). As these examples indicate, the analysis is not exactly systematic.

In book II, which mainly concerns me here, the emotions are treated as dependent variables, to be explained in terms of three aspects of the person who is subject to them.[8] "Take, for instance, the emotion of anger: Here we must discover what the state of mind of angry people is, who the people are with whom they usually get angry, and on what grounds they get angry with them" (1378^a23–26). Among the grounds for anger, he cites the fact of being deliberately slighted. The state of mind of the angry man is "that in which any pain is being felt" (1379^a10–11), as a result of his desire being frustrated in some way. The persons with whom he gets angry include "those who laugh, mock, or jeer at us" (1379^a29). From these and other examples, it appears that emotions, for Aristotle, have two sets of antecedents. On the one hand, they have cognitive preconditions. The relevance of the persons with whom we get angry, for instance, is mediated by our beliefs about them. On the other hand, and this is for us a more unusual insight, they are facilitated by certain noncognitive antecedents, such as being already in a state of distress or pain; Aristotle cites the states of thirst, sickness, poverty and love.[9] Like the emotions, these states may have cognitive antecedents and intentional objects, but, again like them, they are not themselves cognitive states. Nor, as shown by the inclusion of thirst and illness among the examples, are they necessarily themselves emotions in the full-blown sense of the term.

---

8. For discussions of the relation between the treatments of emotions in books I and II, see Frede (1996, pp. 265–72) and Striker (1996, pp. 288–93).
9. In his discussion of "stimulus conditions which facilitate elicitation of emotion without themselves being stimuli for such an emotion," Frijda (1986, p. 283) does not mention preexisting distress. See also n. 30 below.

DEFINITION AND CHARACTERIZATION OF THE EMOTIONS

Aristotle's explicit definition is as follows: "[T]he emotions are those things through which, by undergoing change, people come to differ in their judgments, and which are accompanied by pain and pleasure, for example, anger, pity, fear, and other such things and their opposites" ($1378^{a}21–22$). In the context of Aristotle's other writings, this definition is too wide, incomplete, and misleading. It is too wide, because it also covers physiological disturbances such as headaches.[10] It is incomplete, because it fails to mention other equally invariant features of the emotions. It is misleading, finally, because it defines emotions by their impact on cognition rather than by the fact of being shaped by cognition.[11] When Aristotle considers specific emotions, he consistently analyzes them in terms of their cognitive antecedents rather than in terms of their consequences for cognition. The latter causal connection is contingent: People may be angry or ashamed without having their judgment distorted by the emotion. The former is necessary: Anger cannot arise without an antecedent belief about another person. (But see IV.2 for some qualifications to this statement.)

(1) *Arousal.* In *De Anima*, Aristotle points to the fact that affections of the soul such as "passion, gentleness, fear, pity, courage, joy, loving, and hating" are also affections of the body, and goes on to say that "[h]ence a physicist would define an affection of soul differently from a dialectician; the latter would define e.g., anger as the appetite of returning pain for pain, or something like that, while the former would define it as the boiling of the blood or warm substance surrounding the heart" ($403^{a}17,29–32$). We may note, for future reference, that the "dialectical" definition includes the action tendency of returning

---

10. Fortenbaugh (1970), p. 54.
11. Leighton (1996) offers a systematic analysis of the Aristotelian theory of the emotions in terms of their impact on judgment. He discusses the objection that mere appetites such as hunger and thirst also affect judgment and are accompanied by pleasure and pain: "[T]he alcoholic's thirst may be so strong that the person decides that wood alcohol is not so bad. However, it is not ... the thirst that alters judgment.... Rather, the difference in judgment that may arise in such situations will arise through one's anger, irritation, despair, or reflections upon these matters." But this fails to address the familiar kind of case described by Pears (1985, p. 12): "The driver goes to a party and he judges it best to stop at two drinks in spite of the pleasure to be had from more, because there is nobody else to take the wheel on the way home. Nevertheless, when he is offered a third drink, which, we may suppose, is a double, he takes it. How can he? Easily, if the wish for a third drink biases his deliberation at the party before he takes it."

pain for pain. To use Aristotelian categories, *De Anima* highlights the material cause as well as the final cause of the emotions, while not citing the efficient cause that takes center place in book II of the *Rhetoric*.[12]

(2) *Physiological expressions.* In the *Categories* (9^b27–30), Aristotle draws a distinction between properties such as pallor and darkness, which are permanent qualities, and those that "result from something that easily disperses.... Thus a man who reddens through shame is not called ruddy, nor one who pales in fright pallid." In the *Nicomachean Ethics*, he similarly defines shame as "a kind of fear of disrepute [which] produces an effect similar to that produced by fear of danger; for people who feel disgraced blush, and those who fear death turn pale" (1128^b11–13). Although he clearly knew – how could he not? – that emotions have specific physiological expressions, this feature has no role in his more substantive discussions. He does not mention, for instance, how the expressions of the emotions might be perceived by others and affect their behavior. Nor does he mention the possibility of simulating or suppressing emotional expressions, a neglect that is quite natural given his emphasis on involuntary expressions, as distinct from more voluntary expressions such as smiling.

(3) *Cognitive antecedents.* According to W. Fortenbaugh, Aristotle achieved something like a cognitive revolution in the study of the emotions, in that he clearly and decisively "construes the thought of outrage as the efficient cause" of pain.[13] Before Aristotle, "it was easy to think of emotions as diseases whose victims suffer a misfortune curable only by drugs and inspired incantations."[14] If, however, emotions do not act like charms or enchantments but depend on beliefs, they are amenable to rational argument designed to change the beliefs. Moreover, one can use the cognitive antecedents to distinguish among the emotions: "By building the thought of personal insult into the essence of anger Aristotle could draw a logical distinction between this emotion and the emotion of hate. For the occurrence of hate it is not necessary to believe in personal outrage. It is only necessary to think of someone as a certain kind of person – for example, a thief or a sycophant. In other words, the efficient cause became a powerful tool for distinguishing the logical boundaries

---

12. Fortenbaugh (1975), p. 15.
13. *Ibid.*
14. *Ibid.*, p. 17.

between related emotions."[15] Although these two emotions also differ in other ways, their cognitive antecedents may be the only features
that yield *sufficient* grounds for distinguishing them from each other.

It is not entirely clear, however, that Aristotle thought that emotions
were triggered by beliefs in the usual sense.[16] The words he uses to
denote the antecedents of the emotions may sometimes be rendered
by "impression" rather than "belief," as when I have an impression
that the sun is a foot in diameter while at the same time believing it is
not (*De Anima* 428^{b}1–2). According to Martha Nussbaum, in the context of the *Rhetoric* we are entitled to render these words as "belief."[17]
John Cooper, however, praises Aristotle for being "alive to the crucial fact about the emotions, that one can experience them simply on
the basis of how, despite what one knows or believes to be the case,
things strike one."[18] Independent of Aristotelian exegesis, is this a
crucial fact about the emotions? I return to the question in IV.2, in
the context of a discussion of emotions elicited by works of art.[19]

(4) *Intentional objects.* As noted, Aristotle's general strategy in char-
acterizing the emotions includes the identification of the person with
whom we get angry or of whom we are afraid, envious and the like.
The object of an emotion need not be a person, however, and persons
may play other roles in the emotions besides that of being their objects. The case of shame illustrates both points. The disapproval of
others causes us to feel ashamed by some act we have done (or by
the character revealed by that action).

(5) *Pleasure and pain.* As discussed in IV.2, modern writers tend to
think of an emotion as associated with pleasure *or* pain. Aristotle,
by contrast, seemed to think that an individual emotion typically
is associated with pleasure *and* pain. What for us is the exceptional case of "mixed emotions" was, for Aristotle, closer to being
the typical case.[20] The case of anger is paradigmatic. It "may be defined as a desire accompanied by pain, for a conspicuous revenge
for a conspicuous slight at the hands of men who have no call to
slight oneself or one's friends.... It must always be attended by a
certain pleasure – that which arises from the expectation of revenge"

---

15. *Ibid.*, p. 15.
16. Rorty (1996), pp. 17–20.
17. Nussbaum (1996), p. 307.
18. Cooper (1993), p. 191.
19. See Belfiore (1992, pp. 242–44) for a discussion of this question in Aristotle's philosophy of art.
20. See notably Frede (1996).

($1378^a 31$–33). In fact, "no one grows angry with a person on whom there is no prospect of taking vengeance, and we feel comparatively little anger, or none at all, with those who are much our superiors in power" ($1370^b 12$–13).

According to this analysis, the mixed emotion of anger is caused by the presence of two beliefs: The belief that the other insulted me and the belief that I can take revenge. One belief causes pain, the other pleasure.[21] In many cases, this analysis seems exactly right. I wonder, though, whether we cannot feel angry even when there is no prospect of taking vengeance. Aristotle is aware of the problem. Noting that some might deny that the angry man desires vengeance, "because we become angry with our parents, but we do not desire vengeance on them," he refutes them by observing that "upon some people it is vengeance enough to cause them pain and make them sorry" (*Topics* $156^a 37$–39). Yet even if our parents may indeed suffer when we get angry at them, I do not believe the anticipation of their suffering *invariably* contributes an element of pleasure to our anger, although it may do so on occasion. To such counterexamples we might answer with Fortenbaugh that "there is no reason why Aristotle's conception of . . . anger must be exactly like our own," and that Aristotle "does not deny that [an angry] man may on occasion be in a hopeless position and either not realise it or cling to some quite irrational fantasy of safety or revenge."[22] We might add that the anger could itself enter into the causal history of the irrational belief in the possibility of revenge.

Aristotle's claim about anger as a mixed emotion is part of a wider context.[23] Plato had observed that some appetites involve pain and pleasure at the same time, as when the distressing sensation of thirst and the pleasant anticipation of quenching it occur at the same time (*Philebus* 36b). The interruption of the normal state of the body is painful, and the restoration of the normal state is pleasant; hence, through learning, the anticipation of that restoration itself becomes a source of pleasure. This idea is then generalized to "anger, fear, longing, lamenting, love, emulation, malice, and so forth": They, too, are both "pains of the soul" and "replete with immense pleasures"

---

21. By contrast, the treatment of anger as a mixed emotion in Ortony, Clore, and Collins (1988, pp. 146–53) breaks it down into two *negative* components: disapproving of someone else's blameworthy action, and being displeased about an undesirable event.
22. Fortenbaugh (1975, p. 80, n. 1).
23. The following draws heavily on Fortenbaugh (1975) and Frede (1996).

(*ibid.* 47e). Like Aristotle, Plato cites the Homeric lines about the sweetness of wrath; and like Aristotle he refers to "the pleasures mixed up with the pains in lamentation and longing."

These are phenomenological observations; no explanation is offered. Aristotle, by contrast, suggests an explanation in terms of two simultaneous cognitions. We have seen how this works in the case of anger. "Similarly, there is an element of pleasure even in mourning and lamentation. There is grief, indeed, at his loss, but pleasure in remembering him" (*Rhetoric* 1370^{b}24–26). This might be read as a statement of the endowment-contrast mechanism (I.6): Grief over the person who is dead is mingled with pleasant memories of what he was like when alive. To get the analogy with anger right, however, another reading is required: The person who is mourned is absent rather than dead, and the pain of his absence is mingled with the pleasure of the memory-triggered *anticipation* of seeing him again.

The idea may be further generalized. Fear and pity are painful, but there may also be a pleasurable element in the thought of salvation. (But the dreaded outcome might be certain. In that case, Aristotle says [1308^{a}5–8], no fear will be felt.) Envy is distressful but may go together with the pleasurable anticipation of the destruction of the envied object or its possessor. (But the costs of destruction might be prohibitively high.) If we disregard Aristotle's implausible claim that hatred is a painless feeling, this emotion may also be analyzed as involving pain combined with the pleasurable anticipation of the destruction of its object. (But the hated tyrant might be invulnerable.) Guilt is horrible but can be alleviated by the prospects of confession and reparation. (But the person whom we wronged might be dead.)

I return to these connections in IV.2, from a different perspective. There, I argue that emotional life may be a succession of episodes, each of which has an internal structure, rather than a simple succession of experiences. The disturbance of an initial equilibrium generates a negative emotion, which in turn induces an action tendency, a desire to reestablish the equilibrium, the fulfillment of which generates a positive emotion. Plato and Aristotle took the further step of assuming that the last step can be *foreseen* and thus generate pleasures of anticipation simultaneously with the occurrent pains. But as indicated in the parenthetic observations in the previous paragraph, the restoration of equilibrium may be impossible or prohibitively costly. In such cases, and perhaps also when restoration is possible but unlikely, there may not be any pleasures of anticipation. Conversely – a more controversial point – when the future satisfaction is *certain* there may be *no* pain in the present. The analysis clearly does not have the full generality that Aristotle claimed for it.[24] It is simply not true that all emotions are mixed.

I believe, nevertheless, that the analysis captures an important aspect of emotional experience. When an emotion generates an action tendency, the mind may race ahead of itself and consume the outcome of the action even when effective action is blocked. Observing the greater fortune of another, I may feel a brief pain of envy and an equally fleeting joy at the thought of destroying his possessions, before I come to my senses and dismiss the former as unworthy and the latter as both unworthy and impractical. In some cases, as Fortenbaugh notes, daydreams and fantasies about revenge or destruction may persist for longer periods.

(6) *Action tendencies.* The intimate relation between anger and revenge shows that Aristotle believed action tendencies to be features of some emotions. Because the most extensive discussion of the emotions occurs in the part of the *Rhetoric* that deals with the relation between judgment and emotion, rather than between emotion and action, it is more difficult to say whether he ascribed this tendency to all emotions. Among the emotions that I shall discuss, action tendencies are explicitly associated with anger, fear, emulation, envy, and hatred, but not with the others. He certainly does not say about any specific emotion that it has no action tendency, or desire, associated with it.[25] It has been claimed that some of the emotions he discusses, such as shame, pity, and indignation, do not or need not have any action tendency associated with them.[26] This might seem puzzling. Shame, for instance, is strongly linked with the urge to hide or to disappear. The solution to the puzzle may lie in Fortenbaugh's comment that "[i]n extreme cases an ashamed man may commit suicide, but in doing this he is not rectifying the past."[27] This suggests that an action tendency, for Aristotle, would always have to be a tendency to restore the natural equilibrium that has been interrupted by the emotion-generating event. It is hard to see, however, how that

24. Striker (1996), pp. 291–92.
25. Fortenbaugh (1975, p. 82) claims that "Aristotle is . . . clear that [indignation] need not be manifested in action," but the passage from the *Rhetoric* that he cites to support this view does not speak to this issue.
26. Fortenbaugh (1975, pp. 15, 81–82); Striker (1996), p. 293. Striker also cites the fact that emotions such as pride and relief, although based on desire-fulfillment, are not themselves desires. These do not, however, belong to the Aristotelian list of emotions
27. Fortenbaugh (1975), p. 81.

argument would apply to a positive emotions such as love or joy, which induce a tendency to prolong their causes rather than to end them. Given Aristotle's silence on the subject, these are somewhat idle speculations.

ARISTOTLE ON SPECIFIC EMOTIONS

Having discussed Aristotle's view of what emotions are, let us now consider his account of which emotions there are. I disregard his comments on the states that we call emotions but that he does not refer to as *pathe*, such as pride (*Nicomachean Ethics* 1123a–1125a) or two of the motives that are said to trigger anger in others, spite and *hybris* (*Rhetoric* 1378^{b}16–31). Although for us the latter might seem to be emotions when viewed from the point of view of the subject who is experiencing them, Aristotle considers only how their expression through behavior may induce emotions in others.

In the *Nicomachean Ethics* (1105^{b}21–24), Aristotle offers the following list of the passions: "Appetite, anger, fear, confidence, envy, joy, love, hatred, longing, emulation, pity, and in general the states of consciousness that are accompanied by pleasure or pain." The list is overly inclusive, as it allows us to count as passions pleasurable or painful states not triggered by cognition, such as hunger or thirst. The discussion in book II of the *Rhetoric* is more consistent. Here Aristotle discusses how the orator can induce the following psychic states: Anger, calmness, friendship, hatred, fear, confidence, shame, kindness, unkindness, pity, indignation, pleasure at the deserved misfortune of another (gloating), envy, delight at the misfortune of another (malice), emulation, and contempt.[28] It is not clear whether all of these are emotions as we would use the term. Calmness and confidence, for instance, seem to be defined more by the absence of their opposites than by any positive features. Be this as it may, I shall disregard them here, as they are less important for my purposes. In fact, I shall limit myself to anger, hatred, fear, shame, pity, indignation, gloating, envy, malice, and contempt. For the analysis of social and political phenomena, these (mostly dark) emotions seem to have the greatest explanatory relevance.

---

28. Although a far from ideal term, "gloating" is the closest word I could find for pleasure at the deserved misfortune of another. It is embodied in a famous description by Tertullian of the joys of the saved in heaven when they contemplate the sufferings of the damned (cited in Nietzsche 1956, pp. 183–85).

(1) *Anger.* This emotion is said to be triggered by an undeserved slight or belittling, and in turn to trigger the desire for revenge.[29] Whereas I shall argue (IV.2) that mere desire-frustration without intent to slight can also trigger anger, it is less likely to give rise to the desire for revenge. Hence Aristotle's anger may be a different emotion from what we call anger, and more accurately captured by the term "wrath."[30] As noted above, the slighting can take the form of contempt, spite, or insolence. I discuss contempt in a later subsection. Spite is defined as "thwarting another man's wishes, not to get something for yourself but to prevent his getting it. The slight arises just from the fact that you do not aim at something for yourself: Clearly you do not think that he can do you harm, for then you would be afraid of him instead of slighting him, nor yet that he can do you any good worth mentioning, for then you would be anxious to make friends with him" (1378^b16–22). A's anger, in other words, is induced by what he perceives to be B's malicious frustration of his wishes. Anger can also be induced by the perception of B's contempt for an *independently* caused state of wish-frustration: "[P]eople who are afflicted by sickness or poverty or love or thirst or any other unsatisfied desires are prone to anger are easily roused: Especially against those who slight their present distress" (1379^a15–18). As this statement would make little sense if the distress was itself caused by the offending person, as is the case with spite and *hybris*, I infer that Aristotle here is referring to contempt.

Insolence (*hybris*) is an even more intensively interactive phenomenon. Rather than merely frustrating the wish of the other, it embodies deliberate humiliation of the other – "doing and saying things

---

29. Aristotle is concerned with a slight *to oneself*. In *Les Passions de l'âme* (Art. 195), Descartes observes that there is a characteristic emotion, which he calls "indignation," which arises when A observes B slighting C. When A loves C, this indignation is indistinguishable from anger (Art. 201).

30. Frijda (1994), p. 265. Aristotle also claims, however, that wish-frustration as a state of mind may induce anger (1379^a10–22). Cooper (1993, p. 196) argues that this is a case of one emotion (distress) preparing the ground for another (anger). To render Aristotle consistent with himself, one would have to assume that in addition to the cause for distress (wish-frustration) a separate cause of anger (intentional slighting) has to be present. Some of the things Aristotle says in this passage support this reading; others suggest that wish-frustration by itself is enough to induce anger. Cooper seems to have the second idea in mind when he writes that "[t]he upset feeling that belongs to anger in all these cases is an offshoot of the antecedent upset feeling the person has been experiencing in having some aroused, but unsatisfied appetite. It is as if a pre-existent energy, the appetite, gets redirected when one feels oneself blocked or obstructed in satisfying it, and becomes or gives rise to this new feeling of distress, the anger."

that cause shame to the victim, not in order that anything may happen to yourself, or because anything has happened to yourself, but simply for the pleasure involved. (Retaliation is not insolence, but vengeance.) "The cause of the pleasure of the insolent man is that he thinks himself greatly superior to others when ill-treating them" ($1378^{b}24$–26).[31] *Hybris* is when you give offense neither for profit nor in revenge,[32] but simply because you delight in inflicting shame on the other. It follows from Aristotle's analysis that the victim of *hybris* feels both shame and anger: Shame before third parties at what has been done to him, and anger at the person who has done it.[33] I say more about *hybris* in III.4.

Another connection between anger and shame is that they involve exposure before (roughly) the same categories of persons. We feel anger when slighted before "our rivals, those whom we admire, those whom we wish to admire us, those for whom we feel reverence, those who feel reverence for us" ($1379^{b}25$–27). We feel shame if thought badly of by "those who admire us, those whom we admire, those by whom we wish to be admired, those with whom we are competing, and those whose opinion of us we respect" ($1384^{a}27$–29). Anger, for Aristotle, was an intensely social emotion. Although it can occur in dyadic encounters, the central cases involve the triadic relation of *being slighted before an audience*. Although Aristotle's Athens may not have been a full-blown "culture of honor," it certainly had many of the elements that characterize such cultures (see III.4).

The social aspect of anger is also brought out by Aristotle's curious (to us) notion of what constitutes a "justified" slighting. The Greek text in the definition of anger ($1378^{b}1$) is ambiguous, as shown by comparing the Oxford and Loeb translations. The former says that anger is caused by a slight "at the hands of men who have no

31. The Loeb and Kennedy translations render the last sentence by the more general idea that people feel superior when ill-treating others, without specifying (as in the Oxford translation that I cite in the text) that they feel superior *to those whom they are mistreating*. As we see in section III.4, some recorded instances of *hybris* can plausibly be understood in the more restricted sense (Meidias slapping Demosthenes in public), whereas in other cases the structure is that A feels superior to B because unlike B, A can get away with ill-treating C. The case of Alcibiades committing *hybris* against his wife by bringing his *hetairai* into the house illustrates this idea.

32. We see in section V.3, however, that excessive revenge was often interpreted as a form of *hybris*.

33. See Lewis (1992, pp. 149–53) for a recent discussion of anger triggered by shame (and sometimes triggering shame in return). It is not clear, though, that the concepts of anger and shame are those that Aristotle had in mind.

call to slight one," the latter that it is caused "when such a slight is undeserved."[34] For a modern reader, the latter idea is the more natural. We get angry if someone slights us and we have done nothing that would justify the treatment. Aristotle, by contrast, thinks that we get angry when someone offends us who is not in a social position to do so. He notes, namely, that "we feel particularly angry with men of no account at all if they slight us. For *we have supposed* that anger caused by the slight is felt towards people who are not justified in slighting us, and our inferiors are not thus justified" (1379^{b}11–12; my italics).

(2) *Hatred*. Aristotle offers insightful but puzzling discussions of hatred, differentiated from anger as follows:

Enmity may be produced by anger or spite or calumny. Now whereas anger arises from offences against oneself, enmity may arise even without that; we may hate people merely because of what we take to be their character. Anger is always concerned with individuals – Callias or Socrates – whereas hatred is directed also against classes: we all hate any thief and any informer. Moreover, anger can be cured by time; but hatred cannot. The one aims at giving pain to its object, the other at doing him harm; the angry man wants his victim to feel, the hater does not mind whether they feel or not.... And anger is accompanied by pain, hatred is not; the angry man feels pain, but the hater does not. Much may happen to make the angry man pity those who offend him, but the hater under no circumstances wishes to pity a man whom he once hated; for the one would have the offenders suffer for what they have done; the other would have them cease to exist. (1382^{a}2–16).

A similar analysis is offered in the *Politics:*

There are two chief motives which induce men to attack tyrannies – hatred and contempt. Hatred of tyrants is inevitable, and contempt is also a frequent cause of their destruction. Thus we see that most of those who have acquired, have retained their power, but those who have inherited it, have lost it, almost at once; for living in luxurious ease, they have become contemptible, and offer many opportunities to their assailants. Anger, too, must be included under hatred, and produces the same effects. It is often even more ready to strike – the angry are more impetuous in making an attack, for they do not follow rational principle. And men are very apt to give way to their passions when they are insulted. To this cause is to be attributed the fall of

---

34. The rendering in Cope (1877) is the same as in the Loeb translation, which makes it hard to understand why in his rendering of 1379^{b}11–12 Cope refers back to the definition given in 1378^{b}1. The translation in Kennedy (1991) preserves the ambiguity of the original.

the Peisistratidae and of many others. Hatred is more reasonable, for anger is accompanied by pain, which is an impediment to reason, whereas hatred is painless. ($1312^b19\text{--}34$)

In anger, my hostility is directed towards another's action and can be extinguished by getting even – an action that reestablishes the equilibrium. In hatred, my hostility is directed toward another person or a category of individuals who are seen as intrinsically and irremediably bad. For the world to be made whole, they have to disappear. This distinction is valuable, and largely neglected by modern emotion theorists. In his brief discussion of the issue, Nico Frijda argues that hatred is to anger what shame is to guilt: The first member in each pair is based on an "object evaluation," the second on an "event evaluation."[35] Hatred says that "he is bad," anger that "he did something bad to me." Analogously, shame reflects the idea "I am bad," guilt that "I did something bad" (III.2). Frijda captures part of Aristotle's intuition, but not the idea that hatred can be directed towards categories of individuals as well as against specific persons.[36] None of five other authoritative texts that I consulted characterize hatred; and in fact only one of them mentions it at all.[37] The two texts that discuss the closely related idea of prejudice spell it out in terms of contempt rather than hatred.[38]

The puzzling feature of Aristotle's analyses is the assertion that hatred is unaccompanied by pain. Concerning the first of the two passages that I cite here, it has been suggested that Aristotle treats hatred as an emotional disposition rather than as an occurrent emotion;[39] concerning the second, that it "makes one almost think he is talking about no emotion or passion at all, but a fully reasoned dispassionate

35. Frijda (1986), p. 212. The analogy with guilt and shame is mine, not Frijda's. In fact, he suggests that guilt is based on an object evaluation "because, or to the extent that, this implies self-hatred" (*ibid.*, p. 213).
36. Aristotle himself is unclear on this point. By treating hate and love (or "liking") together (1380^b34) he seems to imply that hate is the opposite of love, and yet the latter emotion is always directed towards specific individuals rather than against categories of individuals.
37. These are Tomkins (1992), Ekman and Davidson (1994), Lewis and Havilland (1993), Izard (1991), and Oatley and Jenkins (1996). The last text makes a few references to hatred, but does not try to characterize it. Perhaps one can reconstruct their idea of hatred from the claim that "envy is hatred arising from comparison of oneself with another person" (p. 88). The hostility in envy, however, differs from the hostility in hatred as, following Aristotle, I construe it here.
38. Izard (1991), p. 274; Oatley and Jenkins (1996), p. 308.
39. Leighton (1996), pp. 232–33, n. 14. See IV.2 for the distinction between occurrent and dispositional conceptions of the emotions.

65

rejection and dislike."[40] Yet as these commentators recognize, these observations do not do away with the problem: Aristotle explicitly says that hatred is a *pathos* and that a *pathos* is accompanied by pain and pleasure. If we assume, more than plausibly, that hatred is not accompanied by pleasure, there is a stark contradiction.

Whatever solution one adopts to the exegetical issue, understanding hatred merely as a disposition does not make substantive sense. It follows from first principles that the immediate cause of behavior must be an occurrence rather than a disposition. My irascibility does not serve as a direct cause of behavior, although it might enter indirectly into the causation of my action, for example through my awareness of it.[41] Only the occurrent emotion of anger can serve as a direct cause of behavior. Similarly, my misogyny – a disposition to hate women – cannot be the proximate cause of my behavior. What causes me to act must be an occurrent emotion that has the same relation to misogyny that anger has to irascibility – but what emotion is that? "Hatred" may do as well as any other term, as long as we keep in mind that the word is also used in the dispositional sense. Although Aristotle's statement that hatred is unaccompanied by pain makes sense if applied to the disposition rather than to its occurrent manifestations, the contrast with anger is misleading, as irascibility is not accompanied by pain either.

Finally, it would seem that hatred does involve pain. For the prejudiced or the fanatic, the thought that the earth is inhabited by what he perceives as evil creatures – members of another race, ethnic group, or religious community – can be intensely painful. One can imagine, to be sure, that the offending category is viewed with "fully reasoned dispassionate rejection and dislike." Some of those who advocate the death penalty for certain crimes may believe, dispassionately, that those who commit such crimes ought to die. But given the undeniable reality of passionate hatred, it is confusing to use the same word about dispassionate reasoning that happens to yield similar conclusions.

The other contrasts that Aristotle draws here between anger and hatred are more valid. Compared with anger, hatred is more compatible with rational calculation. The greatest act of hatred in history, the Holocaust, was carried out in a methodical and systematic way. Although hatred is painful, it does not cloud the mind as anger or

---

40. Cooper (1993), p. 193.
41. For other (nonmental) ways in which dispositions can enter into causal explanations, see Cohen (1982).

fear do. Although frequently based on irrational beliefs, the behavior it triggers need not be irrational, given those beliefs. For this reason, I cannot fully accept Aristotle's argument that "[o]f those who attempt assassination they are the most dangerous, and require to be most carefully watched, who do not take care to survive, if they effect their purpose. Therefore special precautions should be taken about any who think that either they or those for whom they care have been insulted; for when men are led away by a passion to assault others they are regardless of themselves. As Heracleitus says, 'It is difficult to fight against anger; for a man will buy revenge with his soul'" (*Politics* 1315ª25–31). Although the angry man may indeed be willing to take risks that a calculating hater would avoid, his lack of instrumental rationality detracts from his chances of success. The net impact on how dangerous he is for the ruler, compared with someone motivated by hatred, could go either way (see Chapter I).

The statement that anger wants the offender to suffer whereas hatred wants him to cease to exist also makes good sense. Commenting on the genocidal tendencies of the Spanish Inquisition, B. Netanyahu writes that "the extreme, irreparable evil which allegedly inhered in the Jewish nature had to be treated in an extreme manner: Since it was incorrigible, it had to be annihilated."[42] Torture, in the Inquisition, was used not for the purpose of making the victims (Jews converted to Christian faith) suffer, but to coerce them into fictitious confessions of being secret "Judaizers" that would justify their persecution and execution. The Holocaust, too, was based on the desire to extinguish the Jews, not to make them suffer.

Although talk about hatred is not unusual in everyday life, it often means nothing but a strong feeling of anger. "I hate him for what he did to me." In my opinion hatred, in Aristotle's technical sense, is a crucially important emotion in explaining many forms of behavior, notably political behavior. What allows us to differentiate it from other emotions is, as Aristotle said, the belief that a certain person or a certain category of people are intrinsically bad. The link to behavior is not that "because they do bad things, they are bad," but the converse, "because they are bad, they do bad things." Thus evidence about their actual behavior will not affect the belief that they are bad, any more than evidence about the apparently mature behavior of a small child will affect our policy of assuming that he or she is likely to behave childishly. "Their true nature will come out." Thus according to the

42. Netanyahu (1995), p. 990.

racist theory underlying the Spanish Inquisition, "the Jewish moral propensities, inherited by the Marranos from the Jews, must sooner or later determine their religion – which means that those who are *racially* Jews are also, or will be, *religiously* Jews."[43]

(3) *Fear, pity, envy, indignation, gloating, malice.* I treat these emotions together, because of their close relations to one another. They are characterized in terms of three pairs of concepts: Whether something good/bad that is deserved/undeserved is predicated about oneself/others. Here, "undeserved" should be distinguished from "nondeserved." If I get rich by stealth, it is undeserved. If I get rich by hard work, to use a non-Aristotelian example, it is deserved. If I win the big prize in the lottery, it is neither deserved nor undeserved, it is nondeserved (and nonundeserved). Similarly, if I am punished for a crime I committed, my fate is deserved. If I am punished for a crime I did not commit, it is undeserved. If I am hit by a meteor, it is neither deserved nor undeserved.

The notion of desert used here is spelled out in Aristotle's discussion of indignation, caused by the sight of the undeserved good fortune of others. From his discussion, it is clear that my example of desert (wealth achieved by hard work) is indeed non-Aristotelian. Although this *topos* does occur in speeches from the period,[44] Aristotle does not mention it. Instead, he elaborates as follows:

> Indignation is roused by the sight of wealth, power, and the like – by all those things, roughly speaking, which are deserved by good men and by those who possess the goods of nature – noble birth, beauty, and so on. Again, what is long established seems akin to what exists by nature; and therefore we feel more indignation at those possessing a given good if they have as a matter of fact only just got it and the prosperity it brings with it. The newly rich give more offence than those whose wealth is of long standing and inherited.... Further, it is not any and every man that deserves any given kind of good; there is a certain correspondence and appropriateness to such things; thus it is appropriate for brave men, not for just men, to have fine weapons, and for men of family, not for parvenus, to make distinguished marriages. Indignation may therefore properly be felt when anyone gets what is not appropriate for him, though he may be a good man enough. (1387^{a}14–32)

This passage, which could have been used as an epigraph by Proust or Edith Wharton, reflects very much an upper-class attitude.

43. *Ibid.*, p. 983.
44. Ober (1989), p. 221.

Although Aristotle himself may not have shared it, he seems to be advising speakers about how to address an upper-class audience, or at least an audience for which upper-class values had some appeal.[45] Yet Aristotle also entertained the more natural (to us) idea that desert is related to behavior: "If you are pained by the unmerited distress of others, you will be pleased, or at least not pained, by their merited distress. Thus no good man can be pained by the punishment of parricides or murderers" ($1386^b26–28$). In the previous cited passage, note the acute observation that the sheer passage of time can give rise to a belief in entitlement, a theme to which I return in V.2.

Fear is produced when something bad is about to happen to oneself. Although Aristotle does not mention desert in this context, one might imagine a finer differentiation according to which the bad thing is deserved, undeserved, or neither. *Pity* is produced when an undeserved bad happens to another. Although Aristotle asserts (1382^b26, 1386^a28) that what causes fear if it happens to ourselves is also what causes us to feel pity when it happens to another, this claim is somewhat undermined by the lack of reference to desert in the definition of fear. *Envy* is produced when another possesses a good that I lack. *Indignation* is produced when an undeserved good is possessed by another. In the case of envy, therefore, the good must be either deserved or nonundeserved, two cases that might give rise to subtle differences in the envy that is felt. *Malice* is produced by the distress of another. *Gloating* is produced when the other's distress is deserved. Malice, therefore, will occur only when the bad is undeserved or nondeserved. Again, the two cases might yield different emotional nuances. Although Aristotle does not mention hope, that is, the emotion or emotions that arise when a deserved, undeserved, or nondeserved good is about to happen to oneself, the analyses of anticipated pleasure referred to above may partly fill this gap.

The conditions under which we feel fear include (beliefs about) both the motives and the opportunities of those whom we fear. We need not fear them, obviously, if they have no power to harm us.

---

45. For this distinction, see Dover (1994, pp. 34–35); also, at greater length, Ober (1989, pp. 141 [the social composition of the Athenian jury was representative of the population at large], 287 [the jurors were not hostile to the idea of personal superiority], and *passim*). His explanation of the suspicion of the nouveaux-riches differs from Aristotle's: "Basic to the topos was the assumption that since they had started with nothing, the newly wealthy politicians must have accrued their wealth dishonestly" (Ober 1989, p. 235).

Their motives to do us harm include hatred, anger, and, strikingly, fear. People fear "those who have done people wrong, if they possess power, since they stand in fear of retaliation" (1382^b11–12). Aristotle does not mention envy or malice in others as a reason for fearing them. The reason might be that envy is felt by inferiors, who rarely have the power to harm one. Yet one person might have reason to fear the envy of many inferiors when joined together, as Aristotle recognizes in the *Politics* (1304^a37).

The conditions under which we feel pity and envy also include similarity of situation with the pitied or envied man. With regard to pity, Aristotle says that "we pity those who are like us in age, character, disposition, social standing, or birth; for in all these cases it appears more likely that the same misfortune may befall us also" (1386^a25–27). With regard to envy, he says that "we feel it towards our equals . . . ; and by 'equals' I mean equals in birth, relationship, age, disposition, distinction, or wealth" (1387^b23–26). Or again, "we envy those who are near us in time, place, age or reputation" (1388^a6). In both cases, then, the cognitive antecedents for the emotions include the thought "it could have been me," which I discuss in III.3 with regard to envy. A similar condition obtains, as we shall see, in some cases of shame.

(4) *Shame.* In the *Nicomachean Ethics* Aristotle writes that shame

is not becoming to every age; but only to youth. For we think young people should be prone to shame because they live by passion and therefore commit many errors, but are restrained by shame; and we praise young people who are prone to this passion, but an older person no one would praise for being prone to the sense of disgrace, since we think he should not do anything that need cause this sense. For the sense of disgrace is not even characteristic of a good man, since it is consequent on bad actions . . . ; and it is a mark of a bad man even to be such as to do any disgraceful action. To be so constituted as to feel disgrace if one does such an action, and for this reason to think oneself good, is absurd; for it is for voluntary actions that shame is felt, and the good man will never voluntarily do bad actions. But shame may be said to be conditionally a good thing; *if* a good man did such actions, he would feel disgraced; but the excellences are not subject to such qualifications. And if shamelessness – not to be ashamed of doing bad actions – is bad, that does not make it good to be ashamed of doing such actions. (1128^b10–33).

This austere-sounding passage can be read in conjunction with two others, which create a more nuanced picture:

Citizens seem to face courage because of the penalties imposed by the laws and the reproaches they would otherwise incur, and because of the honours they win by such action; and therefore those peoples seem to be bravest among whom cowards are held in dishonour and brave men in honour.... This kind of courage... is due to shame and to desire of a noble object (i.e., honour) and avoidance of disgrace, which is ignoble. One might rank in the same class even those who are compelled by their rulers; but they are inferior, inasmuch as they act not from shame but from fear, and to avoid not what is disgraceful but what is painful. ($1116^a 18$–32)

[While arguments] seem to have the power to encourage and stimulate the generous-minded among the young, and to make a character which is gently born, and a true lover of what is noble, ready to be possessed by excellence, they are not able to encourage the many to nobility and goodness. For these do not by nature obey the sense of shame, but only fear, and do not abstain from bad acts because of their baseness but through fear of punishment. ($1179^b 7$–12)

Although the reading of these and related passages is difficult, the following propositions may, perhaps, be defended. "The many," although shameless, are kept in check by the fear of physical punishment. Aristotle makes it clear that shame operates through the immediate feeling of disgrace rather than through any material sanctions that might accompany it. Second, among the young and immature, shame acts as a useful passion that counteracts other passions. Third, shame may serve the role of fixing the end of action rather than that of shaping each and every action. Commenting on the second passage, Myles Burnyeat writes that "the only thing that is 'second best' about this form of courage is that the citizen soldier takes his conception of what is noble from the laws and other people's expectations rather than having his own internalized sense of the noble and disgraceful."[46] Fourth, shame may be a stage in moral learning – Burnyeat calls it "the semivirtue of the learner."[47] Finally, once that learning has been accomplished, shame plays no further role. Acting courageously then flows from one's nature, like water seeking its natural downhill course. In battle, some soldiers refrain from cowardly behavior because of the fear of being punished by their superiors, whereas others are held in check by the shame they would feel before

---

46. Burnyeat (1980), p. 89, n. 13; see also Belfiore (1992), p. 202; and Cairns (1993), p. 419.
47. Burnyeat (1980), p. 78.

their equals. The truly excellent man thinks neither of his superior nor of his equals.

In the *Ethics*, shame is induced by the fear of disgrace from acting ignobly. The *Rhetoric* covers a wider range of grounds for shame. In general, "Shame may be defined as pain or disturbance in regard to bad things, whether present, past or future, which seems likely to involve us in discredit" (1383^b15–16). Here, too, it is clear that the pain is intrinsic rather than consequential: "[W]e shrink from the disgrace itself and not from its consequences" (1384^a24–25). Some of the things that induce disgrace are, as in the *Ethics*, due to badness: Cowardness, licentiousness, meanness, flattery, boastfulness, and so on. In addition, "another bad thing at which we feel shame is, lacking a share in the honourable things shared by everyone else, or by all or nearly all who are like ourselves... Once we are on a level with others, it is a disgrace to be, say, less well educated than they are; and so on with other advantages; all the more so, in each case, if it is seen to be our own fault" (1384^a9–15). Here, shame shades over into envy, which is also felt of "those whose possession or success in a thing is a reproach to us: These are our neighbours and equals; for it is clear that it is our own fault we have missed the good thing in question" (1388^a17–19). As already noted shame can also shade over into anger, if we are submitted to hybristic behavior (e.g., rape). In this section, however, Aristotle adds that the shame arises when we submit to *hybris* without resisting, for such behavior is "due to unmanliness or cowardice" (1384^a21). I do not know whether he meant to suggest that in such cases, our co-complicity in the act defuses anger so that only shame remains.

(5) *Contempt.* In III.2 I argue that shame and contempt are correlated emotions. We feel shame if and only if we are the targets of the actual or anticipated contempt of others. Although Aristotle discusses both emotions, he does not draw this connection. Rather, as we have seen, he cites (what we translate as) contempt as a source of anger in the target. Quite possibly, he had a somewhat different emotion in mind. This interpretation is also supported by the fact that he cites contempt, along with hatred, as a source of opposition to tyrants. In fact, he does not state that the persons whose disapproval causes us to feel shame feel any emotion at all.

Aristotle's explicit discussion of contempt as an emotion occurs in his discussion of emulation, an emotion related to envy but different in that "it is felt not because others have [highly valued goods], but because we have not got them ourselves... Emulation makes us take steps to secure the good things in question, envy makes us take steps to stop our neighbour having them" (1388ᵃ33–36). In his enumeration of those who are the object of emulation, Aristotle includes

those who have . . . courage, wisdom, public office . . . Also those whom many people wish to be like; those who have many acquaintances or friends; those whom many admire, or whom we ourselves admire; and those who have been praised and eulogized by the poets or prose-writers. Persons of the contrary sort are objects of contempt: for the feeling and notion of contempt are opposite to those of emulation. Those who are such as to emulate or be emulated by others are inevitably disposed to be contemptuous of all such persons as are subject to those bad things which are contrary to the good things that are the objects of emulation, despising them just for that reason. Hence we often despise the fortunate, when luck comes to them without their having those good things which are held in honour. (1388ᵇ15–28)

Like hatred, contempt is triggered by the belief that a person is intrinsically bad. Whereas the badness of the person we hate is related to his ineradicably evil character, the badness of the person towards whom we feel contempt is based on his utter lack of worth. In Aristotle's case the lack of worth was expressed as lack of honor, but that is a contingent feature. Lord Chesterfield, writing to his son, certainly thought women were inferior, but not because they lacked honor:

Women, then, are only children of a larger growth; they have an entertaining tattle, and sometimes wit; but for solid reasoning, good sense, I never knew in my life one who had it, or who reasoned or acted consequentially for four and twenty fours together . . . A man of sense only trifles with them, plays with them, humors and flatters them, as he does a sprightly forward child; but he neither consults them about, nor trusts them with serious matters, though he often makes them believe that he does both; which is the thing in the world that they are most proud of . . . Women are much more like each other than men; they have in truth but two passions, vanity and love; these are their universal characteristics.[48]

If I hate another and I have the power to harm him, he is likely to be afraid (1382ᵃ32). If I express my contempt for him, he is likely to be angry. (That presumably is why Lord Chesterfield thought one should

---

48. Cited in Allport (1979), pp. 33–34.

make women believe they were trusted.) Hate can be symmetrical, as shown by the fact that Aristotle sometimes uses "hatred" and "enmity" as near-synonyms (1382^a1-3). It can also be asymmetrical, as shown by the hatred of thieves and informers. Contempt, by contrast, is usually asymmetrical: If I believe another to be utterly lacking in worth or honor, he is unlikely to think the same of me. As mentioned above, prejudice can take the form either of hatred or contempt. When President Reagan referred to the USSR as "the evil empire," he expressed hatred, not contempt. Lord Chesterfield expresses contempt for women, not hatred. Followers of Hitler thought Jews evil but Slavs inferior.[49]

The emotion of contempt is likely to be particularly strong if the person or group believed to be inferior is also seen as more powerful than oneself. An example is found in Aristotle's comment on the contempt for tyrants. Another example occurs when a regime change propels into power a group viewed as inferior by the traditional elite. Thus Aristotle cites several examples to show that contempt can cause the fall of democracies, "when the wealthy despise the disorder and anarchy which they see prevalent" (*Politics* 1302^b29-30). In this case, contempt is close to resentment, defined by Roger Petersen as "the emotion that stems from the perception that one's group is located in an unjust subordinate position on a status hierarchy."[50]

The antecedents of these emotions are quite varied. They include beliefs about *actions* and the motivations behind them (anger, shame, pity, fear), *possessions* (envy, indignation, emulation, gloating, malice), and *character traits* (hatred, contempt). More simply, they include beliefs about what people – others or oneself – do, have, and are. In addition, some emotions (pity, fear) can be triggered by *events*, that is, by what happens in the nonhuman world. The actions, possessions, traits, and events may lie in the past (one is ashamed of what one has done), in the present (one is angry when struck by another), or in the future (one is afraid of something that is about to happen) or extend over time (one hates people for constant character traits). Aristotle also takes account of counterfactual beliefs: When he observes that we feel shame and envy by failing to achieve what others like us have

---

49. Goldhagen (1996), p. 469.
50. Petersen (1997). As an example, he cites the resentment felt towards Jews by the general Lithuanian population during the period of Soviet occupation in 1940 and 1941, when Jews briefly acquired positions of political influence they had never had before. See also III.1 for further comments on this concept of resentment.

achieved, it is presumably because we think that we, being like them, could have done what they did.

CONCLUSION

Aristotle's analyses of the emotions are extremely instructive. They illuminate his world, or his emotional world, as well as the emotions more generally. The passages I have cited suggest an emotional world that differs from our own. It is intensely confrontational, intensely competitive, and intensely public; in fact, much of it involves confrontations and competitions before a public. It is a world in which everybody knows that they are constantly being judged, nobody hides that they are acting as judges, and nobody hides that they seek to be judged positively. It is a world with very little hypocrisy, or "emotional tact." People did occasionally try to misrepresent their emotions (V.3), but to a much smaller extent than in other societies. Also, the Athenians were relatively unselfconscious. They did not have the idea that emotions could be the object of (as distinct from the effect or the cause of) cognition, nor a fortiori the idea that emotional reactions might themselves give rise to further emotional reactions *in the same subject*. As far as we can tell from the texts that have come down to us, being ashamed of one's anger was not a typical Greek reaction.

From the point of view of emotion theory, many of Aristotle's insights have become so much part of our thinking that we scarcely feel any intellectual surprise when we encounter them in his writings. Let me mention, nevertheless, some of the ideas that remain relatively undeveloped. First, Aristotle's elaboration of Plato's view of the mixed nature of the emotions, as comprising both pain and pleasure, offers a line of argument that seems worthwhile to pursue. Second, his refined analyses of the cognitive antecedents of the emotions go beyond any other discussion known to me. Although we may quarrel with some details and be puzzled by the extreme brevity of many formulations, the basic principles of his approach are sound and not, I think, fully explored. Third, his idea that the antecedents of the emotions also include noncognitive (and nonemotional) mental states such as distress is valuable and, I believe, neglected. Finally, although his analysis of the emotions of prejudice – hatred and contempt – is very sketchy, it still goes beyond almost anything to be found in the modern literature.

II.3. THE FRENCH MORALISTS

After Aristotle, the next major advance in understanding the emotions came with the French moralists, from Montaigne to La Bruyère. Their main contribution, I believe, was to identify *causal effects of emotions on mental life*. Aristotle focused primarily on how emotions are triggered by external causes, and secondarily on how they trigger behavior directly, that is, by spontaneous action tendencies. He did not, in any sustained manner, discuss how emotions may affect judgment, generate other emotions, or induce what I shall call transmutation of motivations.[51] A fortiori, he did not discuss how emotions may affect behavior indirectly, by generating other mental changes that in turn affect behavior.

For a brief illustration, consider the effects of envy (see also III.3). For Aristotle, envy makes us want to prevent others from having a good we lack, for example by destroying it. This is a *direct behavioral effect*. From a different perspective, La Rochefoucauld observes, "The very pride that makes us condemn failings from which we think we are exempt leads us to despise good qualities we do not possess" (M462).[52] Here, the behavioral effects of envy are preempted by the

---

51. As we have seen, the impact of emotion on judgment is actually part of Aristotle's definition of emotion. And in one important passage (*Rhetoric* 1377^{b}30–1378^{a}4) he suggests that the impact tends to be a self-serving one. Although Leighton (1996) argues that Aristotle has a systematic theory of the impact of emotion on judgment, I do not believe his examples support his view. He writes, for instance, "Should one be moved to anger, one thereby views the object of anger as having insulted one (1378^{a}31–33). Becoming ashamed of a person involves being brought to view the person as involved in misdeeds that bring dishonor (1383^{b}15–16)" (p. 209). What he says about anger could be read either as saying that it is accompanied by a judgment that one has been insulted or as saying that it causes that judgment. The first reading, although plausible and perhaps trivial, does not support a causal theory. The second reading does support a causal theory, but not one that lends itself to generalization nor one that Aristotle can plausibly be said to have had in mind, namely the idea that a spontaneous reaction of unjustified anger may invent a reason for itself. This would be the case of an irrational emotion (IV.3); but not all cases of anger are cases of irrational anger. Similar comments apply to what Leighton says about shame; in addition, it should be noted that the passage he cites from the *Rhetoric* is in fact not about vicarious shame.

52. I refer to La Rochefoucauld's *Maxims* as "M" followed by their number in the final (fifth) edition, by "MS" followed by their number in the "Maximes supprimées" and by "MP" followed by their number in the "Maximes posthumes." All of these are included in the Penguin Classics translation by Leonard Tancock, although the numbering of the Maximes supprimées and Maximes posthumes differs from that of the standard edition of the *Maximes* (Truchet 1992) which I follow here. I refer to maxims from earlier edition as "M" followed by a roman numeral to indicate the edition and an Arabic numeral to indicate the number of the maxim, and

mental operation of devaluing the good. Why destroy an object in another's possession when we can persuade ourselves that it is not worth having? This is a *purely psychic effect* of envy. La Rochefoucauld also observes that "[w]e often make envenomed and backhanded compliments, the effect of which is to show up in those we praise faults which we dare not point out in any other way" (M145). As I argue later (III.3), the emotion of envy may be so shameful that we cannot give vent to it directly. Damning by faint praise may, therefore, be an *indirect behavioral effect* of envy, a compromise between the emotions of envy and shame.

The four writers I discuss – Montaigne, Pascal, La Rochefoucauld, La Bruyère – mark the beginning and the end of the greatest era in French intellectual and cultural history. A fuller study of the views of the emotions in this period would have to include many other writers. In *Les passions de l'âme* Descartes offered a systematic analysis of the emotions that in many ways goes far beyond what we find in the moralists.[53] Although some of his analyses are intimately tied to idiosyncratic elements of his general philosophy, others are independently insightful. In other ways – and this is the aspect that concerns me here – Descartes attempts and achieves less than the moralists. Like Aristotle, he ignores the psychic effects and the indirect behavioral effects of the emotions. He is little concerned with the corrosive and transmuting effects of the desires for esteem and self-esteem. Among the moralists, for instance, the idea of prideful humility was a commonplace. Descartes, by contrast, discusses pridefulness ("orgueuil") and "vicious humility" in terms of their common cause, namely lack of self-knowledge, rather than explaining the latter by the former (PA§§157,159,160).

If Descartes falls short of the moralists in these respects, Pascal is much more than a moralist. Although Pascal has penetrating observations on the passions in his *Pensées*, they form only a part of the whole. Also, they mostly touch on vanity, pridefulness, and their foundation in *amour-propre*, more rarely on other emotions. Yet when he deals with these issues, his debunking of human virtue and human knowledge is as radical as anything found in La Rochefoucauld. They both subscribed to a principle that La Bruyère was to formulate as follows: "Men are very vain, and of all things hate to be thought

to maxims in the Liancourt manuscript as "L" followed by their number. These maxims are all found in Truchet's edition. Rochefoucauld's *Réflexions Diverses* are cited from the same edition.

53. Referred to below as PA.

so" (*Characters* XI.65).[54] Pascal, in fact, used this axiom as an argument for the authenticity of the Scripture or the saintliness of the Evangelists or both:

The style of the Gospels is remarkable in so many ways; among others for never putting in any invective against the executioners and enemies of Christ. For there is none in any of the historians against Judas, Pilate or any of the Jews. If this restraint of the Evangelists had been put on [*affectée*], together with many other features of such fine character, and if they had only put it on in order to draw attention to it, not daring to remark on it themselves, they would not have failed to acquire friends to make such remarks for their benefit. But, since they acted as they did without any affectation and quite disinterestedly, they did not cause anyone to remark on it. And I believe that many of these things have never been remarked on before. That shows how coolly the thing was done. (*Pensée* 658)[55]

In fiction, the work of Corneille, Molière, Racine, and La Fontaine often expresses attitudes very similar to those of the moralists. Racine's *Andromaque*, for instance, is a study in emotional self-deception that is easily intelligible in light of their main tenets (II.4). La Rochefoucauld has been likened both to Alceste and to Philinte in *Le Misanthrope*.[56] Among theologians, the writings of Bossuet, Fénelon, and especially Nicole testify to many of the same concerns.[57] Finally, there is a large undergrowth of minor seventeenth-century moralists, notably Jacques Esprit and the Spanish writer Gracian whose book on the courtier was translated into French in 1684 but known in La Rochefoucauld's circles well before that time. Where Gracian's *Oracula* is "almost entirely concerned with worldly one-upmanship"[58] and therefore only superficially related to the concerns of the moralists, Esprit's *De la Fausseté des Vertus Humaines* is a morose piece of Jansenist moralizing rather than an exercise in moral psychology.

---

54. I cite La Bruyère's *Les Caractères* in the translation by Henri van Laun (1885). The first number indicates the chapter (not enumerated in all editions), the second the place of the proposition within the chapter.
55. In citing the *Pensées*, I use the now-standard numbering from the edition by Sellier (1991). This is a bit awkward, as I mainly use the translation by A. J. Krailsheimer in Penguin Classics, which relies on another numbering. Both editions, however, include concordances. I have also consulted the (incomplete) translation by Honor Levi in Oxford's World's Classics series.
56. Hippeau (1978), Chapter 7.
57. For several striking passages in Nicole's writings see Lafond (1986, pp. 27, 110, 191).
58. Thweatt (1980), p. 58.

Among the briefer writings assembled by Jean Lafond in *Moralistes du XVIIe Siècle*, the most remarkable are perhaps the 49 posthumous *Pensées* by Jean Domat (a close friend of Pascal) and the *Discours sur les passions de l'amour*, of unknown authorship (previously attributed to Pascal).[59]

The emphasis I give to La Bruyère may need some explanation. As a thinker, he does not even begin to compare with Montaigne or Pascal, and he is distinctly less penetrating than La Rochefoucauld. His longer character portraits are grotesque descriptions of maniacs that more than anything resemble his own portrait of the "blockhead" or *sot*: "an automaton, a piece of machinery moved by springs and weights, always turning him about in one direction; he always displays the same equanimity, is uniform and never alters; if you have seen him once you have seen him as he ever was, and will be" (*Characters* XI.142).[60] In his more abstract vein, he can be trivial and heavy-handed. Yet at his not-infrequent best he can be very acute, as I hope will become clear. And if for no other reason I want to include him because of a stunning formulation that serves as the matrix for Chapter V: "Nothing is easier for passion than to overcome reason; its greatest triumph is to conquer interest" (*Characters* IV.77).

The French moralists from 1580 to 1680 can be placed in a broader context. Montaigne was constantly inspired by Seneca and Plutarch (*Essays* II.32). La Rochefoucauld defined himself explicitly against Seneca's moral philosophy (the frontispiece of the *Maximes* shows a smiling bust of Seneca unmasked to reveal the grimacing face behind). Pascal, too, saw the presumptuous Stoic philosophy as a main temptation to be avoided. Nevertheless, Seneca's moral psychology contains many insights that, perhaps mediated by Montaigne, reappear in Pascal and la Rochefoucauld. Two examples from *On Anger* show the kind of reasoning I have in mind. "Men whose spirit has grown arrogant from the great favor of fortune have this most serious fault – those whom they have injured they also hate (*quos laeserunt et oderunt*)."[61] Also, "Reason wishes the decision that it gives to be just; anger wishes to have the decision which it has given seem the just decision."[62] I return to both ideas in Chapters IV and V, when discussing irrational emotions.

---

59. Lafond (1992). He also reproduces the "Maximes" of Mme. de Sablé, a close collaborator and inspirator of La Rochefoucauld.
60. See Gray (1986) for an elaboration of this theme.
61. *On Anger*, II.xxiii.
62. *Ibid.*, I.xviii.

In *Reflections on Human Nature*, A. O. Lovejoy showed that the concerns of the French moralists were shared by many English and American writers in the seventeenth and eighteenth centuries. More recently, Albert Hirschman and Morton White have explored the role of La Bruyère's trio of motivations – interest, reason, and passion – in eighteenth-century philosophical and political thought.[63] In France, the work of the moralists was continued by Vauvenargues, whose *Réflexions et Maximes* were modeled on La Rochefoucauld. Also, the publication in 1889 of Montesquieu's *Pensées* shows that his mind was very much like that of the moralists. An example at random: "When a man lacks a certain quality that he cannot obtain, vanity comes to his help and makes him imagine that he has it. Thus an ugly woman believes herself to be beautiful, and a foolish man to have wit. When a man feels the lack of a quality that he can obtain, he compensates himself by jealousy. Thus one is jealous of the rich and the great. The true reason is that vanity cannot fool itself about riches and greatness."[64]

MAXIMS, PROVERBS, AND MECHANISMS

The moralists, notably La Rochefoucauld and La Bruyère, expressed many of their insights in the form of *maxims*, brief epigrammatic statements, usually with a paradoxical twist. Often, these rely on mechanisms in the sense of Chapter I. Sometimes, they rely on what I shall call *reverse mechanisms*. Although maxims are sometimes contrasted with proverbs,[65] they are in many ways quite similar to the latter. Montesquieu, for instance, said that "The *Maxims* of M. de

63. Hirschman (1977), White (1987).
64. Montesquieu (1991), *Pensée* 106. It is not clear however, that Montesquieu was right in stipulating the coincidence of these two criteria. There are qualities, such as height, that one can neither obtain by effort nor fool oneself into thinking that one has.
65. For Lafond (1986, p. 136) proverbs are "truisms" that are ratified by "the impersonal wisdom of the nations." Maxims, by contrast, are closer to the paradox and to what he calls the "antiproverb." As we saw in Chapter I, however, many antiproverbs are themselves proverbial truths (see also Saulnier 1950, p. 88). Rather than distinguishing between maxims and proverbs, I would group them together and oppose both to *aphorisms*. The latter "have the air of brittle special cases," whereas proverbs and maxims "convey a substantial portion of a philosophy of life" (Kenner 1983, pp. 84–85, cited after Mieder 1993, p. 35).

la Rochefoucauld are the proverbs of *des gens d'esprit*."[66] A maxim accentuates one aspect of human experience, often contrary to the accepted or conventional wisdom. To make an impression, the author may state it as a universal truth,[67] whereas in reality it is only intended to counterbalance popular opinion. As Jean Lafond observes, "this is only an artifice and a cunning of style: the author offers *one* truth, to which the elliptical turn of phrase confers the status of *the* truth."[68] When La Rochefoucauld in later editions attenuated his formulaic statements by inserting qualifiers such as "often," "usually," or "most people,"[69] the reason may be that he wanted to avoid giving the impression that virtue was impossible, but it could also be that he realized that the aesthetic requirements of the maxim might conflict with the demand for accuracy.[70]

As with a proverb and its contrary, a maxim and its contrary might both be true, or rather, sometimes true. Thus where the first edition says that "[t]o feel confident of pleasing is often a way of being thoroughly displeasing" (MS46), the manuscript says that "[t]o feel confident of pleasing is often a way of being thoroughly *pleasing*" (L134; italics added). To the proposition that "[w]e have not the strength to follow our reason all the way," Mme. de Sévigné opposed, as more plausible, that "[w]e have not the reason to follow our strength all the way."[71] Both ideas, in fact, can be defended. In a letter, Mme. de Lafayette offered a choice between two maxims: "One may forgive an infidelity, but not forget it," and "[o]ne may forget an infidelity, but not forgive it."[72] Neither appears in the *Maximes*, but both can be defended. Whereas a published maxim has "It is easier to fall in love when you are out of it than to get out of it when you are in it" (MS55), a manuscript has "more difficult" instead of "easier."[73]

---

66. Montesquieu (1991), *Pensée* 667.
67. In the Preface to his *Characters*, La Bruyère said that maxims are "as laws of morality" (Garapon 1990, p. 64), adding that he had "neither sufficient authority nor genius for a legislator."
68. Lafond (1986), p. 138. This is also how I read Tocqueville's lapidary statements in *Democracy in America* (Elster 1993a, Chapter 3).
69. For examples and quantitative assessments, see Truchet (1992, p. xxv) and Hippeau (1978, p. 168).
70. Lafond (1986), p. 140.
71. Truchet (1992), p. 16, n. 1.
72. Lafond (1986), p. 127, n. 48.
73. Truchet (1992), p. 400, n. 2.

The relation between jealousy and its cognitive antecedents offers a particularly striking example. For Descartes, the question was simple. Jealousy is a species of fear (PA§167). In general, "when fear is so extreme that it leaves no room for hope, it turns into despair" (PA§166). It follows that jealousy turns into despair when and because the fear of losing what one has turns into a certainty. La Rochefoucauld did not adopt this deterministic line of reasoning but offered instead an account in terms of mechanisms. In the manuscript, the effect of attaining certainty is expressed in a disjunction: "The remedy for jealousy is the certainty of what one fears, because that will either cause the end of life or the end of love" (L240). The first edition simplifies: "[O]ne ceases to be jealous when one is illuminated about the cause of the jealousy" (MI35). The second edition opts for the opposite simplification: The jealousy "becomes a frenzy as soon as one goes from doubt to certainty" (MII35). All the later editions use a variant of the manuscript formulation: "Jealousy feeds on doubts, and as soon as doubt turns into certainty it becomes a frenzy, or ceases to exist" (M32). Another disjunctive maxim says that "[a]varice often produces opposite effects; countless people sacrifice all their wealth to vague and distant hopes, while others scorn great future advantages for the sake of small present gains" (M492).

La Bruyère offers another striking instance of mechanism thinking:

Disgrace extinguishes hatred and jealousy. As soon as a person is no longer a favorite, and when we do not envy him any more, we admit that his actions are good, and we can pardon in him any merit and a good many virtues; he might even be a hero and not vex us.

Nothing seems right that a man does who has fallen into disgrace; his virtues and merit are slighted, misinterpreted, or called vices. If he is courageous, dreads neither fire nor sword, and faces the enemy with as much bravery as Bayard and Montrevel, he is called a 'braggadocio,' and they make fun of him, for there is nothing of the true hero about him.

I contradict myself; I own it; do not blame me, but blame those men whose judgments I merely give, and who are the very same persons, though they differ so much and are so variable in their opinions. (*Characters* XII.93.)

None of these examples of mechanism reasoning indicates when one or the other of the opposite effects will be triggered. The only attempt to consolidate opposed mechanisms into a law is the one I cited in I.6: "Absence lessens moderate passions and intensifies great ones, as the wind blows out a candle but fans up a fire" (M276). The moralists were mainly concerned with showing up the insufficiencies of conventional wisdom, rather than with identifying the exact conditions under which it might in fact be true.

The rhetorical device of "reverse mechanisms" is strikingly illustrated by the concluding maxim in the *Characters*: "If these CHARACTERS are not appreciated, I shall be astonished; and if they are, my astonishment will not be less." As we have seen, one way of generating maxims is by using the strategy of mechanisms. If the accepted wisdom is that "if A, then always B," one can shock the reader by substituting "if A, then always C," where B and C are incompatible. One can also, however, reverse the procedure. If the accepted wisdom is "if B, then always A," one can substitute "if C, then always A," where again B and C are incompatible. Unlike the mechanism approach, the appeal to reverse mechanisms does not pose any problems of logical consistency as long as B and C are offered as sufficient conditions rather than sufficient and necessary. Both are rhetorical devices used to generate surprise, but when appealing to reverse mechanisms there is no need to exaggerate.

La Rochefoucauld uses this strategy in several maxims. "Greater virtues are needed to bear good fortune than bad" (M25). "The evil we do brings less persecution and hatred upon us than our good qualities" (M29). The strategy may also be embodied in a pair of maxims, as when we compare "people are never deceived so easily as when they are out to deceive others" (M117) with "intention never to deceive lays us open to many a deception" (M118). Many writers emphasize the similar effects of the ancient and the new. Thus Pascal: "[L]ongstanding impressions are not the only ones that can mislead us; the charms of novelty have the same power" (*Pensée* 78); La Rochefoucauld: "The charm of novelty and long habit, poles apart though they may be, both prevent our realizing the shortcomings of our friends" (M426); La Bruyère: "Two qualities quite opposed to one another equally biases the mind: custom and novelty" (*Characters* XII.4). Earlier, Montaigne had devoted the first of the *Essays* to this idea: "We reach the same end by discrepant means," showing how bravery and submissiveness in defense may both induce forgiveness in a victorious enemy. Yet, as he goes on to point out, the example of Alexander's treatment of the commander of Gaza shows that bravery in defense can also induce cruelty in the attacker; hence reverse mechanisms and mechanisms may coexist.

HUMAN MOTIVATIONS

Alone among the moralists, La Rochefoucauld offered something like a theory of human motivations. In fact, his views about unconscious motivation and unconscious cognition are probably more valuable than anything found in twentieth-century psychology.[74] To some extent it is true, as Jean Lafond says, that "a certain verbal exuberance together with the exaggeration required for an original assertion turns this psychology into a mythology."[75] Yet, as I shall try to show, some systematic views can be extracted from what first appears as a random collection of diamond-like maxims.

Before I discuss La Rochefoucauld, let me say a few words about the three other moralists. To simplify – hugely – Montaigne saw the ideal human life to which he aspired as guided in equal parts by reason and pleasure, and actual human beings as guided in equal parts by passion and pleasure. He was acutely aware of the role of the emotions in supporting social norms and, through them, in encouraging deception and hypocrisy. He was only dimly aware, by contrast, of the importance of self-deception in human affairs and of the role of self-image in sustaining it. In La Rochefoucauld and in Pascal, these are among the most central issues. As Lovejoy comments, "There is little in La Rochefoucauld with which Pascal would have disagreed, however much he might have added."[76] I shall in fact ignore the metaphysical and theological aspects of Pascal and cite only his comments on human affairs.

La Bruyère's distinction among interest, reason, and passion, although very useful, is not offered as an exhaustive classification. In fact, he also seems to sketch a theory of *addictive motivations* that do not fall in any of the three categories. In the town, people "cannot do without the very same people whom they dislike and deride" (*Characters* VII.1). Similarly, "the court does not satisfy any man, but

---

74. Although Freud never cites La Rochefoucauld, he is frequently cited by Jacques Lacan, who refers for instance to "that resistance of *amour-propre*, to use the term in all the depth given it by La Rochefoucauld, and which is often expressed thus: I can't bear the thought of being freed by anyone other than myself" (Lacan 1977, p. 13; see also Doubrovsky 1980). Among the other great debunkers of the modern era, Nietzsche refers frequently to La Rochefoucauld.

75. Lafond (1986), p. 181.

76. Lovejoy (1961), p. 18. This claim presupposes that La Rochefoucauld, like Pascal, was an Augustinian at heart. Although this view has been contested (Hippeau 1978), I believe the arguments that favor it are stronger (see notably Lafond 1986, Thweatt 1980).

it prevents him from being satisfied with anything else" (*ibid.* VIII.8). Like La Rochefoucauld – although he does not accord it the same central role – he also refers to "indolence" (*paresse*) as a source of action or inaction: "It is weakness which makes us hate an enemy and seek revenge, and it is indolence which pacifies us and make us neglect it" (*ibid.* IV.70).

For La Rochefoucauld, to whom I now turn, the fundamental human motivation is *amour-propre*: "[T]he love of oneself and of all things in terms of oneself" ("*l'amour de soi-même et de toutes choses pour soi*") (MS1). Exactly what he means by *amour-propre* and how it works is the major question for any serious study of the *Maximes*. Although I do not pretend to be able to answer it fully, I believe the following observations are supported by the text. They are organized around the distinction between esteem and self-esteem, with the concomitant distinction between deception and self-deception.

(1) *Amour-propre* is protean and can take on indefinitely many forms (MS1). Its most striking expression is pridefulness (*orgueil*), which is "inseparable from *amour-propre.*"[77] This statement might seem hard to reconcile with the maxim that "pridefulness refuses to owe, *amour-propre* to pay" (M228). As Vauvenargues observed in his comment on this maxim, however, "pridefulness is nothing but an effect of *amour-propre*, and hence it is *amour-propre* which does not want to owe as well as it is *amour-propre* that does not want to pay."[78] In a given situation, *amour-propre* may induce *several* motivations with opposite implications for behavior. "Hence there is nothing to be surprised at if it sometimes throws in its lot with the most rigorous austerity and brazenly joins in its own destruction, for the moment of its defeat on one side is that of its recovery on another" (MS1).

(2) *Amour-propre* or pridefulness takes two main forms: a desire for esteem (Lovejoy refers to this desire as "approbativeness") and a desire for self-esteem. We are concerned both with the image others have of us and with our self-image. As we shall see, these two concerns generate, respectively, deception and self-deception. As an example of the effect of the desire for esteem, we may take the idea that the "desire to talk about ourselves and to show our failings from the viewpoint we ourselves would choose, accounts for a great deal of our candor" (M383). As an example of the effects of the desire for self-esteem, we may take the maxim that "nature has given us

77. *Réflexions diverses*, p. 224.
78. Vauvenargues (1970), p. 82.

pridefulness to spare us the unpleasantness of seeing our own imperfections" (M36). These two maxims do not, however, exhaust the ways in which we deal with our own flaws. We can also try to hide them from others (M494) or try to make them into virtues (M442).

(3) In some maxims, it is not clear whether La Rochefoucauld appeals to the desire for esteem or to the desire for self-esteem. When he says that "[p]ridefulness, which makes us so envious, also helps to keep envy within bounds" (M281), the reason may be that one does not want to be seen as envious or that one does not want to see oneself as envious. Also, both desires may operate simultaneously. If the desire for esteem and the desire for self-esteem point in opposite directions, one may give up the former the better to satisfy the latter. "Pridefulness always finds compensations, and even when it gives up vanity it loses nothing" (M33). As Lovejoy notes, "those who give alms in secret perhaps gain more in enhanced self-approval than they lose through the repression of their approbativeness."[79] Even better, of course, would be to be known as an anonymous donor – Valmont's strategy when he makes sure that an agent of Mme. de Tourvel, whom he hopes to seduce, observes him handing out money to some poor cottagers.[80]

(4) From a maxim cited above (M36), it would appear that *amour-propre* and pridefulness are part of a beneficial natural design. In a similar vein, La Rochefoucauld writes that "*[a]mour-propre* is more capable (*habile*) than the most capable man in the world" (M4). Commenting on this maxim, Vauvenargues objected that "the most capable *amour-propre* does much damage to its own interest."[81] La Rochefoucauld was aware of this fact, however. "The most dangerous effect of men's pride is blindness. Pride maintains and increases this blindness which prevents men from seeing the remedies that might lighten their burden and cure their faults" (MS19). In different language, the self-deception induced by *amour-propre* may serve the pleasure principle, but not the reality principle. To believe that we have no faults may give us a short-lived sense of well-being, but to know our faults would enable us to navigate better in the long run. Against this argument, however, our need for self-esteem may cause us to acquire virtues and not only to hide our defaults: "Our wish to deserve the praise of others fortifies our virtue" (M150). Also, as

79. Lovejoy (1961), p. 101.
80. de Laclos (1782), letter XXI.
81. Vauvenargues (1970), p. 76.

noted above, the very pridefulness (whether in the form of a desire for esteem or a desire for self-esteem) that causes envy may also keep it within bounds.

(5) Thus at the level of the individual, the need for self-esteem may lead either to vice or virtue. At the level of society, La Rochefoucauld agrees with the other moralists that civilized life is held together by the desire for esteem or *vanity*, which has the miraculous capacity to mimic virtue. Whereas the Epicureans and Descartes thought that enlightened self-interest was enough to generate the appearance of virtue,[82] Montaigne, Pascal, and La Rochefoucauld thought it necessary to enlist *amour-propre* in the form of the desire to be esteemed by others. Lovejoy observes that "this conception . . . of the irrational approbativeness of men as the dynamic of good conduct was one of the favorite themes of social psychology from the sixteenth to the late eighteenth century. This . . . motive is the next best thing to actual virtue, and serves much the same purpose."[83] According to La Rochefoucauld, vanity and the desire for *gloire*[84] is the cause or a cause of clemency (M16), courage (M220), female virtue (M220), loyalty (M247), civility (M260), generosity (M263), candor (M383), and compassion (M463).[85] A similarly reductionist attitude is found in Pascal, for whom *amour-propre* and pridefulness are at the root of humility (*Pensée* 539), compassion (*Pensée* 541), and courage (*Pensée* 654).

(6) *Amour-propre* is doubly perverse. The *malignity* of our nature (a common Augustinian phrase) is such that we draw pleasure from the faults and failures of others. "If we had no faults we should not find so much enjoyment in seeing faults in others" (M31). Our desire to find faults in others is so strong that it often helps us to find them: "Our enemies are nearer the truth in their opinion of us than we are

---

82. For Descartes, see his letter to Elisabeth of January 1646; for the Epicureans, see Hippeau (1978, pp. 156–57).
83. Lovejoy (1961), p. 156.
84. In the *Maximes*, vanity and the desire for glory are synonymous, as shown by M141 or by comparing M213 and M220.
85. Two additional remarks are in order, however. On the one hand, vanity can also induce socially undesirable behavior, such as flattery (M158), stubbornness (M424), spite (M483), and even crime (MS68). On the other hand, La Rochefoucauld does appeal to interest in the explanation of social virtues, such as disinterestedness (M39), friendship (M83), advising others (M116), praising others (M144), desire for learning (M173), gratitude (MS223), respecting justice (MS14), and blaming vice (MS28). As we shall see, however, his idea of interest is not as neatly distinct from vanity as in some contemporary writers; thus the reduction of virtue to interest is hard to distinguish from a reduction of virtue to the desire for esteem.

ourselves" (M458). Yet, even if our enemies are closer to the truth, they err too, even if they err less, from the opposite direction. (On a scale from 0 to 10, if I am 6, I'll think I am 9, and my enemies will think I am 4.) In fact, the *weakness* of our nature is such that we tend to believe what we would like to be true. "The head is always fooled by the heart (*L'esprit est toujours la dupe du coeur*)" (M102). Often, both perversities occur together. "What makes us believe so easily that others have faults is our ability to believe what we wish" (MP25).

An important special case is our cognitive and motivational response to the superior fortune of others. (What follows are reactions to what I refer to below as the "first-order pain" of envy.) On the one hand, we may rewrite the script so as to make others less consistently superior. "There is no man alive who thinks he is inferior, in each of his qualities, to those of the man he most respects" (M452). Also, we feel better if we can denigrate those who possess what we covet: "Hatred of favorites is nothing but love of favor. Resentment at not enjoying it finds consolation and balm in contempt for those who do" (M55). On the other hand, we can devalue the possessions that we lack rather than their possessors: "The very pride that makes us condemn failings from which we think we are exempt leads us to despise good qualities we do not possess" (M462). For instance, "[T]he scorn for riches displayed by the philosophers was a secret desire to recompense their own merit for the injustice of Fortune by scorning those very benefits she had denied them" (M54). As we saw in section I.6, Montaigne, citing the example of Thales, anticipated and refuted this argument. Some grapes *are* sour.

(7) The desire for esteem can take two forms: desire for praise and fear of blame. In La Rochefoucauld's explanation of courage, both have their place: "Love of fame, fear of disgrace (*honte*), schemes for advancement, desire to make life comfortable and pleasant, and the urge to humiliate others are often at the root of the valor men hold in such high esteem" (M213). Commenting on Locke's *Essay on Human Understanding*, Lovejoy notes that Locke is unusual in recognizing "both the positive and the negative aspects of approbativeness." For the most part, "those who were keenly aware of the potency of the 'love of praise' were rarely equally sensible to the potency of the fear of blame, and *vice versa*."[86] Rochefoucauld, in the cited maxim

86. Lovejoy (1961), pp. 135–36.

and elsewhere (M220), was also aware of both – and, as the maxim shows, of many other motives. Lovejoy also notes that, for Locke, fear of blame was a "more prevalent and potent motive" than desire for praise. In the first edition, La Rochefoucauld similarly asserts a hierarchy of motives: Courage is explained "by love of fame *and even more* by fear of disgrace" (MI206; italics added).[87] To achieve fame, one typically has to show more courage than what is needed to avoid disgrace.[88] Hence: "In time of war most men will face just enough danger to keep their honor intact" (M219).

(8) The moralists were highly aware of what one may call the *paradox of honor* – that people seek the esteem of those whom they do not themselves esteem. Montaigne cites Cicero to the effect of, "Can anything be more stupid than to value collectively those whom we despise as individuals?" (*Essays*, p. 709). La Rochefoucauld notes that "we let our reputation and good name depend upon the judgement of other men, all of whom are ill disposed towards us either through jealousy, concern with their own affairs, or lack of sense" (M268). Echoing Montaigne, Pascal writes that "those who most despise men, and put them on the same level as the beasts, still want to be admired and trusted by them" (*Pensée* 707). La Bruyère asks, finally, "Can we imagine that men who are so fond of life should love anything better, and that glory, which they prefer to life, is often no more than an opinion of themselves, entertained by a thousand people whom either they do not know or do not esteem?" (*Characters* II.98).

---

87. In a finer analysis we need to distinguish between three courses of action: doing less than one's duty (to satisfy an interest), doing one's duty (and renouncing an interest), and doing more than one's duty (and sacrificing an even greater interest). According to La Bruyère, "To do our duty is an effort to us, because when we do it we only perform our obligation, and seldom receive those eulogies which are the greatest incentive to commendable actions" (*Characters* XI.104). In a footnote to this text, the editor (Garapon 1990, p. 331) cites a text by Bourdaloue (citing St. Chrystosome) to the effect that because of the "glory" attached to supererogatory actions "we have much less difficulty in doing more than our duty than in doing our duty." Yet in this instrumental perspective (which I criticize in III.3) everything depends on the precise costs and benefits associated with the three courses of action. Doing our duty might be preferable both to doing less and to doing more, if the blame attached to doing less and the sacrifice attached to doing more are great enough. Moreover, taking the point of view of the spectator (who must be assumed to take a noninstrumental perspective), a supererogatory action is worthy of his praise only if the value of the praise to the actor is insufficient to offset the sacrifice he performs.
88. See the preceding note.

(9) The moralists were also aware of another paradoxical aspect of pridefulness, namely that people hide their pride out of pride, their vanity out of vanity. In the continuation of a maxim cited above, La Bruyère says that "[a]ll men in their hearts covet esteem, but carefully hide their anxiety to be esteemed" (*Characters* XI.65).[89] Along similar lines, but with more emphasis on the passive aggressiveness involved, La Rochefoucauld wrote that "[h]umility is often merely feigned submissiveness assumed in order to subject others, an artifice of pridefulness which stoops to conquer (*qui s'abaisse pour s'élever*)" (M254). Lovejoy identifies the paradox with great accuracy:

James's approbation becomes effective as an influence upon John's behavior through John's approbativeness. In so far, then, as approbativeness is disapproved, approbation works against itself, tends to weaken the force through which it functions. It is probably incapable of greatly weakening the subjective *desire*; but it forces that desire to conceal itself and so gives rise to a vast deal of insincerity, and it deprives that useful desire of some of its natural ratification. Disapprobation of approbativeness or of the candid manifestation of it, ought, I suggest, to be disapproved.[90]

(10) *Amour-propre* – love of self – is closely related to interest. In one of his more obscure and eloquent maxims, La Rochefoucauld tells us that "interest is the soul of *amour-propre*; hence, even as the body, cut off from its soul, is without sight, hearing, consciousness, feeling, or movement, so *amour-propre*, severed, so to speak, from interest, ceases to see, hear, feel, or stir" (MP26). The further development of the maxim, suggesting that *amour-propre* is moved only by what matters for the self, is also unhelpful. The maxim was not included in the

89. By contrast, "some among the ancient Greeks and Romans apparently regarded this desire [for approbation] as not only pardonable but laudable" (Lovejoy 1961, p. 96). Aristotle, for instance, said that unambitious people care *too little* about esteem and honor, while ambitious people care too much (*Nicomachean Ethics* 1107^b22–30).

90. *Ibid.*, pp. 97–98. In modern language, we might say that because approbation does not extend to behavior intended to elicit it is not *incentive-compatible*. A standard example of incentive-incompatibility is the following. (i) Soldiers are chosen on the basis of physical fitness. (ii) This criterion gives young men an incentive not to increase but to reduce their physical fitness, for example, by mutilating themselves. The application to approbativeness would be as follows. (i) Good behavior is rewarded by approbation. (ii) This gives people an incentive not to increase but to reduce their search for approbation. The latter holds only when the desire for approbation induces disapproval rather than approval and the desire is difficult to conceal from others. In ancient Greece, where the former did not hold, reward by approbation was incentive-compatible.

final edition. Instead, La Rochefoucauld there states in the Preface to the reader that "by the word *Interest* one does not always mean a material interest (*un intérêt de bien*), but most often an interest of honor or of glory." This suggests that interest is closely related to the desire to be esteemed as well as to the desire for material goods. By contrast, the desire for self-esteem is *not* an interest; hence, if this reading is correct, *amour-propre* need not be accompanied by interest. Interest is engaged in the world, whereas the desire for self-esteem is entirely internal.

(11) A famous maxim says that " [h]ypocrisy is a tribute vice pays to virtue" (M218). This mechanism belongs to the realm of esteem. Its parallel in the realm of self-esteem is, I believe, another famous maxim: "[t]he head is always fooled by the heart" (M102). To see the parallel, we may simply ask: Why should the heart bother to fool the head? Can't it just get on with it and do whatever it wants? An answer very much in the spirit of La Rochefoucauld was provided by Jean Domat: "We do not act by reason, but by love, because it is not the mind that acts, but the heart that governs, and *the deference of the heart towards the mind is such that even if it does not act by reason it must at least believe that it acts by reason.*"[91] It is an important part of our self-image that we believe ourselves and want ourselves to be swayed by reason rather than by passion or interest; hence conscious hypocrisy in the realm of esteem has a parallel in unconscious self-deception in the realm of self-esteem. I develop this comparison at greater length in Chapter V.

(12) The needs for esteem and for self-esteem give rise to what I shall call a *consistency constraint* (see section V.2) on the otherwise opportunistic expressions of *amour-propre*. When La Rochefoucauld writes that "[n]othing is more certain to lower our self-satisfaction than realizing that at one moment we disapprove of what we admired at some other" (M51), the implication must be that this threat to our self-esteem will keep us from changing our mind, at least for a while. He also observes that one source of constancy in love comes from "making it a point of honor to remain constant" (M176). Also, "we remain true to our commitments out of honor, by habit, and because we are not assured of our change of mind."[92] One of the minor moralists, Abbé d'Ailly, summed it up very well: "One often believes to have a sincere love and a disinterested friendship for a

91. Lafond (1992), p. 611; italics added.
92. *Réflexions diverses*, p. 222.

person of great fortune; but one can only be certain when the person is deprived of his power. One is then able to disentangle the source of this friendship: if it was based on interest, honor will sustain it for a while, and then tire of supporting it."[93] In these texts, honor refers to the satisfaction of social norms, that is, to the need for esteem rather than to the need for self-esteem.

(13) Going beyond La Rochefoucauld to some of his contemporaries, we may observe that *amour-propre* can turn against itself. Nicole said that "one can desire from *amour-propre* to be released from *amour-propre*."[94] Because of their *amour-propre* people do not want to see themselves or be seen by others as acting out of *amour-propre*. They sometimes, therefore, lean over backward to avoid the appearance (to themselves or others) of *amour-propre*. In reality, though, this is only *amour-propre* of the second degree. Pascal notes, for instance, that "[o]ur own interest is [a] wonderful instrument for blinding us agreeably. The fairest man in the world is not allowed to be judge in his own case. I know of men who, to avoid the danger of partiality in their own favor, have leaned over to the opposite extreme of injustice. The surest way to lose a perfectly just case was to get close relatives to recommend it to them" (*Pensée* 78). In a footnote, the editor cites a passage from a contemporary writer, Guez de Balzac, to the effect that he has "seen some who, to be admired for their integrity, preferred the interest of a stranger over that of a relative or a friend, even though reason was on the side of the relative or the friend."[95] Whereas Pascal is most plausibly read as explaining the counterinterested behavior in terms of self-esteem, Balzac appeals to the desire for esteem. In Chapter V I argue that the need not to be seen by oneself or by others as too obviously motivated by interest or passion creates an *imperfection* constraint that, jointly with the consistency constraint, ensures that concerns for justice and reason have independent causal force rather than being mere rationalizations after the fact. The need for esteem or for self-esteem induces a double deception or self-deception: Motivation X for professing Y is transformed into motivation Z for professing W.

(14) La Rochefoucauld is one of the main originators of what has been called the *hermeneutics of suspicion*. All apparent virtue is suspect

---

93. Lafond (1992), p. 266. La Rochefoucauld believed that all friendship for superiors was based on self-interest (M85).
94. Cited after Lafond (1986), p. 24.
95. Sellier (1991), p. 178, n. 24.

and in fact fraudulent. This is more than Hume's pragmatic proposition that "*every man must be supposed to be a knave*; though, at the same time, it appears somewhat strange, that a maxim should be true *in politics* which is false *in fact*."[96] Rather, with his Augustinian background La Rochefoucauld assumed (with qualifications discussed below) that the maxim was "true in fact." To be sure, debunking of virtue was not a novel exercise. In one of Cicero's writings, his Epicurean opponent is made to assert that the motive for various great deeds "was not a love of virtue for and in itself," but concerns of security, honor, and esteem. Any apparent acts of sacrifice can be explained by "the principle of forgoing pleasures for the purpose of getting greater pleasures, and enduring pains for the sake of escaping greater pains."[97] Yet La Rochefoucauld carried unmasking and debunking further than anyone before him. Others may have said much the same *en gros*, but nobody with the same force and penetration *en détail*.

To identify the basic principle of his reasoning I first go back to Montaigne. He pointed to what we may call the "uncertainty principle of virtue": the very fact that we come to know about an apparently virtuous act suggests that it cannot have been performed for the sake of virtue. How can we know that the acts that impress us were not made in order to impress? "The more glittering the deed the more I subtract from its moral worth, because of the suspicion aroused in me that it was exposed more for glitter than for goodness: goods displayed are already halfway to being sold" (*Essays* pp. 1157–58). At the limit, the only virtuous acts are those that never come to light. Along similar lines, Pascal wrote that "the finest things about [fine deeds] was the attempt to keep them secret" and that "the detail by which they came to light spoils everything" (*Pensée* 520). Even the philosophers who write against vanity "want to enjoy the prestige of having written well, those who read them want the prestige of having read them, and perhaps I who write this want the same thing, perhaps my readers ..." (*Pensée* 529 bis). Montaigne cites Cicero as the crown example of this attitude – "the vainest man in the world" preaching against vanity (*Essays* p. 1158).

La Rochefoucauld took this line of argument one step further, by denouncing virtuous acts performed for an *inner audience* – oneself. The act of hiding one's virtue that Montaigne and Pascal found so

96. Hume (1963), p. 42.
97. *De Finibus* I.x.35–36.

virtuous cannot be hidden to oneself. The very act of renouncing the outer audience is applauded by the inner audience and may be performed for the sake of that applause rather than for its own sake. Virtue, if it exists, cannot also be conscious of itself.[98] "If pure love exists, free from the dross of our other passions, it lies hidden in the depths of our hearts and unknown even to ourselves" (M69). Here he rejoins Pascal, who said about Man, "If he exalts himself, I belittle him; if he belittles himself, I exalt him" (*Pensée* 163), and "there are only two kinds of men, the righteous who think they are sinners and the sinners who think they are righteous" (*Pensée* 469). For this set of statements to be logically consistent, the sinners cannot *know* that their awareness of being sinners ipso facto makes them righteous.

The notion of an inner audience requires that of an unconscious motivation. The idea of conscious simulation of virtue in order to deceive and please an outer audience is perfectly meaningful. Montaigne found "no quality so easy to counterfeit as devotion unless our morals and our lives are made to conform to it; its essence is hidden and secret; its external appearances are easy and ostentatious" (*Essays*, p. 916). Many people donate money or time to charities for the sake of being approved by others, while professing that they do so for the good of the cause. By contrast, the idea of conscious dissimulation to oneself is meaningless. If the anticipation of self-approval serves as a conscious motive, there will be nothing to approve of. If I approve of my own contributions to charity it can only be because my conscious aim is something else than that very same approval. The desire for self-esteem or self-approval must, therefore, work unconsciously, "behind the back" of the agent. We can never know, therefore, whether our motivations are pure or impure, because in either case they are sure to appear to us as pure. As Nicole observed, this uncertainty works both ways: We always risk "mistaking charity for *amour-propre* and *amour-propre* for charity."[99] Hence the argument of the preceding paragraph must be slightly modified: Rather than claiming that virtue can never be conscious of itself, it appears that it can never be certain of itself. The conclusion is that every person should apply Hume's maxim to himself: Although it is false in fact that every man is a knave, he should always assume himself to be so.

(15) The preceding discussions suggested a rigid separation between deception and self-deception, or between conscious hypocrisy

98. Lafond (1986), p. 11.
99. Cited after Lafond (1986), p. 191.

and the unconscious self-serving operations of the mind. This distinction is certainly useful, and in fact is the organizing principle of Chapter V. Yet it is also somewhat fragile. Montaigne noted that "[t]hose who conceal [a vice] from others usually conceal it from themselves as well" (*Essays*, p. 953). La Rochefoucauld, too, thought that outward hypocrisy combined with inner lucidity was an unstable state. "Would-be gentlemen (*les faux honnêtes gens*) disguise their failings from others and themselves; true gentlemen are perfectly aware of them and acknowledge them" (M202). Coming from La Rochefoucauld, the second half of the maxim is surprising – perhaps it only expresses an unattainable ideal – but the first points to an important idea. Elsewhere it is expressed as follows: "We are so used (*accoutumés*) to disguising ourselves from others that we end by disguising ourselves from ourselves" (M119). Here, the reason why deception and self-deception go together is that the former causes the latter by the mechanism of habit (*coutume*) – not a very satisfactory explanation.

A more plausible mechanism might be that a durable discrepancy between private beliefs and a public view induced by *amour-propre* is itself offensive to *amour-propre* (see section V.2). We want to be esteemed by others as well as by ourselves. To be esteemed by others, we may have to deceive them, by professing motivations and beliefs we do not in fact have. "We should often be ashamed of our noblest deeds if the world were to see all their underlying motives" (M409). At the same time, this perpetual public lying may offend our self-esteem. If we have to choose, we may stop deceiving others, lose their esteem, and maintain our self-esteem. But we may also be able to have it both ways, by fooling ourselves into thinking that we really hold the beliefs and motivations we show to others. On this account, what offends our self-esteem is not the content of the thoughts we hide from others, but the fact that we hide them. On an alternative account, we hide the thoughts from ourselves because they offend our self-esteem directly. "Pridefulness conceals our faults from others and often from ourselves" (M358). This was also Pascal's view: *Amour-propre* "takes every care to hide its faults both from itself and from others" (*Pensée* 743).

THE PASSIONS

None of the moralists offered a theoretical treatment of the passions comparable to those of Aristotle or Descartes. In their writings we

95

find no enumeration or classification of the emotions; no systematic analysis of their cognitive antecedents; and no sustained discussion of their physiological concomitants or of their action tendencies. They present a number of punctual insights that can be used as primary material, as it were, for more general mechanisms. An especially important set of ideas – related to the theme of *amour-propre* – turn on the *willingness to acknowledge* one's emotions, to oneself or to others. Another set of ideas, less central but suggestive, turn on the *ability to detect* one's emotions as they arise. A further set, related to the first, concern the possibility of *irrational emotions*.

(1) In the analysis of how emotions are presented to others we may distinguish between *veil* and *mask* – between hiding an emotion one feels and showing an emotion one does not feel. In the courtly society that formed the background for the moralists, these were pervasive phenomena. "In every walk of life each man puts on a personality and outward appearance so as to look what he wants to be thought: in fact you might say that society is entirely made up of assumed personalities (*composé de mines*)" (M256). Only exceptionally does it happen that a person casts off the mask: "Pridefulness, as if weary of its own artifices and changes of face, after having played single-handed all the parts in the human comedy, puts on its natural expression and reveals itself as arrogance" (MS6).

The need for concealment also applies to the emotions, notably to love. Among the many combinations, one is that the man wears a mask while the woman wears a veil: "It sometimes happens that a woman conceals from a man the love she feels for him, while he only feigns a passion he does not feel" (*Characters* III.67). Whether the deception succeeds is another matter. Sometimes, it may succeed too well. Montaigne writes that he has "known women who have hidden their true affections under pretended ones, in order to divert people's opinions and conjectures and to mislead the gossips. But one I knew got well and truly caught: by feigning a passion she quitted her original one for the feigned one" (*Essays*, p. 942).

According to La Rochefoucauld, in matters of love neither masks nor veils are likely to succeed, but veils even less than masks: "Where love is, no disguise can hide it for long; where it is not, none can simulate it" (M70); "It is harder to disguise feelings we have than to put on those we have not" (MP56). The efficacy of a mask may equally be affected by the need to put on a veil, if we have to hide what we feel towards one person while simulating the same feeling towards another. According to La Bruyère, the veil reduces the efficacy of

the mask: "A man may deceive a woman by a pretended inclination, but then he must not have a real one elsewhere" (*Characters*
III.69). According to the unknown author of *Discours sur les passions
de l'amour*, it is the other way around: "It is almost impossible to
feign love if one is not already close to being lover, or at least loves
somewhere (*aime en quelque endroit*)."[100] Our ability to pierce a veil or
a mask may also be affected by the veils or masks we are ourselves
putting on. According to La Bruyère, the habitual masker easily un-
masks others and is easily unmasked: "Knaves easily believe others
as bad as themselves; there is no deceiving them, neither do they long
deceive" (*Characters* XI.25). For La Rochefoucauld, as we saw, it is the
other way around: "People are never deceived so easily as when they
are out to deceive others" (M117).

To be sure, a mask can also serve as a veil. Montaigne often de-
nounces vicious emotions that are veiled by a mask of virtue. He
refers to "that fine adage used as a cloak by greed and ambition,
'That we are not born for ourselves alone but for the common weal'"
(*Essays*, p. 266). According to La Rochefoucauld, such dissimulations
rarely succeed: "Whatever care a man takes to veil his passions with
appearances of piety and honor, they always show through" (M12).
Yet – to go beyond the texts of the moralists while remaining in their
spirit – a veil that is not also a mask may equally fail to carry conviction. Above, I cited the *Discours sur les passions de l'amour* to the effect
that A's simulation of love for B is more likely to succeed – that is, to
be taken at face value by B – if A has a genuine love for C. Similarly,
A's concealment of love for B is more likely to be taken at face value by
B if A simulates love for C. This was Julien Sorel's strategy in *Le Rouge
et le Noir*. Acting on the advice of a Russian nobleman friend, he engages in a fake courtship of Mme. de Fervaques in order to persuade
his real love, Mathilde de la Mole, that he no longer loves her.

(2) In theory, people might have a similarly dual attitude when
presenting their own emotions to themselves. They might try to persuade themselves that they have emotions they do not have but feel
they should have, or that they do not have emotions they have but
believe they ought not to have. To my knowledge, the moralists did
not discuss the first issue (which I consider in III.3 and IV.3). On the
second question, the only unambiguous statement I have found is
by La Bruyère: "All passions are deceptive; they conceal themselves
as much as possible from others *and from themselves as well*. No vice

100. Lafond (1992), p. 630.

97

exists which does not pretend to be more or less like some virtue, and which does not take advantage of this assumed resemblance" (*Characters* IV.72; italics added). The phrase suggests that an emotion may induce a pressure to conceal another emotion for the inner audience, not only by veiling it but by putting on a mask of virtue.

If this sounds obscure, let me use envy to illustrate the kind of thing La Bruyère may have had in mind. If I envy someone else what he has, the feeling is doubly painful. On the one hand, having less than he has makes me feel that I am less, which is painful. I shall call this *the first-order pain of envy*. On the other hand, the perception that I am envious together with the belief that envy is a sign of moral inferiority also offends my *amour-propre*. I shall refer to the pangs of shame or guilt induced by the pangs of envy as *the second-order pain of envy*. The first-order pain of envy can induce behavior to destroy the envied object or its possessor; alternatively, as we saw above, it can trigger cognitive adjustments so as to enhance the perceived flaws of the other and thereby make him less enviable. The second-order pain can also induce a rewriting of the script, but of a different kind. I can tell myself a story in which the other obtained the envied object by illegitimate and immoral means, and perhaps at my expense, thus transmuting the envy into indignation or anger, in the Aristotelian senses of these terms. The process – which I discuss at greater length in V.2 – is illustrated in Fig. II.1.

There is no textual basis for imputing this specific mechanism to La Bruyère, but it is at least consistent with the text I cited. It is also consistent, albeit more tenuously, with the writings of La Rochefoucauld. He certainly thought that the acknowledgment of certain base emotions is inconsistent with our *amour-propre*. Envy, in particular, is "a timid and shamefaced passion we never dare acknowledge" (M27). That is why "pride, which makes us so envious, also helps to keep envy within bounds" (M281). Or again, "Encouragement given to those just entering society often comes from unacknowledged (*secret*) envy of the well established" (M280). In another comment, which similarly relies on the idea of a mask that is also a veil, he writes, "Coquettish women make a point of being jealous of their admirers so as to hide their envy of other women" (M406).

Yet these texts pose a problem. Hide – for whom? Acknowledge – to whom? To others, or to oneself? Or rather – as deception and self-deception tend to go together – is the concealment motivated by the desire for esteem or by the desire for self-esteem? It makes a big difference whether we first conceal our envy to others out of shame and

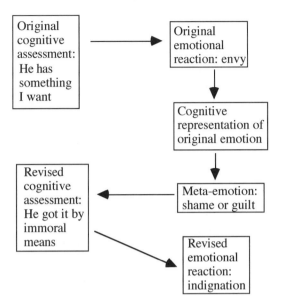

Figure II.1.

then to ourselves out of habit or for the sake of dissonance-reduction, or whether the self-concealment is directly motivated. La Rochefoucauld does not provide an answer. True, he does emphasize our tendency to hide our imperfections from ourselves (M36). Also, as argued by Vivien Thweatt, he appears to have thought that envy was the greatest of all imperfections: "[I]n the world of La Rochefoucauld's *Maximes*, there is no more predatory manifestation of unregenerate nature, animal or Augustinian, than the weakness that finds its outlet in the subterranean *force* of invidious malice."[101] Yet unless the subject of envy also thinks of it as an imperfection, it does not follow that he would tend to hide it from himself. It is a tempting premise and a plausible conclusion, but strict textual evidence is lacking.

(3) Before one can form the intention to hide an emotion, one has to notice it. With regard to the deception of others, this statement is uncontroversial. With regard to self-deception, it is vastly controversial. *The* problem of self-deception is in fact that it appears to be a logically incoherent idea: To hide something for oneself one must first notice it, but once it is noticed one cannot hide it. There is no

101. Thweatt (1980), p. 183.

doubt that the phenomenon exists,[102] but we still do not quite understand how it can exist. The moralists were aware of a particular aspect of this paradox, namely the intention to forget. Montaigne observed that "there is nothing which stamps anything so vividly on our memories as the desire not to remember it" (*Essays* p. 551); for La Bruyère, "the desire to forget someone is to think about that person" (*Characters* IV.38). Yet they did not confront the more general problem of self-deception. Pascal simply stipulated that "[o]rdinary people have the ability not to think about things they do not want to think about" (*Pensée* 659). He had acute insights into the nature of wishful thinking (*Pensées* 458, 804), in which we simply go directly for the belief we wish to be true rather than forming and then rejecting a belief we wish to be false, but he did not confront, much less solve, the problem of self-deception.

Not all ignorance is willful ignorance, however. The moralists argued that one could be in a certain emotional state – be angry, or in love – without knowing it and without the ignorance being motivated by a desire to ignore. With regard to anger, Montaigne noted a basic dilemma: "The infancies of all things are feeble and weak. We must keep our eyes open at their beginnings; you cannot find the danger then because it is so small; once it has grown, you cannot find the cure" (*Essays*, p. 1154). Self-control may be impossible, if the point of no return occurs before the earliest point at which the anger becomes noticeable to the angry person. Others, however, may have noticed it much earlier. We have all heard (or uttered) the angry rebuttal "I am not angry!" to the question "why are you so angry?"

With regard to love, the *Discours sur les passions de l'amour* says that "attachment to one and the same idea wearies and destroys the spirit. That is why the pleasures of love are sometimes more solid and durable if one does not know that one loves."[103] Pascal – who may have inspired the *Discours* even if he did not write it himself – observed about a character in Scudéry's novel *Le Grand Cyrus*, "[W]e like seeing the mistake and passion of Cleobuline because she is unaware

---

102. For a demonstration, see Gur and Sackeim (1979). Mele (1997) argues that most instances of (what I call) self-deception are really instances of (what I call) wishful thinking. Against his view, I find the rebuttals in Bach (1997) and Sackeim and Gur (1997) more convincing. In the words of the latter writers, "[H]ow can we stop the processing of threatening information unless we recognize that the information is threatening?" The questions are complex, however, and deserve a fuller discussion than I can give them here. Some further comments are found in V.2.

103. Lafond (1992), p. 627.

of it" (*Pensée* 528). In a note, the editor cites the following passage from the novel: "Cleobuline loved him without thinking that she loved him, and she was under this illusion for so long that the affection could not be overcome when she finally became aware of it."[104] Once again, there is the suggestion that the point of no return occurs before the point of conscious awareness.

As we shall see in II.4, the theme of love unaware of itself has indeed been central in fiction. In Stendhal's Mme. de Rênal, the unawareness is innocent, as it were, that is, not motivated. In the Princess of Clèves and in Stendhal's Mme. De Chasteller, by contrast, the ignorance is self-deceptive. This phenomenon – willful ignorance of love – is as elusive as other forms of self-deception. By contrast, unmotivated ignorance of one's emotions is no mystery. Having an emotion is being engaged in the world. When I get angry, I focus on the person who offends me; I raise my voice; I gesticulate; utter threatening words or make threatening gestures. Although it would be inaccurate to say that I am unconscious of doing these things, I do not always bring my consciousness of all of them together into the realization that I am angry. When that realization occurs, the emotion may be dampened or consolidated: dampened if the awareness induces shame, guilt, or prudence that urge me to control my anger, and consolidated if the realization that I have no good reason to be angry induces me to find one.

In III.2 and IV.2 I argue that some emotions are not consciously acknowledged as such because the culture lacks the concept of those specific emotional states. There is a hint of that idea in La Rochefoucauld, when he writes that "[s]ome people would never have fallen in love if they had never heard of love" (M136). By and large, however, the moralists did not go beyond asserting that an emotion might remain unacknowledged for a while and then burst into consciousness, which it can obviously do only if the emotion *is* part of the cultural repertoire. To introduce some more terminology, we may refer to *weak proto-emotions* in the case where the culture lacks the relevant concept, and to *strong proto-emotions* when the individual is unaware of the emotion but might or does become aware of it. The former are unacknowledgeable, the latter acknowledgeable but unacknowledged. A further refinement is introduced in IV.2.

(4) The moralists relied heavily on the traditional opposition between reason and passion. Here, *reason* must be sharply distinguished

---

104. Sellier (1991), p. 395, n. 1.

from what we think of as *rationality*. By rationality I mean roughly speaking (see IV.3 for a less rough statement) the instrumentally efficient pursuit of given ends. By reason, I mean – and I believe the moralists meant – any kind of impartial motivation or concern for the common good (see V.1 for a fuller discussion). Following La Bruyère's trichotomy, reason is disinterested as well as dispassionate. We may be rational in the pursuit of a private interest, but then we are not reasonable. We may be reasonable when arguing in terms of the categorical imperative ("What if everyone did that?"), but then we are not rational in the sense in which I use the term. And we may be rational as well as reasonable, if we try to choose the best means to implement a utilitarian conception of the common good.

The concept of rationality was not central to the moralists. They were above the need to husband and economize their resources and, in fact, thought such concerns degrading. Montaigne notes (*Essays*, p. 68) that at one stage of his life he was obsessed with accumulating money, but that "then some good *daemon* or other cast me out of it most usefully . . . and scattered all my parsimony to the winds" (p. 69). By and large, he assumes that any concern for riches will turn into avarice and covetousness: It is a desire that has no nonpathological forms. In La Rochefoucauld, too, the only comments on money making concern its pathological forms (cp. M492 on avarice cited above). Yet the moralists had, I think, an implicit idea of *irrationality*. Moreover, the main instantiation of this idea was (an equally implicit) concept of *irrational emotions*. By definition, all emotions are unreasonable (as I use this term), yet not all are irrational; some are better grounded than others. I discuss the relation between emotions and rationality at some length in IV.3. Here, I shall only present some statements by the moralists that suggest various ways in which the distinction between rational and irrational emotions could be drawn.

According to La Rochefoucauld, envy, as distinct from jealousy, is not only shameful, but irrational. "Jealousy is in some measure just and reasonable (*raisonnable*), since it merely aims at keeping something that belongs to us or we think belongs to us, whereas envy is a frenzy (*fureur*) that cannot bear anything that belongs to others" (M28). In the first edition, the irrational destructiveness of envy comes out more clearly: It is a frenzy "that always makes us wish for the destruction of the good of others" (MI31). Here, the inadequacy or irrationality of envy seems to be linked to its behavioral consequences. Another strange feature of envy is that it outlasts its object: "Our envy always lasts longer than the good fortune of those we envy" (M476).

The last-cited maxim is puzzling but may perhaps be seen as related to the question of irrational jealousy. Although in one sense this emotion is more rational than envy, it also has an irrational aspect. "Infidelities should stifle love, and we should not be jealous when we have cause to be. Only those who avoid giving cause for jealousy deserve to make us so" (M359). On the one hand jealousy presupposes love, but on the other hand a rational love ought to cease to exist when it finds indubitable grounds for jealousy. For La Rochefoucauld, rational love is an emotion that has specific cognitive antecedents and that disappears with them. Irrational love – and irrational jealousy – arise when love persist although its antecedents are no longer satisfied. We saw earlier that the extinction of jealousy is one of the two possible outcomes of the transition from doubt to certainty; we can now add the claim that it is the rational outcome. (This of course still does not tell us when it will occur.)

This idea may be contrasted with the view that "love is not love which alters when it alteration finds" (Shakespeare, sonnet 116). Love is attached to a person and not to specific cognitive antecedents. We may, perhaps, read the following statement by La Bruyère as an attack on the cognitive theory of love: "Those women who do not respect any of our feelings and give us many opportunities of becoming jealous, should not be worthy of our jealousy, if we were guided rather by their sentiments and conduct than by our affections" (*Characters* IV.29). And many would agree with Shakespeare against Pascal's assertion: "[W]hat about a person who loves someone for the sake of her beauty; does he love *her*? No, for smallpox, which will destroy beauty without destroying the person, will put an end to his love for her" (*Pensée* 567). The question becomes more difficult if we ask, "And if someone loves me for my judgement or my memory [sic], do they love *me*, myself? No, for I could lose these qualities without losing my self. . . . Therefore we never love anyone, but only qualities" (*ibid.*).[105]

For a different approach to irrational emotions, we may take as starting point Seneca's observation, cited above, "quos laeserunt et oderunt." The paradox is spelled out by La Bruyère as follows: "Most

---

105. Commenting on this passage, Soble (1990, pp. 309–11) asserts, convincingly I think, that Pascal commits the fallacy of composition when he argues that because a person can lose any one of his properties and remain the same person, he can lose all his properties and still remain the same.

men go from anger to insults; some act differently, for they first give offence and then grow angry" (*Characters* XI.10). On the Aristotelian conception of anger discussed above, a rational person will harm another because he has been harmed himself, with anger acting as the mediating factor. An irrational person, by contrast, becomes angry when and because he has harmed another, even when there was no preexisting cause for anger. Elsewhere La Bruyère notes that "[j]ust as we grow closer in affection to the persons whom we have done a favor, we develop a violent hate of those whom we have strongly offended" (*Characters* IV.68), echoing Montaigne's "[i]t has angered me to see husbands hating their wives precisely because they are doing them wrong" (*Essays*, p. 963). Or again, "is it not one of our beautiful practices today to hound to death not only the man who has offended us but also the man we have offended?" (*Essays*, p. 788). In a variation on the same theme, La Rochefoucauld observes that "[w]e often forgive those who bore us, but we cannot forgive those who find us boring" (M304).[106]

We have established two perverse or irrational patterns: (i) to help another causes me to love him and (ii) to harm him causes me to hate him. Two converse, equally irrational patterns would be (iii) to receive help from another causes me to hate him and (iv) to be harmed by another causes me to love him. Although none of the moralists expresses (iv) in this stark form, La Rochefoucauld combines (iii) with an attenuated version of (iv) when he writes that men "even hate those who have done them kindnesses and give up hating those who have wronged them. The effort needed to reward goodness and take revenge upon evil seems to them a tyranny to which they are loth to submit" (M14).

The hate we feel toward our benefactors is a central theme in the moralists. Ingratitude, for them, was not simply lack of gratitude but an active feeling of hostility. The emotion may arise in two ways, depending on the nature of the relationship between donor and recipient. In a relation between equals, what weighs down the recipient is the fact of being under an obligation. The knowledge that

---

106. According to Saint-Simon's *Mémoires*, La Rochefoucauld himself was not exempt from this mechanism. When the latter asserted in his *Mémoires* that Saint-Simon's father had broken a promise during the Fronde, the father managed to get hold of all copies of the book and wrote in the margin "the author lies." Saint-Simon (1953–61, vol. I, p. 84) adds that La Rochefoucauld and his son "never forgave my father, given that one is less likely to forget the injuries one has done than those one has suffered."

he is expected to return the favor is perceived as constraining his freedom.[107] In a somewhat chilling passage, Montaigne says about himself that "I am so fond of ridding myself of the weight of obligations that I have occasionally counted as gains such attacks or insults or acts of ingratitude as came from those whom, by nature or accident, I owed some duty of affection, taking their offence, as it occurred, as so much towards the settling or discharge of my debts. Even when I continue to pay them the visible courtesies which society requires, I still find it a great saving to do for justice what I used to do for affection and to alleviate a little the inward stress and anxiety of my will" (*Essays*, pp. 1094–5).

In a relation between superior and inferior, what weighs down the recipient is the fact that the superiority of the donor – and the resentment of the recipient – are enhanced rather than attenuated by the act of giving. The resentment is intensified if the recipient suspects that the motive of the donor is in fact to make him or her feel it (see also III.3). A somewhat mysterious statement by La Rochefoucauld may perhaps be understood in this light: "A man's ingratitude may be less reprehensible than the motive of his benefactor" (M96). Otherwise, the theme of humiliating others by benefactions is largely absent in the moralists, surprisingly perhaps, given its prominence in the literature on gift giving.

As we have seen, irrational anger can take the form of inventing a reason for itself. In other cases, it takes the form of substituting one reason for another when the original one is shown to be unfounded. Montaigne has a striking example (taken from Seneca) that is worthwhile citing at some length:

Piso, a great man in every other way, was moved to anger against one of his soldiers. Because that soldier had returned alone after foraging and could give no account of where he had left his comrade, Piso was convinced that he had murdered him and at once condemned him to death. When he was already on the gallows, along comes the lost comrade! At this the whole army was overjoyed and, after many a high and embrace between the two men, the executioner brought both of them into the presence of Piso; all those who were there were expecting that Piso himself would be delighted. Quite the contrary: for, through embarrassment and vexation, his fury, which was still very powerful, suddenly redoubled and by a quibble which his passion promptly furnished him with, he found three men guilty because one had

---

107. For experimental evidence about this effect, see Brehm (1966, pp. 65–70) and Kahn and Tice (1973).

just been found innocent, and had all three of them executed: the first soldier because he was already sentenced to death; the second, the one who had gone missing, because he had caused the death of his comrade; the hangman for failing to obey orders. (*Essays*, p. 813)

This is not the familiar phenomenon that anger caused by frustration in one sphere vents itself in another, as when a person has had a dressing down on the job and takes it out on spouse and children. That, too, is certainly an irrational phenomenon, but it is not the same kind of irrationality. Montaigne describes an emotion that outlasts its cognitive antecedent and then finds a new one, whereas in the example of job frustration we tacitly assume that the original cause continues to operate.

These analyses of irrational love and anger are mostly phenomenological. They draw our attention to the fact that an emotion may arise in a situation in which we would expect the opposite one to be produced – guilt rather than anger, gratitude rather than resentment. For the most part, they are not supported by specific causal mechanisms. *Why* would we hate those whom we harm? Suppose that in the pursuit of his interest a person recklessly harms that of another, who then turns against him in anger. For some individuals, admitting that they behaved badly is intolerable to their self-esteem. Instead, they engage in fault finding, so that they can say about the other, to themselves and to third parties, "He only got what he deserved." This process is closely related to the one depicted in Fig. II.1. I discuss it again in Chapters IV and V.

CONCLUSION

As with Aristotle, the writings of the moralists can teach us much both about the emotions in general and about the place of emotions in the society in which they lived. Their most important novel contribution was to introduce a third dimension in the relation between emotion and cognition. Aristotle emphasized that emotions have cognitive antecedents and cognitive consequences. The moralists added the insight that *emotions can themselves be the object of cognition*. To be sure, they can exist without becoming objects of awareness. In that case, they exist as what I called *proto-emotions*. When we are aware of them, however, the cognitions can trigger second-order emotions or *meta-emotions*. The trigger of the trigger, as it were, is *amour-propre*, in the twin forms of desire for esteem and desire for self-esteem. In its first form, *amour-propre* induces an elaborate game of emotional hide-and-seek. In its second form, the meta-emotion may induce a change in the original cognition and in the corresponding first-order emotion, as shown in Fig. II.1. Admittedly, the moralists did not work out all the causal steps in full detail. Also, I have not tried to draw an accurate historical picture. I have used the writings of the moralists in a deliberately anachronistic manner, taking bits and pieces from each of them to create a composite picture that is of interest in its own right. I believe, nevertheless, that the overall interpretation is consistent with their basic ideas.

The writings of the moralists also cast light on the society in which they lived. They make it very clear that behavior in French courtly society was aggressively self-assertive, but also that the struggle for honor and glory was strongly circumscribed by social norms. The "fashion of the duel" (*Pensée* 529 bis) – the duel is in fact "the triumph of fashion" (*Characters* XIII.3) – was a highly regulated and organized system of self-assertion (see III.4). Also, the self-assertion took place within an elaborate system of veils and masks that is almost a constitutive feature of courtly society. The expression of emotion was also subject to these constraints. Women, as La Bruyère suggested, were supposed to veil their feelings, whereas men were under a social imperative to seduce by putting on a mask of adoration. The rule of courtly behavior was not only to mask and veil one's emotions, but also to unmask and unveil, testing others to reveal their real emotions (see also the discussion below of *La Princesse de Clèves*). Envy was expressed by backhanded compliments, and insults in the form of exaggerated politeness, intended both to humiliate the victim and make him incapable of retaliating. Indirectly, these norms could not help but shape the emotions themselves. By mechanisms that we do not understand very well, emotional life in court society was self-deceptive to an unusual extent.

II.4. EMOTIONS IN LITERATURE

Emotion, I believe, is an important element in all art. Emotion is elicited in readers, listeners, and viewers by formal as well as substantive aspects of works of art. I consider that relation between emotion and the arts in IV.2. Here, I discuss novels and plays for what they tell us about the emotional life of their *characters*. Because authors of fiction are free to construct narrative and characters unencumbered by the irrelevant detail that makes it hard to pierce real-life emotional events, we can read plays and novels as the closest thing to a controlled experiment involving high-stakes human emotions.

To be sure, not all novelists or playwrights will do. Among novelists, for instance, not only second-rank writers like Walter Scott or third-rate writers like Eugène Sue, but even Dickens and Balzac are too obsessed with the picturesque, the melodramatic, or the programmatic to offer reliable character portraits. Ramon Fernandez very appropriately assimilates the characters of Balzac to the *Characters* of La Bruyère: They are illustrations of an abstract principle of human behavior rather than synthetic and fully rounded individuals. As with La Bruyère's more extraordinary creations – Menalque (*Characters* XI.7) or the collector (XIII.2) – Balzac's characters are "monomaniac" in their passions.[108] Rather than using his writings as inspiration and correction for our ideas about emotional life, we must use independently developed ideas to assess the plausibility of his characters.[109]

As moralist as well as novelist, Stendhal presents a particularly significant and paradoxical case. In his odd treatise *On Love*, written before any of his novels, he asserts that "since heaven has denied me literary skill, I have only tried to describe (with all the dourness of science, but also with all its precision) certain facts of which I have been an involuntary witness" (Chapter 24). Yet to test his ideas he had to fictionalize them. His first piece of fiction, "Ernestine or the Birth of Love," was an attempt to create a fictional embodiment of the theory of the seven stages of love. "Strange paradox: the psychological analysis somehow needs fiction to be more *veridical*."[110] Above I warned against the danger of concocting examples to illustrate a theory. In Stendhal's case, however, I believe he was experimenting

---

108. Fernandez (1981), pp. 62, 64. In his comparison of Balzac and La Bruyère, Gray (1986, p. 27) argues that the two are "at antipodes" in precisely the respect in which Fernandez finds them to be similar. Yet it is striking that Gray's characterization of the typical "character" in La Bruyère ("he turns on his own axis, and never deviates from his initial design ... From the moment he is sketched one can foresee how he will end") is almost identical to what Fernandez says about Balzac's characters ("as soon as a passionate character appears in one of his stories one can foresee the further development and the ending of the work").

109. By contrast, Balzac's *sociological* authority is unquestionable. His version of nineteenth-century France "may have struck nearly everyone as being so dense and convincing that no rival account had to be considered" (Pavel 1986, p. 106).

110. Crouzet (1996), p. 304.

rather than merely putting flesh and blood on an abstract idea. He wanted to develop his views through real characters to see if they *rang true*. Elsewhere, I argue that at least one of his experiments turned out to be unsuccessful.[111]

SHAKESPEARE

In Shakespeare's tragedies, some characters are ultralucid about their own behavior. In their asides and soliloquies, Hamlet, Iago, and Macbeth constantly dissect their emotions. Othello and Lear, by contrast, are more unreflectively in their grip. Although the reader or spectator can make inferences about what moves them, the conclusions are necessarily somewhat speculative. If we try to understand Othello's jealousy and in particular why he is so gullible, a plausible answer is that the prejudices to which his skin exposes him (see Brabantio in 1.1 63 ff. and 96 ff.) lend credibility to Iago's suggestion (3.3. 244 ff.) that Desdemona will soon tire of him and seek someone more like herself. Yet the answer *is* inferential. Othello himself does not offer it and, more to the point, could not have offered it, being what he is. He has no soliloquies, no asides.

For insights into the psychology of jealousy in *Othello*, we must, I believe, turn to Iago, who is constantly ruminating on his own envious and jealous feelings. His destruction of Cassio is not only a means towards the ruin of Othello, but also an end in itself. His envy of Cassio shows up twice. In the very opening of the play, it takes the self-deceptive form of denigrating the value of Cassio whom Othello has preferred to him as second-in-command. He dismisses Cassio as a mere "bookish theoric" (1.1. 25) who – unlike Iago – lacks the military experience that would warrant promotion. To explain in a satisfactory way why Cassio was nevertheless promoted, he argues that "[p]referment goes by letter and affection, and not by old gradation, where each second stood heir to the first" (1.1. 37–39). It might seem as if Iago is here complaining on two different grounds – his own superior merit and greater seniority – but perhaps we have to assume that the experience of the more senior person is also the main source of merit. Later, in a shockingly – implausibly? – frank statement, Iago says, "If Cassio do remain, he hath a daily beauty in his life that makes me ugly" (5.1.1 18–20).

111. Elster (in press a), section III.7.

To understand Iago's feelings towards Othello, consider first the Othello–Cassio–Iago triangle. Othello takes something valuable from Iago, an expectation of promotion, and promotes Cassio instead. Would we expect Iago to feel anger towards Othello, envy towards Cassio, or both? Tocqueville, discussing a structurally similar problem in the *ancien régime,* concluded that the bourgeoisie felt envy towards the aristocracy that was preferred to itself by the king rather than anger towards the latter for his favoritism (see III.3). In Iago's case, both emotions are observed. He is angry with Othello, not merely because he frustrated Iago's desire but because in doing so he also violated the norms regulating promotion. In that way, Iago can present his anger to himself as rational or justified (IV.3). Because Cassio's promotion involves norm-violation, his good fortune is doubly undeserved; hence Iago's attitude towards him goes beyond mere envy into indignation, in Aristotle's sense. The perception that Othello has violated a norm thus serves two purposes: the transmutation of irrational anger into justified anger and that of envy into righteous indignation (see also V.2).

Yet although Othello's promoting Cassio over his head is one reason why Iago hates him (1.1. 7–9), it is not the only one. Sexual jealousy also plays a part. At one point Iago says, ambiguously, that

> I hate the Moor
> And it is thought abroad that twixt my sheets
> He's done my office. I know not if 't be true;
> But I, for mere suspicion in that kind
> Will do as if for surety. (1.3. 387–91)

This statement does not make it clear whether it is the public rumor about Othello and his wife Emilia or his own private suspicion that unnerves him. The ambiguity is resolved when he talks about Othello's love for Desdemona, adding that

> Now, I do love her too,
> Not out of absolute lust – though peradventure
> I stand accountant for as great a sin –
> But partly led to diet my revenge
> For that I do suspect the lusty Moor
> Hath leaped into my seat, the thought whereof
> Doth, like a poisonous mineral, gnaw my innards;
> and nothing can or shall content my soul

Till I am evened with him, wife for wife,
Or failing so, yet that I put the Moor
At least into a jealousy so strong
That judgment cannot cure. (2.2 292–303)

Iago's thought – not a full-fledged belief – about Othello and his
wife is sufficient to trigger his jealousy. His first reaction is the desire
to get even, "wife for wife." If that doesn't succeed – and Iago in fact
never tries – he will get even by inducing in Othello a jealousy that will
match his own. To that end he needs a third party to blame, usefully at
hand in Cassio whom he also wants to bring down for other reasons.
In all these machinations, Iago has a plethora of motivations, as we
have seen: envy and indignation at Cassio's promotion, resentment
of the beauty in Cassio's life compared with the ugliness of his own,
anger towards Othello for passing him over for the promotion, and
sexual jealousy towards Othello.

RACINE

Among Racine's plays, *Phèdre* is often singled out as offering the most
vivid portrait of passion, and it is indeed a stunning portrayal of the
power of adulterous love. Stephen Holmes has recently argued for
a connection between Phèdre's psychology and Descartes's *Passions
of the Soul*, emphasizing her weakness of will and inability to control
her emotions.[112] In my opinion Racine has more in common with La
Rochefoucauld. Whether one reads Racine as a Jansenist and therefore
close to La Rochefoucauld,[113] or (less plausibly) as a neo-Epicurean
and *therefore* close to La Rochefoucauld,[114] he is far from the neo-Stoic
views of Descartes.

There is a clear evolution in Racine from his first major play *Andromaque* to *Phèdre*, his last nonreligious play. As noted by Paul Bénichou,
and as will be shown in detail below, *Andromaque* combines "the
violence of passion" with the "follies of reason." After this play, however, "Racine seems increasingly to prefer the portrayal of a lucid
degradation which observes itself with despair and knows itself to be

112. Holmes (1996).
113. Bénichou (1948).
114. Hippeau (1978), Chapter 9. As mentioned previously, Hippeau goes against the
     mainstream by arguing that La Rochefoucauld's Jansenism was assumed rather
     than genuine.

without remedy."[115] Louis Hippeau has drawn attention, however, to a scene in *Phèdre* that involves a form of self-deception similar to that of the earlier play. At the end of the first act, when Phèdre hears the false news that her husband Theseus is dead, her old nurse Oenone encourages her to join forces with Hyppolite, the son of Theseus from an earlier marriage and the object of Phèdre's illegitimate love, so that they can protect her son against Aricie, a pretendant to the succession. Oenone's appeal is based on Phèdre's duty towards her son rather than on her love for Hyppolite, and Phèdre self-deceptively receives it in that spirit. Hippeau comments, "Thus a love that in its principle was a guilty one is metamorphosed into a quite respectable duty, following La Rochefoucauld's recipe," namely that "[v]ices have a place in the composition of virtues just as poisons in that of medicines" (M182).[116]

Andromaque is organized around the unrequited love of Orestes for Hermione, of Hermione for Pyrrhus, and of Pyrrhus for Andromaque, who loves nobody but her young son. In the opening scene, Orestes has just arrived to the palace of Pyrrhus, who keeps Andromaque captive with her son while he is betrothed to Hermione. Orestes tells his friend Pylades that while he was away from Hermione,

> I took my triumph for a burst of hate
> Cursing her frowns, disparaging her charms (54–55).[117]

In this state, he mistook his "transports d'amour" for "transports de haine." Now that he has found her again and heard that she may no longer be attached to Pyrrhus, his hopes rise:

> It is said that my rival shuns Hermione
> Offering elsewhere his passion and his crown [. . .]
> Midst the afflictions that beset her soul
> In mine there arises pleasure, half-confessed
> I triumph, yet delude myself at first
> That my elation springs from my vengeance, but
> The ingrate soon reoccupied my heart.

115. Bénichou (1948), p. 230.
116. Hippeau (1978), p. 234.
117.   Je pris tous mes transports pour des transports de haine
             Détestant ses rigueurs, rabaissant ses attraits.
     The English translation used is that by Cairncross (1967). The translation of "transports" as "triumph" here is misleading.

I saw my passion's embers blaze again;
I felt my hatred was about to end;
Or rather felt that I adored her still. (77–88)[118]

When Orestes hears that Hermione is rejected by Pyrrhus, his reaction is one of joy. First he sticks to the illusion that he hates her, and interprets this reaction as the joy of revenge: if she will not have me, at least she cannot have him. But when his hate turns into love, the joy is reinterpreted as hope.

In a later scene, Andromaque having told Pyrrhus that she cannot love him, he responds as follows:

My passion's violence has gone too far
Ever to halt in mere indifference.
Think well. Henceforth, unless my heart can love
With rapture, it must hate with frenzied rage. (365–8)[119]

Like Orestes, Pyrrhus here asserts that if his love is not reciprocated, it cannot turn into indifference but must change into its opposite, hatred.

In a later scene, Hermione's confidante Cleone asks her why she hesitates to leave Pyrrhus and go away with Orestes:

CLEONE
Did you not tell me that you hated him?

HERMIONE
Hate him, Cleone? Honour so commands,
After so many favours he forgets.
He who was once so dear and has been false!
I've loved too much not to detest him now.

118.   On dit que, peu sensible aux charmes d'Hermione
        Mon rival porte ailleurs son coeur et sa couronne . . .
        Parmi les déplaisirs où son ame se noie,
        Il s'élève en la mienne une secrète joie:
        Je triomphe; et pourtant je me flatte d'abord
        Que la seule vengeance excite ce transport.
        Mais l'ingrate en mon coeur reprit bientôt sa place:
        De mes feux mal éteints je reconnus la trace;
        Je sentis que ma haine allait finir son cours;
        Ou plutôt je sentis que je l'aimais toujours.

119.   Oui, mes voeux ont trop loin poussé leur violence
        Pour ne plus s'arrêter que dans l'indifférence;
        Songez-y bien: il faut désormais que mon coeur,
        S'il n'aime avec transport, haïsse avec fureur.

CLEONE
Flee from him then, and, since Orestes loves . . .

HERMIONE
Ah! Give my fury time to swell. [. . .]
Let us stay on to spoil their happiness. (412–41)[120]

Hermione deceives herself that her love for Pyrrhus is dead, or, more accurately, turned into hate. She nevertheless invents pretexts for staying rather than going away with Orestes. First, she claims that she wants to stay in order to let her anger grow even stronger; next, that she wants to stay so as to disturb the presumed happiness of Pyrrhus and Andromaque by her presence. Both are blatant pieces of self-deception, as Cleone does not fail to point out.

In a later scene, Pyrrhus's mentor Phoenix encourages him to forget Andromaque and marry Hermione instead. Pyrrhus, while seemingly acquiescing, cannot bring himself to decide:

PYRRHUS
                    I see it all.
She counts upon her beauty, and despite my wrath
The haughty girl awaits me at her knees.
I'd see her at my feet and be unmoved.
She's Hector's widow. I'm Achilles's son.
Far too much hate lies between her and me

PHOENIX
Then make a start and talk no more of her [. . .]

PYRRHUS
                    No,
I've not yet said all I must say to her.

120.　　　　　CLÉONE
Ne m'avez-vous pas dit que vous le haïssiez?
HERMIONE
Si je le hais, Cléone! Il y va de ma gloire,
Après tant de bontés dont il perd la mémoire!
Lui qui me fut si cher, et qui m'a pu trahir!
Ah, je l'ai trop aimé, pour ne le point haïr!
CLÉONE
Fuyez-le donc, madame, et puisqu'on vous adore . . .
HERMIONE
Ah! laisse à ma fureur le temps de croître encore! [. . .]
Demeurons toutefois pour troubler leur fortune.

My anger to her but half revealed.
She does not know how strong's my enmity.
Let us go back. I'll brave her to her face.
And give my hate the very fullest scope. (658–78)[121]

Like Hermione, Pyrrhus deceives himself, as Phoenix does not fail to point out. Like her he seeks a pretext for avoiding a clean break, namely that he wants to show Andromaque how much he hates her.

In a later scene, Orestes bursts into rage upon hearing that Pyrrhus intends to marry Hermione after all. He brushes aside Pylades' suggestion that Pyrrhus, like Orestes himself, is to be pitied rather than hated:

No. It is my despair that spurs him on.
He'd scorn her but for me and for my love
Till then he was impassive to her spell.
He takes her to deprive her of me. (737–40)[122]

Here Orestes claims that the only reason why Pyrrhus wants to marry Hermione is Orestes's love for her. It is not entirely clear whether Orestes claims that Pyrrhus now actually loves Hermione (like a small child who only starts wanting a toy when another child starts playing with it), or that Pyrrhus wants to bask in Orestes's unhappiness.

When Hermione learns that Pyrrhus has definitely rejected her, she calls for Orestes and asks him to avenge her:

121.
PYRRHUS
Je vois ce qui la flatte:
Sa beauté la rassure; et, malgré mon courroux,
L'orgueilleuse m'attend encore à ses genoux.
Je la verrais aux miens, Phoenix, d'un oeil tranquille
Elle est veuve d'Hector, et je suis fils d'Achille:
Trop de haine sépare Andromaque et Pyrrhus.

PHOENIX
Commencez donc, seigneur, à ne m'en parler plus [. . .]

PYRRHUS
Non, je n'ai pas bien dit tout ce qu'il lui faut dire.
Ma colère à ses yeux n'a paru qu'à demi.
Elle ignore à quel point je suis son ennemi.
Retournons-y. Je veux la braver à sa vue,
Et donner à ma haine une libre etendue.

122.
Non, non; je le connais, mon désespoir le flatte;
Sans moi, sans mon amour, il dédaignait l'ingrate;
Ses charmes jusque-là n'avaient pu le toucher:
Le cruel ne la prend que pour me l'arracher.

While he still lives, fear lest I pardon him.
Suspect my wavering anger till his death.
Tomorrow I may love him if today
He dies not. (1198–1201.)[123]

Hermione claims that unless Orestes kills Pyrrhus immediately, she might come to love him again. Hence, the murder is a kind of precommitment: Kill him, so that I cannot love him. This passage must be read in conjunction with what Hermione tells Orestes after he has carried out the assignment:

HERMIONE
Why did you murder him? What did he do?
Who told you to?

ORESTES
God! Did you not yourself
Here, one short hour ago, ordain his death?

HERMIONE
Ah! how could you believe my frantic words?
And should you not have read my inmost thoughts? (1542–6)[124]

First, Hermione told Orestes to kill Pyrrhus as precommitment against backsliding. Now, she tells him that he should have understood that she did not really want to be precommitted: that her precommitting self was the inauthentic one, not the self against which the precommitment was directed.

The oscillations between love and hate in *Andromaque* are not "transmutations," in the technical sense of that term used in V.2. They do not, that is, involve meta-emotions – feelings of shame or anger that

123. Tant qu'il vivra, craignez que je ne lui pardonne.
    Doutez jusqu'à sa mort d'un courroux incertain:
    S'il ne meurt aujourd'hui, je puis l'aimer demain.

124.   HERMIONE
    Pourquoi l'assassiner? Qu'a-t-il fait? A quel titre?
    Qui te l'a dit?
          ORESTE
          O dieux! ne m'avez-vous pas
    Vous-même, ici, tantôt, ordonné son trépas?
          HERMIONE
    Ah! fallait-il en croire une amante insensée?
    Ne devais-tu pas lire au fond de ma pensée?

are induced by first-order emotions and in turn induce other first-order emotions. Instead, the emotional dynamics of *Andromaque* could be explained in one of two ways. First, the hate might simply be the feeling of frustrated love.[125] Now, the mere fact of not being loved in return is not a rational ground for hate (IV.3). For the emotion to be rational, it must arise out of a belief that the object of the emotion is intrinsically bad or evil. Racine does not, however, reveal the stories that Orestes, Hermione, and Pyrrhus might tell themselves to justify their hate. We should not conclude, however, that the lack of a cognitive element is a weakness of the play. Rather, it could simply help us to identify the kind of irrationality that is at work. If one invents a story to justify one's emotion, the irrationality is located in the belief: Given the belief, the emotion is rational enough. If one forgoes the story altogether and simply lashes out in rage because one's desire has been thwarted, the irrationality is squarely located in the emotion itself.

Second, the hate might be due to a misattribution. This is the explanation offered by Orestes: He "mistook" his "transports" for hate when they were actually caused by love. As we shall see shortly, the hateful feelings of the Princesse de Clèves towards the Duc de Nemours are due to the guilt she feels from loving him. In her case, the arousal of love combined with the pain of guilt is mistaken for the arousal of hate, just as in the case of Orestes love together with the grief of rejection is mistaken for hate. When strong arousal occurs together with strong pain, the subject may wrongly attribute them to a single emotion (hate) even when they are in reality caused by two different emotions (love together with either guilt or grief). This second explanation is more plausible, I believe, because it accounts better for the instability of the emotions and for the tendency of the characters to act as if in love even as they tell themselves that they hate. The phenomenon of mistaken emotions is discussed more fully in IV.2.

---

125. Soble (1990), pp. 135–6. Baumeister and Wotman (1992, p. 54) state that in their sample of 134 stories of unrequited love, "often would-be lovers are reluctant to allow themselves to feel anger or hatred toward the person they love, but they have no such scruples about the third person whom they regard as 'competition.'" At the same time, "a substantial minority of the would-be lovers did sooner or later direct some negative affect toward the person they loved, whether this was frustration, angry feelings of betrayal, or even an attempt to convince themselves that the grapes were sour – that is, to devalue the person who spurned their love" (*ibid.*, p. 55).

MME. DE LAFAYETTE

We may compare Hermione and Phèdre with a third seventeenth-century heroine, the Princesse de Clèves in Mme. de Lafayette's novel of the same name. All three experience passionate love, yet suffer very different effects. Hermione deceives herself about her emotion. Phèdre remains for the most part lucid but succumbs to weakness of will. The Princesse de Clèves exhibits lucidity *and* willpower, remaining virtuous in the face of a passion for a man other than her husband.

The novel was first published in 1678, the same year as the final edition of La Rochefoucauld's *Maximes*. Mme. de Lafayette and La Rochefoucauld were very close friends and perhaps at one time lovers. Although it was widely rumored at the time that *La Princesse de Clèves* was due to their joint authorship, there is no hard evidence to this effect. The novel in itself does not suggest much of an influence. With an important exception to be discussed below, the "esprit" of the Princess is not the "dupe" of her "coeur." Unlike Hermione, she is lucid; unlike Phedre, she is virtuous – two character traits that La Rochefoucauld does not really allow to be possible.[126] True, the courtly society described in the novel is a good illustration of La Rochefoucauld's maxim that the world is "composé de mines" – of veils and masks. As Mme de Chartres tells her daughter, the future Princesse de Clèves: "If you judge from appearances here, you will often be mistaken; what appears is seldom the truth."[127] This idea, however, was not La Rochefoucauld's most original contribution to moral psychology. His analyses of how people deceive themselves were far more novel than his comments on how they deceive others.

La Princesse de Clèves is a novel about love, requited and unrequited; shame of love; and fear of love. The title character is married to M. de Clèves, whom she does not love, and in love with the Duc

---

126. Although his exclamation, "How a woman is to be pitied when she has love and virtue together!" (MP49), may well have been made with the Princess of Clèves in mind (Truchet 1992, p. 172, n. 1), it constitutes an acknowledgment of the possibility of virtue that goes against the main current of the Maxims. Vigée (1960) offers a reading of the novel that makes it an almost direct transposition of La Rochefoucauld and Pascal. Although there may be nothing in the novel that explicitly contradicts this reading, there is nothing that supports it either. The claim, for instance, that the secret of the final renunciation of the Princess is to be found in La Rochefoucauld's MS1 or in Pascal's *Pensée* 680 seems entirely arbitrary.

127. Lafayette (1994), p. 19.

de Nemours. Initially, however, she does not realize that she is in love with him. The mother of the Princess, perceiving the love of her daughter for the Duc de Nemours, tells her, "It is long since I perceived this affection, but I have been averse to speaking to you about it, lest you should become aware of it yourself."[128] The reader knows, however, that she *had* already made her daughter aware of that love by telling her about the Duke's flighty character and in particular about his great passion for another lady at the court: "It is impossible to express her grief (*douleur*) when her mother's words opened her eyes to the interest she took in Monsieur de Nemours; she had never dared to acknowledge it to herself."[129] The Princess, in other words, deceives herself about her true feelings until she realizes that she is jealous. It is not only that she ignores her love: The ignorance is motivated. Note that what triggers the conscious awareness of her love is her awareness of another emotion, jealousy. As the discussion of Stendhal will show, the latter emotion, too, can remain at the level of unawareness until revealed by another emotion.

Once the Princess has understood that she is in love, an emotional chain reaction is set in motion. "She could not keep from being embarrassed, and yet delighted to see him; but when he was out of her sight and she remembered that this pleasure was the beginning of passion, she felt she almost hated him, so much did the idea of guilty love pain her."[130] The guilt of being in love causes her to hate him. The Duke causes her to have an emotion (love) that causes her to have an emotion (guilt) that it is painful to have, analogously to the second-order pain of envy. Yet the mechanism by which the love appears as hate differs from the mechanism by which envy is transmuted into indignation. A I argue in IV.2, in her case it is a question of misperception of her emotion rather than of a cognitive reframing that induces a new emotion. For another example of how a second-order emotion (of shame rather than guilt) can turn love into hate, the reader is referred to the discussion in V.2 of the relation between Mathilde de la Mole and Julien Sorel.

Later, when M. de Clèves suspects her love, she sends the Duke away when he comes to visit her. That does not help her, however, with her husband, who reproaches her as follows:

128. *Ibid.*, p. 28.
129. *Ibid.*, p. 26.
130. *Ibid*, p. 28; translation slightly modified.

"Then you were ill for him alone" he went on, "since you received everybody else? Why this difference for him? Why is he not the same to you as all the rest? Why should you dread meeting him? Why do you show him that you make use of the power his passion gives you over him? Would you dare to refuse him if you did not know that he is able to distinguish your severity from incivility? From a person like you, Madame, everything is a favor except indifference."[131]

Eleven years later, La Bruyère stated the last idea in epigrammatic form: "A woman who always stares at one and the same person, or who is for ever avoiding to look at him, makes us think one and the same thing about her" (*Characters* III.65). The intentional origin of dissimulation leaves a trace that can often be detected by an acute observer.[132] The Prince believed, correctly we may assume, that his wife's refusal to see the Duke revealed rather than hid her feelings for him. He also believed, correctly perhaps, that the Duke believed this to be the case. Finally, he also believed – but here it is less clear that he was right – that she believed that the Duke believed her refusal to be a sign of his favor. His anger is based on that third-order belief, which may, however, be a result of his jealousy rather than its cause.

At the end of the novel, when her husband is dead and the Duke wants her to marry him, she turns him down with the following words: "Monsieur de Clèves was perhaps the only man in the world capable of keeping his love after marriage. My fate forbade me enjoying this blessing. Perhaps, too, his love only survived because he found none in me. But I should not have the same way of preserving yours; I believe that the obstacles you have met have made you constant."[133] She claims, in other words, that her husband loved her only because she did not love him, and that the Duke loves her only because he cannot have her. There are two ideas involved here. First, even if love necessarily involves the desire for reciprocity,[134] it may not survive the satisfaction of that desire.[135] Second, even if love necessarily involves the desire for consummation,[136] it may not

---

131. *Ibid*, p. 86.
132. Elster (1983b), pp. 71–2.
133. Lafayette (1994), p. 103.
134. Soble (1990), pp. 243–6.
135. In a variant of the Groucho Marx paradox: "Someone who would stoop so low as to love *me* cannot be worth loving."
136. An exception may be certain forms of courtly love, regulated by the idea that "[W]hatever turns into reality is no longer love" (de Rougemont 1983, p. 34).

survive the satisfaction of that desire.[137] Both ideas are expressed in a maxim by La Rochefoucauld: "Love, like fire, cannot survive without continual movement, and it ceases to live as soon as it ceases to hope or fear" (M75).

JANE AUSTEN

As Gilbert Ryle shows in an essay on "Jane Austen and the moralists,"[138] her novels are very much in the critical and debunking spirit of the moralists. The dialogues and authorial asides contain observations that could have come straight from La Rochefoucauld or La Bruyère. In Chapter 9 of *Pride and Prejudice*, for instance, we find an exchange that mirrors La Rochefoucauld's comment on how absence affects love of varying degrees of strength (I.8). Mrs. Bennet, referring to her oldest daughter, says that

"When she was only fifteen, there was a gentleman at my brother Gardiner's in town, so much in love with her, that my sister-in-law was sure he would make her an offer before we came away. But however he did not. Perhaps he thought her too young. However, he wrote some verses on her, and very pretty they were."
"And so ended his affection," said Elizabeth impatiently. "There has been many a one, I fancy, overcome in the same way. I wonder who first discovered the efficacy of poetry in driving away love!"
"I have been used to consider poetry as the *food* of love," said Darcy. "Of a fine, stout, healthy love it may. Every thing nourishes what is strong already. But if it be only a slight, thin sort of inclination, I am convinced that one good sonnet will starve it entirely away."

The emotional register in Jane Austen's novels is less violent than that of sixteenth- and seventeenth-century writers. There are no jealousy killings (Othello); no deaths from grief (M. de Clèves); no madness (Orestes); no suicides (Hermione). Her characters may have strong emotions, but not violent ones, with the exception of Marianne in *Sense and Sensibility* (and not counting the erotic relationship between Henry Crawford and Maria Bertram in *Mansfield Park*). Although each novel ends with at least one happily consummated and

---

137. See for instance the analyses in Grimaldi (1993, pp. 31–2 and *passim*) of the Proustian concept of love.
138. Ryle (1971). He relates her writings exclusively to the British moralists, notably Shaftesbury, without citing any of the French moralists.

fully requited love relation, Austen's treatment of this emotion is often a touch too idyllicizing (an exception being the unsurpassably romantic final chapters of *Persuasion*). She is stronger in her treatment of unconsummated love, notably Henry Crawford's love for Fanny Price and Edward Bertram's love for Miss Crawford. Henry Crawford's courtship of Fanny Price begins as a tease or a bet and then turns into the real thing, similar to Valmont's love for Mme. de Tourvel in *Les Liaisons Dangéreuses*. Unlike Valmont, however, he does not succeed in his seduction plot but spoils his chances by eloping with Maria Bertram. Edward Bertram's love for Miss Crawford follows the opposite course, beginning as a compelling infatuation and ending in disillusionment when he learns that she blames her brother not for what he did but for doing it so publicly. The failure of these two relationships is the closest thing to a touch of tragedy in Austen's work; she indicates in fact that they might have been consummated had it not been for Crawford's akratic behavior. The Crawfords differ in this respect from the otherwise quite similar character of William Elliott in *Persuasion*, who is not even tempted by goodness.

Austen's emotional range is mainly displayed in her social satire. Her novels are populated with comical and vicious characters whose pride, vanity, envy, malice, indolence, and other petty emotions are vividly conveyed in dialogue and monologue the like of which has never been written. I shall consider three emotions that loom large in Austen's universe: pride, vanity, and boredom.

Pride and Prejudice offers a large cast of characters that illustrate the many varieties of pride, ranging from Darcy's basically sane self-approbation, which only needs to be taken down a notch or two, through Sir William Lucas's empty but harmless boasting, to Lady Catherine de Bourgh's malicious gloating and Mr. Collins's absurd combination of self-satisfaction and self-abasement. But rather than going into details of these descriptions, I prefer to use an example from *Mansfield Park*. When Fanny Price goes to her first ball, her aunt Lady Bertram sends her maid Mrs. Chapman to help her dress, quite unnecessarily, as it turns out, because Fanny is already dressed by the time Mrs. Chapman reaches her room. Later, when Fanny receives an offer of marriage from Henry Crawford, Lady Bertram sees it as all her doing: "I am sure he fell in love with you at the ball. I am sure the mischief was done that evening, You did look remarkably well. Every body said so. Sir Thomas said so. And you know you had Chapman to help you dress. I am very glad I sent Chapman to you" (vol. 3, Chapter 2). This is an instance of backward or irrational pride. Rather than being a case of a genuine accomplishment inducing justified pride, Lady Bertram's pride is based on a spurious accomplishment, the belief in which is the effect rather than the cause of the emotion it supports.

Persuasion is among other things a study in vanity. Both Sir Walter Elliott and his daughter Elizabeth are consumed by a selfish concern with appearances. In all other respects, they are emotionally cold and sterile:

Vanity was the beginning and the end of Sir Walter Elliott's character; vanity of person and of situation. He had been remarkably handsome in his youth; and, at fifty-four, was still a very fine man. Few women could think more of their personal appearance than he did; nor could the valet of any new made lord be more delighted with the place he held in society. He considered the blessing of beauty as inferior only to the blessing of a baronetcy; and the Sir Walter Elliott, who united these gifts, was the constant object of his warmest respect and devotion. (vol. 1, Chapter 1)

Being concerned with his appearance and situation, he judges others by the same criteria. It is, in fact, part and parcel of his vanity that he cannot imagine that others do not share his concern with appearances. He is able, moreover, to use that concern as an excuse for his lack of generosity in other respects. Speaking to one of his daughters about another,

'How is Mary looking?' said Sir Walter, in the height of his good humour. 'The last time I saw her, she had a red nose, but I hope that must not happen every day.'
'Oh! no, that must have been quite accidental. In general she has been in very good health, and very good looks since Michaelmas.'
'If I thought it would not tempt her to go out in the sharp winds, and grow coarse, I would send her a new hat and pelisse.' (vol. 2, Chapter 3)

This is the kind of extremely fine-grained observation in which Austen excels. Spurred by vicarious vanity, Sir Walter first seems to entertain the idea that his daughter might need a warm coat so that she would not spoil her looks by a red nose. His pettiness getting the better of him, however, he then turns the argument around: A new coat might encourage her to go outside and ruin her skin in the sharp weather. The causal chain from his vanity to his decision to abstain from the gift has, I believe, the following structure. (i) Because of his all-absorbing vanity, he cannot imagine that others are less vain than he is, or that appearances are not the central part of their well-being. (ii) Because of his all-absorbing vanity, he has no genuine concern for the well-being of others. (iii) Because of the conventional norms guiding relations between parents and children, he nevertheless feels a brief urge to do something when he perceives a threat to his daughter's appearance. (iv) The urge is quenched, however, when his selfishness helps him come up with a script in which his daughter's appearance and his purse would both be better served by her *not* getting the coat.

A similar self-serving justification for meanness occurs in *Sense and Sensibility*, but there the mechanism is more transparent. After his father dies, John Dashwood manages to persuade himself not only that he is under no obligation to provide an annuity for his sister, but that she will actually be better off if he does not: "[W]hatever I give them occasionally will be of far greater assistance than a yearly allowance, because they would only enlarge their style of living if they felt sure of a larger income, and would not be the sixpence the richer for it at the end of the year" (vol. 1, Chapter 2). Such self-serving and self-deceptive practices, based on petty emotions of greed and vanity, form the background for the near-undiluted goodness of the main characters in Austen's novels. Only the Crawfords exemplify moral ambiguity; they are neither petty, nor ridiculous, nor strong enough to be good.

Emma in the novel of that name is the most complex of Austen's heroines. As persuasively argued by Patricia Meyer Spacks, her emotional state in much of the novel is *boredom*. Yet, she "does not understand herself as bored. More precisely, she knows her condition from time to time, in specific situations (in the company of Miss Bates, on the eve of Miss Taylor's wedding), but suppresses her awareness that boredom inheres in her circumstances."[139] Not only does she deceive herself about her emotion, but she also manages to mistake its symptoms for those of love. "In one of Austen's brilliant jokes, Emma actually confuses boredom with erotic feeling. 'This sensation of listlessness, weariness, stupidity, this disinclination to sit down and employ myself, this feeling of every thing's being dull and insipid about the house! – I must be in love.'"[140]

139. Spacks (1995), p. 167.
140. *Ibid.*

STENDHAL

As I have said, Stendhal is both moralist and novelist. In its subject matter, *De l'amour*, especially the "Fragments divers," is in many respects close to La Rochefoucauld and La Bruyère.[141] The work also refers regularly to La Rochefoucauld, not only to the *Maximes* but also to *La Princesse de Clèves*, which Stendhal wrongly attributed to him. When he refers to the Princess or the Duc de Nemours, and to other fictional characters, it is "as if they had existed"[142]; as if, that is, they could provide illustrations or counterexamples for this or that abstract proposition. In this book, I am among other things urging that we follow in his steps.

The essay on love has a key position in Stendhal's life and work. It expresses and condenses Stendhal's great, unhappy love for Matilde Dembowsky, whom he pursued for several years in an unsuccessful, perhaps self-defeating courtship. Much of the book, in fact, can be seen as a somewhat self-serving explanation why his love for her *had* to remain unconsummated. At the same time, the book has been called "the hidden center of his work,"[143] and certainly provides the matrix for at least two of his novels, *Le rouge et le noir* and *Lucien Leuwen*. In these works, Stendhal achieves by proxy what he could not obtain in real life. "In his reveries, he is metamorphosed into Julien, Fabrice, Lucien, Lamiel; he changes his face, his body, his social condition, even his sex – but always to tell his own life by improving his fortune or embellishing his misfortune."[144] The novels are more than daydreams or exercises in wish fulfillment, but they are certainly that too.

De l'amour also remains the best study of what Stendhal called "amour-passion," for which Dorothy Tennov, in a book dedicated to Stendhal, has coined the term "limerence."[145] In the literature on

---

141. The style, by contrast, is unpolished, at times almost stenographic, which for a modern reader can be a virtue. "The arrows of our great moralists are more beautiful, and equally sound, but already stuck in their target; Stendhal's are seen in full flight. It is an impression that only Pascal conveys with greater force" (Prévost 1951, p. 188).
142. Crouzet (1996), p. 309.
143. Crouzet (1990), p. 281.
144. Starobinski (1961), p. 211; see also Elster (in press a), section III.7.
145. Tennov (1979, p. 171) reports that from her reading on the literature of love "apart from Stendhal, I found nothing that can really be considered a systematic and comprehensive approach to the phenomenon." In her interviews with 500 individuals, Tennov found almost all the reactions described by Stendhal. A summary, drawing on both Stendhal and Tennov, is in Brehm (1988, pp. 234–42).

love, the phenomenon is often referred to as "infatuation." As many will know – according to Tennov, some never experience it – it is an all-consuming state, which thrives on uncertainty, fear, and hope and induces utterly distorted and self-serving interpretations of the behavior and utterances of the person one loves. Stendhal's achievement was to perceive an analytical structure and an orderly progression in this apparently opaque emotion.

(1) The relation between love and cognition is an important theme in *De l'amour*. Stendhal offers a cognitive theory of love, although it is very different from Pascal's. The reason for loving another is not the belief that the other has this or that quality, such as beauty or intelligence, but the belief that the other *loves oneself*. "No one can love unless urged by the persuasion of love (the hope of being loved)."[146] In his theory of stages of love, Stendhal stipulates that the first stage is admiration; the second is the thought, "How delightful it would be to kiss her, to be kissed by her" and so on; and the third is hope, that is, the belief that one is loved. Even a "small degree of hope" (i.e., a low probability of being loved) is then sufficient to trigger the fourth stage, love. Certainty of being loved, by contrast, may kill the love as we shall see. Moreover, "even when hope is lacking after a day or two, love will persist" (Chapter 3).

Stendhal does not explain where the triggering belief comes from, for example whether it is based on observation or wishful thinking. What is sure is that once the fourth stage is reached, beliefs lose touch with reality. "From the moment he falls in love even the wisest man no longer sees anything *as it really is*.... He no longer admits an element of chance in things and loses his sense of the probable; judging by its effect on his happiness, whatever he imagines becomes reality" (Chapter 12). Stendhal does not say, however, whether the transition from the second to the third stage is similarly guided by the pleasure principle. The issue is complicated by the fact that the third-stage belief as well as the fourth-stage passion may be unconscious. In the short story "Ernestine," the heroine receives a rose from the unknown

146. Stendhal (1980), p. 279. Some years before the publication of *De l'amour*, Jane Austen made an apparently similar observation in *Northanger Abbey*, when describing Henry Tilney's love for Catherine Morland: "[T]hough Henry was now sincerely attached to her, though he felt and delighted in all the excellencies of her character and truly loved her society, I must confess that his affection originated in nothing better than gratitude, or, in other words, that a persuasion of her partiality for him had been the only cause of giving her a serious thought" (vol. 2, Chapter 15). Yet Stendhal would have said that the *certainty* of her calf-love would have made it impossible for him to love her.

young man who has been depositing flowers and letters in her garden and finds herself crying. "What did those tears mean? Ernestine did not know.... We who have fewer illusions can recognize the third stage of the birth of love: the appearance of hope. Ernestine did not realize that her heart was saying, as it contemplated the rose: 'It is certain now that he loves me.'"[147] Later, she also makes the transition to the fourth stage without being aware of it:

Ernestine was very far from recognizing the nature of the feelings which held sway in her heart. Had she been able to foresee whither they were leading her she would have had a chance of escaping their dominion. A young German, English, or Italian girl would have recognized love; however, our wise educational system having chosen to deny the existence of love to young girls, Ernestine was only vaguely alarmed by what was taking place in her heart; on profound reflection she could see nothing there but simple friendship. If she had taken that one rose it was because she feared lest in doing otherwise she might have hurt her new friend and driven him away. 'And besides,' she told herself, after much thought, 'one must not be found wanting in politeness.'[148]

This analysis invites several remarks. First, I do not think unconscious beliefs and unconscious passions necessarily go together. One can imagine an unconscious belief triggering a love that is aware of itself. Second, it is hard to tell whether Ernestine's ignorance of her love is motivated or unmotivated. The second half of the passage suggests that Ernestine is searching for *excuses* to keep the flower, which indicates a self-deceptive ignorance rather than an entirely innocent one. Third, however, the reference to French culture suggests that the ignorance is genuine: Her love is only a proto-emotion because she does not have the necessary conceptual framework to see it for what it is. Finally, Stendhal confirms an idea we met above, that in the development of love there is a point of no return and that immediate recognition of the emotion is necessary to nip it in the bud.

(2) A clear-cut case of self-deceptive ignorance of love occurs in *Lucien Leuwen*.[149] In the early part of the novel, Lucien and Mme. de Chasteller have come to love each other deeply yet are uncertain about each other. She fears that he may be no more than a rake, he that she does not really love him. Whenever he makes a clumsy and

147. *Ibid.*, p. 297.
148. *Ibid.*, p. 298.
149. The following is more fully developed in Elster (in press a), section III.7.

tentative advance, she sees it as a reason for doubt about his character; she grows haughty, he is made desperate, and, through his desperation, redeems himself for a while. Gradually they grow closer to each other. Lucien writes her a letter; she, after some soul-searching, replies in what she believes to be a severe and uncommunicative tone. In an authorial aside, Stendhal comments as follows:

Why note that her reply involved a studied attempt at the haughtiest turns of phrase? Three or four times Leuwen was urged to abandon all hope, the very word *hope* was avoided with an infinite adroitness that made Mme. de Chasteller very pleased with herself. Alas, without knowing it she was the victim of her Jesuitical education; she deceived herself, in applying badly, and unawares, the art of deceiving others which she had been taught at the Sacré-Coeur. She *answered*: everything lay in this word, which she preferred to ignore.[150]

As an analysis of self-deception, this is strikingly similar to Sartre's example of the woman who lets a man take her hand yet refuses to admit to herself the meaning of this act.[151] Sartre's woman lets her companion take her hand and finds refuge in lofty and exalted conversation; Mme. de Chasteller replies to Lucien's letter and finds refuge in the severity of her tone.

By contrast, an unambiguous case of innocent ignorance is that of Mme. de Rênal in *Le rouge et le noir*. For a while she is unaware of her love for Julien Sorel. Although thinking about him constantly, she has not put a name on her feelings. The triggering event is her happiness when she learns that Julien is not, as she feared, about to marry her maid Elisa: "[U]nable to resist the joy which, after so many hopeless days, swept like a torrent in flood through all her being, Mme. de Rênal falls into a dead faint. When she has recovered consciousness and was comfortably settled in her own room, she sent everyone away. She was deeply amazed. Can it be that I'm in love with Julien? she said to herself at length."[152] One emotion, love, goes unperceived until it is revealed by another emotion, happiness, which is induced by the relief from a third (unperceived) emotion, jealousy. Unlike Mme. de Chasteller, she does not display any resistance to the idea of being in love. Although raised like her by the Jesuits, "Madame de

150. Stendhal (1952), p. 959.
151. Sartre (1943), p. 94 ff.
152. Stendhal (1952), p. 261.

Rênal had possessed enough good sense to forget, as something quite absurd, everything she had been taught in the convent,"[153] including the art of self-deception.

(3) From the fourth stage in the development of love there is a short step, or rather no step at all, to the fifth stage: *crystallization*. This is the best-known idea in *De l'amour*, and of considerable interest in its own right. Before I discuss it, it is worthwhile observing, however, that unlike many other ideas in that work it plays no role in Stendhal's novels. The heroes and heroines of the novels are, without exception, just as wonderful as the heroines and heroes believe them to be. The "angelical sweetness" of Mme. de Rênal, Mme. de Chasteller, and Clélia Conti may be a result of the author's crystallization around Matilde Dembowsky,[154] but owes nothing to crystallization in their fictional lovers.

The origin of the term is as follows: "At the salt mines of Hallein near Salzburg the miners throw a leafless wintry bough into one of the abandoned workings. Two or three months later, through the effect of the waters saturated with salt which soak the bough and then let it dry as they recede, the miners find it covered with a shining deposit of crystal. The tiniest twigs no bigger than a tom-tit's claw are encrusted with an infinity of crystals, scintillating and dazzling."[155] In a story about the Salzburg bough, Stendhal has one of his friends drawing the analogy with love: "[F]rom the moment you begin to be really interested in a woman, you no longer see her *as she really is*, but as it suits you to see her. You're comparing the flattering illusions created by this nascent interest with the pretty diamonds which hide this leafless branch of hornbeam – and which are only perceived, mark you, by the eyes of this young man falling in love."[156]

As with the influence of love on the perceived probability of being loved, crystallization is a form of irrational belief formation, inducing an exaggerated belief in the "beauty and the merit" of the other person. For Pascal, the perception of these qualities is the cause and justification of the love; for Stendhal, love is first caused by the (relational) belief that one may be loved and then causes the (monadic) belief about the other that justifies the emotion. Again, the emotion works

153. *Ibid.*, p. 251.
154. Crouzet (1990, p. 289) suggests that if Stendhal "had been more lucid and less infatuated, he would have found her *emphatic*."
155. *Ibid.*, p. 284.
156. *Ibid.*, p. 287.

backward, to invent its own justification. For La Rochefoucauld, the mechanism at work in such cases is *amour-propre*. "Our *amour-propre* magnifies or minimizes the good qualities of our friends according to how pleased we are with them" (M88). My desire for self-esteem leads me to believe that somebody who is the object of *my* love must be an exceptional person. My desire for esteem leads me to believe that a person who loves *me* has exceptional qualities that enhance the value of the love.

This explanation cannot, I think, be imputed to Stendhal. If crystallization were always a product of *amour-propre*, it would always tend to satisfy our desire for esteem or for self-esteem. It could never work to make us unhappy. In his discussion of jealousy (*De l'amour*, Chapter 35), however, Stendhal makes it clear that crystallization has the power to make us miserable: "Though the same habit [crystallization] persists, the moment you become jealous it produces the opposite effect. Far from giving you sublime joy, every perfection added into the crown of your beloved, who perhaps loves another, is a dagger-thrust in the heart" (Chapter 35). Whereas in the pre-jealous state "no matter what you see or remember . . . , you are always finding . . . new and apparently ideal ways of making her love you more," jealousy has the opposite effect: "[I]nstead of suggesting new ways of increasing her love, [what you see or remember] indicate more of your rival's advantage. You see a pretty woman galloping in a park, and the rival is immediately famed for his fine horses." Moreover, in jealousy "you overrate your rival's success, and the insolence resulting from it." Stendhal also cites from *Othello*:

> Trifles light as air
> Seem to the jealous confirmation strong
> as proofs from holy writ. [338–40]

In jealousy there is, in other words, a constant tendency to *counter-wishful thinking* (I.6) that is hard to explain as a result of *amour-propre*. To my knowledge, none of the major French seventeenth-century writers on the passions noted the tendency of jealousy to confirm its own fears, against the evidence.[157] Those who believe *amour-propre*

---

157. Descartes might seem an exception: "Jealousy . . . has reference to our desire to retain possession of some good. It arises not so much from the strength of the reasons making us judge that we might lose it as from our great esteem for it, which causes us to examine even the slightest grounds for suspicion and regard them as reasons worth serious considerations" (PA§167). The passage is

is the mainspring of human action should, if anything, argue that it leads us to *underestimate* the evidence in support of our jealousy. (This is in fact the reaction of M. de Rênal in *Le rouge et le noir* when he receives an anonymous letter stating that his wife and Julien Sorel are lovers. His love, however, is what Stendhal called *amour de vanité*, which may plausibly be seen as guided by *amour-propre* only.) The jealous person is doubly irrational: Having his beliefs shaped by his desires is irrational in itself, but having them shaped so as to frustrate the desires instead of satisfying them violates the pleasure principle as well as the reality principle. If crystallization can have this effect in jealousy, there is no reason to believe that it invariably follows the pleasure principle in love.

(4) What I have discussed so far is what Stendhal calls passionate love (*amour-passion*), the only kind of love worthy of a superior being and the only one he gives to his main characters. Other varieties of love include mannered love (*amour-goût*), vanity–love (*amour de vanité*), and love through pique (*amour par pique*). The first two are closely related. "If you take away vanity, there is very little left of mannered love" (Chapter 1).[158] Stendhal points to two features of passionate love that we may use to distinguish it from mannered love and vanity–love respectively. On the one hand, "while passionate love carries us away against our real interest, mannered love as invariably respects those interests" (Chapter 1). On the other hand, "the ridiculous consequences of grand passion are the only proof I will admit in evidence of its existence" (Chapter 5). Yet even those harboring the lesser forms of love may demand to be loved passionately: "Whatever kind of love one lover feels, no sooner is jealousy arisen that the other lover is required to fulfill all the conditions of passionate love. Vanity produces all the needs of a tender heart in the jealous lover" (Chapter 36).

Stendhal's idea of love through pique (Chapter 38) is an entirely original if not always convincing construction. It arises when A falls in love with B simply because A's rival C is in love with B. As

ambiguous. It could mean that if there is a low probability for a very bad outcome the badness of the outcome causes us to overestimate the probability (Holmes 1996, p. 98). More plausibly, perhaps, it could be read simply as saying that the badness of the outcome compensates for the low probability.

158. In a puzzling observation (Chapter 38) he also subsumes love through pique under mannered love, saying that the element of pique is "the best test for distinguishing between mannered and passionate love." Yet that statement is not consistent with the views that in mannered love people never act against their interest and that amour through pique may lead people to kill themselves (Chapter 38).

René Girard notes, we find this triangular pattern in the relation between Julien Sorel and two prominent members of the local gentry, M. de Rênal and M. Valenod. As preceptor of the children of M. de Rênal, Julien becomes more desirable when it becomes known that M. Valenod would like to hire him to teach his children.[159] I disagree with Girard, however, when he also finds the same pattern in the relation between Julien Sorel, Mathilde de la Mole, and Mme. de Fervaques. He asserts that Mathilde's love for Julien is resurrected only when he appears to be the object of desire on the part of Mme. de Fervaques, because "a certain prestige is attached" to the latter. Mathilde, however, has nothing but contempt for her rival. Her emotion is based on the thought that "he loves her, so he cannot love me," not on the thought that "she loves him, so he must be worth loving."

The relation between jealousy and love through pique has a rough resemblance to the Aristotelian distinction between hatred and anger (II.2). "Jealousy desires the death of the rival it fears. A man suffering from pique, on the other hand, wants his enemy to live and above all to witness his triumph." In pique the rivalry predates the love, which is only a means of getting back at the other. Although the love induced by rivalry among Opera girls may be real enough to "drive them to suicide," it "dies the moment their rival is sent packing." What matters in love through pique is defeating the other rather than attaining one's goal. "A man suffering from pique . . . would be loth to see his rival give up the contest, because the rival might be insolent enough to think: '. . . if I had cared to pursue the struggle I should have got the better of him . . .'" This is a rarefied cognitive antecedent – A's belief about B's belief about B's counterfactual victory over A – but the emotion is plausible enough.

Although a man who loves passionately may find no other way of having his love requited than by creating an *amour par pique* in the woman he loves, he may find that this is not how he wanted to be loved. In fact, being loved for this reason "is perhaps, after jealousy, the most cruel unhappiness of all. There is a great city where people still remember a gentle, sensitive man, overcome with fury of this kind, who killed his mistress because she only loved him through pique against her sister." Thus we find Stendhal asserting that when a woman A loves a man B out of pique against her rival C, the relation can unravel in one of two ways. As we just saw, B may kill A because

159. Girard (1961), pp. 19–20. He does not cite *De l'amour*.

she is the source of his misery. Alternatively, if C kills herself, A's love, which depends on the existence of C to witness her triumph, will also die. In his novels Stendhal never tried, perhaps wisely, to create relations of this complexity.

(5) The relation between Julien Sorel and Mathilde de la Mole in *Le rouge et le noir* is prefigured in the analyses of *De l'amour*. The see-saw nature of their relationship – when one is up the other is down – is foreshadowed in the earlier work. (As we shall see in V.2, the transmutations of Mathilde's feelings have a further and rather different explanation, related to her alternations between pride and shame.) "The loves of two people in love with each other are almost never the same. Passionate love has its phases, when first one partner and then the other will be more in love" (Chapter 36). Moreover, one feels more *because* the other feels less and vice versa. The mechanism here is that spelled out by La Rochefoucauld: "[L]ove ceases to live as soon as it ceases to hope or fear" (M75). We have seen that Stendhal disagrees with one half of this statement: Although the onset of love requires a belief that the other may love one, it can persist even when the belief is replaced by the certainty that the other does not love one. He fully embraces, however, the second and more paradoxical half: Love cannot outlast the certainty that the other *does* love one.

In a famous line from *Andromaque* (1365), Hermione asks Pyrrhus: "I loved you wayward. Faithful what would I have done? (*Je t'aimais inconstant; qu'aurais-je fait fidèle?*)" Stendhal's answer is the opposite of the one implicit in this rhetorical question. He would say that if Pyrrhus had been faithful to her, Andromaque would have loved him less, not more. "The pleasures of love are always in proportion to the fear" (Chapter 59). He notes that "a woman suspected of inconstancy leaves you because she is too sure of you. You have removed fear, and the little doubts of happy love no longer occur" (Chapter 36). Love – *amour-passion*, the thing that keeps one awake at night – is nurtured by the perpetual overcoming or suspension of uncertainty. Note that the grounds for uncertainty as well as the grounds for suspending it may be figments of the imagination. The former is the case for Lucien Leuwen in his relations with Mme. de Chasteller, the latter for Stendhal himself in his relations with Matilde Dembowsky, who probably never loved him the way he sometimes thought she did.

(6) *Lucien Leuwen* is the novel that is most closely related to *De l'amour*, not surprisingly, as both works reflect his unhappy love for

Matilde Dembowsky.[160] Of all his heroes, only Lucien has Stendhal's timidity in the presence of the woman he loves – the fear of always saying too much or too little. Chapter 24 of *De l'amour* offers an explanation and justification of this behavior. "You reproach yourself for lack of wit or boldness; but the only way to show courage would be to love her less." In fact, this behavioral expression of genuine passion provides "a clear distinction which women can draw between passionate love and mere gallantries, between the tender soul and the prosaic soul. At these critical moments the one gains where the other loses; the prosaic soul acquires just that hint of warmth which it usually lacks, while the tender soul loses its wits from excess of feeling, and from trying to hide its folly, which is even worse." Immediately after the passage cited in (4) above to the effect that passionate love can be recognized by its tendency to induce ridiculous behavior, he goes on to say that "[s]hyness, for instance, is a proof of love" (Chapter 5). Here, Stendhal seems to confuse necessary and sufficient conditions. Even if all genuine love must take the form of shyness, one cannot expect a woman to take shyness as an infallible indicator of genuine love. The fallacy, as Aristotle noted (*Poetics* 1460^{a}17–25), is a natural one, and becomes even more so when the agent is motivated to commit it.

In Chapter 26, "On Modesty," he turns to the expression of love in women. This chapter, too, is about why appearances are misleading. "It is obvious that every tender and proud woman – and these two qualities seldom exists apart, since they are cause and effect – must assume habits of coldness which are labeled 'prudishness' by those whom they disconcert." In the further development of this argument, Stendhal again comes very close to the self-deceptive confusion of necessary and sufficient conditions. A woman may affect modesty, thinking, "My lover will respect me the more for it." Hence, Stendhal seems to think, a man who finds himself refused by the woman he loves should not let himself be discouraged too easily. Commenting on Stendhal's feelings towards Matilde Dembowsky, Michel Crouzet writes, "So much anger, so many scruples, so many defenses and so much severity could only be proofs of [her] love: it is only against an all-powerful emotion that one barricades oneself. She turns into an exemplary fictional heroine: the more she rejects him the more she belongs to him."[161]

---

160. For a fuller discussion of *Lucien Leuwen*, see Elster (in press a), section III.7.
161. Crouzet (1990), p. 292.

We saw earlier that M. de Clèves offered a similar explanation of his wife's refusal to see the Duc de Nemours. In his case, the account is plausible because there is no other reason why she should refuse his visits. Matilde Dembowsky, however, had all sorts of other reasons for refusing to see Stendhal or rationing his visits to twice a month. He was making a thorough nuisance of himself, courting her in precisely the calculated manner[162] that he elsewhere (*De l'amour*, Chapter 24) claims to be incompatible with passionate love. Both his life and his theoretical transposition of it in *De l'amour* bear witness to the love-induced self-deception that is one of the major themes of that work. In *Lucien Leuwen*, he wants to show that it is possible that he was right. Stendhal makes sure that the readers know that Lucien's timidity and Mme. de Chasteller's severity are in fact expressions of their love for one another. When she barricades herself by only allowing him to visit her in the presence of a companion, Stendhal makes it clear that she needs to protect herself against her love for him rather than against him.

GEORGE ELIOT

Stendhal wrote both as moralist and as novelist, but he kept the two separate from each other. In George Eliot, the novelist and the moralist coexist on the same page. In *Middlemarch*, to which I limit myself here, she is constantly commenting on the interplay between emotion and cognition in the characters rather than letting the reader infer these psychological mechanisms from what they say and do. For this reason, and also because of her occasionally impenetrable prose, the novel is somewhat heavy-handed. Yet we do not feel (at least I don't) that her characters are mere cardboard illustrations of more abstract propositions. The comments are *comments* – inspired by the development of the characters, not inspiring it.

Middlemarch is a study in moral psychology, and especially in the psychology of self-deception. The characters deceive themselves about their emotions and are led by their emotions to deceive themselves about other matters. Thus Ronald de Sousa is able to use a passage from *Middlemarch* to illustrate the idea of irrational or self-deceptive emotions. He first observes, "If I learn that you did not steal my bicycle, I may look around, self-deceptively, for something

162. *Ibid.*, p. 296.

135

else to blame you for. But that is clearly irrational."[163] The point is then effectively driven home through an example from George Eliot's novel. "When Mrs. Farebrother learns that Lydgate is not the natural son of Bulstrode, she does not think this to be sufficient grounds for ceasing to think ill of Bulstrode. 'The report may be true of some other son.'"[164]

Middlemarch is especially interesting and intriguing in what George Eliot has to say about the mental readjustments and realignments that go into the alchemies of the mind. I'll have more to say about those aspects of the novel in V.2. Here I just offer some samples of her insights. When Dorothea tells her sister that she can keep all the jewels from their mother, "Celia felt a little hurt. There was a strong assumption of superiority in this Puritanic toleration, hardly less trying to the blond flesh of an unenthusiastic sister than a Puritanic persecution" (Chapter 1). In Dorothea's case, the act of renouncing the jewels is entirely innocent. Although it produced resentment and humiliation rather than gratitude in the recipient, she did not act to produce that effect.

A less innocent show of generosity is observed in the relation between her husband Casaubon and his cousin Will Ladislaw, whom Dorothea marries after Casaubon's death. Will writes to Casaubon that he has decided to give up the financial support he has been receiving from him, stating as his reason that he "had come to perceive that his defects – defects which Mr. Casaubon had himself often pointed to – need for their correction that more strenuous position which his relative's generosity had hitherto prevented from being inevitable" (Chapter 30). The actual reason, however, was his desire to be liberated from an obligation: "If he . . . left off receiving favours from [Casaubon], it would clearly be permissible to hate him the more" (Chapter 22). For symmetrical reasons, Casaubon resents Will's giving up the dependence on his generosity:

Mr. Casaubon . . . had disliked Will while he helped him, but he had begun to dislike him still more now that Will had declined his help. That is the way with us when we have any uneasy jealousy in our disposition: if our talents are chiefly of the burrowing kind, our honey-sipping cousin (whom we have grave reasons for objecting to) is likely to have a secret contempt for us, and any one who admires him passes an oblique criticism on ourselves. Having the scruples of rectitude in our souls, we are above the meanness of injuring

163. de Sousa (1987), p. 165.
164. *Ibid.*, p. 199. The episode takes place in Chapter 26 of *Middlemarch*.

him – rather we meet all his claims on us by active benefits; and the drawing of cheques for him, being a superiority which he must recognise, gives our bitterness a milder infusion. Now Mr. Casaubon had been deprived of that superiority. (Chapter 37)[165]

The passage may be contrasted with a similar analysis by La Bruyère, to show how the same material may be handled in very different ways:

Though the charge of maintaining a poor person may be very burdensome to us, yet a change of fortune, which makes him no longer our dependent, gives us no great pleasure, in the same way as our joy at the preferment of a friend is somewhat tempered by the small grudge we bear him for having become our superior or our equal. Thus we agree but ill with ourselves, for we should like to have others dependent on us, but it must cost us nothing. (*Characters* IV.51)

Or as La Rochefoucauld might have said, "Pridefulness wants to be owed, *amour-propre* to be paid" (Cp. M228 cited above). To these abstract ideas George Eliot adds detail that make them vivid and compelling. By telling a story in which the reason for the initial benefaction was to offset a feeling of inferiority, she makes the donor's reluctance to see the recipient become independent more fully intelligible.

CONCLUSION

There is no common set of insights we can draw from these novels and plays. The French moralists have, taken collectively, something like a theory of human motivation, and a relatively coherent view of the relation between emotion, cognition, and behavior. The authors I have discussed are so diverse that no similar construction can be imputed to them.

It is clear that novelists and playwrights recognize the two major roles of the emotions, in generating behavior and in generating other mental states. In Shakespeare and Racine, the first aspect may seem to dominate. Yet as we have seen, *Othello* is not only a play

---

165. In his analysis of this scene, Oatley (1992, p. 259) argues that "jealousy is one of the emotions that Casaubon feels with the arrival of Ladislaw's letter." Actually, I believe, that emotion does not appear until Chapter 42, with Ladislaw's return from abroad.

about murder but also about self-deceptive emotional phenomena. A similar remark applies to *Andromaque*, if not to Racine's later plays. This being said, compared with the seventeenth-century writers whom I have cited, the nineteenth-century writers emphasize the second aspect more heavily. It is not that Jane Austen, Stendhal, and George Eliot ignore the role of the emotions in generating behavior. Rather, they identify more complex causal chains by which emotions jointly with their psychic effects generate behavior. Consider Sir Walter Elliott. If he had decided to offer himself a coat, it could have been a straightforward effect of his vanity. The decision not to offer a coat to his daughter does not have a similarly simple explanation in terms of vanity, yet, if my reading is accurate, it can be indirectly explained in terms of that motivation.

Chapter III

Social Emotions in Historical Context

III.1. INTRODUCTION

Some emotions are essentially social: They are triggered only by beliefs that make a reference to other people. Nobody feels envious of birds for their ability to fly; "envy occurs only between man and man."[1] Other emotions are contingently social, in that the beliefs that trigger them may or may not contain a reference to other people. One may be afraid of an avalanche as well as of a bully. In this chapter I discuss some essentially social emotions: shame, envy, and the cluster of emotions related to the pursuit and defense of honor.

Because my aim is to discuss emotional patterns that are related to general features of social life, I try to go beyond individual reactions. I shall not consider idiosyncratic instances of raw emotions that make newspaper headlines, as when a high-school student sues her school for naming another student covaledictorian with herself,[2] a college student disfigures a former roommate out of envy,[3] or a woman solicits a man to kill the mother of her daughter's chief rival for the cheerleading team, hoping that the mother's death will distract the rival from the competition.[4] By contrast, the Jacobins who wanted to destroy the cathedral spires of Chartres and Strasbourg because their "domination over other buildings was contrary to the principles

---

1. Plutarch, "On Envy and Hate" 537B.
2. "Courts, and Not Grades, May Decide Who Is the Valedictorian of a High School," *New York Times* (12 June 1996).
3. "Co-ed Chopped in Envy May Be Disfigured," newspaper headline cited in Schoeck (1987, p. 130).
4. "Rah, Rah, Rah, Sis . . . Boom? In Texas, Cheerleading Is Serious Business, Maybe as Serious as Murder," newspaper headline cited in McAdams (1992, p. 2, n. 1).

of equality,"[5] acted within a social system with strong norms that make their behavior intelligible. Similarly, I shall not consider people who kill themselves because of unrequited love[6] or depression.[7] By contrast, the American admiral who committed suicide when it was shown that he was not entitled to the decorations he was wearing,[8] or the six Frenchmen who killed themselves in 1997 after they were caught in a crackdown on pedophilia, can be understood in light of the social emotions of shame and contempt.

The impact of social emotions on behavior is in fact highly dependent on the social norms to which actors subscribe. Much of the chapter, therefore, deals with the relation between emotions and social norms. In III.2, I argue that social norms in general operate through the emotions of shame and contempt. In III.3 and III.4 I argue that the behavioral manifestations of envy and honor can be amplified or dampened by the operation of social norms, mediated by feelings of shame.

Because social norms vary across societies, one cannot get a good understanding of the social emotions by considering only contemporary Western societies. In going beyond this domain, one could remove the spatial limitation, the temporal limitation, or both. I mainly keep my discussion within the confines of Western history, because the cultures that have shaped the society in which I live are more accessible to me than, say, ancient China or contemporary Polynesia. The variation in my case studies is not so great, therefore, as what could have been achieved by considering a wider range of societies. The cases I discuss are ancient Greece (III.2, III.3, and III.4), medieval Iceland (III.4), seventeenth-century France (III.4), eighteenth-century France (III.3), nineteenth-century America (III.3), and nineteenth-century Mediterranean societies (III.4). In doing so I rely on a range

5. Réau (1994), pp. 14, 377.
6. Thus according to Tennov (1979, p. 149) "seventeen percent of [her core sample of 500 persons] indicated that they had 'often thought of suicide,' and 64 percent *of those* claimed to have 'seriously attempted to commit suicide.' That figure represents more than one out of every 10 (11 percent) of a set of college students who otherwise appeared perfectly normal!"
7. "In a lifetime, 15% of patients with major depression will eventually die of suicide" (Maxmen and Ward 1995, p. 233).
8. See Boyer (1996) for an account of this episode and the norms that explain it. The following comment seems appropriate: "A code of honour is a set of rules for behaviour. The rules are observed because to break them provokes the distressing emotions of guilt or shame. Whereas guilt is a product of knowing that one has transgressed and therefore might be found out, shame results from actually being found out – in military circles traditionally the greater crime!" (Dixon 1976, p. 197).

of remarkable books by François Billacois, David Cohen, Kenneth Dover, N. R. E. Fisher, William Miller, Alexis de Tocqueville, Peter Walcot, and Stephen Wilson. In addition, I draw on the writers discussed in Chapter II: on Aristotle for the study of Athenian society and on the French moralists for seventeenth-century France.

A discussion of emotions in their historical context must address the question of whether people in all societies have the same range of emotions. I do not have a firm answer to this question, but I discuss it on various occasions. In II.3 I mentioned La Rochefoucauld's observation that some people might not have fallen in love had they never heard of love; I return to that idea in IV.2. In III.3 I draw on Bernard Williams's work to argue that although the ancient Greeks did not have our concept of guilt and for that reason could not feel guilt as we do, they probably felt guilt in the form of what I called a *strong proto-emotion*. Two other instances are cited in IV.2. In all these cases, a modern Western observer may be able to identify the emotion by its written or behavioral expressions. Nevertheless when an emotion is not consciously acknowledged as such by the agent or by other members of the society, it is a less important part of social life.

Before I proceed to the case studies, some classificatory remarks about the social emotions may be useful.

(1) The social emotions divide into *emotions of comparison* and *emotions of interaction*.[9] Emotions such as malice or envy may be triggered by favorable or unfavorable comparisons with individuals with whom we will never interact. An academic may take a malicious pleasure when a book by a better-known colleague whom he has never met receives a negative review. Other emotions, such as anger or shame, arise only when there is social interaction, either face-to-face or indirectly, for example by writing the negative review oneself. A desire for superiority may be satisfied by a comparison between oneself and another, or by interaction with another in which one shows oneself to be superior.[10]

For an example of this distinction at work, consider La Bruyère's observation that "[w]e feel somewhat ashamed of being happy at the sight of certain miseries" (*Characters* XI.82; see also V.23). This

9. For a similar distinction, see Hirshleifer (1987).
10. I am deliberately not saying that both are instances of *the* desire for superiority. I conjecture that the evolutionary explanations of the desires for comparison-superiority and for interaction-superiority, if and when we find them, will turn out to be very different from one another.

statement may be more plausible if "in the sight of" is taken to imply interaction than if only comparison is involved. Thus Norbert Schwartz and Fritz Strack report some intriguing findings on reports of subjective well-being in personal interviews and questionnaires. On the one hand, "respondents reported higher well-being in personal interviews than in self-administered questionnaires. Moreover, this difference was more pronounced when the interviewer was of the opposite sex, but was not obtained when the interviewer was severely handicapped. Respondents apparently hesitated to tell someone in an unfortunate condition how great their own life is." On the other hand, "the mere presence of a handicapped confederate was sufficient to increase reported subjective well-being under self-administered questionnaire conditions, presumably because the confederate served as a salient standard of comparison."[11]

In many cases, comparison and interaction are at work simultaneously.[12] In Chapter II, I cited Roger Petersen's definition of resentment as caused by "the perception that one's group is located in an unjust subordinate position on a status hierarchy." This is not merely a question of status inconsistency, in which group A is higher than group B on one dimension of comparison and lower on another (e.g., education and wealth). Rather, group A perceives itself as higher than B on a dimension of comparison while at the same lower than B on the interactive dimension of power and subordination. As Petersen shows in the case of Lithuanian politics in 1940 and 1941, this particular constellation can produce particularly virulent feelings in group A, and a tendency to engage in persecution of group B once an occasion presents itself.

(2) The distinction between comparison-based and interaction-based emotions can be supplemented by another. Suppose A has an occurrent emotion induced by a belief about B, such as anger, envy, spite, malice, envy-enjoyment, or the like. I shall call the emotion *internal* if the beliefs that generate it include a belief about B's attitude towards A. It is *external* if the beliefs do not contain any such reference. I believe, for instance, that the emotion of shame is internal, whereas the emotion of contempt that triggers it is external (III.2). Envy and malice are external, comparison-based emotions. Envy-enjoyment is an internal comparison-based emotion, because A's enjoyment is triggered by the belief that B envies him. Similarly,

11. Schwartz and Strack (in press).
12. I am grateful to Roger Petersen for pressing this point on me.

B's resentment at A's enjoyment of B's envy of A is, unlike envy itself, an internal comparison-based emotion. A's pleasure in seeing B humiliated is an external comparison-based emotion. It is an external interaction-based emotion if A engenders B's humiliation in secret, so that B will not know that A is the source of his downfall. It is an internal interaction-based emotion if A humiliates B and makes sure that B knows it.

In general, interaction-based emotions are more intense (with respect to both arousal and valence) and have stronger behavioral manifestations than the comparison-based ones. Being badly off is bad enough; being made badly off by behavior instigated for that sole purpose adds insult to injury. Also, internal emotions are stronger than external ones. It is only when we learn that others rejoice in our suffering that it becomes really insufferable, as Aristotle says in a passage from the *Rhetoric* (1379^a15–18) cited in II.2. Beyond a certain level of satisfaction of material needs, our need for the esteem of others is more important than anything else, except perhaps our need for self-esteem; and their withholding of esteem can be intensely painful. Thus Lovejoy quotes Voltaire as saying, "To be an object of contempt to those with whom one lives is a thing that none has ever been, or ever will be, able to endure"; Adam Smith as asserting, "Compared with the contempt of mankind, all other evils are easily supported"; and John Adams to the effect of, "The desire of esteem is as real a want of nature as hunger; and the neglect and contempt of the world as severe a pain as gout and stone."[13]

(3) The social emotions may be further classified into those that involve an evaluation of the object of the emotion and those that do not. The nonevaluative emotions include notably embarrassment, envy, and malice. The evaluative emotions can be further subdivided along three dimensions. First, the belief that triggers the emotion can target either oneself or others. Second, the object of the belief can be either an action of the targeted person or the character of the person as a whole. Third, the evaluation can be negative or positive. Combining these yield the following emotions:

- Shame: a negative emotion triggered by a belief about one's own character
- Contempt and hatred: negative emotions triggered by beliefs about another's character

13. Lovejoy (1961), pp. 181, 191, 199.

- Guilt: a negative emotion triggered by a belief about one's own action
- Anger: a negative emotion triggered by a belief about another's action
- Pridefulness: a positive emotion triggered by a belief about one's own character
- Liking: a positive emotion triggered by a belief about another's character
- Pride: a positive emotion triggered by a belief about one's own action
- Admiration: a positive emotion triggered by a belief about another's action.

Except for liking and admiration, these emotions all are discussed in the previous chapter or in this one. As will become clear, their evaluative aspect is closely linked to social norms that regulate character as well as behavior.

(4) The social emotions mentioned so far are all dyadic. Many emotions, however, are triadic: They are triggered by beliefs that make reference to two other persons. Although jealousy is the only example known to me of a triadic emotion that is named in ordinary language, there are many others. In II.4 I discussed Iago's emotion towards Othello when Cassio is promoted over his head, and Stendhal's notion of *amour par pique*. Other triadic emotions involve audience effects. A's emotion may be triggered when he witnesses the behavior of B towards C. In II.3, for instance, I noted that for Descartes indignation is the emotion that arises in A when he sees B mistreating C. Also, A's emotion may be triggered by B's behavior towards himself in the presence of C. In III.4 I consider the emotions generated when A humiliates B in front of C, arguing that the presence of an observer solves a paradox inherent in Hegel's master–slave dialectic. Very much of social interaction, in fact, takes place before an audience, and the emotions triggered in the actors depend both on the presence of an audience and on what kind of audience it is.[14] The

14. In their study of the "culture of honor" in the American South, Nisbett and Cohen (1996, Chapter 4) report that when they staged a scene in which Southern subjects were insulted by a confederate, they expected but did not find a difference in cortisol and testosterone levels between subjects who were insulted in the presence of third parties and those who were insulted without witnesses; nor did they find a difference in behavioral responses (as measured, for instance, by the choice of the aggressive strategy in a game of chicken) between the public and private conditions. To explain these puzzling results, they comment, "In retrospect . . . it is

emotion felt by a boy who receives a dressing-down from his mother in the presence of a friend is likely to be very different from what he feels in the presence of his father, and both reactions will differ from what he would feel were no third party present. The three cases might, for instance, yield shame, fear, and anger respectively. (See also the passage from Sylvan Tomkins quoted in the next section.)

III.2. SHAME AND SOCIAL NORMS

I have argued elsewhere that social norms are an immensely powerful influence on behavior.[15] I now think, however, that I had the emphasis somewhat wrong. I first state the idea of social norms that I relied on, and still rely on, and then explain the change of emphasis. Roughly, I now think that the emotion of shame is not only a support of social norms, but *the* support.

EMOTIONS AND SOCIAL NORMS

Social norms as I understand them are characterized by four features. First, they are non–outcome-oriented injunctions to act. In their simplest form, they take the form of unconditional imperatives: "Always wear black at funerals." They may be contrasted with conditional, outcome-oriented imperatives: "Always wear black in strong sunshine" (as do people in Mediterranean countries to maintain circulation of air between the clothes and the body). In a more complex form, they can be conditional imperatives that make the action contingent on the past behavior of oneself or others rather than on future outcomes to be achieved. Norms of reciprocity have this form: Help those who help you, and harm those who harm you. Second, social norms are shared with the other members of one's society or of some relevant subgroup. Moreover, "the sharing itself is shared," as Charles Taylor writes in a different context.[16] All members know

not clear that our manipulation was a very good one. The [public insult] occurred in front of people the subject had never seen and likely would never see again." The authors also report that the first type of audience effect that I discuss in the text is not more prominent among Southerners: "[T]hey were not more likely [than Northerners] to approve of a man's hitting another person if that person 'was beating up a woman'" (Nisbett and Cohen 1996, p. 30).

15. Elster (1989b,c).
16. Taylor (1971).

that all are subject to the norms, and know that all know this, and so on. Third, because all share the norms, group members can enforce them by sanctioning violators. Sanctions range from various forms of avoidance behavior through social ostracism to outright persecution. Finally, norms are also sustained by the internalized emotion of shame.

Although not wrong, this account is misleading. It gives the impression that the enforcement of norms is overdetermined, by two sufficient causes: external sanctions and internalized emotions. If this were the case, the account of norms that views them simply as systems of material sanctions[17] would be incomplete rather than false. I now believe it to be false, because sanctions do not work by imposing material losses on their targets. When I refuse to deal with a person who has violated a social norm, he may suffer a financial loss. Far more importantly, however, he will see the sanction as a vehicle for the emotions of contempt or disgust and suffer shame as a result. The material aspect of the sanction that matters is *how much it costs the sanctioner to penalize* the target, not how much it costs the target to be penalized. The more it costs me to refuse to deal with you, the stronger you will feel the contempt behind my refusal and the more acute will be your shame. (Thus the phrase "this hurts me more than it hurts you" may be intended to add to the punishment, not to soften it.) Although high costs to the sanctioner often go together with high costs for the target, as when the sanctioner renounces the opportunity for a mutually profitable business transaction, this need not be the case; and even when it is the case, my claim is that the costs to the sanctioner are what makes the sanction really painful to the target. It tells him that others see him as so bad that they are willing to forego valuable opportunities rather than to have to deal with him.

The emotional meaning of sanctions was recognized by Aristotle, who wrote that "[s]hame is the imagination of disgrace, in which we shrink from the disgrace itself and *not from its consequences*" (*Rhetoric* 1384a; italics added). In the seventeenth century, the English naturalist John Ray expressed the same ideas as follows:

I cannot but admire the Wisdom and Goodness of God, in implanting such a Passion in the Nature of Man, as Shame, to no other Use or Purpose, that I can imagine, than to restrain him from vicious and shameful actions.... Now

17. Axelrod (1986); Abreu (1988); Akerlof (1976, 1980); Coleman (1990).

Dishonour is nothing else but men's ill opinion of me, or Dislike and condemnation of my Actions, in some way declared and manifested to me; which, why I should have such an Abhorrence of, and why it should be so grievous and tormenting to me, there seems to be not a sufficient Ground and Foundation in the Nature of Things, *supposing such as have this Opinion have neither Power nor Will to hurt my body.*[18]

In his discussion of this issue, Nico Frijda initially hesitates when he writes, "Being rejected from the group and other forms of social isolation are potent sources of distress; they may lead to suicide or woodoo death. . . . However, they are perhaps to be understood as exemplars of loss of satisfying, or merely of familiar, conditions."[19] But the last suggestion can't be right: The emotional reactions of outcasts and emigrants are not the same. The latter are affected only by their state of isolation from others, the former also and mainly by the way it is brought about. Later, Frijda recognizes as much, when he writes that in Western cultures "social rejection constitutes severe punishment, and most likely *not merely because of its more remote adverse consequences.*"[20]

Sylvan Tomkins has given a vivid description of the importance of social norms in generating shame. In the following vignette, a person is put through the wringer by successive exposure to three very different sets of social norms:

Our hero is a child who is destined to have every affect totally bound by shame. We see him first with his age equals. He is a friendly, somewhat timid child, who is being bullied. He is not angry with the bully, indeed he is a little afraid of him. His reluctance to fight evokes taunts of "sissy," "chicken," "yellow" from those who themselves may be shamed by this timidity. Rather than tolerate his shame he will permit himself to be coerced into flying in the face of fear and fight the dreaded bully. The same timid one, coerced into tolerating fear by his age equals and into fighting the bully, may return home to be shamed into mortification for having fought. "Nice little boys don't fight like ruffians. Mother is ashamed of you. Whatever got into you? You know better than that." The timid one now starts to cry in distress. The feeling of shame has passed a critical density, and tears well up in the eyes and add to the intensity of his sobbing. At this point his father,

18. Cited after Lovejoy (1961, p. 165; italics added). My point is that even when others have the power and will to hurt my body, that can matter much less than their power to hurt my mind.
19. Frijda (1986), p. 274.
20. Frijda (1986), p. 351; italics added. See also *ibid.*, p. 291.

attracted by the childlike, even effeminate display of tears, expresses manly contempt for such weakness. "What are you crying for, like a two-year old? Stop it – you make me sick."[21]

From the opposite end of the behavioral spectrum, the role of shame in behavior can be illustrated with some examples from military life. As shown for instance in John Marquand's *Melville Goodwin, USA*, this is one of the most highly norm-regulated spheres of society. In an entertaining and instructive book on *The Psychology of Military Incompetence*, Norman Dixon gives several examples to show how fear of shame can undermine rational self-interest. "A factor which plagued British military thinking then [during the Boer war], as at other times, was the tendency to equate war with sport. The notion that certain acts were not 'cricket' was carried to such absurd lengths that the trooper was given no training in the 'cowardly' art of building defensive positions or head cover."[22] The behavior of Japanese soldiers during World War II provides an example of "another difficulty with behaviour directed *solely* by a sense of honour," namely that "if its incentive is no more than an avoidance of shame, the resultant behaviour may be irrational and the very strictness of the code have quite unforeseen consequences for the military way. So unthinkable was it that Japanese soldiers would ever surrender to the enemy that they were not instructed as to how they should comport themselves if they did. As a consequence, Japanese prisoners of war were a relatively fruitful source of interrogation for Allied interrogators."[23]

In a similar vein, referring to events that took place more than 2,000 years earlier, Kenneth Dover writes that

The fear of being judged inferior is the kind of fear which overrules rational calculation; in Thucydides viii 27.2 f., Phrynikhos just succeeds in dissuading his colleagues in command from a disastrous course of action by pointing out that however "shameful" it might seem to them to withdraw in the face of a Peloponnesian fleet, it would be a great deal more shameful for Athens if she suffered final defeat through their sensitivity. The Athenian envoys at Melos were right to say that fear of being shamed leads nations to take action entirely contrary to their own interests (v 111.2 f.). The Athenian force in Sicily was lost largely because Nikias preferred to lose it and die with it

21. Tomkins (1992), vol. II, pp. 228–9.
22. Dixon (1976), pp. 54–5.
23. *Ibid.*, p. 199.

rather than order a retreat and possibly be condemned for doing so on his return (Thucydides vii 48.4).[24]

Shame belongs to a bundle of "self-conscious emotions": embarrassment, shame, guilt, pride, and pridefulness.[25] Of these, embarrassment is caused by the mere exposure to others,[26] without any evaluative components. The other four emotions, by contrast, presuppose negative or positive evaluations by oneself or others. Here, I focus on the contrast between guilt and shame, an opposition that can be described in terms of cognitive antecedents, intentional objects, or action tendencies.[27] I discuss pride and pridefulness in III.4.

As indicated above, shame is triggered by the contemptuous or disgusted disapproval by others of something one has done.[28] It is an internal interaction-based emotion: I feel shame in your presence because I know you disapprove of me. The emotions that convey disapproval can, by contrast, be purely external: If my disapproval of you takes the form of an involuntary grimace of disgust I need not give any thought to the shame I thereby induce in you. The deliberate induction of shame – sometimes referred to as "shaming" – involves an internal emotion, in which my disapproval is mingled with the pleasure of making you aware of it. Because it is a form of humiliation shaming can easily misfire, by making the target feel anger rather than shame.[29] In fact, shaming rests on an *incoherent intention*, by which I mean the intention to induce emotion X by behavior that would

24. Dover (1994), p. 237.
25. For a survey, see Tangney and Fischer (1995). These emotions are self-conscious in the sense that their cognitive antecedents include beliefs about what the subject is, has, or does, not in the sense that the subject is necessarily aware of the emotion. The self-conscious emotions may even remain at the level of strong proto-emotions – unactualizable in a given society, not merely unactualized on a particular occasion. This may have been the case, as we shall see below for guilt in classical Greece.
26. Lewis (1995).
27. The two emotions can also be distinguished by their physiological expressions. We blush in shame, not in guilt. Although Darwin claimed that people sometimes blush when they are alone, he also asserted that "when a blush is excited in solitude, it is almost always related to the thoughts of others about us" (1872, p. 335).
28. Miller (1997), p. 34.
29. See the comment by June Tangney cited in "Crime and Punishment: Shame Gains Popularity as an Alternative to Prison," *New York Times* (16 January, 1997). For a general discussion of the relation between shame, shaming, and anger, see also Lewis (1992, pp. 149–53).

induce X if it was spontaneous but that induces emotion Y if believed to be motivated by the intention to induce X.[30] Involuntary recoil is more effective in inducing shame, because it does not give the target the option of rewriting the script in terms of a blamable intention to slight (II.2) on the part of the sanctioner.

Although shame typically involves something one has done, it can also be induced by something that is done to one or by entirely unrelated events. The tendency of rape victims to blame themselves, for instance, may take the form of shame ("I am the kind of person who attracts trouble") as well as of guilt ("I shouldn't have let someone I didn't know into the house").[31] Also, "the occasion of shame may be something one could not conceivably do anything about, such as having poor parents or growing old."[32] These might seem to be irrational phenomena, until we look at them from the point of view of the shame-inducing observer. A rape victim may feel ashamed if he believes that others believe that he could and should have taken greater precautions or put up greater resistance.[33] An old person may well feel shame in the face of someone who expresses his disgust with old age. (Yet even if his shame is not irrational, the disgust may be; see IV.3.) I do not think, however, that these explanations account for all instances of apparently irrational shame. A rape victim might well feel shame even if met with universal compassion. To account for such cases, we cannot appeal to the "just-world hypothesis," the idea that people have a need to believe that what happens in the world generally and to them in particular is just; hence a tendency, for instance, "to view the rape as a punishment for some prior behavior."[34] This mechanism should induce guilt, not shame. I do not know what the right explanation is.

Although guilt does not involve exposure to an actual audience, it may be triggered by beliefs about a hypothetical audience. Sometimes we ask ourselves, "What would they have thought?" where the reference group consists of internalized role models who may be absent or long dead. Yet the reference to models is not necessary for the production of guilt. Feelings of guilt often occur when we have violated

---

30. See also Elster (1983b), Chapter II.
31. Janoff-Bulman (1979), p. 1806; see also Lamb (1996), p. 30 ff.
32. Taylor (1985), p. 90.
33. The use of the male pronoun is not inappropriate, given Aristotle's discussion in the *Rhetoric* (1373^a35, 1384^a20) which may refer to homosexual as well as heterosexual rape.
34. Lamb (1996), p. 31. For the just-world theory, see Lerner (1980).

a *principle* that we view as binding, even if it is one that is entirely of our own making. The person who violates a self-imposed pruden- tial rule never to drink before dinner may well feel guilty.[35] Moral principles can also operate without any anchor in a model.

It is tempting (and not uncommon) to *define* guilt in terms of the violation of a principle, whether it is moral or prudential, anchored in an internal model or not. Many well-recognized cases of guilt do not, however, fit this definition. One counterexample is "survivor guilt," which has been observed in "survivors of family suicide or death, survivors of plane or car accidents, spouses of rape victims, war vet- erans who have witnessed the death of fellow soldiers, and Holocaust survivors."[36] Often, the survivors know that there was something they *could have done* that would have averted the disaster or shifted its burden from others to themselves. Because of "counterwishful thinking" (I.6), they often ignore the fact that they *could not have known* at the time what to do. Perhaps this is irrational guilt, but it is no less guilt for that. Other cases of guilt are even more blatantly irrational. Thus when I have friends visiting from out of town, I feel guilty when it rains during their stay.[37] I do not know whether the fact that I feel no pride when the sun shines makes me more irrational or less.

Shame, as I have said, arises when something one has done causes others to express disapproval. Because the disapproval takes the form of contempt or disgust rather than anger, it attaches to the person rather than to the act (II.2). Correlatively, shame is "characterolog- ical" or "global" rather than "behavioral" or "specific."[38] In shame, one thinks of oneself as a bad person, not simply as someone who did a bad thing. As Michael Lewis observes, one is forced into this attitude by the attitude of the observer: "The disgust/contempt of another . . . forces us into a global attribution. It is very difficult to envision someone making a specific attribution in the face of

---

35. Ainslie (1992), pp. 194, 322–3. See also Taylor (1985), p. 88: "I may feel guilty because I watch that silly television serial rather than improve my mind by read- ing great literature . . . The crucial thought here is just that what I am doing is forbidden."
36. Lindsay-Hartz et al. (1995), p. 293. See also Morris (1987), pp. 232–7.
37. Conjecturally, the mechanism that produces guilt in this case might be the follow- ing: Because they are having less of a good time when the weather is bad, I try to come up with something else to make their stay pleasant. I am, as it were, trying to undo the damage caused by the weather. Because much undoing is related to harm caused by one's own actions, the behavior may trigger the emotion that normally gives rise to it. I do not suggest, however, that this mechanism accounts for all cases of irrational guilt.
38. Janoff-Bulman (1979).

another's disgusted/contemptuous look because the look says, 'You disgust me.'"[39] The paradox of shame is that it "involves taking a single unworthy action or characteristic to be the whole of a person's identity."[40] An action is taken to be indisputable proof of the *character* of the person rather than an isolated piece of behavior that may be ascribed to negligence or weakness of will.[41]

Conversely, guilt attaches to specific actions rather than to one's character as a whole. Once again, this reaction is correlated with specific observer reactions. As Bernard Williams notes, "What arouses guilt in an agent is an act or omission of a sort that typically elicits from other people anger, resentment, or indignation.... What arouses shame, on the other hand, is something that typically elicits from others contempt or derision or avoidance."[42] Although accurate and important,[43] this observation is also potentially misleading. Shame typically *needs*, for its actualization, the presence of others; guilt does not.[44] In guilt, there is a correlation between what the agent feels and

39. Lewis (1992), p. 102.
40. Lindsay-Hartz et al. (1995), p. 297.
41. I believe Niedenthal et al. (1994) make a conceptual mistake when they single out "transient qualities of self," such as "I wish I hadn't been so absent-minded," as triggers of shame. This amount to asserting that acts of omission trigger shame, whereas acts of commission trigger guilt. I believe, on the contrary, that we often feel very guilty about neglectful behavior. We may even do so, irrationally, when the appropriate emotion is one of regret ("If I had only called him up, he would have left later and not been killed in the accident").
42. Williams (1993), pp. 89–90. Rozin et al. (1993, p. 588) "propose that contempt is the middle ground between anger and disgust" on a continuum of hostile emotional reactions. For some purposes, for example to study the physiological expression of the emotions, the idea of a continuum may make sense. If we want to understand the role of the emotions in social life, however, a dichotomous distinction between anger on the one hand and disgust or contempt on the other, corresponding to the distinction between guilt and shame, seems more useful.
43. I believe, for instance, that in the light of this comment it is hard to defend the assertion by Ekman (1992a, pp. 65–6) that "[t]he distinction between shame and guilt is very important, since these two emotions may tear a person in opposite directions. The wish to relieve guilt may motivate a confession, but the wish to avoid the humiliation of shame may prevent it." By confessing that one has violated a moral principle, one may induce anger in others but not the reaction of contempt or disgust that would cause one to be ashamed.
44. I say "typically," as I do not want to deny that shame can be triggered by thoughts about what others *would have thought* rather than by what they actually think; cp. the comments on blushing in n. 27. One might also cite the comments of Max Weber (1968, p. 576) on "that distinctive type of 'shame' [mistranslated as 'guilt'] ... which characterizes modern secular man precisely because of his own *Gesinnungsethik* ... Not that he has *done* a particular deed, but that by virtue of his unalterable qualities, acquired without his cooperation, he *'is'* such that he *could* commit the deed – this is the secret anguish born by modern man."

what others *would have felt* had they known what he did. In shame there is a causal connection between what others *actually feel* and what the agent feels.

The two emotions can be distinguished, finally, by their action tendencies. In shame, the immediate impulse is to hide, to run way, to shrink – anything to avoid being seen. If one cannot run away, suicide may be the only solution. Other reactions to shame are also possible. Williams observes that "shame may be expressed in attempts to reconstruct or improve oneself."[45] That can indeed be a very important effect of shame in some cases, but it is not its automatic or primary action tendency. Sometimes, shame can induce aggression, not only as a reaction to shaming as discussed above but also as a way of leveling the playing field. "By putting another down, one may attempt defensively to repair and in comparison raise up one's shattered sense of self-worth."[46] Once again, this can hardly be the primary action tendency of shame. Perhaps, like a trapped animal, we strike out when we find that we cannot run away; but our first impulse is to run away.

The basic action tendency of guilt is to make repairs, to undo the bad one has caused. In addition, there is often a strong urge to confess, preferably to the person one has harmed. Both tendencies are expressions of a more general tendency to restore an equilibrium that has been upset (II.2). Another equilibrium-restoring action tendency commonly observed in guilt is the impulse to harm oneself by seeking punishment, so as to match the harm one has done to others and in some magical way take the sting out of it.[47] Conjecturally, this irrational action tendency is especially likely to arise in cases of irrational guilt. Although the psychoanalytic theory of guilt is too complex and (to me at least) too obscure to be discussed here, this conjunction of irrational guilt and irrational reactions to guilt seems to be an important component in it.[48]

45. Williams (1993), p. 90.
46. Lindsay-Hartz et al. (1995), p. 296.
47. Fenichel (1945), p. 105; Taylor (1985), p. 89.
48. Suppose that A has inflicted wrongful harm on B, making A feel guilty and B feel angry. The action tendencies of these two emotions could be harmonized in one of two ways. On the one hand, B might want A to make repairs and A might want to make repairs. On the other hand, B might want to make A suffer and A might want to make himself suffer. In the account of the emotions I have been proposing, the action tendencies are typically *not* harmonized: B wants A to suffer and A wants to make repairs. Even though making repairs typically is costly and thus in a sense involves suffering, this is not the same as saying that the

THE REGULATION OF BEHAVIOR

It is generally agreed that the burning feeling of shame is more intensely painful than the pang of guilt.[49] In shame, both the need for self-esteem and the need for esteem are frustrated. To think of oneself as a bad person is bad enough; the additional thought that others view one in the same light is nearly intolerable. Hence we often do everything we can to avoid the feeling of shame. Most obviously, the anticipation of shame acts as a powerful regulator of behavior. We avoid doing things that might otherwise benefit us because we fear that we might be discovered and put to shame. In contrast to guilt, we cannot easily avoid shame by self-deceptive maneuvers. As La Rochefoucauld says, "Our misdeeds are easily forgotten when they are known only to ourselves" (M196); conversely the accusing stare of others cannot be wished away.

There is another, related reason why shame cannot be easily preempted by self-deception. Shame, typically, is triggered by behavior, independently of the mental states that produced it and of the outcome it produces. Guilt, by contrast, often involves the antecedents as well as the consequences of behavior, as when it is triggered by the perception that the action produced a bad outcome that was either foreseen or foreseeable. It is hard to deny behavior. If I am caught picking my nose in public, I cannot point to my neighbor and say, "He did it." By contrast, if I drive carelessly and hit a pedestrian I can deny that I was careless (self-deception about the mental state behind the action) or claim that he was careless (self-deception about the causal process that brought about the outcome). Because avoidance of shame cannot take the easy option of self-deception, it has to use the hard option of behavior modification. Another reason why guilt is less important than shame in the regulation of behavior is that being "less intense, it may not convey the motivation necessary for change or correction."[50]

I have argued that social norms regulate behavior through the twin mechanisms of shame in the subject and disgust or contempt in the

spontaneous action tendency of A is to make himself suffer. It is only in the case of irrational or neurotic guilt that the action tendencies of A and B converge towards A's suffering. Yet even in this case the harmony is not complete, for B's desire is typically that *he*, B, be the one who makes A suffer. Preemption of punishment by self-punishment may not be enough to restore equilibrium.

49. Lewis (1992), p. 77; Tangney (1990), p. 103.
50. Lewis (1992), p. 77.

observer. Norm-guided behavior may also, however, be upheld by more positive emotions in the subject. One may feel passionately about what the norm requires one to do. Vengeance, for instance, may be sustained by anger or wrath, not only by fear of shame (III.4). More generally, the behavior of those who *induce* shame by showing their disgust and contempt cannot itself be explained by their fear of shame, at least not if we go sufficiently high up in the hierarchy of actions and reactions to them. In any system of norms, there must be some unmoved movers – sanctioners whose disapproval of others cannot itself be explained by the fear of disapproval.[51]

In fact, most individuals, being actors as well as observers in social life, are subject to both tendencies. Their adherence to the norm may not be so strong that they would follow it were they not afraid of the disapproval they would incur if they didn't, but strong enough to make them sanction the noncompliance of others without fear of disapproval being the ultimate motive. Assume, for specificity, that I stand to gain $2,000 from violating the norm, and that if I violate it my neighbor will impose material sanctions on me that cost me $500 and him $500. Assume, moreover, that I, too, would be willing to give up $500 rather than violate the norm, but that I would not be willing to sacrifice $1,500 for the norm's sake. I might still abide by it, however, if my neighbor's willingness to give up $500 signals a degree of contempt that is strong enough to induce a sufficiently strong sense of shame.

I am not saying that shame is a "cost" that can be added to other costs of action. Just as emotions can override interest, interest can override emotions, but that is not to say that emotions are arguments in a cost–benefit function. For some purposes, shame may be usefully modeled as a cost,[52] but only as a rough approximation and in an "as-if" sense. A person who thought of shame as a cost, similar to a parking fine, would probably not feel any. Similarly, as I argue in IV.3, a person who thought of guilt as a cost that could be eliminated by taking a guilt-erasing pill would probably not feel any.

---

51. Elster (1989a), pp. 132–3. In their theory of guilt and shame among workers in a firm, Kandel and Lazear (1992, p. 813) try to deal with this problem by arguing that "the firm can be thought of as a circle. As long as a worker is told only that he is to punish the neighbor on his right or suffer punishment from the one on his left, he will carry out the punishment." I fail to see what this means or how it solves the difficulty.

52. Illuminating uses of this approach include Petersen (1989) and Laitin (1995, 1998).

The role of shame in decision making depends on whether it is anticipated or experienced. Following George Loewenstein's theory of the role of visceral factors in behavior,[53] I suggest that compared with its role in a cost–benefit model shame is weighed too little when anticipated and too much when experienced. As is clear from the passages quoted above from Voltaire, Adam Smith, and John Adams, shame is an intensely painful experience. We would expect, therefore, people to be very careful not to get caught engaging in shameful activities and to avoid engaging in them altogether if there is even a small chance of getting caught. Whereas the first prediction seems to be born out, casual observation suggests that the second is not. Even if we can anticipate the objective chances of being caught cheating at an examination, we are probably less good at anticipating the devastating subjective impact of being caught.

The fact that the experience of shame is so overwhelmingly painful also ensures that it will not enter into decision making merely as a cost. When people kill themselves under the impact of shame, it is often, I believe, because the overwhelmingly strong emotion blots out any rational concern with the future. The fine grain of this effect remains to be understood. One possibility is that shame, like certain drugs, induces a temporary heightening of the rate of time discounting. The agent may know that the feeling of shame is unlikely to last, but she or he does not care. Another is that a person in the grip of shame is unable to imagine that it will not last forever. Whatever the exact mechanism, the emotion of shame works not only as a very strong current (negative) reward, but also as a causal force that shapes the assessment of other rewards. In the choice between suicide and (say) moving to another part of the country under a new name, the shame has the dual effect of enhancing the value of the former option *and* of devaluing the latter.[54]

NORMATIVE REGULATION OF THE EMOTIONS

Norms are regulated by emotions and regulate them in turn. There are normative expectations about which emotions one should *express* under specific circumstances, and even norms regulating what

53. Loewenstein (1996).
54. Katz (1988), pp. 24–5. He refers to humiliation rather than to shame, but in their ability to undermine the credibility of comforting thoughts ("time heals all wounds," etc.) the two emotions seem very similar.

emotions one is expected to *feel*. Consider first the regulation of emotional expressions. *Hypocrisy* is organized around such "display rules," as Paul Ekman calls them.[55] When it is not the homage that vice pays to virtue, hypocritical behavior is dictated by social norms. In some societies, such as the former USSR or China under Mao, hypocrisy has had an extreme or pathological character: Everybody knew that everybody's enthusiasm for fulfilling the plan or hatred of the class enemy was entirely faked, and yet one would lose one's job or be expelled from the party if one failed to conform. Contrary to what Timur Kuran argues, these "cultures of hypocrisy" did not rest on horizontal conformity, induced by the fear of sanctions imposed by one's equals.[56] In totalitarian regimes, the authorities ask citizens to inform on each other (a vertical communication) precisely because they cannot count on them censuring each other (a horizontal communication). And to the extent that there is horizontal pressure, it is caused by vertical pressure. If some individuals speak out against the system others will indeed withdraw from them, but only because they are afraid the authorities will otherwise see them as guilty by association.[57]

Under normal conditions, hypocrisy is part of what makes the world go around, not so much by forcing us to express emotions we don't have as by keeping us from expressing those we have. In everyday life under nonpathological conditions, veils are more important than masks. There are even norms regulating the emotions that are appropriate to express as sanctions for norms violation. Although society would be a horrible place if norms of politeness and minimal helpfulness were not respected and enforced, it would not be much better if norm-violators were consistently terrorized. These metanorms are also sustained by emotions. The target of moralizing, as noted above, may feel anger rather than shame. Third parties may express disapproval of moralizers who express their disapproval too strongly. In Tahiti, there is both control by shame (*ha'ama*) and control of shame: "Although gossip is an important part of 'shame control,' the words designating gossip have a pejorative tone, and gossiping is said to be a bad thing to do. Ideally, the behavior which would produce shame on becoming visible has to spontaneously force its way into visibility; people are not supposed

55. Ekman (1980).
56. Kuran (1995); see also the review in Elster (1996a).
57. See for instance Margolin (1997, p. 530).

to search out shameful acts. Such a searching out is itself a *ha'ama* thing."[58]

Norms directed at the emotions themselves, not simply their expression, constitute a deeper issue. Emotions, like thoughts, are not under one's immediate control (see IV.3). Hence injunctions about what to feel or not to feel, as well as rules about what to think and not to think, might seem pointless. Yet Christianity enjoins us to refrain from even thinking about our neighbor's wife, and middle-class American mothers used to tell their daughters that good girls don't even think about sex. If taken to heart, such injunctions can produce a state of hopeless confusion and guilt in the recipient. The same is true about the social norms that regulate the emotions. Failure to conform to the norm that one ought to grieve when a close relative dies, or to be happy on one's wedding day, tends to induce guilt.

Violation of feeling rules may also produce shame rather than guilt. Consider an example from Arlie Hochschild. "Each of two mothers may feel guilty about leaving her small child at day care while working all day. One mother, a feminist, may feel that she should not feel as guilty as she does. The second, a traditionalist, may feel that she should feel more guilty than, in fact, she does feel."[59] When giving talks on the emotions, I have asked several hundred people for their intuitions about this case. The large majority confirmed my hunch, which is that the feminist mother would be ashamed at feeling guilt in this situation. By contrast, they thought – and so do I – that the traditionalist mother would typically feel guilty about her lack of guilt.

For another contrast, compare the Princess of Clèves, whose love for the Duc de Nemours makes her feel guilty (II.4), with Mathilde de la Mole, whose love for Julien Sorel makes her feel ashamed (V.2). In this case, the difference between the emotions is clearly linked to the difference between the norms whose violation triggers them. By loving someone else than her husband, the Princess goes against a moral as well as a social norm; by loving the son of a carpenter, Mathilde de la Mole goes against a purely social norm. A similar distinction may underlie the different reactions of the two mothers. The feminist mother may be concerned with what her feminist friends would think if she were to express her guilt, whereas the traditionalist mother is motivated by what she perceives as the moral demands of being a mother.

58. Levy (1973), p. 340.
59. Hochschild (1979), p. 567.

This being said, it is a puzzle why emotions should trigger either guilt or shame. From the premises that (i) guilt attaches to voluntary action and (ii) the emotions are involuntary, it follows that emotions should not trigger guilt. But they do. From the premises that (iii) shame is induced by the disapproving stare of others and (iv) the emotions are unobservable, it follows that emotions should not trigger shame. But they do. One solution to the puzzle is to assume that the agent irrationally denies (ii) or (iv). Another is to assume that the agent accepts (ii) and (iv) but irrationally feels guilt or shame nonetheless. I return to this thorny question in IV.3.

SHAME IN ANCIENT GREECE

The Greeks, by and large, had no conception of guilt, or at least not the modern conception of guilt.[60] Theirs was a shame culture, not a guilt culture. Yet the issue is somewhat more complicated, as I shall try to show, drawing on Bernard Williams's discussion of the relation between guilt and shame in ancient Greece. Two points stand out. First, he observes that in ancient Greece guilt existed as a *proto-emotion* (II.3). The Greeks were concerned with many of the things that we associate with guilt rather than shame, such as indignation, reparation, and forgiveness. What they lacked was the concept of this concern: "*What people's ethical emotions are depends significantly on what they take them to be. The truth about Greek societies . . . is not that they failed to recognise any of the reactions that we associate with guilt, but that they did not make of those reactions the special thing that they became when they are separately recognized as guilt.*"[61] The sentence that I have italicized expresses a very general truth, the implications of which are further discussed in IV.2.

Second, Williams observes how in ancient Greece something like the shame–guilt distinction reappears within the concept of shame itself. "By the later fifth Century the Greeks had their own distinction between a shame that merely followed public opinion and a shame

---

60. In his discussion of "conscience" Dover (1994, pp. 220–3) by and large agrees that the Greeks did not have our (nonreligious) concept of guilt but also cites "passages which seem to carry a suggestion (perhaps in some cases illusory) that self-respect and the prospect for self-contempt are genuine motives" (p. 221). Cairns (1993, pp. 27–47) argues against a sharp distinction between shame cultures and guilt cultures but also asserts that different societies occupy different parts on a guilt–shame spectrum and that the ancient Greeks were closer to the shame end.
61. Williams (1993), p. 91.

that expressed personal conviction."[62] The idea is illustrated with examples from Euripides's *Hippolytus*. We find a related distinction in Aristotle's treatment of shame.[63] He writes that we are not "ashamed of the same things before intimates as before strangers, but before the former of what seem genuine faults, before the latter of what seem conventional ones" (*Rhetoric* 1384^b25–27). Also, he notes, we feel friendly "towards those with whom we are on such terms that, while we respect their opinions, we need not blush before them for doing what is conventionally wrong; as well as towards those before whom we should be ashamed of doing anything really wrong" (1381^b19–21). There is no conception of guilt here, but a distinction between types of spectators and a distinction between types of acts. Something like the shame–guilt distinction appears here, then, as a distinction between shame before strangers and shame before friends, or, equivalently, between shame for conventionally wrong actions and shame for genuinely wrong actions. (For the latter distinction see also *Nicomachean Ethics* 1128^b23–5.) The picture would have been even clearer if shame before friends or for genuine faults was associated with indignation, reparation, and forgiveness, but Aristotle does not make this connection.

Kenneth Dover, on whom I draw heavily in the following, observes that "in cases where a modern speaker would probably make some reference to good and bad conscience the Athenians tended instead to use expressions such as 'be seen to . . .,' 'be regarded as . . .,'" referring for instance to the desire to be seen as honest rather than the desire to be honest. For them, "goodness divorced from a reputation for goodness was of limited interest."[64] Also, their strongest term of censure was "shameless" rather than, as among ourselves, "immoral." A truly bad man was one who showed that he did not care about the opinions of others. Yet the difference between Athenian and modern attitudes to wrongdoing is not only that in Athens shame overshadowed guilt, which existed only in the form of a proto-emotion. There are also differences in the grounds on which people were made to feel ashamed and in the ways in which they were made to feel so.

---

62. *Ibid.*, p. 95.
63. As Williams points out to me, the distinctions, although related, are not quite identical. Aristotle does not, for instance, entertain the idea that the audience before which one feels shame may be oneself.
64. Dover (1994), p. 226. The gap between this attitude and that of Pascal and Montaigne, for whom a reputation for goodness inevitably detracts from it (II.3), could not be greater.

In their moral psychology the Greeks placed less emphasis on the intention and other mental antecedents of action than we tend to do. Theirs was not only a "shame culture" but also a "results culture."[65] Their notion of responsibility was similar to the legal idea of strict liability, for which intention and knowledge are irrelevant.[66] Or, to put it in slightly different terms, they were quick to assume the worst:

Shame at defeat or failure, even if I know perfectly well that I did my best and was worsted by overwhelming force or by dishonesty so alien to my character as to be unintelligible and unforeseeable, can still be felt very keenly because I am aware that other people cannot know all the circumstances and may therefore believe that I lacked courage, determination, prudence or common sense. There are few shaming situations to which this consideration is inapplicable, and after all, failure *is* commonly the consequence of sloth, negligence or remediable ignorance. We tend to give the benefit of the doubt, and the Greeks ... tended not to.[67]

A citizen of a modern Western society might not feel any shame at all in this situation. A general who is blamed by his compatriots for a defeat he suffered through no fault of his own might feel bitter, resentful, indignant – but not ashamed. The disapproval of others might be neutralized by one's own knowledge that there is nothing to disapprove of. Also, in our societies there is no shame attached to losing in a competition, as long as one is thought to have done one's best. The Greeks thought differently (see III.4).

One reason for the ascription of blame by observers and feelings of shame in the agent in such cases can be found in the religious views of the Greeks. If an action produces a bad outcome in what appears to be an accidental way, observers and agent may suspect that the situation was engineered by the gods to punish him for some blamable prior deed. *There are no innocent accidents.* The following summary by Dover of a passage in Antiphon provides an illustration of this line of reasoning, with an ironic final twist:

The prosecutor of a young man who has accidentally killed a boy while prac-ticing javelin-throwing argues that the young man may have been guilty of

---

65. Adkins (1972), p. 61. For some political implications of this attitude, see Elster (in press d). For other examples of strict-liability societies see Edgerton (1985, pp. 161–2).
66. Williams (1993), pp. 57, 64.
67. Dover (1994), p. 238. See also *ibid.*, pp. 159–60, for some rule-utilitarian arguments for this attitude.

an impiety and so, being "stained," was maneuvered by the gods into a predicament which would result in his condemnation for accidental homicide; while the defendant argues that if it was the divine will that the boy should die, it would be impious to condemn the young man who was the instrument of death.[68]

Dover also argues that because of their emotional frankness or lack of emotional tact the Greeks expressed feelings of disapproval – and induced shame – on grounds that we today would find unacceptable. Whereas "we tend to feel that if we admit to being repelled by ugliness and suffering" we are lacking in compassion, the Greeks were ready "to use the word *aishkros* of what was repellent *for any reason*."[69] What we think of as morally arbitrary properties such as beauty or ugliness were for them part of the moral order. Thus the term of praise *kalos* was used to denote beauty as well as other forms of excellence; conversely its antonym *aishkros* could mean "shameful" as well as "ugly."[70] Referring to Alcibiades and his exceptional beauty, Jacqueline de Romilly writes that in his time "beauty was openly recognized and celebrated as a merit."[71] Conversely, the partial blurring of aesthetic and ethical qualities induced a tendency to view ugliness as repulsive on both grounds.

Also, "wealth and the achievements made possible by wealth are *kalos*, while poverty and the limitations which it imposes are *aishkros*. This is one reason why *aishkros* was sometimes applied to behavior which was not the fault of the agent."[72] Joshua Ober cites a reference to a law "that forbade anyone to reproach any Athenian, male or female with working in the agora,"[73] presupposing both a tendency to disapprove of such work and a tendency to disapprove of the disapproval. In our society, the latter is sufficient to neutralize the former, either because the one is very strong or because the other is very weak. Among the Greeks, the relative strengths of the two tendencies were such that a law was needed.

For us as well as for the Greeks, observable achievements and appearances are grounds for approval and pride. There is a difference, however, in the extent to which *failure* to meet standards of

---

68. *Ibid.*, p. 150; references omitted.
69. *Ibid.*, p. 242.
70. Dover (1994), p. 70.
71. de Romilly (1996), p. 18.
72. Dover (1994), p. 70.
73. Ober (1989), p. 276.

achievement and appearance provide grounds for blame and shame. In our society we do not blame people for what is outside their control. When we express disapproval of – and induce shame in – the obese and the unemployed, it is usually when and because we believe they could have been otherwise had they wanted to and tried hard enough. Conversely, we do not express disapproval of the disfigured or the hardworking street vendor. The Greeks were more consistent. In their society, the irrational admiration of the beautiful or of those born rich was matched by an equally irrational contempt for the ugly or for those born poor. Although Aristotle does not include involuntarily acquired deficiencies among the grounds for shame, the mentality of the ordinary Athenian citizens that Dover reconstructs from the plays and oratory written for them may have been different. To conclude, this difference between the Greeks and ourselves arises because they *felt little shame inducing shame* in others under circumstances in which we would be strongly censured for doing so.[74]

There is a still further reason why the Greeks were more ready to induce shame in others: They enjoyed it. I discuss this aspect of shame among the Greeks at greater length in III.4. Here I shall only indicate the importance of *hybris* – the deliberate infliction of shame on others, for the sheer pleasure of doing so – in Greek society. As N. R. E. Fisher shows in an exhaustive study of the topic, this notion should be understood in the Aristotelian sense cited in II.2. *Hybris* is "behaviour designed to produce shame."[75] This characterization is not quite sufficient, however: "It is from the absence of any motive, good or bad, apart from *the pleasure of insulting*, that one deduces that this is indeed *hybris*."[76] The hybristic person enjoys humiliating others. He derives pleasure not merely from seeing other people being ashamed, but from making them feel ashamed and from their knowledge that he enjoys it. Moreover, the behavior typically takes place before third parties. The hybristic person wants others to know that he can humiliate someone and get away with it.

---

74. Miller (1997, p. 200) claims that in modern societies "we learn to suffer *guilt* from mocking" (my italics). This is certainly often the case. When Emma Woodhouse makes fun of poor Mrs. Bates and receives a scolding from Mr. Knightley, what she feels is definitely guilt rather than shame, as shown by her efforts to make repairs. In other cases, however, what keeps people from mocking are social rather than moral norms, as shown by the fact that what counts as banter in some circles would be seen as mockery in others.
75. Fisher (1992), p. 10.
76. *Ibid.*, p; 11; italics added.

The Greeks in general did not approve of hybristic behavior. To admit to *hybris* would be to admit to shamelessness.[77] Moreover, it happened that "an attempt at *hybris* in fact recoils and brings shame on the insulter."[78] There was a legal category, *graphe hybreos*, which enabled victims (or others) to prosecute hybristic behavior. Yet once again the fact that a certain behavior was forbidden in the law indicates that it could not be kept in check by social norms alone. In contemporary Western societies, the deliberate and gratuitous humiliation of another for the sheer pleasure of enjoying his shame may still occur in youth gangs and among sadistically inclined individuals, but it is a marginal phenomenon. There is no contemporary analogue of a Meidias or an Alcibiades who would slap a rival in public merely to show that he could get away with it, and no need for a law to prevent such behavior.[79]

This way of inducing shame differs from the one considered above. To make another feel ashamed by expressing disapproval for his appearance is to react to a preexisting feature of the person, who may well agree that it is in fact something to be ashamed of. To induce shame by slapping him in public or by beating him up and then urinating on him is to *create* the grounds for the shame. Rather than drawing attention to the other's inferiority and thus making him feel inferior, one causes him to be inferior. The mere expression of disapproval may also, of course, have an element of intentional humiliation. In all societies, I suspect, there are people who get much of their enjoyment from making others feel uncomfortable or ashamed, by reminding them of facts they would rather not be reminded of. To succeed, however, they will have to hide their intention and enjoyment – otherwise they may only induce anger in the target.

III.3. ENVY IN SOCIAL LIFE

Shame is unique among the emotions because it is so intensely unpleasant. Envy is unique because it is the only emotion we do not want to admit to others or to ourselves.[80] Iago's explicit acknowledgment

77. *Ibid.*, p. 123.
78. *Ibid.*, p. 91.
79. See Demosthenes (21.143–8) for a comparison of Alcibiades and Meidias.
80. A central thesis in Schoeck (1987) is that modern writers even find it difficult to admit this emotion *in others*: "[A]t about the beginning of this century authors began to show an increasing tendency, above all in the social sciences and moral

that he envies Cassio because he "hath a daily beauty in his life that makes me ugly" is exceptional. To destroy another's possessions out of envy violates what Leibniz called the principle of "innocent utility," which enjoins us to respect what confers utility on one individual as long as it does not harm anyone else.[81] The envied person is indeed, in the typical case, innocent. He has not done anything to deserve to have his possessions taken away from him. If the envious person nevertheless proceeds to do so, he is behaving viciously. More than that: The envious person does not even benefit in any material sense, nor, as we shall see, in welfare terms.

Because of its vicious character, envy is normally suppressed, pre-empted, or transmuted into some other emotion. When it leads to action, it is usually mediated by the prior transmutation into a more acceptable emotion, such as righteous anger or righteous indignation (V.2). In actual cases, this transmutation may be difficult to document. What we observe is that one person, with no apparent gain or even at some cost to himself, destroys an object in the possession of another or even that other person himself. In many cases we may plausibly infer that the ultimate cause is envy, even though the proximate cause may remain unknown.

In this chapter, I ignore this complication. I refer to people as motivated by envy even when they might vehemently deny this explanation of their behavior. This procedure is justified in part by the fact that other people often see the envy for what it is. La Rochefoucauld's maxim that "[i]t is just as easy to deceive oneself without noticing as it is difficult to deceive others without their noticing" (M115) applies to envy no less than to love. Hence even though A's envy of B might be only the ultimate explanation of A's behavior, it may be the proximate cause of the action B takes to protect himself. Thus most behavioral manifestations of envy probably arise indirectly, mediated either by another emotion in the envious person or by others' perception of his envy.

philosophy. This I regard as a genuine case of repression. The political theorist and the social critic found envy an increasingly embarrassing concept to use as an explanatory category or in reference to a social fact" (p. 13). Conversely, Walcot (1978, p. 7) praises the Greeks for being "honest enough to accept this fact of human nature and to mention it quite openly when discussing human motivation." The question is confounded, however, by the existence, in some societies, of social norms that condemn envy so strongly that people are reluctant to act on it. The paucity of envy-based explanations might at least partly be due to the fact that envy has less explanatory power in some societies than in others.

81. See Elster (1975), p. 135.

Table III.1.

	I	II	III	IV	V
A has	5	3	4	4	4
B has	5	3	5	4	3

ENVY AND MALICE

The pain of envy we feel by observing another's good fortune is matched by the malicious pleasure we take in his misfortune. Envy as well as malice may be weak as well as strong. We may define these concepts in terms of *preferences over distributions,* disregarding the way in which the distributions came about (this distinction will be important later). Consider five situations, presented in Table III.1.

If weakly envious, A prefers **IV** to **III**. If strongly envious, A also prefers **II** to **III**. If malicious, A would prefer **V** to **IV** and, if strongly malicious, **V** to **I**. Like envy, malice makes us wish for the destruction of the goods of others, at no benefit (weak malice) or even at some cost (strong malice) to ourselves. In weak envy and malice, my welfare is lexicographically prior to the illfare of other people: I may wish for the destruction of their assets, but only when it does not hurt myself. In strong envy and spite, there are trade-offs: I am willing to give up some of my welfare for an increase in another's illfare. Whenever there is envy, we usually find both strong envy and strong malice: Lexicographic preferences are rarely found in reality and envy tends to bring malice in its wake. Nevertheless, in some cases the trade-offs may be so steep that the notion of weak envy is useful; and sometimes people may be willing to acknowledge envy as an egalitarian motive and more reluctant to admit the purely destructive motives of malice. In fact, envy towards those who are better off may go together with compassion for those who are worse off.[82] In that case, A's welfare is reduced both when B has more and when he has less. What looks like downward altruism may, however, be an expression of self-interested envy-avoidance or envy-alleviation.

When the envied object is a positional good, envy logically implies malice. If someone has a car I covet, I can try to establish a balance by getting a similar car or by destroying his. If I do the former, I may still

82. Scott (1972), Loewenstein et al. (1989).

do the latter, out of malice, but I need not. If someone is praised as the best writer in his generation, this distinction collapses. I cannot get what he has without taking it away from him. The pleasure of being praised as the best writer is indistinguishable from the pleasure of others receiving less praise. Societies organized around honor, therefore, inevitably involve malice, the desire for others to have less or to be less. They may but need not involve envy. Some people may be willing to obtain the first place by tripping up the competition, but for others this means would detract from the pleasure of the prize. The desire for esteem may urge one to destroy the rival, and the desire for self-esteem hold one back.

Although being envious is horrible, being envied is, for many, a very pleasant experience. Francisco de Quevodo said that "whoever does not want to be envied, he does not want to be a man."[83] Malice differs from envy-enjoyment. Even if I derive no pleasure from the fact that you have little compared with me, and would not mind were you to get more, I may savor your obsessional preoccupation with my fortune. Indirectly, therefore, I may be induced to keep you down. Also, as I remarked in the introduction to the present chapter, envy should be distinguished from resentment at envy-enjoyment. In the terminology introduced there, all these emotions are comparison-based, but whereas envy and malice are external, envy-enjoyment and resentment of envy-enjoyment are internal.

Envy-enjoyment is a murky emotion, similar in that respect to the emotion on which it is parasitic. Envy, to be sure, is a form of esteem; like hypocrisy, it is a homage paid by vice to virtue. It is also, indeed, a vicious emotion. The question is whether the envied can really gain *durable* satisfaction through esteem coming from such a vicious source. Compared with "praise of the good by the good,"[84] the enjoyment of envy is like ashes in the mouth. Envy-enjoyment is also subject to inherent limitations. Your envy would not really be worth having if you were too great a failure. Hence it is in my interest to keep you from slipping down too far. Also, if you fall too far down you might cease to envy me. In the next section I argue that an analogous issue arises in Hegel's master–slave dialectic.

Envy can be multiply harmful to the envious. There is what I called in II.3 the first-order pain of envy: I am less because I have less. If the object of envy is another's happiness rather than his possessions, a

---

83. de la Mora (1987), p. 37; see also the cite from Epicharmus on p. 185 below.
84. Bryson (1935), p. 9.

vicious spiral can be set up. Assume that A's level of well-being is 4 and that of B is 7. When A becomes aware of B's higher level of well-being, the envious awareness of B's prosperity reduces A's well-being from 4 to 3. A then carries out another comparison, between B's level and the level to which he, A, is reduced after the first comparison. This comparison may reduce his welfare even more. At the same time A's envy-enjoyment may raise his level to 8, thus further intensifying B's envy, and so on. These processes could converge to a tolerable level of well-being for A, or drive him to suicide. Also, envy may cause suffering by interaction: If the envied person enjoys my envy of him, he has an incentive to perpetuate my misery.

In addition, there is the second-order pain of envy. The acknowledgment of other painful emotions, such as grief, does not create additional pain, as does acknowledgment of the ignoble feeling of envy. If others infer from my behavior that I'm envious, they can make me feel ashamed by showing their disapproval. If I detect the feeling in myself, I may feel guilt. Now it is far from clear that there is anything to feel guilty about. Aquinas wrote, "In the genus of envy we find sometimes even in perfect men certain first movements, which are venial sins."[85] According to Dr. Johnson, "We are all envious naturally; but by checking envy, we get the better of it."[86] According to Kant, "Movements of envy are ... present in human nature, and only when they break out do they constitute the abominable vice of a sullen passion that tortures oneself and aims ... at destroying others' good fortune."[87] We have nevertheless, I think, a general tendency to infer from the premise that it is bad to act on a certain emotion that it is bad to have it in the first place. Many who would never act on an envious urge, a desire for their neighbor's wife, or an ethnic or sexist prejudice feel guilty for having even a fleeting inclination in that direction.

Whether the condemnation of envy is based on moral principles or on social norms, the fact that these vary across societies implies that the need to hide envy from oneself or others will also vary in time and space. I do not know of any society in which an individual would consciously confess to envy in the Aristotelian sense, that is, hostility towards the nonundeserved fortune of another, and justify aggressive or destructive behavior in terms of this motivation. For that reason,

85. Aquinas, *Summa*, IIaeQu.36, 3d article.
86. Boswell, *Life of Johnson*, Ætat. 69.
87. Kant (1785), pp. 576–7.

Iago is not entirely credible. Yet the concealment of envy may be more perfunctory in some societies than in others. Contemporary Western societies are probably at one extreme on this scale. Here, the envious urge is usually suppressed or preempted, and when it is not it has to undergo more than a superficial transmutation before it can serve as a basis for action. In our societies one rarely justifies aggressive behavior by saying, "He's getting too big for his shoes," or, "Who does he take himself for?" A more elaborate story is usually needed (see V.2 for further discussion). In other societies the story can be very thin indeed.

Norms against envy (and malice) interact with the strength of the emotion to determine which of several possible outcomes will occur. The lowest level of reaction is immediate suppression of the envious urge with no further ramifications for mental life or behavior. The next level is a cognitive reframing to take the sting out of the envy. At the third level we find transmutation of envy into another emotion, which in turn induces behavior. Fourth, we may observe behavior undertaken out of untransmuted envy, consciously and even overtly recognized as such. As I have said, I believe this to be a rare phenomenon. Almost all envy-motivated behavior falls in the third category. Below, I first discuss the second category and then treat the third and fourth categories together. The specific mechanisms underlying the third are further discussed in V.2.

ANTECEDENTS, OBJECTS, AND ACTION TENDENCY OF ENVY

The cognitive antecedents of envy include a belief that another person has something that I want, in both senses of that verb. In addition, they include a counterfactual belief, "it could have been me." Envy presupposes that I can tell myself a plausible story in which I ended up with the envied possession. It is not plausible to imagine that I could have been king if the appropriate baby-switching had occurred after I was born, and it is not even meaningful to imagine that I could have been drop-dead beautiful had I had different genes. For this reason, princes may envy kings and starlets envy stars, but most people envy neither, or only weakly. The objects of envy are thus closely connected with its cognitive antecedents. I envy someone if I believe I could have been like him. The reason I envy rather than try to emulate him is often that I do not believe I *can* become like him – although we were equal at the outset, I have ruined my chances.

This idea of "neighborhood envy"[88] – we envy only our immediate superiors in the relevant hierarchy, but not those who stand far above us – is very prominent in the literature on envy. (We shall see, though, that under conditions of high mobility "envy at a distance" is also compatible with the belief that "it could have been me.") Because he cannot hide his merits, Julien Sorel is the object of the furious envy of his costudents at the religious seminary in Besançon. The situation changes abruptly when he is made tutor in charge of the Old and New Testament: "To his great amazement, he found himself less hated. He had expected that, on the contrary, their hatred of him would have increased" (*Le rouge et le noir* I.29). Later, he achieves an even more stunning success, and "at that moment, envy was at an end" (*ibid.*).

The notion of neighborhood envy, if taken literally, is too simple. More plausibly, the income of others earning more than oneself is felt ever more acutely up to a certain point, beyond which the envious person experiences a release from envy. In the immediate neighborhood of the agent there may be an interval in which others' income has increasing marginal disutility, but this is not the case throughout the whole income range.[89] The intensity of envy, whether measured by arousal or valence, is probably an inverse U-shaped function of the distance between the other and myself. As in many nonmonotonic relationships, there are two multiplicatively related mechanisms at work. On the one hand, the strength of envy depends on how much there is to be envious *about*. If my neighbor earns a hundred dollars more per year than I do, it's hard to get excited about it, unless I care more about the ordinal rank than about the cardinal difference. On the other hand, the strength depends on how plausibly I can tell myself that "it could have been me." If he earns ten times as much as I do, it may be hard to come up with a plausible story. We would expect, therefore, envy to increase with distance up to a point and to decrease thereafter.

Aaron Ben-Ze'ev argues that envy presupposes the idea of *undeserved inferiority*, more specifically the belief that "it is not the case that it should not have been me."[90] This way of spelling out undeserved

88. Bös and Tilman (1985).
89. Brennan (1973) assumes increasing marginal disutility of others' income for the whole income range. I believe this goes in the face of all we know about the psychology of envy. By contrast, Salovev and Rodin (1984, p. 782) argue that "The relationship between the degree of another's superiority and one's experience of jealousy is, perhaps, nonmonotonic."
90. Ben-Ze'ev (1992), p. 563.

inferiority differs from the stronger claim "it should have been me," and both differ from a claim about the other's undeserved good fortune, "it should not have been him." In my opinion, this is a moralized account (IV.2). It may explain what Rawls calls "excusable envy,"[91] but not all envy is excusable. Envy may tend to excuse itself (V.2), but that is justification ex post rather than ex ante. I believe there are many cases of "raw envy," triggered simply by the vivid thought that "*I* could have had that." I may envy my richer neighbor even if the reason why I am poor is that I don't (and didn't) work as hard as he does. Ben-Ze'ev says that my envy would be even stronger if I could ascribe my laziness to an innate disposition, but I think it is the other way around. If I really don't think I *could* work as hard as he does, I have no plausible story to tell myself. It seems inconsistent, therefore, when Ben-Ze'ev also appeals to counterfactual plausibility to account for the strength of envy.[92]

The action tendency of envy is to destroy the envied object or its possessor. It is this fact, combined with the lack of any good reasons to destroy it, that makes envy so unacceptable to oneself and others. One may explain this tendency, perhaps, in terms of a desire to restore an equilibrium. By destroying the superior possessions of someone who is otherwise our equal, we bring about full equality. The urge to destroy is different from a wish or a preference. Most of us have thought occasionally that we wouldn't mind something bad happening to a successful rival, and yet we would never take a step to bring it about, even if we could do so without anybody learning about it. We can distinguish, in other words, among the following states:

A. The status quo
B. The state of the world in which my rival is made worse off, but not as the result of my action
C. The state of the world in which my rival is made off worse off, as the result of my action

My argument is that much envious behavior can be explained on the basis of two assumptions. First, the agent prefers B over A and A over C. (See below for a similar comment on malice.) This doesn't mean that we don't have the urge to destroy the envied possession,

91. Rawls (1971), p. 534.
92. Ben-Ze'ev (1992), p. 568.

only that we may not want to act on it. Second, when people never-theless act on the urge, it is because in their keen desire for the other's misfortune they confuse B and C. They fail to see, that is, that they cannot intentionally bring about a state that is defined by not being brought about intentionally by themselves.[93] Once the deed is done, they discover that they are worse off rather than better.

This account is conjectural, but something like it is needed to ac-count for what I believe to be a robust fact about envy: When people act on their envy they are not relieved of their unhappiness. Rather, they tend to become worse off. It is a general fact about the emo-tions that they can inspire us to take actions that are misguided *from the point of view of the emotion itself.* Rather than restoring the equilib-rium, the action only upsets it further. Fear can make us run when we should have stood our ground, and vice versa. If I try to get even for a small humiliation, my adversary may decide to humili-ate me even more. In envy, this phenomenon seems to be almost universal. Although I do not know of any empirical studies of the question, a dominant theme among all writers on envy is that it de-vours itself no less than others.[94] For this reason, as I argue below, some of the standard social-science analyses of envy are seriously misguided.

COGNITIVE REACTIONS TO ENVY

The first- and second-order pains of envy set up strong psychic pres-sures to get rid of the feeling. Most of us most of the time man-age to do so by a mental shrug of the shoulders and by thinking about something else. We can also, however, reframe the situation so as to stop the urge from arising in the first place. The follow-ing is a brief catalogue of such preemptive mechanisms. I begin, however, by discussing a mechanism that is behavioral rather than cognitive.

93. Cp. also Elster (1983b), Chapter 2. There is an obvious similarity between this argument and the argument I adduced against the idea of shaming. Yet whereas the intention to bring about state B is *logically* incoherent, the intention to induce shame or guilt is incoherent only because people as a matter of fact tend to feel anger when manipulated.

94. The most famous literary description of envy, in Ovid's *Metamorphoses* (II, 760 ff.), brings well out the pathological aspects of envy. Even more poignant is a text by a medieval French writer, Guillaume de Digulleville, cited in Vincentcassy (1980, p. 256).

One can choose one's friends and acquaintances to avoid those of whom one might be envious.[95] Because of the undesirable feelings of dissonance that arise when frequenting those who are better off in some important respect, one seeks out instead individuals less likely to induce envy. By frequenting other mediocrities, a mediocre person may persuade himself that he is as good as anyone and better than some. This is especially tempting, and easy, if the standards for superiority are contested. Within the humanities and the softer social sciences, for instance, the formation of cliques of scholars united by this or that obscurantist theory may at least partly be explained by the fact that by joining forces they avoid exposure to those who might make them feel inferior, especially as the latter also, although for different reasons, tend to shun any contact.

A psychic analogue of this mechanism is the choice of reference group. There are usually many groups that satisfy the constraint of minimal similarity that is necessary for comparisons to arise. The choice of one group among these may be made on various grounds. Anticipatory socialization,[96] induced by the desire to become member of a higher group, need not lead to envy if one believes that one's turn will come one day.[97] In this case the choice of reference group is not made for the sake of its envy-reducing effects. In other cases, the choice of reference group by an individual with little hope of upwards mobility is dictated entirely by the pleasure principle.[98] The individual shops around, as it were, until he finds a group that minimizes felt envy, subject to the similarity constraint. (But see V.2 for a mechanism that might induce him to search for a superior reference group.) There are obviously limits to what can be achieved in this way. Some comparisons just cannot be avoided, however unpleasant they might be for one's self-esteem. Yet a badly paid unskilled worker may to some extent preempt envy of his colleagues by making neighborhood life rather than the workplace the axis of his existence.

A common mechanism is to devalue other aspects of the person whom one would otherwise envy.[99] Thus the stereotype that beautiful blondes are dumb may be due to other women's envy rather than to male chauvinism. Among the strategies for "restoring equality" found in a French village, that of introducing additional criteria of

---

95. Goldthorpe et al. (1969), pp. 109, 141.
96. Merton (1957), pp. 265 ff.
97. Hirschman and Rothschild (1973).
98. Hyman (1968), p. 357.
99. Schalin (1979), pp. 134–5.

evaluation was prominent. "It is possible for a villager to reject or annul almost any bid for prestige or accusation of low status because of the diversity of ranking criteria."[100] La Bruyère noted that some men "allow no one to possess solid qualities when he is agreeable; or, when they think they have perceived in a person some bodily attractions, such as agility, elasticity, and skill, they will not credit him with the possession of those gifts of the mind, perspicacity, judgment, and wisdom; they will not believe what is told in the history of Socrates, that he ever danced" (*Characters* II.34). Moreover, once a person has identified some aspect in which he is superior to the envied person he will tend to value that aspect more highly, a bit like the person who after hesitating between two cars ends up buying one because it is faster and then upgrades the importance of speed relative to other criteria.[101]

Rather than devaluing the envied person, the preemption of envy may take the form of devaluing the envied object so that it does not appear as worth having. This process can take two different forms, which may be illustrated by the story of the fox and the sour grapes. Citing this story, Max Scheler makes a distinction between saying that the grapes are sour and saying that sweetness is bad.[102] The emergence of the latter view is memorably discussed in *The Genealogy of Morals*, notably in a passage on the "manufacturing of ideals":

"There's a low, cautious whispering in every nook and corner. I have a notion these people are lying. All the sounds are sugary and soft. No doubt you were right, they are transmuting weakness into merit."
"Go on."
"Impotence, which cannot retaliate, into kindness; pusillanimity into humility; submission before those one hates into obedience to One of whom they say that he has commanded this submission – they call him God. The inoffensiveness of the weak, his cowardice, his ineluctable standing and waiting at doors, are being given honorific titles such as patience; to be *unable* to avenge oneself is called to be *unwilling* to avenge oneself."[103]

The envious person can proceed in one of two ways. When confronted with the superior fortune of another, one can attempt to

100. Hutson (1971), p. 47.
101. Elster (1989d), pp. 56–7.
102. Scheler (1972), p. 74.
103. Nietzsche (1956), pp. 180–1.

redescribe his situation so as to make it less enviable. My neighbor earns more than me; but he has to work longer hours. Another woman may be more beautiful; but she will regret her looks more when she grows older. ("Better to be foul than to have been fair.") The superior possessions of the other are not denied, but the envious person alleviates their sting by framing them as desirable components of an undesirable whole. Nietzsche and Scheler argued that Christianity resolves the tension in a different way, by declaring that possessions are never desirable and are in fact an obstacle to salvation. This value change offers, as it were, a wholesale rather than a retail solution to the problem of *ressentiment*. Rather than having to debunk each instance of superiority by some ad hoc explanation, the inferior can now tell himself that he is superior by virtue of the very properties that formerly constituted his inferiority.

BEHAVIORAL MANIFESTATIONS OF ENVY

Although the immediate action tendency of envy is to destroy the envied object or its possessor, this is only the most direct behavioral manifestation of envy. There are many other acts that would never have been carried out in the absence of envy. They may be classified along two dimensions. On the one hand, they may be actions undertaken by the envious, by the envied person, or by third parties. On the other hand, they may be undertaken in order to reduce envy or to provoke it. Of the six combinations, we never observe the envious person acting *intentionally* to intensify his envy, although some of his envy-inspired actions may in fact have this outcome. We do, however, observe the other five cases.

(1) The direct behavioral expression of envy is targeted towards the envied person or his possessions. This is the primary behavioral phenomenon from which the others are derived. As a first example, consider the lack of public toilet facilities in New York City. Although these have been successfully installed in many European cities, and an experimental trial in New York was very successful, the idea was eventually scrapped. Spokespersons for the disabled resisted the installment of toilets that could not accommodate them. The authorities resisted the installment of toilets big enough to accommodate the disabled, because they would be "big enough to hold more than one person, and thus big enough to attract drug users, prostitutes, and

vagrants."[104] In theory, both objections could be met by installing separate toilets for the handicapped. "In Europe, wheelchair-ready kiosks are kept locked and can only be used by handicapped people, who have magnetic cards to open them."[105] Yet, "Anne Emerman, director of the Mayor's Office for People with Disabilities ... passionately insisted that under city law, each and every unit must be large enough for a wheelchair."[106] Mayor Dinkins observed that the handicapped "see that to have a special unit that is different than that for others as being discriminatory."[107] Although there is no reason to think that the advocacy for a unified system of large toilets rather than a dual system was due to envy, the preference for no system at all over a unified system of small toilets can more plausibly be imputed to that motive – nobody shall have what not all can have. If this interpretation is correct, the disabled may end up being worse off than before: They do not get the toilets, and others believe them to be envious.

Political systems that are both egalitarian and totalitarian seem to spawn envy. In China, during the Cultural Revolution, farmers with fruit trees were ordered to cut them down.[108] In Eastern Europe, an anecdote about strong envy is told in and about many countries. A fairy visits a farmer and tells him that because she was unable to assist at his baptism, she will now fulfill any wish he might have, on the condition that his neighbor gets twice what he asks for. After a moment's reflection, he asks her to tear out one of his eyes. In III.1 I cited the Jacobin tendency to destroy church spires that were higher than the surrounding buildings. Louis Réau, from whose history of vandalism I take this example, distinguishes between "unavowed" (he means "unavowable") and "avowable" motives for vandalism, envy being one of the former. Among his examples is the tendency for sovereigns to destroy all traces of their predecessors, by destroying their effigies or planishing inscriptions celebrating their exploits.[109] Note that because destruction is costly, these acts illustrate strong rather than weak envy. An important reason why not more spires were destroyed during the French revolution was in fact the cost of demolishing them – indicating a relatively weak degree of envy.[110]

104. *New York Times* (26 February 1994).
105. *Ibid.* (21 May 1991).
106. *Ibid.*
107. *Ibid.* (28 January 1993).
108. Xinxin and Ye (1987), pp. 121, 126.
109. Réau (1994), p. 15.
110. *Ibid.*, p. 378.

The converse case of destruction out of envy is that of construction out of malice. Early German law had statutes forbidding "envious building" (*Neidbau*), defined as "when a prospective building is planned clearly to the detriment of a neighbour and without pressing need, or where such building has little or no purpose, while representing great damage, and loss of light and air, to the neighbour."[111] In English and especially in American common law, we find similar bans on "spite fences."[112] The behavior targeted by such laws would be motivated by malice; in fact, given the costs of construction, by strong malice. The need for the laws suggests that such practices were not uncommon. For another instance of malice, we may take Abram de Swaan's claim that "It is . . . ill-will at the possible advantages of another group in society which colours the resistance of the petite bourgeoisie against the social insurance schemes for industrial workers."[113] The petty bourgeoisie resented that workers were given for nothing the protection against disease and unemployment that they had provided out of their own savings and that was a main status distinction between the two classes. Here, malice is the unavoidable by-product of the search for prestige and status.

(2) Envy-enjoyment may induce various kinds of behavior: Acquiring more than one would have otherwise, displaying one's possessions more prominently than one would have otherwise, undermining the situation of others to stimulate their envy, or improving it for the same purpose.[114] Veblen – the central writer on envy-provocation – emphasizes the first two strategies. He argued that among the "incentives to acquisition and accumulation," a central component was "the desire to excel in pecuniary standing and so gain the esteem *and envy* of one's fellow-men."[115] Conspicuous consumption is an instance of the second strategy: "Costly entertainments, such as the potlatch or the ball, are peculiarly adapted to serve this end. The competitor with whom the entertainer wishes to institute a comparison is, by this method, made to serve as a means to the end. He consumes vicariously for his host at the same time that he is a witness to the consumption of that excess of good things which his

---

111. Schoeck (1987), pp. 137–8.
112. Liebermann and Syrquin (1983), p. 31.
113. De Swaan (1989), p. 268.
114. The qualification "more that one would have otherwise" is important, to avoid the fallacy of thinking that anyone who enjoys the envy of others acts for the sake of that enjoyment (see Elster 1983b, section II.10).
115. Veblen (1965), p. 32; my italics.

host is unable to dispose of single-handedly, and he is also made to witness his host's facility in etiquette."[116] The third strategy is difficult to distinguish from malicious behavior. The referee who writes a negative report on a colleague's grant proposal or votes against his membership in a scientific academy may do so to maintain the other's envy as well as his own feeling of superiority. For the fourth strategy to work, two conditions must be satisfied: The alleviation of B's inferiority caused by A's gift to B must be more than offset by the aggravation of inferiority caused by A's display of generosity, and the subsequent increase in A's envy-enjoyment must be large enough to compensate for his loss of income.

(3) To avoid being the target of destructive envy, one can either divest oneself of one's assets or hide them. As noted above, divestiture may be self-defeating if it takes the form of a transfer to the envious. Outright destruction of assets might not achieve the goal either, because it suggests an enviable lack of concern for the envied goods. The envious will not be content until he sees the envied person being stripped of his assets against his will, a feat that is hard to achieve at will. One may, however, try to create the appearance that the assets were destroyed nonvoluntarily. This strategy is similar to the much more frequent form of envy-reduction that consists in hiding one's assets from the sight of the envious.[117] "In Haiti, G. E. Simpson found that a peasant will seek to disguise his true economic position by purchasing several smaller fields rather than one larger piece of land. For the same reason he will not wear good clothes. He does this intentionally to protect himself against the envious black magic of his neighbours."[118] In Ghana, a man who was believed (correctly) by his relatives to be very rich managed to reduce their envy by building "a house which he purposely left unfinished so that he could tell his relatives, 'You see, I have no more money, I am a poor man.'"[119] In a Mexican village, fear of envy rather then fear of robbery was the main reason for the refusal to install glass windows in the house.[120]

(4) Acts of envy-reduction or envy-avoidance may also be undertaken by third parties. Parents, for instance, will try to minimize envy among siblings, sometimes with the effect of generating resentment towards themselves. A small girl was promised a pair of roller

---

116. *Ibid.*, p. 75.
117. For examples of the hiding strategy see also Foster (1972, pp. 175–6).
118. Schoeck (1987), p. 58, citing Simpson (1941).
119. Schoeck (1987), p. 74.
120. Foster (1965) p. 154.

skates for going to the dentist. The promise was kept, but she was upset when her younger sisters got the same reward without having done anything for it. At a large scale, redistributive tax policies have been interpreted in this light. Tax policies can, in fact, be seen in all three perspectives. If political power is in the hands of the relatively poor, they may impose progressive taxation even beyond the point at which they benefit from it (strong envy).[121] If it is in the hands of the rich, they can tax themselves to prevent the poor from rebelling out of envy. If political power is in the hands of a decaying aristocracy or a middle class of functionaries, they can similarly tax the rich to assuage the envy of the poor. Yet although such envy-based explanations of taxation are quite common, they are also quite commonly based in a right-wing ideology. I have not seen any attempt to provide empirical evidence that this motivation has in fact been operating. If there are cases in which popular demand has forced taxes up to a level at which the negative impact on work incentives is so strong as to decrease total tax revenue, I would suspect that the motive is unenlightened self-interest or a short time horizon rather than envy. Below I discuss other cases – in classical Greece and prerevolutionary France – in which it is hard to prove the superiority of envy-based over interest-based explanations.

(5) Envy can also be provoked by a third party, as part of a divide and conquer strategy. Thus, "[o]ne of the deadliest weapons in the arsenal of psychological warfare is propaganda aimed at convincing some segments of the enemy group that they are suffering more hardships or are gaining fewer benefits than other segments of the group."[122] Here, as elsewhere, it is important to distinguish genuine cases of *divide et impera* from the superficially similar phenomenon of *tertius gaudens*.[123] A's envy of B may de facto work to the benefit of C, but we should avoid the fallacious functionalist inference that C has been instrumental in creating the envy.

DESANITIZING ENVY

Economists capture envy and malice as externalities in the utility function.[124] This sanitized description cannot, however, account for

121. Boskin and Sheshinski (1978), p. 590.
122. Kreech and Crutchfield (1948), p. 411, cited after Heider (1958), p. 289.
123. For this distinction, see Simmel (1908, p. 82 ff).
124. For examples, see Sussangkarn and Goldman (1983), Kirschsteiger (1992), and Mui (1995). This way of representing envy is nevertheless an advance on the

the emotional dynamics of envy. Consider for instance the fact that destroying the other's asset can make one feel more rather than less inferior. One might capture it, perhaps, by saying that if A's income appears with a negative coefficient in B's utility function, utility-maximizing action by B for the purpose of reducing A's income will, as a by-product, increase the absolute value of the coefficient. It is hard to see, however, what would be gained by this redescription. In fact, it would be misleading, by suggesting that a rational B might refrain from acting on his urge if he anticipated that the positive effect on his welfare caused by A's loss would be more than offset by the negative effect caused by the more acute feeling of his own inferiority. This is not how envy works. A person in the grip of envy will not pause to consider the effects of endogenous preference change, discounted to present value.

Nor can the sanitized version of envy capture the idea that A may derive psychic benefits from the suffering that his consumption imposes on B, as in envy-enjoyment. One might try, again, to model the situation as one in which A's utility function has B's utility (rather than his income) as one argument. But this would be to collapse envy-enjoyment and malice. A might not enjoy B's suffering as such, only the suffering caused by B's envy of him. Other forms of suffering might leave him indifferent, or even sympathetic. Also, while the sanitized approach squares with the fact that B feels bad when A makes him worse off out of malice, it does not fit the fact that B may also feel bad when A's malice takes the form of making him better off. That gifts may induce humiliation rather than gratitude is a commonplace – but there is no natural way of capturing it in the language of utility externalities.

Another implausible sanitized theory of envy and malice is to view them merely as processes of comparison that make people feel bad or good. In classical antiquity, Isocrates claimed that "if we encounter those who fare well, our lot is even harder to bear [than if we fall in with the unfortunate], not because we envy them their prosperity, but because amid the blessings of our neighbours we see more

notion of *envy-free* allocations (Foley 1967, Varian 1974), defined not as allocations in which nobody suffers from pangs of envy but as allocations in which nobody would rather have someone else's bundle of goods than his own. Envy-freeness could be violated even if all individuals are nonenvious in the usual sense of the term; conversely an envy-free allocation might give rise to pangs of envy if an individual envies another's utility rather than his bundle of goods. Denoting utility functions by u and bundles by x, $u_i(x_i) - u_j(x_j)$ could be negative even if $u_i(x_i) - u_i(x_j)$ is positive (see also Hammond 1987).

clearly our own miseries" (14. 47). Although he does not assert that envy simply *is* a contrast effect (I.6), he comes close to doing so. An explicit statement to this effect was made by Hume, who claimed to "derive the passions of malice and envy" from the general principle that "objects appear greater or less by a comparison with others." Specifically, "the misery of another gives us a more lively idea of our happiness, and his happiness of our misery."[125] These statements may capture the pain of envy, but not its destructive urge.

More recently, an influential article by Thomas Ashby Wills stipulates as a basic principle that "[p]ersons can increase their subjective well-being through comparison with a less fortunate other" and then derives as one corollary that this effect can be achieved "by actively causing harm to another person, thereby creating the opportunity for comparison with a less fortunate other."[126] In the otherwise richly documented article, Wills does not cite a single plausible instance of behavior illustrating the corollary,[127] probably because there are few examples to be found. To feel good by comparing myself to another whom I have made badly off *for the purpose of enabling me to make a favorable comparison*[128] is like getting pleasure from compliments that I pay another person to make me.[129] Although not an impossible feat to achieve, it would require unusual capacities for self-deception.[130]

125. Hume (1960), pp. 375.
126. Wills (1981), pp. 245–6.
127. Wills (1981, p. 261) claims that studies showing that "subjects who received negative evaluation from partner gave more shocks to partner" or that "subjects who received higher level of shock from partner gave more intense shock to partner" illustrate the corollary. The interpretation of these findings in terms of pleasurable downward comparisons seems contrived.
128. A different matter is the quasi-sadistic pleasure that one may derive from the *act* of making others worse off (see the subsequent discussion of *hybris*).
129. Parducci (1995), p. 92 is perhaps making a similar mistake in his discussion of why people so rarely choose the worst of several alternatives even when the immediate loss would be more than offset by the long-term gains through the contrast effect (I.6). "To do so would go against the immediate preferability of more to less when both are experienced in the same context, as they are at the moment of choice." But I am not sure this identifies the problem accurately. We often choose what looks best at the time, disregarding the impact of the choice on the welfare we will derive from later choices. The theory of melioration offered in Herrnstein and Prelec (1992) rests on a roughly similar mechanism. Yet whereas the subject of Herrnstein's experiments can overcome their tendency to suboptimal behavior once they understand the long-term consequences of their choices, I conjecture that subjects of Parducci-like experiments could not. For a bad event to serve as anchor for a contrast effect it must not be deliberately chosen for that purpose (see also Parducci 1995, p. 121, for a partial recognition of this fact).
130. Elster (1984), p. 179. It is easier to achieve by acts of omission than by acts of commission. Abstaining from helping another – even when it would be at no or

ENVY AND THE GREEKS

In a monograph on this topic Peter Walcot cites a number of discussions of envy by Greek writers in the near-millenium spanning Homer and Plutarch.[131] His purpose is partly to extract general insights into the nature of envy, partly to highlight its importance in Greek history and society. Below, I draw on his discussion and sources as well as on other writings.

(1) The most systematic discussions of envy are found in three essays by Plutarch, "How to Profit by One's Enemies," "On Brotherly Love," and "On Envy and Hate."[132] In his discussion of the antecedents of envy we find an instance of what Montaigne called Plutarch's characteristic tendency to present things in "opposite and contrasting manners" (see I.4). On the one hand, "envy increases with the apparent progress of the envied in virtue" (537F); on the other hand, "supreme and resplendent fortune often extinguishes envy" (538A). In this case, however, the two opposing mechanisms can plausibly be reduced to the lawlike theory of neighborhood envy: As the distance to the envied person increases, envy first increases and then decreases. Similarly, extreme misfortune extinguishes envy (i.e., malice). By contrast, neither great fortune nor great misfortune can extinguish hate. Nobody envied Alexander, Plutarch says, but he was hated by many.

Isocrates implicitly appeals to the theory of neighborhood envy when he argues that "those who live in monarchies, not having anyone to envy, do in all circumstances so far as possible what is best" (3.18). The monarch might, in fact, take active steps to make himself appear beyond envy. According to Herodotus, when the king Deioces surrounded himself with pomp and mystery it was because he feared "that his compeers, who were brought up together with him, and were as of good family as he, and no whit inferior to him in manly qualities, if they saw him frequently would be pained at the sight, and would therefore be likely to conspire against him, whereas if they did not see him, they would think him quite a different being from themselves" (I.99).[133] If the way to assuage or prevent envy is

low cost to oneself – because one enjoys his or her discomfort is psychologically different from inducing his or her discomfort.
131. Walcot (1978).
132. These occupy, respectively, pp. 86B–92, 478–492, and 536E–539 of the standard edition.
133. See Walcot (1978, p. 55) on the relation between envy and pain.

to increase the distance between the ruler and his subjects, he can do so by elevating himself (as in this story) or by keeping them down (as in a story to be told below). In either case, the goal of envy-reduction might be accompanied by and inseparable from sheer malice.

Plutarch notes that "among the disorders of the soul [envy] alone is unmentionable" (537E).[134] The envious person will therefore try to misrepresent his motivation to others (V.2). This is offered as an observation, not as a piece of advice. In his more normative mode, Plutarch states simply that people "should by all means envy no one" (485E). As a realist, however, he knows that this is to ask too much. If people cannot get rid of the tendency to envy others, "they should turn the malignancy outwards and drain it off on those not of their blood, just as men do who divert sedition from the city by means of foreign wars" (*ibid.*). This advice is offered to divert envy from one's siblings. In I.4, I cited a similar passage in "How to Profit by One's Enemies," to the effect that a man would profit from venting his enemy on his enemies so as to divert it from friends and relatives (91F; cp. also 92B). We may ask whether these strategies of cognitive framing could ever be successful. As Plutarch also states in "How to Profit by One's Enemies," envy of your enemy may spill over to friends, and even if the compensation theory were correct, it is not clear that envy can be redirected at will.

Plutarch also considers envy-reduction from above, i.e., by the envied. He observes, very acutely, that generosity will not work. Whereas men forgo hate when they receive a benefit from those they hated as evil, this strategy "actually exasperates [envy]; for enviers eye more jealously those who possess a reputation for goodness, feeling that they possess the greatest blessing, virtue; and even if they receive some benefit from the fortunate, are tormented, envying them for both the intention and the power. For the intention proceeds from their virtue, the power from their good fortune, and both are blessings" (538D). In his discussion of sibling envy, he recommends a more promising strategy, based on the premise that "it is impossible that the one brother should excel at all points and in all ways." Thus the superior brother, "if he does not try to curtail or conceal the advantages of his brother ... but yields in his turn and reveals that

---

134. To my knowledge, there is no suggestion in his writings or in those of other Greek authors that people feel compelled to hide their envy to themselves as well as to others. As far as I can glean from my limited knowledge of the literature, self-deception was not a central topic for Greek thinkers (Chapter III of Pears 1985 is useful on this topic).

his brother is better and more useful in many respects, by thus continually removing all grounds for envy, fuel for fire, as it were, will quench the envy, or rather will not allow it to spring up or begin at all" (485B). Here, Plutarch recommends that to defuse envy the envied person should do what the envious one often does spontaneously, that is, emphasize aspects in which the inferior is superior.

(2) According to the theory of status inconsistency, those who are high on one dimension (e.g., wealth) and low on another (e.g., power) will be subject to an unpleasant tension. The remarks by Plutarch just cited amount to saying that the tension may be relieved if others are respectively low and high on the same dimensions. The more common argument is that those who suffer this tension will engage in individual or collective action so as to occupy the same high status on both dimensions (I.6). According to Joshua Ober, this was the outcome of Solon's reforms: "An elite of wealth, which would be both larger and more permeable to new members, thus replaced the nobility of birth as the exclusive governing elite.... The membership of the new ruling class therefore would be sensitive to economic change; the absence of disparity between economic position and access to political power might defuse intra-elite tension considerably."[135]

Later, Athens extended the political elite so that it included all Athenian citizens and thus ceased to be an elite. This created a social system in which full equality in one respect went together with large degrees of inequality in another. As Aristotle notes in the *Politics*, this is not a stable situation: "For the one party, if they are unequal in one respect, for example wealth, consider themselves to be unequal in all; and the other party, if they are equal in one respect, for example free birth, consider themselves to be equal in all" (1280^b23–25). Thus, whereas both offsetting inequalities and equality across the board may reduce envy, the coexistence of equality and inequality will exacerbate it:

Equality among the full Spartan citizens was something consciously adopted, or so the ancient sources imply, in order to reduce envy among these citizens and thus prevent a Helot revolt. Athenian democracy had no such origin – but a consequence of the development of democracy at Athens was a restriction on the scope offered for feelings of envy because of an equality of voting rights. In one respect at least a citizen could feel himself to be as good as the next citizen, and this was in an area of the greatest importance, political

135. Ober (1989), p. 61.

life. But perhaps democracy actually intensified rather than reduced feelings of envy: the very fact that all citizens were equal as voters in the assembly simply may have made some that much more aware of their inequality in birth or wealth or even good luck, and so Plutarch refers frequently to envy in his biographies of fifth-century Athenians. To put it another way, if one is "entitled" to an equality of rights as a voter, this is a strong inducement to expect a comparable equality across the board. In fact if equality is to curb envy it must be a full equality which covers all of life, and the Spartan system did attempt to be comprehensive.[136]

(3) I have discussed the tension that may arise between envy-enjoyment and fear of the destructive urges in envy. Ideally, I would like to enjoy my material possessions *and* to bask in your envy of them, but if you destroy them I cannot also enjoy them. Walcot refers to this as "the standard paradox for a Greek – one wants to be honoured and this is impossible for a poor man, and yet honour and wealth inspire envy in others and this envy must not be fostered."[137] This, I believe, is a universal phenomenon rather than a specifically Greek one. More unusual – although not unique as we shall see when discussing Tocqueville – is the following variant of the paradox. Suppose that A, subscribing to the Greek dictum that "the man who is not envied is as nothing,"[138] is inspired to great achievements so that he can enjoy the envy of his inferior B. A's wealth, power, or status may then trigger a destructive urge of malice in his superior C, who cannot stand the prospect of his superiority being challenged.[139]

The role of C may be played either by the gods or by the arbitrary, omnipotent tyrant. (And when the gods are in the role of C, tyrants are often in the role of A.) Consider first the "envy of the gods" or, more accurately, the belief in divine envy. There are a number of instances in Greek tragedies and in Herodotus of mortals being struck down by the gods because, in one way or another, they were out of bounds. Drawing on various commentators, we may distinguish three motives for this behavior.[140] First, the gods may punish those who are guilty of some crime, such as *hybris*, toward other mortals. Second, they may punish those who are guilty of a crime towards the

---

136. Walcot (1978), p. 64.
137. *Ibid.*, p. 54; see also pp. 34, 39.
138. Epicharmus, cited in Walcot (1978), p. 39.
139. At the same time, of course, A may be the target of B's destructive envy. Walcot does not consider such double-barreled attacks, which I discuss in a subsequent section on Tocqueville.
140. Ranulf (1933/34); Walcot (1978); Fisher (1992).

gods themselves. Again, *hybris* is a frequently cited crime. Third, the gods may punish outstanding mortals out of sheer malice.

The best-known example involving the third motive is the story Herodotus tells about Polycrates (3.39 ff.).[141] Noticing the "exceedingly good fortune" of Polycrates, his friend Amasis wrote him a letter warning him against the envy of the gods and advising him to choose the one of his possessions he valued most highly and throw it away. Polycrates, finding the advice to be good, decided that the possession it would grieve him most to lose was his signet ring, which he then proceeded to throw into the sea. A few days later, the ring was found in the belly of a fish that was served to the king. Later on, to be sure, Polycrates came to a bad end (3.125). Thus the behavior of the gods matches a phenomenon we found in Plutarch: You cannot escape envy (or malice) by generous or self-sacrificial actions performed for that very purpose. There is no hint, however, that the mechanism is the same in the two cases. In the case of Polycrates, it appears that once his fate had been decided, there was nothing he could do to prevent it.

Tyrants and kings, too, may suffer from malice. According to Demosthenes, Philip of Macedonia was subject to an especially vicious and self-destructive form of royal malice. He "is so jealous that he wants to take to himself all the credit of the chief successes, and is more annoyed with a general or an officer who achieves something praiseworthy than with those who fail ignominiously" (11.12). According to Herodotus, this kind of behavior is endemic in tyrannies:

How can a monarchy be a well-adjusted institution, when it provides the possibility for a man to do what he likes without being subject to any control? To place even the best of all men in such a position of power would place him beyond the reach of customary modes of thought. For in him is engendered *hybris* as a result of the presence of good things, and envy is a natural growth in man from the beginning. ... It is true that the tyrannical man should be free of envy, since he possesses all good things; in fact the opposite occurs in his relations with his citizens. He is envious of the best of them as long as they survive and are alive, and takes pleasure in the worst of the citizens, and is very ready to listen to slander. He is the most inconsistent of all creatures; if you offer him admiration in moderate quantities, he is angry that he is

141. Fisher (1992, pp. 361–4) offers a lucid discussion of this episode, and of the relative importance of the first and third divine motives that I distinguish in the text. For simplicity I only consider the third motive here.

not paid extreme attention, and if someone pays him extreme attention he is angry at him for being a flatterer. (III.80)

(4) I now turn to some Athenian institutions that have been understood as expressions of envy. The most frequently cited is the peculiarly Greek institution of ostracism, involving a ten-year expulsion from the city without loss of property or citizen rights. During the fifth century BC, the citizens held an annual vote to decide whether there should be an ostracism that year. If the vote was favorable, they met again two months later and chose the person to be ostracized. The choice was not a foregone conclusion, as shown by the last recorded episode in which Hyperboles tried to engineer the ostracism of Nicias or Alcibiades, only to see himself selected when they joined forces against him.[142] Although it is tempting to see the two-month interval as a cooling or delaying device, similar to that used by the Athenians in other contexts,[143] this episode shows that it could be used to stir passions up as well as to cool them down.[144]

There is no general agreement on the purpose for which ostracism was established or (a different issue) for which it was used. Three possibilities stand out. First, ostracism could be used to expel a potentially dangerous individual from the city. Second, it could be used somewhat like our general elections, to decide between two alternative policies by expelling the proponent of one of them. And third, it could be a vehicle for envy. To be sure, ostracism would not be explicitly presented and defended in terms of envy. Rather, it can be understood as "a piece of democratic machinery almost ideally contrived to cater for widespread envy, since it allows envy to be expressed legitimately."[145] Again, the analogy with elections is useful, if we follow Tocqueville in his argument that citizens vote to exclude from power those whom they envy. In both cases, an institution purporting to promote the public good may be hijacked to express envy.

A problem with interpreting ostracism in terms of envy is the lack of contemporary statements to this effect. The evidence for this view comes largely from Plutarch, writing some five or six centuries after the events he describes. In his *Lives* Plutarch notably explains the ostracisms of Themistocles and Aristides in terms of envy:

142. Ostwald (1986), pp. 302–5; Kagan (1981), pp. 144–7.
143. Hansen (1991), p. 307.
144. Sinclair (1988), p. 170; see also Elster (in press a), section II.5.
145. Walcot (1978), p. 54.

The Athenians banished [Themistocles], making use of the ostracism to hum-ble his eminence and authority, as they ordinarily did with all whom they thought to be too powerful, or, by their greatness, disproportionable to the equality thought requisite in a popular government. For the ostracism was instituted, not so much to punish the offender, as to mitigate and pacify the violence of the envious, who delighted to humble eminent men, and who, by fixing this disgrace upon them, might vent some of their rancour. (*Life of Themistocles* 22.3)

[The people] banished Aristides by the ostracism, giving their jealousy of his reputation the name of fear of tyranny. For ostracism was not the punishment of any criminal act, but was speciously said to be the mere depression and hu-miliation of excessive greatness and power; and was in fact a gentle relief and mitigation of envious feeling which was thus allowed to vent itself in inflict-ing no intolerable injury, only a ten years' banishment. (*Life of Aristides* 7.2)

Concerning the episode that led to the ostracism of Hyperboles, Plutarch offers two contrasting accounts, one in terms of personalities and one in terms of policies:

The enmity betwixt Nicias and Alcibiades running higher and higher, and the time being at hand for decreeing the ostracism or banishment, for ten years, which the people, putting the name on a sherd, were wont to inflict at certain times on some person suspected or regarded with jealousy for his popularity or wealth, both were now in alarm or apprehension, one of them, in all like-lihood, being to undergo this ostracism; as the people abominated the life of Alcibiades, and stood in fear of his boldness and resolution . . .; while as for Nicias, his riches made him envied, and his habits of living, in particular his unsociable and exclusive ways, not like those of a fellow-citizen, or even a fellow-man, went against him, and having many times opposed their inclina-tions, forcing them against their feelings to do what was their interest, he had got himself disliked. To speak plainly, it was a contest of the young men who were eager for war, against the men of years and lovers of peace, they turning the ostracism upon the one, these upon the other. (*Life of Nicias* 11 1–2)

From these texts, it would appear that the relation between envy and other motives for ostracism is partly one of misrepresentation (V.3), partly one of joint causation or overdetermination. One may envy a powerful man and use fear of tyranny as a pretext. One may also, however, genuinely fear that he could use his power to some dangerous end. Any accumulation of power may be seen as undesir-able because of the uses to which it might be put. Also, one might want to banish a powerful man if he advocates a specific policy judged to be too risky.

We need to look more closely at what Plutarch cites as grounds for envy. In addition to power they include wealth (Nicias), *hybris* (Alcibiades), reclusiveness (Nicias), having made the mistake of being right (Nicias), great love of honor (Themistocles), and sheer goodness (Aristides). Alcibiades was widely seen to be hybristic, and the fear that he might use power to set up a tyranny was not at all implausible.[146] Themistocles was "a great lover of honor," orchestrating his public appearances to create "an appearance of greatness and power." At the meeting that decided the ostracism of Aristides, an illiterate citizen asked him to write *Aristides* on his sherd. He, "being surprised, [asked] if Aristides had ever done him any injury. 'None at all,' said he, "neither know I the man; but I am tired of hearing him everywhere called the Just.'" This is a pure case of envy. Attacks based on wealth and reclusiveness probably also belong here. The other cases are more ambiguous. Love of honor (*philotimia*) becomes *hybris* when taken to excess,[147] and the desire to retaliate against *hybris* springs from anger, not envy. Nor is the desire to get back at someone who has proved one to be wrong a form of envy, but rather an instance of irrational anger.

(5) It is often claimed that income transfers are motivated by envy or fear of envy. Above I expressed some skepticism about this claim as applied to redistributive taxation. Although the Athenians did not use direct taxation, there were other transfers that could be seen, and have been seen, as behavioral manifestations of envy. Among the most important are *liturgies* and *fines*.

Rather than relying on a regular income tax to finance the provision of public goods, the Athenians counted on the rich to volunteer, by subsidizing and organizing public services or "liturgies." In Xenophon's *Economics*, Socrates recites a number of such services:

I notice that you are bound to offer many large sacrifices; else, I fancy, you would get into trouble with gods and men alike. Secondly, it is your duty to entertain many strangers, on a generous scale too. Thirdly, you have to give dinners and play the benefactor to the citizens, or you lose your following. Moreover, I observe that already the state is exacting heavy contributions from you: you must needs keep horses, pay for choruses and gymnastic competitions, and accept presidencies; and if war breaks out, I know that they will require you to maintain a ship and pay taxes that will nearly crush you. (II, 5–6)

146. Fisher (1992), p. 87.
147. *Ibid.*, pp. 20, 23.

As the language suggests, the contributions were not exactly voluntary. At a certain level of wealth citizens were obligated to perform these duties, but some did more than was required, and in fact competed with one another to be the most generous. Services such as manning a ship were necessary for the survival of the city and can hardly be understood in terms of envy. By contrast, when the rich subsidized sacrifices and festivals, the poor may have appreciated the services not only because they made them better off, but also because they made the rich worse off. Drawing on George Foster's idea that the rich can assuage the envious by "throwing a sop" to placate them,[148] Walcot asserts that "the liturgy is perhaps the clearest example of a method for avoiding envy being absorbed within the constitutional framework of the democratic state, for surely the liturgy is simply an institutionalized expression of sop expenditure."[149] He does not, however, offer any further argument or evidence for this interpretation. In particular, he says nothing about what the rich feared might happen if they did not fulfill or overfulfill[150] their duties in this respect, that is, about how the poor would *express* their envy.

A possible argument connects the performances of liturgies to the fear of being fined out of envy. In a comment linking these two issues, Ober writes that

Demosthenes states that in light of the great amounts that they are lucky enough to possess, the rich should willingly expend a small part of their fortune on the *eisphora* [a tax usually grouped with the liturgies] in order that they may be allowed to reap the benefit of their remaining wealth without disturbance. There seems to an implied threat here, that if the rich do not give willingly, they may have their property confiscated. The threat does not refer, however, to a class revolution leading to a general redistribution of property, but to the legal means of recourse by which the money could be extracted from the wealthy shirker.[151]

148. Foster (1972), pp. 177–9. See Elster (1991) for a criticism of the unwarranted functionalist explanations involved in Foster's analysis of this and other aspects of envy.
149. Walcot (1978), p. 59.
150. There are in fact two different explananda. On the one hand, we might try to explain the establishment of the institution of liturgies as an expression of popular envy. On the other hand, we might try to explain the overfulfillment of one's duty as an expression of fear of envy among the rich. Walcot's suggestion – that the *institution* is due to fear of envy – is implausible, given the democratic nature of the process by which it was established.
151. Ober (1989), p. 200.

The legal means in question is the fine that a wealthy defendant might have to pay if found guilty in a lawsuit. The Athenians were extremely litigious,[152] and a wealthy man was always vulnerable to frivolous suits by professional accusers or "sycophants." In the sources we often find references to the idea that the popular jury might impose a heavy fine on a wealthy defendant merely because he was wealthy. That idea is consistent with two different motivations, however. The people might want to take the wealth for itself – or take it away from its owner.

On the one hand, the people – as represented by the large jury – could simply be motivated by *self-interest*. In a hand-to-mouth economy such as Athens there was always "a temptation to jurors to vote in the interest of the treasury when money was short, and an informer dangled before their eyes a fat estate whose owner, he alleged, had been guilty of some serious offense."[153] This motivation might, however, cut both ways, as the defendant might also tell the jury that it would be in their interest to side with him, so that he could go on performing liturgies on a generous scale in the future.[154] The argument might even be presented as an ongoing tit-for-tat: I have given generously in the past so that you might treat me leniently in the court so that I can give generously in the future.[155]

On the other hand, the people could be motivated by *envy*. In a part of a speech where he defends his own character, Isocrates cites the following comment by a friend who was afraid that praising himself might have the opposite effect of what he wanted:

"Some men," he said, "have been so brutalized by envy and want and are so hostile that they wage war, not on depravity, but on prosperity; they hate not only the best men but the noblest pursuits; and, in addition to their other faults, they take sides with wrong-doers and are in sympathy with them, while they destroy those whom they have cause to envy. They do these things, not because they are ignorant of the issues on which they are to vote, but because they intend to inflict injury and do not expect to be found out." (4.142–3)

Several speeches by Demosthenes illustrate the appeal to envy in order to win sympathy among the jurors. Trying to whip up hostility

152. Sinclair (1988), pp. 209–10; Todd (1993), pp. 147–53.
153. Jones (1957, p. 58), citing three speeches by Lysias (30, 27, 19).
154. For examples, see Ober (1989, p. 227).
155. See notably two speeches by Lysias (21.15–20, 25.10–13).

against Meidias, for instance, he plays on their envy as well as resentment at envy-enjoyment:

He has built at Eleusis a mansion huge enough to overshadow his neighbours; he drives his wife to the Mysteries, or anywhere else that he wishes, with a pair of greys from Sicyon; he swaggers about the market-place with three or four henchmen in attendance, describing beakers and drinking-horns and cups loud enough for the passers-by to hear. I do not at all see how the mass of Athenians are benefited by all the wealth that Meidias retains for private luxury and superfluous display. (21.158–9)

It is hard to know how, in practice, we could tell whether a jury which imposed a heavy fine was motivated by envy or self-interest. Aristotle implicitly suggests a way of differentiating the two motivations from one another. In the *Politics*, he notes that "[t]he demagogues of our own day often get property confiscated in law-courts to please the people" (1320ᵃ4–5), because the people has a direct financial interest in the size of the state coffers. He then goes on to recommend "a law that the property of the condemned should not be public and go into the treasury but be sacred. Thus offenders will be as much afraid, for they will be punished all the same, and the people, having nothing to gain, will not be so ready to condemn the accused" (1320ᵃ6–10). In terms of La Bruyère's trichotomy of motives (II.3), Aristotle here claims that if you remove any *interest* the people might have in the outcome, they will decide in accordance with *reason* or justice, thus assuming that they would not be moved by *passion*, for example by envy. As we saw earlier, however, he also claims that jurors are swayed by passion rather than interest (*Rhetoric* 1354ᵇ31–32). The issue could have been decided by implementing his recommendation and observing whether the jurors did in fact refrain from imposing confiscatory fines on the wealthy.

TOCQUEVILLE ON ENVY

Among the major social theorists, Tocqueville is the only who accords major importance to envy. In *Democracy in America* as well as in *The Old Regime*, ideas related to envy, equality, and mobility form a central explanatory cluster. I discuss the books in the chronological order of their subject matter rather than in their order of publication.

(1) *The Old Regime and the French Revolution* is a study of the relations among classes and social groupings in prerevolutionary France.[156] The groups involved are the peasantry, the urban artisans, the urban bourgeoisie, the nobility, the intellectuals, the Church, and the royal administration. In the following, I neglect the intellectuals and the Church. Although important in the overall argument of the book, they are less central to the emotional dynamics I shall describe. The relations among the various classes and between the classes and the royal administration are to a large extent described in terms of interest. Yet what concerns me here is how the clash of interests generates strong emotional reactions – envy, malice, and hatred – that, for Tocqueville, provide the main explanation for the fragility of the old regime and its ultimate downfall.

The Old Regime is a very complex work, yet I believe it can be summarized in a single sentence, "On ne s'appuie que sur ce qui résiste."[157] Tocqueville argued that over the centuries before the Revolution the French monarchy used divide-and-conquer tactics to isolate and weaken the various social classes (OR, p. 136), with the result that when the King finally needed their support to resist the revolution they were too feeble to offer any help.[158] More specifically, by isolating the nobility from the peasantry on the one hand and from the bourgeoisie on the other, the kings deprived their natural ally of the ability to come to their help in a time of crisis. In both cases, the kings proceeded by offering the nobility a poisoned gift – exemption from military service and from paying taxes. As Tocqueville describes the process, it involved shortsighted behavior on both sides. The nobility imagined "that they could keep their lofty status while evading its obligations. At first it seemed they had succeeded, but soon a serious internal malady attacked them, whose effect was, so to speak, to make them gradually crumble up" (OR, p. 135). For a warrior

---

156. References to this work are noted by *OR* followed by the page number in Tocqueville (1955). This translation is utterly unreliable and has been modified in many places. Unfortunately, the new translation in Tocqueville (1998) is even worse.

157. "One cannot get support from what does not offer resistance." Tocqueville does not use this phrase. Stendhal cites it in *Le rouge et le noir*, with the following comment by the editor: "Spoken by François Andrieux to Bonaparte during a discussion of the civil code" (Stendhal 1952, p. 1470).

158. Here and below I exaggerate the intentional nature of the royal decisions that brought about this state of affairs. Tocqueville argued that the isolation of the various classes from one another was also to a large extent a by-product of actions undertaken for other ends (OR, pp. 58, 123). I ignore this exegetical issue, which is somewhat marginal to the present discussion.

caste, lack of obligations is demoralizing (OR, p. 79). The king, on his side, did not see that by weakening the nobility he was ultimately undermining his own power (OR, pp. 122–3, 132).

The French nobility was the target both of the hatred of the peasantry and the envy of the bourgeoisie. In the comparative perspective that Tocqueville sketches at the beginning of the work – why the revolution took place in France rather than elsewhere – we can explain the calmer social climate in Germany and especially in England by the absence of one or both of these emotions. In France, the peasants hated the local lord because he exploited and oppressed them without offering anything in return (OR, p. 30). In Germany and England, by contrast, the local nobility retained a hand in the local administration that could justify their extractions (OR, p. 27). Also, whereas the French nobility did not pay taxes, the German and especially the English nobility paid disproportionately *higher* taxes (OR, pp. 87, 98). In these countries, the upper classes did their part in a quid pro quo, whereas the French nobility became entirely parasitic and hence more hateful.

According to Tocqueville, the French nobility was also more exposed to envy, at least compared to England. In Germany, the class of higher functionaries – superior to the bourgeoisie while inferior to the nobles – were in a situation similar to that of the French bourgeoisie. In a classic case of status inconsistency, their increasing influence together with their exclusion from the Court caused them to feel "hurt" and "irritated" by the privileges of the nobility, and "prepared the ground for an initially favorable reception of the French revolution in Germany" (OR, p. 229). In Britain, where the caste system separating nobility and commoners had been totally abolished (OR, p. 82), there were no grounds for class envy.

Of these two emotions, hatred is the stronger one.[159] In hate, the action tendency is to destroy the person who is the object of the

159. Tocqueville's use of the words "envie" and "haine" is roughly consistent with the Aristotelian senses in which I use the terms "hatred" and "envy" here. Sometimes he uses both "envie" and "haine" to characterize a relation that I would refer to only by "hatred" (e.g., p. 31); at other times he seems to use "envie" in the sense of "hatred" (e.g., p. 204). More frequently, however, he uses "envie" in the Aristotelian sense of the term (pp. 89, 92, 127, 186, 187). The most puzzling passage is one in which he refers to the attitude of commoners towards the nobility as "haine" and their attitude towards the recently ennobled as "envie" (p. 89). I do not quite know what to make of this text. It is clear from the passage in OR (p. 87) cited in the text that the bourgeoisie were envious of the tax privileges of the nobles. If they also harbored an emotion that could be described as hatred, it was in any case much less virulent than the hatred of the peasantry towards the lord.

emotion. In envy, it is to destroy his property. The destructive urge in envy is directed against a person only if I envy him for something that cannot be destroyed separately, such as his goodness.[160] The fury of the French peasantry was a driving force in the violence of the French revolution (OR, pp. 134–6). The envy felt by the bourgeoisie, by contrast, did not go beyond the abolition of feudal privileges. This refers, of course, to the situation up to and including 1789. The violent bourgeois hatred of the *"ci-devants"* that was to emerge a few years later was triggered by their counterrevolutionary rather than by their prerevolutionary behavior.

From these general considerations I turn to the role of envy and malice in Tocqueville's argument. I begin with malice, which is the easier issue. Tocqueville observes several times that before the revolution French society became increasing obsessed with status. In their contempt of the recently ennobled, "the nobles refused to tolerate in their electoral body anything that savored in the least of the bourgeoisie" (OR, p. 89). As for the latter, it was equally jealous of the prerogatives that set it apart from the petty bourgeoisie. In fact, "what perhaps strikes us most in the behavior of the eighteenth-century bourgeoisie is their fear of being assimilated to the mass of the people" (OR, p. 93). Within the bourgeoisie, finally, questions of precedence took on all-consuming importance, wigmakers protesting what a contemporary source calls their "rightful pain (*juste douleur)"* when the bakers were given pride of place (OR, p. 95).

In this struggle for status, the upwardly mobile came under fire from both ends, suffering both envy from below and malice from above. "Far from reducing the hatred of the nobility felt by the commoners, the practice of ennoblement had the opposite effect, and became even more intensified by the envy which the newly ennobled inspired in his former equals" (OR, p. 89). In fact, "in some provinces newly ennobled men were given the cold shoulder from one side because they were not thought to be noble enough, and from the other side because they were found to be too much so" (*ibid.*).

Status *comparison* was important because occasions for *interaction* were lacking. Although interaction can be destructive, it can also take the form of cooperation for mutual benefit. Comparisons, however, are intrinsically sterile. Self-government of the towns was a mere

---

160. "Therefore when they were gathered together, Pilate said unto them, Whom will ye that I release unto you? Barabbas, or Jesus which is called Christ? For he knew that for envy they had delivered him." (Mtt 27:17–18).

sham, as all political power belonged to the Intendant as representative of the king (OR, pp. 44–6). As for interaction between bourgeoisie and nobility, it was spoiled by the tax exemptions that the king had granted to the nobles. "As there is almost no public matter that does not arise from an existing tax or the imposition of a new one, it is obvious that when the two classes are no longer subject to taxation on an equal basis, they have almost no reason to engage in common decision making and no cause for common needs or feelings. Thus little or no effort is required to keep them apart, since one has taken away from them all opportunities and incentives to act in concert" (OR, p. 88).

This is not the place to discuss Tocqueville's analysis of how the nobles got and kept their tax exemption, except to say that it was essentially a bribe offered them by the king so that he could exploit the rest of the population without having to call a meeting of the Estates-General (OR, pp. 98, 100). Instead, I cite his comments on the psychological consequences of the phenomenon:

The most odious privilege, that of exemption from taxation, became progressively more valuable from the fifteenth century up to the Revolution. ... So long as the *taille* was the only impost to which the rest of the population was subject, the nobleman's immunity attracted little attention. But when taxes of this order were multiplied under a host of other names and in various forms; when four other imposts were assimilated to the *taille*; and when obligations unknown in the Middle Ages – notably forced labor requisitioned by the Crown for public works and compulsory service in the militia – were superadded, with the same disregard for equality, the exemption for the nobility appeared enormous. True, the inequality, though great, was not as bad as it seemed, since the nobleman was often affected indirectly, through his tenants, by taxes from which he himself was exempted. But in these matters the inequality you see hurts more than the one you feel (*l'inégalité qu'on voit nuit plus que celle qu'on ressent*). (OR, pp. 86–7)

The last remark is not entirely clear. Tocqueville may simply be making the trivial point that bourgeois envy could not be relieved by burdens on the nobility that the bourgeoisie weren't aware of ("what you don't know can't help you"). But he may also be making the stronger claim that even though the bourgeoisie had the cognitive prerequisites to reframe the situation of the nobility to make it less enviable, they either did not do so or, if they did, it did not take the sting out of their envy. Some forms of envy may be so burning that they cannot be alleviated by cognitive preemption.

The converse of what I called the "trivial point" is that you cannot envy advantages that you ignore ("what you don't know can't hurt you"). Tocqueville makes this observation in one of his most brilliantly ironical chapters, entitled "How the People Was Aroused by Attempts to Relieve It." The root of the problem was the inability of the nobles to understand that the people were human beings like themselves, speaking the same language and subject to the same emotions. Tocqueville recounts a story told by Voltaire's secretary, about Mme. Duchâtelet who "had no scruples about undressing in the presence of her manservants, being unable to convince herself that lackeys were men" (OR, p. 183). Similarly, expressions of sympathy for the peasantry were made in condescending and contemptuous terms, as if the nobles "were living in some backward country such as Galicia, where the aristocracy speaks a different language from the lower classes and cannot be understood by them" (OR, p. 185).

Because of their lack of imagination the nobles might inadvertently provoke envy by calling attention to inequalities that might otherwise have gone unnoticed. Tocqueville writes that in 1788 a provincial assembly sent out a letter to the inhabitants of the parishes inviting them to give an account of all their grievances. They wanted, obviously, to get all details about taxes imposed on the peasants, but

the curiosity of the provincial assembly did not stop with this. They also wanted to know the number of persons in each parish – nobles, clergy and commoners – who enjoyed any special privileges as regards taxation, and in what these privileges consisted. . . . But even this was not enough. Supposing, they said, equality of taxation came into practice and exempted persons were required to pay their share, at what figure might be assessed the sums they would contribute under the heads of the *taille* and its accessories, poll tax and forced-labor dues? This could not but arouse each individual man to passion by detailing his miseries and pointing to those responsible for it, embolden him when he saw how few they were, and kindle greed, envy and hatred in his heart. (OR, p. 185–6)

This case illustrates how an attempt to reform the old regime might elicit envy. Elsewhere, Tocqueville argues that the unreformed regime produced the same effect. Referring to the arbitrary and ferocious methods of tax collection, he writes that

the French peasant . . . acted much as the Jews did in the Middle Ages. Even when he was a man of means he put up a show of poverty, knowing that any sign of wealth was dangerous. . . . In its 1761 report the Agricultural society of Maine mentioned that it had the idea of awarding cattle as prizes and encouragements. It goes on to say that "the idea had been dropped because of the risk that the winners would be exposed to a mean-spirited jealousy, which might take advantage of the arbitrary methods of tax-assessment to make them suffer in the following years." In this system of taxation, every taxpayer had an urgent and permanent motive for spying on his neighbors and promptly notifying the tax collector of an increase in their means; they were all trained in envy, delation and hatred. (OR, p. 127)

As in the case of envy as a motivation for income transfers among the Greeks, the imputation of this motive is questionable. Just as the Athenian demos had an interest in imposing heavy fines on the rich, Tocqueville makes it clear that the peasant had an interest in denouncing his wealthy neighbor. As the tax collector in the village was assigned annually a fixed sum to bring in (OR, p. 125), the peasants knew that their burden would be eased if they could get someone else to pay more. And as in the Athenian case, a test of the envy hypothesis would require the removal of a self-interested motive, for instance by looking at societies in which taxes are assessed on an individual rather than a collective basis and that do not offer any rewards to informers. Whether we deal with Ancient Greece, prerevolutionary France, or modern capitalist societies, there is a tendency among scholars to explain income transfers by appealing to envy where mere interest seems sufficient. Although some of these may be cases of causal overdetermination, that remains to be shown.

Although the French revolution ended with the destruction of the monarchy, it began with the destruction of the nobility. It was not at all foreordained that it would have to go beyond this stage. Had it not been for the utter ineptitude of Louis XVI, a constitutional monarchy might have been established. This is a speculative assertion and not really required for the point I want to make, which is that at the outset of the revolution the hatred and envy of peasantry and bourgeoisie were directed exclusively at the nobility and not at all towards the king. In the case of bourgeois envy, this fact might seem puzzling. The nobility, to be sure, was exempt from taxes, but they obtained the exemption from the king. Would not anger at the king rather than envy of the nobility be the more appropriate emotion? This may not, however, be the way these emotions work. If A causes B to have more than C, C may direct his emotions towards the proximate rather than the ultimate cause of his feeling of inferiority. Iago, to be sure, hated Othello as much as Cassio, but this may not be the typical pattern.

Or perhaps we should think of the situation in terms of emotional mechanisms in the sense of Chapter I: Whether C mainly expresses anger towards A or envy towards B may depend on triggering factors that we have not yet identified.

(2) In *Democracy in America*, envy is central. In fact, envy is "the democratic sentiment" (DA, p. 310). It expresses a "debased taste for equality," as distinct from the "legitimate passion for equality which rouses in all men a desire to be strong and respected" (DA, p. 57). It is not entirely clear, though, what the target of democratic envy is supposed to be. Tocqueville's language is ambiguous, much more so, in fact, than in *The Old Regime*. I believe, nevertheless, that an argument can be made for a distinction between the hatred of privilege and the envy of economic superiority.

In prerevolutionary France, privilege was seen as a good whose possessor was to be envied; after 1789, privilege was seen as a hateful bad to be eradicated completely (OR, p. 204). This latter idea is central in *Democracy in America*, in which Tocqueville refers to the "ever-fiercer fire of endless hatred felt by democracies against the slightest privilege" (DA, p. 673; see also p. 630). Tocqueville's terminology is hard to understand, however, as he goes on to say that this hatred "favors the gradual concentration of all political rights in those hands which alone represent the state. The sovereign, being of necessity and incontestably above all the citizens, does not excite their envy." Here, hatred and envy seem to be used interchangeably. Also, there are closely parallel passages on how even the smallest inequality (DA, p. 538) *or* the smallest privilege (DA, pp. 672–3) stands out on an otherwise uniform background. Yet whereas he does argue that democratic society aims at the complete abolition of all legal privilege, complete economic equality is *not* among its ends. "It is not that in the United States, as everywhere, there are no rich; indeed, I know of no other country where love of money has such a grip on men's hearts or *where stronger scorn is expressed for the permanent equality of property*" (DA, p. 54; my italics). In democratic societies, privilege excites hatred because it is unambiguously bad. Superior economic status, by contrast, is similar to privilege before 1789: It is envied because it is a good, not hated because it is bad.

In general, as we have seen, envy is triggered by a perception of equality. It is limited to those about whom one can say, "It could have been me." The existence of legal barriers to mobility sets barriers to the imagination and hence to envy, whereas the removal of the barriers facilitates it:

As long as the Negro is kept as a slave, he can be held in a condition not far removed from that of a beast; once free, he cannot be prevented from learning enough to see the extent of his ills and to catch a glimpse of the remedy. There is, moreover, a curious principle of relative justice very deeply rooted in the human heart. Men are much more struck by inequalities within the same class than by inequalities between classes. Slavery is understood, but how can one allow several million citizens to live under a burden of eternal infamy and hereditary wretchedness? The free Negro population in the North feels these ills and resents these injustices, but it is weak and in decline, in the South it would be numerous and strong. (DA, p. 355)

The absence of legal barriers to mobility facilitates envy. An even more important factor, which presupposes the first but does not follow from it, is the presence of high de facto rates of mobility. In America, "wealth circulates with incredible rapidity, and experience shows that two successive generations seldom enjoy its favors" (DA, p. 54). In a society where fortunes are constantly being made and unmade, a poor man looking at a rich man can tell himself, plausibly: It could have been me. "In America I never met a citizen too poor to cast a glance of hope and envy towards the pleasures of the rich or whose imagination did not snatch in anticipation good things that fate obstinately refused to him" (DA, p. 531). Mobility induces hope as well as envy, because it allows both the thought "I may get it" and the thought "I could have had it."[161]

Tocqueville draws attention to cognitive as well as behavioral manifestations of envy. Concerning the first, he writes that "private citizens see men rising from their ranks and attaining wealth and power in a few years; that spectacle excites their astonishment and their envy; they wonder how he who was their equal yesterday has today won the right to command them. To attribute his rise to his talents or his virtues is inconvenient, for it means admitting that they are less virtuous or capable than he. They therefore regard some of his vices as the main cause thereof" (DA, p. 221). The operative causal factor in this tendentious interpretation is what I called (II.3) the first-order pain of envy, the damage done to one's self-esteem by admitting the superiority of another. Because an ordinary citizen will not envy a criminal his success, he adopts a view of politicians as corrupt that

161. Hirschman and Rothschild (1973) also emphasize this duality. In contemporary China, however, the culture of envy is so strong that the leaders feel compelled to emphasize that "it is ideologically correct for some of the citizens to become rich first" (*Renmin Ribao* 1984, cited after Mui 1995).

can short-circuit his feeling of inferiority. The counterfactual thought that "it could have been me" is irrelevant if it presupposes behavior he would be ashamed of engaging in.[162]

Considering behavioral expressions of envy, Tocqueville uses an historical analogy that we have already encountered: "Take a look at this opulent citizen. Might one not think him a medieval Jew afraid that his wealth should be suspected?" (DA, p. 179). Wealthy democratic citizens do everything to avoid being noticed and envied. Moreover, they also eventually come to understand that conferring benefits on the less wealthy will intensify envy rather than assuage it. "For benefits by their very greatness spotlight the difference in conditions and arouse a secret annoyance in those who profit from them" (DA, p. 512). Therefore the rich "are at pains not to get isolated from the people" (DA, p. 511), knowing that "what is wanted is not the sacrifice of their money but of their pride" (DA, p. 512).

The lack of outstanding politicians in democracies is due to fear of envy among the eminent as well as to envy among the less eminent. On the one hand, envy is the "secret instinct leading the lower classes to keep their superiors as far as possible from the direction of affairs" (DA, p. 198). On the other hand, because of the pervasiveness of envy the wealthy "prefer to leave the lists rather than to engage in an often unequal struggle against the poorest of their fellow citizens" (DA, p. 179). To the extent that the citizens knowingly exclude competent citizens from holding office,[163] they are cutting off their nose to spite their face (strong envy). Although they would benefit materially from having competent leaders, they are prepared to give up material benefits to assuage their envy. It is only in times of crises that these two obstacles disappear: "Then genius no longer hesitates to come forward, and the people in their fright forget their envious passions for a time" (DA, p. 199).

Envy preemption may also be behind the institution of compulsory military service, by which "the burden is spread equally and without discrimination among all the citizens. That too is a necessary result of their way of life and thought. A democratic government can do pretty well what it likes, provided that its orders apply to all and at the same moment; it is the inequality of a burden, not its weight, which

---

162. See also V.2 for a strikingly similar analysis in Netanyahu (1995) of the relation between the Spanish "conversos" and Old Christians.
163. The qualification is needed, as Tocqueville also suggests that the citizens may simply not be capable of distinguishing the more competent from the less competent politicians (DA, p. 198).

usually provokes resistance" (DA, pp. 651–2). To be sure, the move to compulsory military service or other impersonal modes of selection such as the draft lottery could also be motivated by considerations of fairness.

In democracies, "salaries seem to diminish as the power of the recipients increases" (DA, p. 213).[164] Tocqueville offers two explanations of this fact. On the one hand, "a poor man has no distinct idea of the needs which the upper classes of society may feel. What seems a moderate sum to a rich man strikes the man accustomed to be satisfied with necessities as prodigious, and he supposes that a state governor with his six thousand francs must feel himself lucky and be the object of envy" (DA, p. 213). This explanation relies on the lack of imagination of the citizens rather than on any particular motivation. The ordinary citizen is not said to envy the governor his income, only to assume that because he is generally envied he must be sufficiently paid. On the other hand, "the secondary official is almost on a level with the people, whereas the higher one dominates it. Thus the former may still excite its sympathy (*intérêt*), whereas the latter rouses envy" (DA, p. 213). Although the argument is far from clear, one reading is as follows. Because the lower official occupies a position deemed to be within reach of the ordinary citizens they do not begrudge him his salary, whereas the higher positions are so inaccessible that they have no personal interest in the salaries and thus are free to give vent to their envy. With regard to the lower positions, they think not only "I could have had that" but also "I can still have that," hope serving to temper envy. With regard to the salaries of higher officials, there is no brake on envy.

CONCLUSION

Some tentative conclusions to emerge from this discussion of envy in three societies – ancient Greece, prerevolutionary France, and nineteenth-century America – are the following. (i) The idea of neighborhood envy is generally confirmed. (ii) The object of envy can be a constant-sum good such as status or a variable-sum good such as income. Not surprisingly, status envy was central in the two status societies. (iii) As we would expect, malice or downwards jealousy is

164. The context makes it clear that this is not be taken literally; what he means is that in America "officials of secondary rank are better paid *than elsewhere*, but higher officials are much less well paid" (p. 212; italics added).

also important in these societies. (iv) Claims about envy-motivated income transfers in the status societies may be true but have not unambiguously been shown to be true. (v) Envy from below and malice from above may target the same individual, who is caught in a bind between enjoying the envy of his inferiors and fearing the malice of his superiors. (vi) Direct behavioral manifestations of envy are found mainly in the political realm: ostracism in Greece, voting for mediocrities and compressing the salaries of public officials in America. (vii) The indirect behavioral manifestations of envy – caused by fear of envy or the enjoyment of envy – take different forms in the three societies. Only in Greece do we find evidence for the existence of envy enjoyment and envy provocation. In the French village and in America, the rich hide their wealth rather than flaunting it. (viii) In both Greece and France we meet the idea that attempts to assuage envy by generosity is bound to backfire. These conclusions are obviously not based on in-depth study of any of the three societies. They are offered mainly to illustrate the idea that the social emotions and their expression are indeed shaped by the social context in which they arise.

III.4. HONOR, DUELS, AND FEUDS

Envy and malice are comparison-based emotions. In this section I discuss the interactive emotions clustered around the phenomenon of *honor*. More specifically, I consider the institutions of dueling and feuding that in many societies have served as vehicles for acquiring, maintaining, and losing honor.

The general idea of honor has, I believe, two main variants. For simplicity, I henceforward refer to the first as "glory," reserving "honor" for the second and more intensely interactive form. To understand glory, we can begin with the truism that in all societies certain actions, achievements, possessions, or character traits are valued or seen as "good." Instances of socially defined goodness include the ability to suffer pain without showing it, courage in the face of danger, military prowess, wealth or learning, modesty and humility, beauty, and strength. The members of society may, first, simply want to be good (a monadic property). Second, they may want to be better than others (a dyadic relation). Third, they may want to be seen to be good (another dyadic relation). Finally, they may want to be *seen as better than (all) others* (a triadic relation). Attainment of this end constitutes glory in its full-blown form.

Glory may be dyadic as well as triadic, if opposition and audience coincide. Yet in the cases I discuss here, the desire for glory is a desire to be viewed as superior by third parties. The desire to *be* good or better or the best may but need not coexist with the desire to *be seen as* good or better or the best. Although the overarching motivation of *amour-propre* generates both the desire for esteem and the desire for self-esteem, sometimes one is sacrificed for the sake of the other (II.3). In this section, I largely ignore such conflicts between *percipi* and *esse*. I also disregard the complication, briefly mentioned below, that the pursuit of glory may involve four categories of actors rather than three.

As defined here, glory seems entirely based on comparison rather than interaction. In practice, however, those who compete for the top rank are rivals who compete with an eye to each other as much as to the audience. It is not as if they first try to do as well as they can and then enjoy the limelight if they happen to come out on top. Rather, each is spurred to achievement by the presence and excellence of the competition. The reward from glory comes in no small part from knowing that the rival knows and resents that others believe him to be inferior to oneself. The cognitive antecedents of the emotion have at minimum three layers: I believe that he believes that others believe me to be superior. Higher-order phenomena are probably frequent.

To motivate the distinction between glory and honor, consider the difference between figure skating and boxing as competitive sports. In the former, each competitor is judged separately. At the end, the winner is declared to be the one with the best score. The participants never fight against each other. In boxing that is all they do. Here, competing takes the form of a face-to-face confrontation in which moral qualities such as courage are as important as skills. Now, courage can also be important in sports that do not involve face-to-face interactions. In alpine sports, for instance, "nerve" is very important. Yet in boxing – and by extension in feuding and dueling – it is a matter of showing courage towards another human being who is determined to hurt you. Boxers who lose their nerve, as did Ingemar Johansson in the 1956 Olympics, are accused of cowardice. Downhill skiers who lose their nerve are not.

I define honor, then, as being seen to show courage when trying to inflict damage on someone who tries (or might try) to do the same to oneself. Moreover, there can be no certainty of winning; some risk of losing is necessary if the behavior is to confer honor. This stipulative definition may not include all the phenomena that have been referred to under the heading of honor and are not instances of glory as just defined, but I believe it covers the central cases that I discuss below. Unlike glory, honor does not require success in the undertaking, as we shall see. For related reasons, honor, again unlike glory, is not a zero-sum phenomenon. A final difference is that whereas the pursuit of glory is often optional, the defense of one's honor is always mandatory. Again, I refer to the discussions below.

Like glory, honor may be dyadic as well as triadic. To show why in some cases three parties are needed to establish honor, let me first define a notion of *protohonor*, arising from the relation of domination and subordination described in Hegel's master–slave dialectic.[165] In a struggle for life and death, one of the protagonists surrenders to the other, thereby showing himself more attached to the material side of existence. He becomes the slave of the other, who emerges as the master. By risking his life, the master showed that he was more concerned with the recognition (*Anerkennung*) by the other of his superiority than with material security and well-being. Yet the master's satisfaction proves illusory, for who can gain honor from being recognized by a slave? The lack of worth of the slave also devalues any deference he confers on the master.

The master's search for recognition by the slave is inherently self-defeating as long as only these two actors are involved. The paradox is dissolved, and protohonor transformed into honor, when we add a third party – a public. By exposing oneself to the risk of death in the presence of a third party, one gains stature in the eyes of the onlooker. To be sure, a triumph over a known coward can never confer honor; in fact, it might detract from it.[166] But if it is only by backing down that the challenged person shows himself to be a coward, the challenger's honor is nevertheless enhanced, because *for all he knew* the challenge might have been taken up. The action has to be both courageous ex ante and recognized ex post by a party capable of conferring honor. A triadic relation satisfies both conditions. Yet honor can also be established in two-party interactions, if both fight valiantly and the loser is wounded but not mortally. In pistol dueling honor was enhanced even if neither party was hit, because for all they

165. Hegel (1982), pp. 112–6. See also Elster (1976b) and Elster (Chapter 4, 1978).
166. Billacois (1986, p. 359) cites from an Italian text from 1572: "The more we hold our opponent to be a man of honor, the greater will be our reputation and honor. Whereas if we hold him in contempt, if we try to make him out to be base and without honor, our own shame will grow by the fact that we pick a quarrel of honor with such a miserable person."

knew they might have been hit. Each of the two was then the witness and guarantor of the other's honor.

In ancient Greece, Kenneth Dover writes, "To earn the ultimate praise it was necessary either to win or to die."[167] There was no honor for surviving losers. Yet in less result-oriented cultures, demonstrable signs of having shown courage in the face of danger can be highly valued. In imperial Germany, for instance, facial scars left by saber dueling were highly prized as a sign of masculinity. Thus "[i]n a 1912 session of the Reichstag, one deputy contended that hardly anyone achieved high state office who had not undergone the requisite facial."[168] As this example shows, a presumably noninstrumental courage could have great instrumental value. I return to this point below.

We can distinguish among several types of emotions that arise in this context. The pursuit of glory and honor may be accompanied by specific emotions. Those who achieve these goals have characteristic emotional reactions, as do the losers. Also, observers may react with specific emotions to the attainment of, or failure to attain, glory and honor. Consider first the pursuit of honor. Because the pursuit of honor is strongly shaped by social norms, we would expect failure to act honorably to trigger the norm-related emotions of contempt in the observers and shame in the subject. Although the emotions triggered by the pursuit and achievement of honor do not have equally familiar names in English, they can be very strong, as we shall see.

Consider next the pursuit of glory. Because, as I said, this activity is often optional rather than mandatory, there is not necessarily any stigma of inferiority attached to those who do not join the competition (but see below for an exception). Those who do join, and then fail, may feel shame, humiliation, or just disappointment, depending on the social norms regulating the competition. In modern societies, winning an election is an occasion for glory, but there is no shame attached to losing. In early seventeenth-century England, as Mark Kishlansky has shown, the disgrace of losing an election was felt so keenly that people hesitated to stand unless they were sure to win; in fact, they might hesitate if they *had to* win, if they had to face an opposition. "Freely given by the will of the shire or the borough, a place in Parliament was a worthy distinction. Wrested away from

---

167. Dover (1994), p. 162.
168. McAleer (1994), p. 149. As very few duelists were actually killed in these encounters, it is perhaps more appropriate to refer to the test as one of showing courage in the face of *pain* rather than danger. (I owe this point to David Cohen.)

competitors in a divisive contest, it diminished the worth of both victor and vanquished."[169]

In societies or in spheres of social life where outcomes are regulated by competition, the emotion experienced by the winners is a variety of pride, triggered by the belief in one's own (socially defined) goodness. In general, pride does not require interaction with others. It can arise even in the monadic case: I may be quietly proud of my donations to charity, and even prouder of the fact that I hide them to others. It can also arise in either of the two dyadic cases that I described. Pride is likely to be especially intense, however, in the triadic case, in which esteem, self-esteem, and feelings of superiority merge into one delicious emotion.

Above I related shame and guilt to the beliefs, respectively, that one is a bad person and that one has done a bad thing. Several writers have drawn a similar distinction between the emotion resulting from the belief that one is a good person and the one arising from the belief that one has done a good thing.[170] I denote the former by pridefulness and the latter by pride. (The former term is also the one I used to translate "orgueil" in II.3.) Like pride, pridefulness can arise in the monadic case, in the two dyadic cases, and in the triadic case. Full-blown pridefulness stems from the belief that one is, and is thought by all to be, superior to all. Among the classical "exemplars," this megalomaniacal attitude is perhaps best instantiated by Alcibiades. "He had everything going for him. He had too much. How could he not think that his person came before everything else? . . . Beautiful, noble and rich, he ceased to take any account of others and thought that, in practice, everything was his due."[171]

HONOR BY ASCRIPTION OR BY ACHIEVEMENT

Honor, to be kept intact, must not suffer insults. Yet this is only one half of the story. The other half is that sometimes honor must be created before the need to preserve it can arise. Honor-based societies differ in this respect. In some societies, there is a presumption in favor of honor. Although it can be lost by shameful behavior, one

169. Kishlansky (1986), p. 17.
170. Tangney (1990) refers to these emotions as alpha and beta pride respectively. Lewis (1992, pp. 78–9) refers to them as hybris and pride. Montaigne draws a similar distinction between vainglory and glory in *Essays* II.17 and II.16.
171. Romilly (1996), pp. 32, 37.

does not have to – indeed, one cannot – acquire it through action. For women in Mediterranean societies, the analogue of honor is "shame" (sexual modesty), an attribute that "is negative, absolute (a woman either has it or does not – there are no degrees of shame), cannot be increased and can be demonstrated, as it were, only in the breach."[172] An analysis of feuding in Pakistan suggests that the same could be true of moral honor (*ghrairat*), as distinct from political honor (*aizzat*). "*Ghrairat* is perhaps best understood as personal worth or integrity. As Kohistanis explain, *ghrairat* is natural, a part of *imam*, and therefore a gift from God (in fact, God's most valuable gift). Every Muslim is born with *ghrairat*, and although it can be polluted by the actions of others, as one's shoe is polluted by stepping in manure, it can only be lost by the failure of its owner to protect it."[173] Contrasting French and Spanish notions of honor, François Billacois writes that "in a country where honour was not a conquest in which a man had to be recognized by his *fellow*, his equal, against whom he measured himself, but was instead a family treasure, an inheritance exclusively and passively held by women, which could be taken away at any moment by an *other*, someone irreducibly foreign, reparation was no longer a matter of duels, but of vendettas."[174]

In other societies, including some feuding and dueling societies, honor has been a matter of achievement rather than ascription. Before the age of the duel, one could achieve honor in tournaments. "As military exercises and warlike displays, they exalted the personal bravery of the winner, covering the warrior who showed cowardice, weakness or lack of skill in shame and ignominy."[175] In dueling societies, many engaged in deliberate provocation, to insult or offend another. Moreover, one could not achieve it by insulting just anybody. In Iceland, "The possession of honor attracted challenges, because that was where honor was to be had."[176] For a medieval knight, the "prime concern must be pursuit of distinction, and a challenge should never be rejected. Rather he should go out of his way to confront others."[177] Montaigne refers to "what is said by the Italians

---

172. Black-Michaud (1975), p. 218.
173. Lincoln-Keiser (1986), p. 500.
174. Billacois (1990), p. 39.
175. *Ibid.*, p. 16. Either my analysis is mistaken, or the assertion that defeat through lack of *skill* entailed shame and ignominy is.
176. Miller (1990), p. 33.
177. Kiernan (1986), p. 33. According to Veyne (1976, p. 382), however, honor was a matter of achievement in classical antiquity, but a matter of ascription in the Middle Ages.

when they wish to reprove that rash bravery found in younger men by calling them *bisognosi d'honore*, 'needy of honour:' they say that since they are still hungry for that reputation, which is hard to come by, they are right to go and look for it at any price – something which ought not to be done by those who have already acquired a store of it."[178] In many feuding societies, many acts are undertaken with the knowledge that a feud might ensue, and undertaken only because a feud might ensue, although not for the purpose of causing a feud.

The two concepts of honor – by achievement and by ascription – may coexist within a given society. In a study of urban gangs in contemporary America, Martín Sánchez Jankowski refers to the ascriptive concept as "honor" and the achieved one as "respect," differentiating them as follows:

"Respect" is something that is active – that is, it is the act of achieving deference. A gang member has to earn respect; it is not something that everyone has. In addition, once a person has earned respect, he must be willing to protect it, because a person's reputation depends upon respect, and reputation is an essential source for success. In contrast, "honor" is a passive trait that equates with dignity. Honor, for Chicano gang members, does not have to be earned. It is something that Chicano culture imparts to every person, but it is the recipient's obligation to preserve it. Thus, Chicanos enter the gang with honor, whereupon they must guard against it being taken away through the actions of others. Honor carries with it far more responsibility than respect. The Chicano gang member's honor is integrally tied to that of his entire family; he must protect both his honor and that of other members of his family.[179]

Among the societies I discuss here, honor in ancient Greece and seventeenth-century France seems to have been mainly by achievement, whereas Icelandic and Corsican honor was mainly by ascription. Yet the distinction should not be pushed too far. As noted previously, even in feuding societies people often go out of their way to insult others in order to gain honor or "respect." To achieve this end, actual fighting is not necessary. (Nor, as we shall see, is winning necessary if a fight occurs.) Honor – or "respect" – can be achieved or maintained by any act that carries with it a real risk of escalation into a fight, a duel, or a feud. The offender tries to capture or steal the honor

178. Montaigne (1991), p. 839. Bryson (1935, p. 28) cites a sixteenth-century Italian writer to the effect that "giving [insults] pertains to the nature of man; because everyone seeks distinction, one mark of which is to offend fearlessly."
179. Jankowski (1991), p. 142.

of the other, by betting that the other's instinct for self-preservation will be stronger than his feeling of outraged honor. The insulting party may also take care to leave the door open for several interpretations, if his goal is to humiliate the other rather than to provoke him into a fight. The target's desire for survival and his capacity for self-deception may deter him from retaliating, yet unbiased third parties will know that the challenger has won. Some individuals were no doubt addicted to violence: They issued provocations because they wanted to fight, not to gain a reputation by making the other back down.[180] Others might have wanted to fight because they perceived that it is more difficult to gain honor by issuing a challenge that is not taken up. But many engaged in brinksmanship, trying to have it both ways. Their desire for self-preservation was strong enough to make them phrase the challenges in ambiguous terms, in the hope that the other's desire for self-preservation would make him back down.

HONOR AND GLORY AMONG THE GREEKS

The pursuit of glory through competitive excellence was at the center of Greek society, by which here, as elsewhere, I mainly mean Athenian society in the fifth and fourth centuries B.C. I have already cited Kenneth Dover's observation that for the Greeks, "goodness divorced from a reputation for goodness was of limited interest." But what the Greeks sought was not simply a reputation for goodness, in the way labor arbitrators try to obtain a reputation for fairness or a car dealer a reputation for honesty. They chose arenas of interaction in which they might show that they were *better* than their rivals. To heighten the effect of praise, Aristotle says we may "point out that a man is the only one, or the first, or almost the only one who has done something, or that he has done it better than anyone else; all these distinctions are honourable" (*Rhetoric* 1368^{a}11–13). One might demonstrate superiority by objective criteria, as in sports, or by the judgment of third parties. Even in the former case, however, there must be an audience, which in the latter case also serves as judges of the performance. Functionally, in fact, the pursuit of glory involves four categories: The agent, his rivals, his audience, and his judges. I

---

180. A French duelist of this variety is described in Chapter 13 of Billacois (1990), who concludes by saying that he offered to his contemporaries an image "which had something of both Don Quixote and Don Juan about it" (p. 159).

shall, disregard, however, the distinction between the third and the fourth categories. In Athens, for practical purposes, the demos as a whole was audience as well as judge.

For the Athenians, *philotimia* or "love of honor [i.e., glory]" was a pervasive motivating force. Dover writes that "the Greeks tended to judge people not on a 'pass or fail' criterion, but by deliberately imparting a competitive character to as many aspects of life as possible (e.g., plays, songs and dances at festivals), and the wide difference between the treatment of winners and the treatment of losers augmented the incentive to excel."[181] Aeschylus, for instance, "wrote his plays for performance at a dramatic competition with the hope presumably of securing first prize"; hence when he left Athens for Sicily "it will occasion no surprise that one reason advanced in antiquity for his departure from Athens was professional chagrin, defeat at the hands of the young Sophocles or at the hands of Simonides."[182] Losing is always shameful; in fact "defeat is *aischron* [shameful] even when the gods cause it."[183]

The value attached to glory in the Greek world was so strong that shame could attach not only to losers but also to noncontestants. Thus in Xenophon's *Memorabilia* (III.7.1) Socrates and Charmides agree that "a man who was capable of gaining a victory in the great games and consequently of winning honour for himself and adding to his country's fame, and yet refused to compete" could only be a coward. Failure to compete for one's country because of fear of the shame of losing is as cowardly as failure to fight for one's country because of fear of dying. In fact, Dover observes that sometimes "patriotic" rather than "ambitious" is the proper translation of *philotimos*.[184] Yet it seems that the patriotic urge was typically secondary to ambition, in the sense that the desire to bring glory to the country was itself motivated by the glory that accrues to anyone who brings glory to his country. The opposite conclusion would violate Dover's axiom that "goodness divorced from a reputation for goodness was of limited interest." Thus the man who refuses to compete is ultimately shamed for failing to seek glory for himself. Thus for the Greeks, both the refusal to compete and loss in competition were causes for blame and shame. For us, neither is blameworthy or shameful.

181. Dover (1994), p. 232.
182. Walcot (1978), pp. 50, 51.
183. Adkins (1972), p. 60.
184. Dover (1994), p. 231.

The search for glory was often inextricably linked to the search for honor. In a study of Athenian litigation, David Cohen emphasizes both comparative and interactive aspects of the struggle for preeminence. In the first place, plaintiff and defendant were rivals: "[F]or those skilled in such activity, litigation provides a competitive setting where one seeks the pleasure of victory in a way comparable to gambling, hunting, or athletic competition."[185] It was not simply a question of being seen to be right in the particular case at hand. The participants were animated by pridefulness rather than by pride; they wanted to be seen as better *persons*. Because of the special features of the Athenian legal system, cases were won by persuading the jurors of one's own goodness or the opponent's badness, by (what appears to us to be) boasting and mudslinging. The paucity of written records often made it difficult to establish exactly what the facts were. To do so one had to rely on witnesses, which were notoriously unreliable. As a witness could not be cross-examined, he should be seen "not so much as a means of discovering the truth, but rather as a supporting actor who was offering to share the risks faced by his principal."[186]

In this situation, the jurors "could rely on little other than a general assessment of the character and standing of the parties and a calculation of what result will best serve an amalgam of justice and the interests of the *demos*."[187] There seem to be two independent but converging causes behind the (for us) extraordinary emphasis on character and personality. First there are the technical problems of Athenian litigation just mentioned. If you could establish that your opponent was a man worthy of contempt or hatred (II.2), you could argue to the jurors that the act he was accused of was "just the kind of thing he would do" even if you could not establish that he actually did it. The same argument applies in reverse to praise of oneself. Second, the tendency of the Greeks to think in terms of shame rather than guilt also made it natural for them to focus on characters rather than on actions.[188]

At the same time, Athenian litigation had strong elements of feuding and vengeance. "A long-standing feud, year after year of

185. D. Cohen (1995), p. 66.
186. Todd (1993), p. 96; see also D. Cohen (1995), p. 111.
187. D. Cohen (1995), p. 130; see also Todd (1993), p. 162, n. 20. For the role of interest in legal decisions, see the discussion of envy among the Greeks in the previous section.
188. Cairns (1993), p. 45.

provocation and retaliation, is a conspicuous phenomenon of the upper-class society with which, in the main, extant Attic oratory is concerned."[189] Cohen offers many examples to show that lawsuits were often part of an ongoing interaction in which the parties tried to humiliate each other by various means, litigation being only one. As in later times, these feuds had two goals. Initially, one party might seek to gain ascendancy on another by humiliating him. In subsequent stages, the goal was to achieve some kind of balance – to undo a wrong, to redress a harm. As we saw (II.2), these are also features of the Aristotelian conception of revenge. The balance, again as in later feuds, was notoriously hard to establish.[190] What was sufficient for one party might be too much or too little for the other. What La Rochefoucauld says about reciprocation for a gift also applies to retaliation for an offense: The response may seem inappropriate "due to the pridefulness of both giver and receiver, for they fail to agree upon the value of the kindness" (M225).

In legal feuds, the participants ascribed a number of motives to themselves and to the opponent: Justice, revenge, private interest, and envy. With regard to social acceptability, the motives seem to have been ranked in the order I have listed them. For my purposes here I want to emphasize how the revenge motive, occupying an intermediate position in the hierarchy, can be asserted in order to refute charges of an inferior motivation *or* denied in order to assert a superior one. Thus in a speech by Lysias (24.1–3), the orator anticipates that his opponent will claim to have acted for the sake of revenge and refutes him in advance by arguing that he only acted out of envy. Similarly, to deflect suspicions of frivolous prosecution, the plaintiff "could declare that the accused was his personal enemy and that he was using his citizen right to prosecute for revenge and not for gain."[191] Conversely, in his speech against Meidias Demosthenes (21.29–35) "emphasizes over and over again that to punish a transgressor of public order is not to deliver that transgressor over to his private enemy for vengeance."[192] Elsewhere Demosthenes admits to

189. Dover (1994), p. 182; also D. Cohen (1995), Chapter 5 and *passim*.
190. Todd (1993), p. 161.
191. Hansen (1991), p. 195. He also argues that this claim would be more credible than the claim to be acting in the public interest. It is easier for interest to misrepresent itself as passion than to present itself in the guise of reason (see also V.3).
192. D. Cohen (1995), p. 95; see also Dover (1994), pp. 188–9 for a similar case. Immediately before the cited passage, Demosthenes had tried to deflect suspicions that he was acting out of interest by pointing out that he chose to bring a public suit rather than a private suit that might have brought him financial gains. In

the motive of revenge but emphasizes that his suit was "a favourable opportunity for doing the State a service, and at the same time getting satisfaction for the wrongs I had suffered" (24.8). Being an emotional motivation, the desire for revenge was seen as inferior to the disinterested pursuit of justice, yet among the emotions it was much more acceptable than envy. I pursue this general theme in V.3.

As I noted above, love of honor could easily turn into *hybris*. In his exhaustive study of this notion in Greek literature and politics, N. R. E. Fisher argues convincingly (as far as I can judge) that it should not be understood in the modern sense of "excessive self-confidence." Rather, as I mentioned earlier, it must be understood as the deliberate humiliation of others for the sheer pleasure of the act. Although *hybris* typically refers to a specific kind of behavior, I shall also use the term to refer to the emotion associated with that behavior. It is closely related to pridefulness, in the full-blown variety that involves the belief that one is intrinsically superior to all others. It involves the pleasure of being able to do evil with impunity, the most potent of all rewards from wealth and power; the malicious pleasure of watching another squirm or shrink in shame; and the sadistic pleasure of being the one who makes him suffer. A paradigm of *hybris* is Meidias's public slapping of Demosthenes, expounded and condemned at length in the latter's speech against the former. A temporally extended paradigm is offered by the life of Alcibiades, "the most hybristic of those who lived under the democracy" in Xenophon's words (*Memorabilia* 1.2.12). For an analysis of the finer nuances of *hybris* I also refer to an extended quotation from Fisher's work in V.3.

The relation between *hybris* and honor is complex. Although Fisher does not explicitly assert that the pursuit of honor was an invariable component of *hybris*, he comes very close to saying so when he asserts that "the essential meaning of *hybris* for Aristotle [is] the deliberate insulting of other people, in pursuit of one's own *honour* and pleasure" and that "Aristotle's account is an essentially accurate representation of the Greek concept."[193] I shall assume, therefore, that he does hold this view. Fisher also asserts, quite unambiguously, that *hybris* always involved the (pleasurable) dishonoring of others. He seems committed, therefore, to the zero-sum view of honor: The interaction that adds to one person's honor must detract from that of another.

the end, however, he did gain financially, when Meidias paid him to drop the suit. According to his enemy Aeschines (3.52), his motives were dishonorable; according to Plutarch's *Life* (12.2), they were not.

193. Fisher (1992), pp. 25, 7; my italics.

Before I proceed, we must ask whether the idea of honor involved here is the same as the one I gave earlier. The behavior of Meidias fits well with the definition of honor as an attempt to inflict damage on another at some cost or risk to oneself. Slapping someone in public is a paradigmatic case of struggle between equals for the purpose of gaining honor at the other's expense. Meidias took a risk and in fact had to pay a cost (he paid Demosthenes to drop the case). Other cases, which do not involve equals, are more puzzling. They do not involve honor as I defined it; moreover, there does not seem to be *any* plausible concept of honor in which these interactions had a zero-sum nature.

Consider first *hybris* against inferiors, notably slaves, women, and youth. One might think (i) that a slave had no honor to lose, and (ii) that no honor could be gained from insulting him. Arguing against the first proposition Fisher asserts that "while of course it is a recognised principle that slaves may be judicially tortured or punished by corporal beatings which would be a denial of a free man's status, some brutal and degrading physical maltreatment, or non-judicial torture, could seem to be a denial of a slave's status and honour as human beings, and therefore could be *hybris*, especially if done, as it might well be, for the sadistic delight in exercising such power."[194] He does not, however, try to establish the second proposition. In particular, he does not mention the idea that if *hybris* against slaves was against someone else's slave, it could be seen as a vicarious attack on the honor of the owner and thus confer honor on the hybristic person.

By contrast, Fisher does mention that *hybris* against women, whether in the form of rape or of seduction, could be undertaken to shame the male members of their household.[195] Similarly, a man who has a homosexual relation with a boy still under the guardianship of his father commits *hybris* against the latter.[196] This argument does not apply to the behavior of Alcibiades, however, when he committed *hybris* against his own wife by bringing *hetairai* into his house so that she had to leave. It may have given him pleasure to flaunt his immorality and go in the face of social norms – but it is hard (for us) to imagine that it could also have brought him honor. Similarly, there were charges of homosexual *hybris* that did not involve third parties.[197] Once again, it is hard to see how honor could be gained by

194. *Ibid.*, p. 59.
195. *Ibid.*, p. 105.
196. *Ibid.*, p. 42.
197. *Ibid.*, pp. 108–10.

inflicting "disgusting practices" on one's boyfriend. In upshot, *hybris* against an inferior confers honor only if it also dishonors a person of equal status to oneself who is responsible for him or her.

There are also instances of *hybris* being committed *by* inferiors. "From the point of view of those who feel they are in a superior position, to be treated 'familiarly,' as an equal, to be disobeyed or to be given orders by those whom one believes to be beneath one, is demeaning, insulting or outrageous and can be called *hybris*."[198] In this case, too, it is hard to see that the hybristic inferior gains in honor what is lost by the target or object of the *hybris*. A slave who gets away with disobeying his master might gain prestige among other slaves, but that is hardly what the Greeks or anyone else have understood by honor. I conclude, therefore, that in general one cannot obtain honor by hybristic acts. The conclusion is reinforced by the fact, mentioned above, that the Greeks strongly disapproved of hybristic behavior. In fact, as we shall see in V.3, the general disapproval of *hybris* created an inducement to present hybristic acts as really caused by other motives – anger, sexual desire, revenge, or drunkenness. If honor is valued, as it certainly was among the Greeks, any act conferring honor should also be valued. As *hybris* was not valued, it could not confer honor. The Greeks were certainly fascinated by Alcibiades, but they did not honor him.

FEUDS AND DUELS

Among the Greeks, the aim of the elite feuding I have described was not to kill the opponent, but to dishonor and humiliate him in public. Moreover, the target of revenge had to be the very person who had offended one; retaliation against a brother or cousin was not a full substitute. Finally, the means employed in the feuds were largely unconstrained by social norms. These generalizations may admit to exceptions, but I believe they are roughly true, at least when we compare the Greek feuds with the Icelandic and Mediterranean feuds that I discuss below. In these societies, feuding was murderous, took place between families rather than between individuals, and was highly regulated by social norms.

A phenomenon that has similarities with both is the duel. Like the vendetta, duels are murderous and highly norm-regulated. Like

198. *Ibid.*, p. 117.

feuding among the Greeks, the duel targeted individuals rather than groups. (An exception arises when seconds join in the fighting.) An implication of the fact that the duel was both murderous and involved specific individuals was that it usually came to a definite end when one of the enemies had been killed. By contrast, nonmurderous individual feuding (as in Greece) or murderous family feuds (as in Iceland or the Mediterranean countries) can go on for a long time, within and across generations, whence the importance of "balance."

Feuds and duels involve what looks like pointless killing, a meaningless waste of human lives. Historians and social scientists are often reluctant, however, to admit this perspective. Instead they try to account for these institutions in terms of some individual or social purpose they might serve. First, revenge behavior might have a genetic basis, based on the higher reproductive fitness of vindictive individuals. Evolution could develop "vengeance genes" that predispose individuals to seek revenge when their reproductive interests are harmed, even if the retaliation involves some cost or risk to the avenger in excess of the extent, if any, to which the original damage is undone. Second, revenge might be individually rational, an argument that comes in two versions. On the one hand, an individual might rationally seek to develop a reputation for being irrationally vindictive; on the other hand, revenge might be part of a tit-for-tat equilibrium in iterated games. Third, even if individually irrational these practices might serve some wider social function, such as maintaining an exclusive elite (duels), regulating population size (vendettas), or keeping conflicts down to a tolerable level (vendettas).

I shall not repeat the arguments that I have offered elsewhere against these reductionist theories.[199] Broadly speaking, their common flaw is their highly speculative nature. They are based on "as-if" or "just-so" stories of one kind or another, without any serious attempt to provide evidence and mechanisms. Nor shall I try to provide an alternative explanation of these behavioral propensities. Instead, I shall try to sketch some of the modalities of interaction of emotion, social norms, and rational self-interest that we observe in duels and vendettas. I am too impressed by the variety and diversity of these phenomena to be tempted to construct an all-encompassing theory that would account for them all. Although some general ideas will emerge, they are more of the nature of mechanisms than theories.

199. Elster (1990).

FEUDING IN MEDIEVAL ICELAND

In *Bloodtaking and Peacemaking* William Miller provides a rich account of feuding in medieval Iceland. In addition to legal documentation, the book relies heavily on fictional sources, the sagas. As many of these stories were written centuries after the events they describe, they can hardly be taken for veridical historical records. Miller argues, and I have no reason to disagree, that they nevertheless provide reliable insights into Icelandic social structure. They identify the social norms that prescribe or proscribe specific forms of behavior in conflictual situations, and they help us understand how the actors were able, within limits, to manipulate these norms in their own interest. As in the case of dueling, the ostensibly noninstrumental goal of honor was pursued with a great deal of regard for material benefits and sheer survival.

Miller defines the feud by the following features: (1) It is a hostile relation between two groups. (2) It is different from ad hoc revenge killing. (3) Unlike war, a feud does not involve large mobilization. (4) A feud involves collective liability. (5) A feud is governed by alternations (taking turns). (6) People keep score. (7) The feud is related to a culture of honor. (8) The feud is governed by norms that limit the class of possible expiators and the appropriate responses. (9) There are culturally acceptable means for settling conflicts.[200] To these features we might add the following, also taken from Miller's account. (10) The tit-for-tat aspect of the feud is closely related to the norms of gift-giving. "The model takes over the entire vocabulary of exchange and inverts it."[201] (11) The interval between each killing should neither be too short nor too long. As one saga has it, "Only a slave avenges himself immediately, but a coward never does."[202] (12) In feuding, "success was more important than glorious failure. ... Parties showed little hesitation in taking advantage of uneven odds."[203]

Feature (11), in particular, throws light on the motivation behind feuding. "The fact that the next move belonged to the members of the avenging party conferred a power on them. It was the power to terrorize, the power to instill fear and anxiety, the power to impose the very real costs of being on the defensive.... Saga characters speak

200. Miller (1990), pp. 180–1.
201. *Ibid.*, p. 182.
202. *Ibid.*, pp. 83, 193.
203. *Ibid.*, p. 195.

of the deliciousness of the slow hand. 'And the longer vengeance is drawn out the more satisfying it will be.'"[204] This analysis has a number of implications. First, we recognize a theme from Aristotle: Vengeance should aim at making the enemy suffer rather than die. Second, in a typical feud the enemy ultimately *has* to die, because his suffering is caused by and is indissociable from his fear of death. Third, the enemy suffers not only materially and emotionally: He is also attained in his honor. The taking of precautions is easily interpreted as a sign of dishonorable pusillanimity.[205] Fourth, although it is not clear why immediate revenge is dishonorable, one possibility is that it indicates a lack of self-control characteristic of slaves.[206] Another possibility is that immediate revenge suggests a dishonorable fear of a preemptive attack, in case the opponent should break the norm of my-turn-your-turn or the norm itself yield ambiguous predictions. Fifth, indefinite delay of revenge might induce suspicion that the offended party is motivated by fear rather than by a desire to savor the opponent's fear.

Miller does not make the suggestion that feuds were initiated for the purpose of self-affirmation or the attainment of honor. Rather, he describes a society in which people were extremely quick to take offense at any action that might be seen, however remotely or improbably, as an attack on their honor. As in ancient Greece, the idea of accidentally caused harm was not credible. "Neither law nor society was especially amenable to claims of accident when made by the injured party ... it was more than a misfortune to be a victim of an accident, it was also a dishonor ... Close friends and kin have accidents, enemies do not; a hostile intent will be supplied."[207] Even requests to purchase a good could, under suitable circumstances, be read as insulting. Thus in one story A asks B to sell him hay which A is to give to his tenant C, when A could also have obtained the hay from his friend D. B's surly refusal to sell, triggering A's taking

---

204. *Ibid.*, p. 193.
205. *Ibid.*, pp. 193–4.
206. William Miller (personal communication) adds that "immediate revenge is dishonorable also because it is stupid, another characteristic of slaves. It relinquishes too cheaply the advantage of being able to terrorize your opponent and to make him suffer by fearing whether or not he will disgrace himself." We may note that duels are different in this respect. "Once resolved on, combats took place with only brief delay ... Any long interval would have suggested to busybodies that one or both parties were hesitating" (Kiernan 1986, p. 146); same observation in Billacois (1990), p. 239.
207. Miller (1990), pp. 66, 67.

that "no one would consider his [bleeding and fainting] shameful." But because of the general nervousness about shame in this society, Thorhall is not appeased by the judgment of his friends. He is only too aware of the style of competition which would use any ambiguous unconventional act to the detriment of someone's reputation if it could be so used: "and he said nothing could stop what people would say."[215]

Again, Thorhall's reaction might be due to the ambiguous relations of expression to emotion. Because he believes that observers might ascribe his fainting to a shameful emotion such as fear, he is doubly eager to take revenge, not only to undo the affront but also to dispel any erroneous impressions about his lack of courage.

Miller's recent book is a useful supplement to his first. It shows that the concern for honor does not generate behavior directly, but that the link is mediated by a complex set of emotional states. These include not only emotions triggered immediately by behavior, but also emotions caused by thoughts about other people's emotions and by thoughts about their thoughts about one's own emotions. The thought that others might think one afraid was fueled by the knowledge that they were eager to put the worst possible construal on one's behavior. In this atmosphere of intense suspicion it took little to trigger revenge and feuds. To some extent, to be sure, this atmosphere also had a deterrent effect. If the slightest slight can escalate into a full-blown feud, there is an incentive to be circumspect in words and behavior. Against this, however, there is the fact that too much circumspection is dishonorable. Medieval Iceland was a minefield in which even being immobile might get you blown up.

DUELING IN EARLY MODERN EUROPE

Among the various modes of confrontation discussed in this section, the duel demonstrates most vividly the tension between the demands of honor and the demands of self-interest. Given the ideology according to which the duel embodied "the proud indifference to consequences,"[216] any kind of instrumental concern was dishonorable. The purpose of the duel is not to win, but to expose oneself to danger. Montaigne argued, for instance, that the use of skill in face-to-face confrontations is dishonorable:

215. *Ibid.*, p. 102; brackets in original.
216. Kiernan (1986), p. 161.

And as I myself know from experience [fencing] is an art which has raised the hearts of some above their natural measure; yet that is not really valour since it draws its support from skill and has some other foundation than itself. The honour of combat consists in rivalry of heart not of expertise; that is why I have seen some of my friends who are past masters in that exercise choosing for their duels weapons which deprived them of the means of exploiting their advantage and which depend entirely on fortune and steadfastness, so that nobody could attribute their victory to their fencing rather than to their valour. When I was a boy noblemen rejected a reputation for fencing as being an insult; they learned to fence in secret as some cunning craft which derogated from true inborn virtue.[217]

Unlike Montaigne's friends, these latter noblemen didn't mind being good at fencing, but they minded being seen as having taken steps to acquire the skill. The grip of honor on their minds was not complete, because they did learn to fence, but the norms of honor did force them to learn in secret. They wanted to be seen as honorable – but also to survive. We also find Pascal and La Rochefoucauld discussing this issue, with opposite conclusions. The former asserts, "We even die gladly provided people talk about it" (*Pensée* 521). La Rochefoucauld – who like Montaigne had seen a great deal of military action – had a more realistic perspective. "In time of war most men will face just enough danger to keep their honour intact, but few are prepared to go on doing so long enough to ensure the success of the enterprise for which the danger is being faced" (M219).

The history of dueling is full of similar compromises. Frederick Bryson observes, for instance, that in sixteenth-century Italy it made a great difference whether one insulted by word or by act.[218] To an insult by words, such as, "You are a traitor," the proper response usually was to give the lie to the other person. To redress his honor, the latter might then issue a challenge to duel, in which the insulted party would then have the choice of arms. To an insult by act – a kick, blow, or slap – the proper response often was a challenge to duel, in which the insulting party would have the choice of arms. A further complication arose if the accusation by word was known to be true. The insulted could then not give the lie, "but one might answer, 'In saying so-and-so you have acted unjustly,' whereupon the first speaker could reply, 'In saying that I have acted unjustly, you lie'. The other party would then, in case of a duel, become the challenger

217. Montaigne (1991), pp. 790–1; see also pp. 237–8.
218. Bryson (1935), p. 39 ff.

submitted to it without the least cheerfulness.... 'They often do it to keep up appearances rather than because they want to,' said P. Caussin in 1624. 'Their blood runs cold at the thought of the danger to which they are exposing themselves.' Some fought out of conformism; others to glorify their difference. To fight a duel was to set oneself off from society (*se mettre en marge*). To shy away from a duel was also to set oneself off.[227]

Initiation of a duel may be triggered by "boiling anger" at some real or imagined offense, or by a "furious passion" for distinction. The appearance of either motivation, however, could merely be instrumental rationality in disguise. "How many times did cold calculation concerning ways to distinguish oneself and advance one's career lie behind the unthinking intoxication of public display of courage?... Montaigne's brother-in-law Pressac ... observes that those who are punctilious about honour act no differently from ... 'those who parade their desire for such fights and who, voluntarily, seek them out, assuming that they will thus acquire the reputation of being men of worth and of good service: in which they are in practice doing nothing other than seeking personal profit and advantage.'"[228] Dueling, on this reading, was a form of signaling – an enterprise that is inherently pointless apart from revealing the possession of qualities that might be useful in other contexts.[229] This rational-choice explanation of dueling differs from the usual tit-for-tat explanation of revenge behavior. The latter can at most explain retaliation against violence, not the initiation of violence.

Pascal did not see that the dueling could be due to a passion for distinction – a desire to stand out rather than a desire to conform. According to Billacois, he also missed another important aspect of the duel: "Pascal understands nothing of reparation which is not vengeance, of a fight desired and agreed upon by both parties, a confrontation which is the outcome of a pact, a murder which is proof of esteem for the victim, indeed which gives him back this esteem, and which can be a proclamation of profound solidarity between the two combatants."[230] In this slightly opaque passage we need only retain the idea that honor is not a constant-sum phenomenon. Defeat in a duel does not imply dishonor. As a contemporary put it, "no

227. Billacois (1986), p. 136.
228. Billacois (1990), p. 78.
229. This suggests a "screening theory of dueling," analogous to the screening theory of education (Spence 1973).
230. Billacois (1990), p. 138.

one loses in this game unless he surrenders like a coward to save his life."[231]

Defeat and *surrender* are in fact entirely different outcomes. To fight a duel and lose (while surviving) is to show a courage that confers honor: Not only does the loser not lose honor, he gains it. "A death he has not sought to flee transfers the loser into a hero. It could almost be said that it did not matter whether or not a duelist lost, as long as he proved his courage."[232] In this case, honor is positive-sum. Surrender, by contrast, is entirely dishonorable. As Hegel noted, in purely dyadic terms the implication is that a duel that ends because one party surrenders is negative-sum in honor. The party who surrenders loses his honor, and *for that very reason* the other gains no honor from the victory. To be recognized as superior by a person without honor does not confer the *recognition* that is at the core of honor, whence the need for a third-party audience.

Yet even when the loser suffers defeat rather than surrenders, his recognition – although in this case worth having – is not the main goal of the duel. The duelists sought general reputation rather than merely recognition by the adversary. According to Billacois, publicity was in fact essential for the duel. Unlike the Spanish, who took revenge in secret, sometimes using hired killers, the French gentleman wanted to be seen, hence the tension generated by the royal ban on duels: "[E]ven though gentlemen practiced duels *alla macchia* (constrained to do so by the antithetic requirements of honour and prohibition), they did not like them, and indeed disapproved of them. For the practice ran contrary to the very reason underlying the phenomenon of the duel, the importance of appearances. How indeed could one prove one's worth without the presence of witnesses, and how could one found a reputation on a furtive, dissimulated act?"[233]

In dueling, what mattered was winning rather than killing. According to Billacois, the ideal-typical duel (although not necessarily the most important statistically) brought together "men without anger or

---

231. *Ibid.*, p. 52. It follows that in the case of defeat (as distinct from surrender), the winner should never force the loser to beg for mercy (*ibid.*, p. 214). In practice, however, this principle was not always respected. Thus Saint-Simon (1953–1961, vol. 1, p. 82) recounts how his father, having disarmed his opponent in a duel, "wanted him to beg for his life; but he would not do so. My father said that he would at least disfigure him; [his opponent] said he was too generous to do so, but that he would admit to being defeated." Here, it is clear that the duelist wanted his opponent to suffer, either psychologically or physically.
232. *Ibid.*, pp. 52–3.
233. Billacois (1990), p. 121.

hatred and free of everything in vengeance that is stained with emotion. In practice, as is abundantly apparent in the French sources, this requirement produced two attitudes: respect for the opponent (before the fight) and the absence of any intention to kill him (even if a duelist did his best to kill his opponent, and sometimes succeeded)."[234] The most convincing argument for this view is found in the importance of seconds, who risked their lives because they were under the pressure of strong social norms that made it dishonorable to refuse a demand to serve as a second.[235]

This is not to say that dueling had no emotional roots. As we have seen, action guided by social norms is ultimately supported by emotions. Moreover, the initiation of a duel for the purpose of self-affirmation and recognition by competent others must in many cases have had a strong emotional component. Young men who are *bisognosi d'honore* may not feel shame, as long as there is no particular occasion on which they fail to do what is required, yet they will feel an anguish of incompleteness until they have proven themselves. Finally, many of those who were arbitrarily singled out as occasions for the self-affirmation of others must have taken up the challenge out of anger rather than from fear of social ostracism.

THE MEDITERRANEAN VENDETTA

The best-studied cases of feuding involve the Mediterranean societies. Although there are many useful accounts by local observers, travelers, or anthropologists,[236] the outstanding work on the topic is by an historian. Stephen Wilson's *Feuding, Conflict, and Banditry in Nineteenth-Century Corsica* provides an immense wealth of detail and insights that is not matched, even remotely, by any other study. Once again I do not try to summarize his findings, but focus on the aspects of the analysis that are most relevant for the present purposes.[237] Occasionally I shall also cite studies of other countries in the region to illustrate specific points, on the assumption that the Mediterranean

---

234. *Ibid.*, p. 213.
235. *Ibid.*, p. 66.
236. For Corsica, see Busquet (1920). For Albania, see Hasluck (1954). For Montenegro, see Boehm (1984) and Djilas (1958). For a wider Mediterranean perspective, see Black-Michaud (1975).
237. In the following, parenthetical page references are to Wilson (1988). Citations within the cited passages are taken from contemporary records.

feuding societies were roughly similar in most relevant respects. As the assumption may be controversial, I do not rely heavily on these other studies.

The very richness of Wilson's study is based on a feature of Corsican society that also makes it somewhat atypical, namely that it "belongs to that small number of societies where feuding survives into the modern period within purview of agents of a relatively efficient bureaucratic State" (p. 17). Legal and administrative records provide extremely detailed accounts of feuds – their origin, their development, their settlement, their reemergence, and so on. Because vendettas led to murders and the judicial system had the task of capturing, prosecuting, and convicting the killers, the bureaucracy inevitably gathered a great deal of information about the feuds. But the state apparatus was an actor as well as an observer – an actor, moreover, whose presence changed and modified the vendetta compared with feuding societies in which the state had more of a low-level presence. Many feuds were in fact largely conducted through the court system. Conversely, the legal procedures were heavily shaped by the background environment of feuding. I shall ignore this issue, which is incidental to my purpose here, but the reader is strongly encouraged to read Wilson's fascinating chapter on feuding and the courts.

In nineteenth-century Corsica, vengeance killings had an extent and an intensity rarely seen elsewhere. "Corsica was ... at the upper end of any scale of human societies measured by the incidence of killing and interpersonal violence within them. Significantly higher homicide rates are only found regularly among certain 'primitive' peoples addicted to warfare ... or for very brief periods and among limited sections of 'advanced' societies" (p. 15).[238] As for the sheer ferocity of the killings, we may cite an instance from 1845 in which "Antono Santalucia ... shot Antono Quilichini, the sixth of the witnesses against his brother in the 1840 trial to be killed" (p. 30), and one in which "a notary from Novale was convicted of homicide on false testimony and subsequently died in prison. His brother became a bandit and over a period of years killed all 14 prosecution witnesses" (p. 280). Another episode that provides a glimpse into this mental universe occurred in 1881, when a woman killed her rival's "ten year

238. Nisbett and Cohen (1996, p. 1) cite calculations that imply even substantially higher rates of homicide in certain regions of the American South – another "culture of honor."

old son when she was unable to find any other target. She then gave herself up and received a very lenient sentence, which reflected the view that she had been largely justified in her action" (pp. 100–1).

We may distinguish among several "decision points" in a feud.[239] There is the decision to initiate a feud (A), the decision to retaliate (B), and the decision to stop (C). The second decision can be repeated several times. As Montaigne said, "The first acts of cruelty are done for their own sake; from them there is born a fear of just revenge; that produces a succession of fresh cruelties, each intended to smother each other" (*Essays*, p. 793). The basic structure of a feud is, therefore, {A,B,B ... B,C}. As we shall see, the whole cycle could itself be repeated several times, thus generating feuds of indefinite duration.

According to a nineteenth-century writer cited by Wilson (p. 197), "there were four circumstances which justified or required vengeance: when a woman had been dishonoured, when an engagement had been broken, when a close relative had been killed, and when false testimony in court led to the conviction of a member of one's family." These are all cases of vengeance for the sake of maintaining one's honor. The system of honor also included, however, actions undertaken for the purpose of gaining honor (pp. 99, 100, 173), notably by young men who are "needy of honor." Such actions were risky, and in fact undertaken because they were risky. As Christopher Boehm writes about feuding in another Mediterranean society, "a Montenegrin male ... had to take into consideration the possibility of starting a feud whenever he asserted himself in such a way as to impugn seriously the honor of another person. While offering insults was an expected mode of maintaining honor, he also knew that his stronger provocations might get him killed."[240]

Envy could also be at the origin of feuds:

[An] example of the hatred which the *nouveau riche* could attract was seen at Ampriani in 1832, where the mayor Giovan-Battiste Lota was killed by Pasquale Negroni. Lota was a wealthy pharmacist who came originally from Penta-di-Casinca, and 'the fortune which he had acquired, the influence which he exercised in the region, excited the envy of Negroni, who could not stand seeing an outsider dictating to the inhabitants of his village.' (p. 85)

The conflict which we have described reflects an intense competition for scarce material resources, and this was perceived by actors and observers

239. Boehm (1984), Chapter 8.
240. *Ibid.*, p. 145.

at the time. 'The ordinary acts of revenge carried out in the Tallano district for some time now,' the subprefect commented in 1820, 'are to destroy livestock, to throw down enclosures, to cut fruit trees and to damage vines. Everyone seeks to impoverish his antagonist.' But land and property were not . . . simply an economic resource; they were a means to power and prestige. . . . This is well conveyed by an anecdote from a village in La Rocca. . . . A young boy heard that a man had been killed and asked his father why. 'He had cleared some land' was the only reply. The man had in effect wished to increase the amount of land which he cultivated. This would have in turn increased his income and thus enhanced his political influence, something which his enemies could not tolerate. The same point was made, with different emphasis, by the Corsican writer Salvator Viale in 1853: 'The wealth and dignity of a man, and his credit, can create enmities towards him among the people of his village; sometimes the acquisition or extension of a field, a new house or the improvement of an old one, even putting up shutters or hangings by windows, can be the origin of envy and ill-will.' Conflicts of material interest and conflicts of honour were thus inextricably linked in Corsica. (p. 89)

Both passages assert that envy can create new enmities. The second adds that it can also reinforce existing ones to the point at which a killing follows. From the second we also learn that behavior that might seem like sheer envy, destroying another's property at no profit to oneself, could in fact be a low-grade form of vengeance. Wilson has extensive discussions of such nonmurderous forms of vengeance directed against property or animals (e.g., pp. 51, 69–70, 76–84), adding that they could easily escalate into vengeance killings.

Feuds could also arise by accident. As in Greece and Iceland, actions were judged mainly by their outcomes rather than by their intentions. Specifically, the Corsicans seem to have been reluctant to draw a distinction between accidental and intentional murder. When Giuseppo Petrignani was killed by a salvo fired during a celebration, "a man called Peretti was arrested and convicted of involuntary homicide, but the Petrignani refused to believe that the killing had been an accident and Giuseppo's father 'manifested the intention of seeking revenge'" (p. 43). In general, "little distinction was drawn at village level between accidental and deliberate killings, though the courts drew the distinction very clearly. Antono Belfini of Zicavo, for example, was sentenced to only eight months' imprisonment around 1830 for the accidental killing of Silvestro Giordani of Bastelica. The latter's family saw this as a totally inadequate punishment and arranged to have Belfini killed by bandits when he came out of prison" (pp. 289–90). The Corsicans, again like the Greeks and the Icelandics, were quick to believe the worst. Thus unsubstantiated rumor and gossip could have severe consequences:

Once a girl had been compromised or seduced, and particularly if she were pregnant, pressure was brought on the man and his family to agree to a marriage.... Sometimes the mere rumour that a seduction had occurred was sufficient to set this procedure in motion. In 1840, for example, 'at the time of the wheat hoeing,' Cornelia Cartucci of Arbarella had gone down to the plain of Taravo with several other people, including Antono Rutilj. Although they claimed that they had not even spoken to each other, some children spread the rumour that there had been intimacy between the two. 'From that moment Cornelia believed not only that her honour had been compromised, but also that it was Rutilj's duty to marry her.' Her brother and her uncle concurred in this view and informed Rutilj accordingly. When he protested that he had had nothing to do with her as she well knew, she agreed but added that 'the fact is that because of you, no one else will marry me.' Rutilj maintained his refusal despite further threats and was eventually killed by Cornelia's brother. (p. 104)

Once an initial offense had occurred, for whatever reason, subsequent acts of violence could be rooted in one of three emotions: anger, hatred, and fear. Anger – or "wrath" as we should probably say here (II.2) – was the dominant emotion. In revenge societies the spontaneous urge to retaliate against an offender is immensely strengthened by social norms requiring retaliation. As Wilson's administrative sources has nothing to say about the subjective experience of revenge, we must supplement him by other sources. For a sixteenth-century French writer on duels, "vengeance is pure voluptuousness."[241] In an account of life in his childhood Montenegro, Milovan Djilas elaborates on the same theme:

This land was never one to reward virtue, but it was always strong in taking revenge and punishing evil. Revenge is its greatest delight and glory. Is it possible that the human heart can find peace and pleasure only in returning evil for evil?... Revenge is an overpowering and consuming fire. It flares upon and burns away every other thought and emotion. It alone remains, over and above everything else ... Vengeance ... was the glow in our eyes, the flame in our cheeks, the pounding in our temples, the word that had turned to stone in our throats on our hearing that blood had been shed ...

241. Cited after Billacois (1986), p. 358.

Vengeance is not hatred, but the wildest and sweetest kind of drunkenness, both for those who must wreak vengeance and for those who wish to be avenged.[242]

In general, the intoxication subsided when the vengeance had been accomplished and the equilibrium restored. In some feuds, however, the driving emotion seems to have been hatred of the opposing family rather than anger at a specific action. "There are indications that the killing of children characterized feuds of particular bitterness or 'bad feuds' aimed at the total extinction of rival families" (p. 209). Also killing of women "was indicative of a 'bad feud,' in which women were involved as victims not only in themselves but also as future child-bearers. In such feuds the aim was to eliminate one's enemies completely" (p. 218). These "'[b]ad feuds,' in which enemies swore to exterminate each other and where immunities were flouted, were clearly the most disruptive but they were not the most common form" (p. 239).

The role of fear is more complex. Let me postpone the issue of fear of the shame one would incur by failure to fulfill one's duty to take revenge and consider only killing undertaken out of fear for one's life. It is important here to distinguish between two concepts of fear.[243] On the one hand, talk about fear may simply refer to a certain complex of beliefs and desires. We believe that unless we do something to prevent it, X will happen. We don't want X to happen. Hence if it is not too costly or difficult, we try to prevent it. All of this can obtain in the absence of any emotional reaction whatsoever, as when we say we're afraid of getting wet in the rain. On the other hand, talk about fear may refer to the visceral emotional state, as when we believe ourselves to be in acute and imminent danger. Hence killing someone out of fear might be either a rational preemptive action or a (possibly counterproductive) act of panic.

Drawing on Prosper Mérimée's novella *Colomba*, which takes place in Corsica, Russell Hardin argues that vengeance killings were rational, preemptive acts undertaken out of self-interest.[244] Killing the children of your enemy is a rational way to prevent them from killing

---

242. Djilas (1958), pp. 86, 105, 106, 107.
243. Gordon (1987), p. 77 and *passim*.
244. Hardin (1995), pp. 120–2. He does not cite textual evidence in the novella, however, to favor this prudential interpretation over one that imputes hatred to the protagonists, nor have I found any such evidence in the work.

you when they grow up. Wilson notes in fact that "sons might be killed in order to prevent their avenging their fathers. This was apparently the motive which led the Susini of Figaro to kill Santo, the teen-age son of Matteo Maisetti in 1848" (p. 191). He does not cite any other examples, however. One might think that the "bad feuds" could have been undertaken out of this motive. In my opinion, Wilson's description of these feuds is more strongly suggestive of hatred than of fear. Also, if his exhaustive study of hundreds of feuds cites only one example of rational preemptive killing, it would be surprising if this were a common phenomenon. Moreover, he explicitly asserts that bad feuds were not the most common form.

Wilson does not cite any examples of murders undertaken out of fear in the full-blooded emotional sense. If such cases existed, the murderer would certainly have an incentive to hide the motive. In all societies where honor is important, fear – in either of the two varieties – is frowned upon. In fact, we know a great deal about the disapproval meted out to those who *abstained* from killing because they were (thought to be) afraid. Social contempt was expressed by the *rimbecco*, "a deliberate reminder of the unfulfilled revenge. It could take the form of a song, a remark, a gesture or a look, and could be delivered by relatives, neighbours or strangers, men or women. It was a direct accusation of cowardice and dereliction" (p. 203). A vivid description is provided in an earlier account:

The life of the individual who is exposed every day to the *rimbecco* is hell . . . "Whoever hesitates to revenge himself, said Gregorovius in 1854, is the target of the whisperings of his relatives and the insults of strangers, who reproach him publicly for his cowardice." . . . "In Corsica, the man who has not avenged his father, an assassinated relative or a deceived daughter *can no longer appear in public*. Nobody speaks to him; he has to remain silent. If he raises his voice to emit an opinion, people will say to him: avenge yourself first, and then you can state your point of view." The *rimbecco* can occur at any moment and under any guise. It does not even need to express itself in words: an ironical smile, a contemptuous turning away of the head, a certain condescending look – there are a thousand small insults which at all times of the day remind the unhappy victim of how much he has fallen in the esteem of his compatriots.[245]

The decision to pursue a feud could, therefore, involve a number of motivations. First, there was often an urge of anger, a burning desire

245. Busquet (1920), pp. 357–8. For a subtle discussion of the predicament of the man who fails to avenge an offense, see also Bourdieu (1969).

to take revenge or a specific action. Second, there may have been hatred, a burning desire to exterminate an enemy and his family. Third, there may have been fear of being killed or injured by the enemy if one tried to take revenge. Fourth, there may have been fear of being killed or injured by the enemy if one didn't. Either of these fears could exist in either of the two forms I just described. Fifth, there was the shame incurred though the *rimbecco* if one failed to take revenge. Finally, there were material costs of failing to take revenge, ranging from being unable to find a wife to leaving oneself without allies in future conflicts, not to speak of the increased risk of conflict to which the lack of allies would expose oneself. In most situations, several of these motivations must have been present, fused together in ways that language does not describe very adequately and our theories do not help us explain.

The decision to terminate a feud could be unilateral or bilateral. Unilateral termination would be the rule in bad feuds, if one family achieved its goal of exterminating the other. In most feuds, however, the termination was by mutual agreement that a balance had been achieved. In some cases, the agreement included actions to redress the balance or to prevent it from being disturbed. The basic principle was that peace is made "when the number of dead is equal on either side" (p. 253). Yet "hostilities usually involved a whole series of incidents and the calculation of equivalents was not easy. Conventions about how injuries compared with deaths, blows from one weapon with those from another, deaths of women with those of men, and so on, were only very rough, and notions of honour, which the escalation of violence brought to the fore, militated against such calculations" (*ibid.*). Just as insistence on equality of weaponry might be seen as dishonorable in the duel, so could insistence on equality of sacrifice in the vendetta.

I conclude with some comments on the role of honor in the feud. As I read Wilson, there was some difference between the strictness of honor requirements in stages A, B, and C of the feud. In the first stage, the defense of honor seems to have been paramount. In the pursuit and settlement (or pseudosettlement) of the feud, by contrast, dishonorable means were not infrequently observed. In theory, the defense of honor could only employ honorable means (cp. the comments above on Montaigne and the duel). In practice, the means included subterfuge, deceit, and other violations of the norms of honor.

For an instance of the requirements of honor in the first stage, we may consider the norms of courtship, stated as follows by a contemporary writer. "It is not the young man in Corsica who asks first for the hand of a girl in marriage; for, if he were refused, he would be the butt of ridicule among his comrades; and no other girl of his condition would afterwards consent to marry him. She would believe herself to be humiliated if she took a man whom another had refused" (p. 113). For this reason, various indirect arrangements existed by which a young man could signal a marital intention without running the risk of dishonor. Yet these arrangements could fail, in which case the rejected suitor could reassert his honor in either of two ways. On the one hand, he could kill his rival if the girl who rejected him later married another. In fact, "some women preferred not to marry, if their parents opposed their first choice, for this reason" (p. 112). On the other hand, he could try to dishonor the girl, for instance by raping her, so as to prevent her from finding another husband (p. 113). In the first case, the logic is "if I can't have her, nobody shall"; in the second, "if you won't have me, I'll make sure that nobody wants you." Although not exactly instances of vengeance, these were acts committed for the purpose of redressing a balance of honor.

Once the feud was underway, it was supposed to respect certain norms, notably with respect to who could be chosen as targets for retaliation. There was a rough consensus that targets (as well as recruitable allies) included male relatives to the second, often the third, and occasionally the fourth degree (pp. 189–90). Although these expectations were somewhat ambiguous, "the difficulty of knowing who was a legitimate target in a feud was to some extent overcome by requiring that the protagonists make a clear declaration on the subject. Robiquet stated in 1835 that at the outset of a feud a family "would let it be known to what degree of kinship the hostilities would extend"' (p. 190). Yet even this practice left "plenty of room for misunderstanding," and

sometimes misunderstandings were deliberately created. In course of a feud between the Giacomi and the Tomasi of Gavignano, a Giacomi was killed in 1838. "The relatives of the victims resolved to take reprisals and in order better to achieve this they declared emphatically that they wished only to punish the killer himself and not members of his family. Tricked by this deceitful declaration, the latter took no precautions," and two of them were ambushed shortly afterwards. (p. 190)

"The ostensible aim of vengeance . . . was not to destroy one's enemy but to restore one's own honour . . ., and this might be damaged by behavior that was too ruthless" (p. 246). Yet the norm of excluding women, children, and old men as targets was frequently violated (pp. 208–19). Some of these killings were more or less accidental. Others occurred as part of a "bad feud." Still others occurred when women and children were chosen as second-best targets. Also, "attacking women and children may ... have been a deliberate act of provocation when one side refused to respond to normal insult and the killing of men" (pp. 41–2). Although the picture is obviously complicated, there was still a general sentiment that "only male blood could really satisfy the need for vengeance" (p. 223). In contrast to the "cold" norm violations involved in ambushing an enemy who had been led to think he was immune, these violations of the norms defining who where acceptable victims occurred in hot blood: "[O]nce feuding had begun, rules as to who was or should be involved might be set aside 'in the intensity of passion unleashed'" (p. 195).

Norm violations could also occur in the third stage. In theory, peace settlements were supposed to be "sacrosanct" and "religiously observed" (p. 263). Moreover, signatories to a peace treaty often included third parties who staked their reputation and sometimes their financial assets on adherence to it (*ibid.*). In practice, however, treaties were "very frequently broken soon after being signed" (p. 264), one of the reasons being that "a peace or peace negotiations could be entered into with duplicity as a ploy in a feuding situation" (*ibid.*; see also pp. 253–4 and 291–2 for examples). These violations, too, were carried out in cold blood, and presumably were more blamable than the ones due to "the intensity of passion unleashed."

CONCLUSION

This discussion of glory and honor in four very different societies has shown several recurrent themes, which may be briefly summarized as follows. (i) Actions undertaken for the sake of glory aim, by definition, at excelling and standing out from others. Some actions undertaken for the sake of honor have the same aim, whereas others aim at redressing a balance of honor. (ii) Whereas glory, again by definition, is constant-sum, this is not necessarily the case for honor. In the Corsican vendetta, honor seems to have been constant-sum, but not in the Icelandic feud or the seventeenth-century French dueling. (iii) When honor is not constant-sum, the interaction can leave the parties with a larger total amount of honor, as when both fight honorably and both survive, or with a smaller total, as when a man of honor engages in a fight with his social inferior. (iv) The calculus of honor is almost always in dispute, and agreement that a balance obtains is difficult to reach, because each party tends to put the best interpretation on its own behavior and the worst on the opponent's. (v) The pursuit of honor is often tempered with self-interest, and notably with an interest in survival. (vi) Moreover, the pursuit of honor may be an investment in material self-interest, if the reputation for courage can serve to advance one's career. (vii) The pursuit of honor is often pursued by dishonorable means, which include not only means that show an excessive concern for survival but also means that violate norms of immunity, promise-keeping, and truthfulness. (viii) The spectrum of emotions triggered in the pursuit of honor and glory is very broad, including contempt, shame, pride, pridefulness, anger, hatred, fear, and envy. Although some of these emotions occur in spontaneous, presocial form, they are often focused and intensified by social norms and in particular by codes of honor.

Chapter IV

Rationality and the Emotions

IV.1. INTRODUCTION

The relation between reason and passion is one of the oldest questions in philosophy. A different and more narrowly defined issue is the relation between rationality and the emotions. To shed some light on this topic is the main aim of the present chapter, and notably of section IV.3. To do so, however, I first need to say something about the nature of emotion in general. Drawing on Chapters II and III and on modern studies of the emotions, this is what I try to do in section IV.2.

To inquire into the nature of emotion and into the relation between rationality and emotion seems to presuppose that the concept of emotion is coherent and well-defined, or, equivalently, that emotions form a *natural kind*. Following Roy Wise and Michael Bozarth, we may distinguish between homology and analogy as explanatory heuristics.[1] Whereas analogies do not necessarily extend beyond the superficial similarities that define them, homologies, resulting from common causal mechanisms, do allow such predictive extensions. Consider the diagram in Fig. IV.1.

A key problem in the study of the putative emotions is whether they are related to each other as bats to birds and whales to sharks, or unified by a common causal mechanism as in the case of bats and whales.[2] Although there may be some purposes for which the concepts "creatures that fly" (including flying fish!) or "creatures that

1. Wise and Bozarth (1987).
2. In Elster (in press b, Chapter 3) I similarly ask whether the *addictions* are unified by a common causal mechanism or whether they are simply lumped together on the basis of phenomenological similarities.

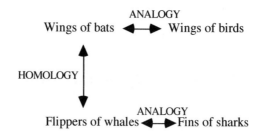

Figure IV.1.

live in the sea" are useful, the concepts of mammals, birds, and the various classes of fish are indispensable for scientific purposes. Similarly, it is not very useful to define emotion phenomenologically as, say, "action readiness accompanied by physiological arousal" if different emotions arise in different ways and are linked to behavior by different pathways. Thus I agree with the following programmatic statement by Joseph LeDoux:

To the extent that emotional responses evolved, they evolved for different reasons, and it seems obvious to me that there must be different brain systems to take care of these different kinds of functions. Lumping all of these together under the unitary concept of emotional behavior provides us with a convenient way of organizing things – for distinguishing behaviors that we call emotional (for example, those involved with fighting, feeding, sex, and social bonding) from those that reflect cognitive functions (like reasoning, abstract thinking, problem solving, and concept formation). However, the use of a label, like "emotional behavior," should not necessarily lead us to assume that all of the labeled functions are mediated by one system of the brain. Seeing and hearing are both sensory functions, but each has its own neural machinery.[3]

The class of what we think of as emotions might, therefore, be like the class of creatures that fly – a classification that is useful for some purposes but too crude for others. On the one hand, all flying creatures are subject to the same aerodynamic constraints. To understand how bats manage to stay in the air it's probably going to be useful to know how birds do it. On the other hand, if we want to understand the reproductive system of bats there is no point in considering that

3. LeDoux (1996), pp. 126–7; see also LeDoux (1995), pp. 1049–50.

of birds. Similarly, emotions that are produced by entirely different neural pathways may have features in common that make it useful to group them together for specific purposes, whereas for other purposes they must be treated as entirely heterogeneous phenomena.

The possibility that "the emotions" may not be a coherent and theoretically useful concept is reflected in the following discussion. Although I shall characterize the emotions in terms of seven specific features, I also note that for each feature (except the first) there are some (putative) emotions in which it is absent. One could, of course, define the emotions by stipulating that for something to be an emotion it has to possess (say) four of the seven features, but that would not be very useful.[4] I prefer to leave the concept open-ended and ambiguous, in the hope that at some future time we may come to understand it better. Perhaps it will turn out that the unruly category of "the emotions" encompasses several, internally homogeneous classes of phenomena.

The lack of agreement about what emotions are is paralleled by lack of agreement on what emotions there are. As Malcolm Budd says, "the emotions undoubtedly form a heterogeneous class, and one, moreover, of which the membership is uncertain."[5] Among the states that unambiguously qualify as emotions we may first mention the social emotions enumerated in III.1: anger, hatred, guilt, shame, pride, pridefulness, admiration, and liking. Second, there are emotions generated by good or bad things that have happened or will happen: joy and grief. There are emotions generated by thoughts of good or bad things that may happen in the future (hope and fear) or of good or bad states of affairs that may obtain in the present (love and jealousy). Fourth, there are the emotions enumerated by Aristotle (II.2) that are triggered by the thought of the good or bad of others: sympathy, pity, envy, malice, gloating, indignation. Fifth, there are counterfactual emotions generated by thoughts of what might have happened but didn't – regret, rejoicing, disappointment,

---

4. A definition of this kind has been offered for addiction. Thus in the *Diagnostic and Statistical Manual of Mental Disorders, 4th edition* (American Psychiatric Association 1994, p. 181) substance dependence is identified by the copresence of any three of seven defining features. Although this criterion may be justified by pragmatic diagnostic needs, it cannot serve as a definition for more theoretical purposes.
5. Budd (1985), p. 14. I also agree with the immediately following sentence: "In this situation it is better to forgo the attempt to capture the essence of an emotion in a definition of the form 'Each emotion is. . .,' and, instead, to provide a model to which many emotions conform but from which other emotions or states of mind diverge in various ways and to different degrees."

elation – and wistful subjunctive emotions generated by thoughts of what might still happen, albeit with insufficient probability to generate hope or fear. Borderline or controversial cases include surprise, boredom, interest, sexual desire, enjoyment, worry, and frustration. Given what I have said, it would be premature to try to eliminate this fuzziness.

There is also little agreement on the classification of the emotions. Each of the many typologies that have been proposed may capture some aspect of the emotional landscape, but none of them seem compelling or canonical.[6] Even the fundamental distinction between basic and nonbasic emotions commands little agreement. Some ground it in the idea of an emotional chemistry, with the molecular emotions being assemblies of atomic ones.[7] Others use the analogy of primary and compound colors, with the nonbasic emotions being blends of the basic ones.[8] Also, the basic emotions identified by various writers vary enormously. There is not a single emotion that is found in all of the fourteen lists of purportedly basic emotions accumulated by Andrew Ortony, Gerald Clore, and Allan Collins.[9] Taking account of linguistic variations, anger and fear occur in all but two of the lists, joy in all but six, sadness and disgust in six, shame and love in three. These writers also offer their own list of twenty-two basic emotions;

6. Thus Ortony et al. (1988) distinguish among three types of emotions, depending on whether they are caused by events, agents, and objects (e.g., people and things), as assessed by the criteria of desirability, praiseworthiness, and appealingness. For instance, resentment is elicited by an event presupposed to be desirable for someone else, reproach by the disapproval of someone else's blameworthy action, and so on. For Russell (1980), emotions can be organized in a two-dimensional space with the axes defined by high–low arousal and pleasant–unpleasant. For Rolls (1995, p. 1092) the emotions may be grouped according to whether they are caused by the presentation of a positive reinforcer, the presentation of a negative reinforcer, the omission of a positive reinforcer or the termination of a positive reinforcer, or the omission of a negative reinforcer or the termination of a negative reinforcer.
7. This analogy suggests that the component emotions remain identifiable within the more complex one, as when hydrogen and oxygen combine to give water. Lazarus (1991, p. 229) asserts, for instance, that "[w]hen I say that smugness is a combination of contempt and pride, I mean that to feel smug is to feel both contemptuous of those who are below *and* proud to be superior." I should add that Lazarus is not a basic-emotion theorist.
8. This analogy suggests that the component emotions lose their identity in the compound, as when blue and yellow are blended to yield green. Ortony et al. (1988, p. 24) write, for instance, that "[g]ratitude is not simply the cooccurrence of admiration for an agent and happiness for the resulting desirable outcome. It is a unified emotion in which the constituents need not necessarily be independently experienced."
9. Ortony et al. (1988), p. 27.

although longer than any other list, it does not include anger. All of this suggests skepticism, and some humility.

Finally, there is very little agreement on a number of substantive issues involving the emotions. As documented in a useful volume, *The Nature of Emotion*, edited by Paul Ekman and Richard Davidson, even on the most basic issues there is amazingly little agreement among students of the emotions.[10] They asked specialists in the field to answer twelve questions:

- Are there basic emotions?
- How are emotions distinguished from moods, temperament, and other related affective constructs?
- What is the function of emotions?
- How is evidence of universals in antecedents of emotion explained?
- What are the minimal cognitive prerequisites for emotion?
- Is there emotion-specific physiology?
- Can we control our emotions?
- Can emotions be nonconscious?
- What is the relation between emotion and memory?
- How do individuals differ in emotion-related activity?
- What develops in emotional development?
- What influences the subjective experience of emotion?

In their introduction the editors write, "There is no commonly accepted answers to the questions that form this book – that is why they were chosen." Given this disagreement among specialists, a non-specialist must tread carefully. Although I address some of the twelve questions, I do so at an intermediate-depth, commonsense level that does not prejudge what the ultimate answers will be. Because my main interest is in the consequences of the emotions, I do not need to go deeply into questions about their origin – a task for which I am not equipped in any case.

In the rest of this chapter I proceed as follows. In section IV.2, I try to characterize the emotions in terms of their phenomenological or observable qualities, drawing on current theoretical writings on the emotions as well as on the case studies in Chapters II and III. I also draw on some of the writings that deal with emotions induced by works of art, a body of literature that is briefly expounded at the

10. Ekman and Davidson (1994).

beginning of the section. From a conceptual point of view, the aesthetic emotions are important because they can provide counterexamples to what might otherwise seem obvious claims about the nature of emotion. Among the seven qualities that I single out for analysis, the cognitive antecedents of emotion receive by far the most extensive discussion. In IV.3 I build on this theoretical discussion and on previous chapters to address three aspects of the relation between emotions and rationality. There is the question of whether emotions detract from or on the contrary enhance the instrumental rationality of behavior; whether emotions themselves can be viewed as more or less rational; and whether emotional states can be the object of rational choices. In an appendix to the chapter I enumerate some main ways in which emotions affect behavior – either directly or through the generation of mental states that in turn are capable of shaping behavior.

IV.2. THE NATURE OF THE EMOTIONS

The word "emotion" can be taken either in an occurrent or in a dispositional sense. Occurrent emotions are actual episodes of experiencing anger, fear, joy, and the like. Emotional dispositions are propensities to have occurrent emotions, such as irascibility, faintheartedness, or what we call a "sunny disposition." Prejudices such as misogyny or anti-Semitism are also emotional dispositions. The disposition might be characterized in terms of the threshold for triggering the emotion (e.g., irritability), in terms of the strength of the emotion when triggered (e.g., irascibility), or both. Even irascible people are not angry all the time, and an angry person need not be irascible, so the two phenomena are distinct. For many questions, it matters a great deal which of the two meanings we have in mind. They yield very different interpretations, for instance, of the idea of "rational emotions" (IV.3). I might acutely desire never to experience shame but also desire to have a disposition to feel shame – in fact, the latter desire presupposes the former. It will usually be clear from the context whether I refer to occurrent emotions or the dispositions to have them. In the present section, I mainly discuss the occurrent sense.

EMOTIONS AND THE ARTS

Before I proceed to characterize the occurrent emotions, I need to introduce a set of emotions that I have neglected so far in the book.

These are the emotions produced in us by works of art, most vividly by literature, film, and music.[11] These emotions form two quite distinct sets. On the one hand, works of art have the capacity to induce emotions that we also experience in ordinary walks of life, such as joy, grief, terror, and the like. Although the emotion I feel when listening to Johnny Hodges playing "Jump for Joy" with Duke Ellington's orchestra lacks some features of the joy one may feel when a proposal of marriage is made or accepted, it is unmistakably the same emotion. Also, although the vicarious joy felt by the reader when Captain Wentworth proposes to Anne Elliott in *Persuasion* differs from the emotion generated by a similar real-life situation, it is a kind of joy nonetheless. The reasons for the differences will be made clear when we consider the phenomenology of emotion. Here, I only want to insist on the similarities. It is, for me, an indubitable introspective datum that joy induced by music or fiction is appropriately called "joy," by virtue of its similarities with joy as experienced in encounters with the world.

On the other hand, there are the specifically aesthetic emotions induced by the formal organization of a work of art. They include wonder, awe, surprise, humor, relief, and release. When a character in a novel finds himself able to resolve an apparently insuperable problem, the reader may experience the vicarious emotion of (nonaesthetic) relief or release. If that event also takes place in such a way that it enables the reader to solve cognitive puzzles created by earlier events in the novel, he may experience the *aesthetic* emotion of release that we have when things are seen to fall into place. In some works of music, these aesthetic emotions dominate completely. The ordered and supremely controlled complexity of Bach's Goldberg Variations, for instance, generates emotions of awe and wonder that may not have any nonaesthetic equivalent at all.

As we shall see, both the aesthetic and the nonaesthetic emotions generated by works of art create puzzles or constitute counterexamples for some well-known theories of emotion. "Appraisal theory," for instance, which asserts that all emotions are triggered by a cognitive appraisal of a situation,[12] cannot account for feelings of joy generated by a joyous piece of music, and only with difficulty for the feelings of terror generated by a horror movie. Similarly, either

---

11. Some aspects of this issue are more fully discussed in section III.4 of Elster (in press a).
12. Lazarus (1991).

variety of art-induced emotion is hard to square with the view – further discussed in IV.3 – that emotions are actively chosen rather than passively undergone.

To characterize occurrent emotions I use the criteria that I adopted in my discussion of Aristotle's theory of the emotions. They are states of the organism that can be characterized in terms of seven features:[13]

- Qualitative feel
- Cognitive antecedents
- An intentional object
- Physiological arousal
- Physiological expressions
- Valence on the pleasure–pain dimension
- Characteristic action tendencies

The first criterion (which is added to the Aristotelian list) is an *intrinsic* feature of the emotional experience. The second and the third are *cognitive* attributes. The last four criteria are *visceral* attributes, in the sense that they are common to the emotions and other visceral states such as pain, hunger, or thirst.[14] Each of these criteria can serve one or both of two functions. On the one hand, they can help us decide whether a state of the organism is an emotion or something else, such as a cognition, a craving, or a sensation of pain. On the other hand, assuming the first question to have been decided, they can help us decide which particular emotion is involved.

13. In the following I draw heavily on the outstanding synthetic exposition by Frijda (1986). Ekman (1992b) offers a list of nine features that characterize the emotions of anger, fear, sadness, enjoyment, disgust, and surprise, and possibly also contempt, shame, guilt, embarrassment, and awe. The features are distinctive universal signals, presence in other primates, distinctive physiology, distinctive universals in antecedent events, coherence among emotional response, quick onset, brief duration, automatic appraisal, and unbidden occurrence. He downplays cognition and, especially, valence. I argue that in studying the role of the emotions in complex social situations these aspects are crucial. If shame, for instance, can regulate social life (III.2), it is because it is intensely unpleasant. Moreover, the two-way interaction between emotion and cognition is central to understanding what Ekman (1992a) refers to as emotional "wildfires."
14. For the idea of "visceral factors," see Loewenstein (1996).

As I noted in the discussion of two concepts of fear in III.4, visceral arousal is an important criterion for deciding that a state is an emotion rather than a simple belief–desire complex. By contrast, we cannot use fine-grained differences in arousal patterns to decide whether the organism is experiencing envy or indignation, anger or hatred, shame or guilt, regret or disappointment.[15] Nor can physiological expressions reliably serve the same purpose.[16] Conversely, we may use action tendencies to distinguish among the emotions, but not to decide whether a state of the organism is an emotion or not. Shame and guilt can be distinguished by their action tendencies, yet the urge to undo a harm one has caused can arise without feelings of guilt. According to Weber, the institutionalization of confession and penance in the Catholic Church went hand in hand with "weakening the demands of morality upon the individual ... The vouchsafing of grace ... largely spares him the necessity of developing an individual life based on ethical foundations."[17]

QUALITATIVE FEEL

The most striking phenomenological feature of the emotions might seem to be what they *feel like*. There is in fact a strong temptation to think that each emotion has a separate "quale" or qualitative feel. In the somewhat analogous case of colors,[18] one could argue that no amount of knowledge about wavelengths and other measurable features of colors can substitute for the experience of what a given color looks like. Similarly, one might argue that an emotional experience is something over and above the various features that I have listed, or rather, something over and above the subjective perception of these

---

15. In a literature survey, Levenson (1992) reports consistent autonomic nervous system differences among anger, fear, disgust, sadness, and happiness but adds that even with more research "the final tally of distinctions is likely to be small" (p. 26).
16. Carroll (1996, p. 131) observes that to convey emotion in movies, showing the human face may not be sufficient. "In order to arrive at a more fine-grained and unambiguous characterization of the emotion, we depend on knowing the object or cause of the emotion in question"; hence in editing "that is devoted to conveying the emotional state of a character, we move from the glance to the target, in order to ascertain the particular emotion of the character." Cp. also the remark from Miller (1993, p. 103) cited in III.4: "[S]omatic displays are often susceptible of more than one emotional meaning."
17. Weber (1968), p. 561.
18. For another aspect of this analogy, see n. 8.

features. The felt difference between guilt and shame, for instance, does not seem to be merely the perception of different action tendencies, of different forms of physiological arousal, and so forth. Rather, each emotion seems to be a pure and qualitatively unique experience, much like a unique shade of red or blue.

Although the analogy with color is dubious, there is a case to be made for the existence of "pure emotions." One piece of evidence comes from music. Malcolm Budd argues, for instance, that "when you hear music as being expressive of emotion E – when you hear E in the music – you hear the music sounding like the way E feels."[19] Another piece of evidence is provided by the finding that the emotions can be produced by direct electric stimulation of the brain:

Upon stimulating his left amygdala at 1 mA, he had a feeling "as if I were not belonging here," which he likened to being at a party and not being welcome. ... Right hippocampal stimulation at 3 mA induced anxiety and guilt, "like you are demanding to hand in a report that was due 2 weeks ago ... as if I were guilty of some form of tardiness."[20]

If emotions are induced in subjects by injecting them with procaine, they report "a range of affective experiences, including euphoria, sadness, fear and anxiety ... [These] procaine-induced experiences seem related to the essential 'qualia' of some emotional states such as euphoria or fear. Subjects are able to unambiguously name their experience, yet, they cannot report cognitions or environmental clues that could have evoked this affect or even justify its experience *a posteriori*."[21]

These various arguments and findings make it quite plausible, in my opinion, that each emotion has a unique quale or feel to it. If the neuroscientists are right in that "it should be possible to identify central nervous system patterns of coactivation that are characteristic of a particular qualia,"[22] one might inversely rely on these patterns to identify emotions in animals that are incapable of saying what they feel, assuming that the basic neurobiology of the brain is similar enough. These, however, are ideas that lie in the future. They play no role in the following discussion.

19. Budd (1995), p. 136.
20. Gloor (1986), p. 164, cited after Brothers (1995), p. 1111.
21. Servan-Schreiber and Perlstein (1997).
22. *Ibid.*

COGNITIVE ANTECEDENTS

Emotions differ from other visceral factors, such as pain, bodily pleasures, thirst, or hunger in two respects. Emotions have cognitive antecedents, the latter do not; emotions have intentional objects, the latter do not.[23] Otherwise, the other visceral motivations share or may share the four other features that I use to characterize the emotions. Thus emotion and cognition are intimately connected. That is, in fact, why emotion can distort cognition in the ways to be discussed in IV.3 and V.2. Here, I shall only explore the causal link from cognition to emotion. As this relation is the central issue in the study of human emotions, I discuss it at some length.

To illustrate the difference between emotions and other visceral states, consider Michael Liebowitz's claim that "the chemistry of love" is like that of the amphetamines.[24] Being in love can indeed induce many of the same properties as being high on amphetamines: acute awareness, heightened energy, reduced need for sleep and food, feelings of euphoria. Yet the differences are also striking. In particular, the amphetamine-induced euphoria runs a predictable course, lasting for several hours and then turning into a depression. Love-induced euphoria, by contrast, can last for weeks and then change into black dysphoria and despair at a second's notice, on learning that the love one thought requited really isn't.[25] Although it is possible that amphetamine and love recruit some of the same neural circuitry, some important mechanisms must be entirely different. Because of the different reaction times, the pathway from ingestion of a chemical substance to a feeling of elation must differ in important respects from the pathway that begins with the *belief* that one's love is requited and ends in the emergence of a somewhat similar feeling. Whereas the former pathway is now being elucidated, fine-grained knowledge of the second lies at best in the distant future and may in fact never be attainable.

(1) Sometimes, emotions are said to be triggered by events or states of affairs. Strictly speaking, this is misleading, just as it is misleading to say that rational agents choose the best element in the feasible set. In the latter case, we should say that the agents choose the best of

23. The distinction is due to Hume (1960, p. 278): "We must ... make a distinction betwixt the cause and the object of these passions; betwixt that idea, which excites them, and that to which they direct their views, when excited."
24. Liebowitz (1983), pp. 92–103.
25. See for instance the many vivid descriptions in Stendhal (1980) and Tennov (1979).

the elements that they *believe* to be feasible (IV.3). In the case of the emotions, the appropriate statement is that emotions are triggered by *beliefs* about events or states. In both cases we may use (as I have been doing) the convenient and innocuous shorthand of saying that actions or emotions are induced by events or states, without adding each time that the effect is mediated by the beliefs.[26] In both cases, the beliefs may or may not be accurate; more relevantly, they may or may not be well grounded in the evidence available to the agent. Beliefs that are not well grounded in evidence are *irrational*.[27] By implication, actions based on irrational beliefs are irrational. By a further implication, one might argue that emotions based on irrational beliefs are irrational. I postpone that issue until the next section.

(2) There is another normative issue that I want to take up here, however. Consider the cognitive antecedents of anger. In *The Cognitive Structure of Emotions*, Andrew Ortony, Gerald Clore, and Allan Collins argue that anger is caused by a perception of standard-violation. Anger, on their view, is triggered by blameworthy actions that cause undesirable outcomes.[28] I submit that this is a *moralized definition*. Perhaps it captures the occasions on which we are entitled to feel angry, but these are not all the occasions on which people get angry. Often, anger is triggered simply by goal-frustration, as stated in the "frustration-aggression hypothesis."[29] Car drivers get angry with bicyclists simply because they prevent them from driving as fast as they want. An instance of this tendency was reported to me by a therapist. Upon learning that there had been a burglary in the house while his wife had been absent, the husband asks her, angrily, "Why did you have to choose this day to visit your mother?" The thought that "[i]f she had not gone to see her mother, there would have been no burglary" is enough to trigger his anger. The additional thought, "She should have known that if she went to see her mother and left the house empty, there might be a burglary," is not required. The husband's anger may be irrational (IV.3), but it is still anger. In such cases, there may be a tendency to justify the anger, originally induced by goal-frustration, by presenting it (to oneself or others) as caused by standard-violation, yet the latter idea need not enter into the original emotion.

---

26. See also Fortenbaugh (1970), n. 30.
27. I simplify. For a fuller statement, see IV.3 .
28. Ortony et al. (1988), pp. 148–53. For a similar view, see Solomon (1993), p. 126.
29. Krebs and Miller (1985), pp. 39–42.

(3) The exact relation between the antecedents and the emotions is a matter of some controversy. Jan Smedslund is perhaps the most explicit advocate of a position that is implicit in many other writings on the emotions, namely that the link is logical or conceptual rather than empirical.[30] For him it is a necessary or conceptual truth that anger arises if and only if one is the target of intentional slighting, to use Aristotle's phrase (II.2).[31] But this is a moralized definition. It may capture cases of rational or subjectively justified anger, but not all cases are of that kind. Another view is that the link is empirical and lawful. Emotions, as other phenomena, are the target of covering-law explanations. I have said what I think about this idea in Chapter I. I agree, therefore, with Roy Schafer that "predictability of emotions depends on a number of usually unspecified conditions being met."[32] Goal-frustration without standard-violation or intentional slighting may cause anger but need not do so; moreover, the conditions under which it does so are too numerous and too varied to be enumerated.

I believe, therefore, that the mechanism approach is the appropriate one. Consider first type A mechanisms. La Rochefoucauld claimed, "Jealousy feeds on doubts, and as soon as doubt turns into certainty it becomes a frenzy, or ceases to exist" (M32). The certainty that another is preferred may kill the jealousy – or exacerbate it. Also, just as fear may induce either flight or fight, a given set of antecedents may induce either fear or anger, depending on conditions that generally elude us. (As anger also tends to induce fight, this means that the same conditions can induce fighting by two different pathways.) Anger and fear may also illustrate type B_1 mechanisms. A given set of antecedents may induce fear *and* anger, with the net effect on behavior or action tendency being in general indeterminate. On the one hand anger may help one overcome fear in battle;[33] on the other hand anger may be kept in check by fear.[34] Bittersweet emotions of interpersonal and intrapersonal comparison also fall in this category. Below, I give some examples of mechanisms of type B_2.

---

30. Smedslund (1992, 1993). Cp. also Solomon (1993), p. 126: "A change in my beliefs (for example, the refutation of my belief that John stole my car) entails (not causes) a change in my emotion (my being angry that John stole my car). I cannot be angry if I do not believe that someone has wronged or offended me." This assertion may be usefully contrasted with the passage from de Sousa (1987, p. 199) cited previously.
31. Smedslund (1993). I simplify.
32. Schafer (1976), p. 335.
33. Montaigne (1991), pp. 638–9, 816.
34. Seneca, *On Anger*, XXX.

Type A mechanisms are important when the antecedents include conditions for several emotions with different intentional targets. If we are humiliated in front of others, we may feel anger at the person who humiliates us *or* shame before the audience (III.2). If a parent gives a toy to one child but not to another, the latter may feel envy at the sibling *or* anger at the parent. Finally, when A causes B to hurt C, C's anger may be directed at B *or* at A. To borrow an example from James Fearon and David Laitin, suppose that member A of ethnic group X hurts member B of ethnic group Y, and that members of Y retaliate with a general attack on all members of X. In that situation, a member of X may either feel anger at his co-member A *or* direct his anger at Y.[35]

(4) Because cognitions are vulnerable to framing effects, the same holds for the emotions they trigger.[36] Two logically equivalent ways of describing a situation can generate very different emotions. In V.2 I cite, as an example, how Mathilde de la Mole frames her love for Julien Sorel in two different (although equivalent) ways that trigger the meta-emotions of pride and shame respectively. Also, workers in a firm might feel ashamed if the state subsidizes their wages, but not if it offers cheap energy to the firm for the explicit purpose of enabling the firm to keep them on the payroll. The aluminum industry in Western Norway demands and gets huge subsidies in the form of cheap energy, partly because the workers do not want wage subsidies. The government has tried to offer the fishermen in Northern Norway direct labor subsidies, only to be met with the response that they prefer subsidies to be given to the shipowners. In both cases observers emphasize that accepting wage subsidies is perceived to be like begging. Workers in the textile industry, in which direct wage

---

35. Fearon and Laitin (1996) distinguish between two ways in which interethnic cooperation can be maintained. On the one hand, there can be a "spiral-equilibrium" in which each member of a group is deterred from defecting in interactions with members of another ethnic group by the knowledge that his defection will trigger defection by all members of the other group in interactions with all members of his group. On the other hand, there can be an "in-group policing equilibrium" in which defection in out-group interaction is prevented by the knowledge that it will be punished by defection in interactions with other members of his own group. In the first case, there is the possibility of the two emotional reactions discussed in the text. The first reaction – anger at one's co-member who has triggered the massive retaliation – might transform the spiral-equilibrium into an in-group policing equilibrium. The second reaction – anger at the other group – would support the spiral equilibrium. As David Laitin points out to me, political leaders might be decisive in determining which reaction is in fact triggered.
36. On framing effects, see Tversky and Kahneman (1981).

subsidies *are* given, envy the aluminum industry its energy require-ments which justify less transparent income transfers.[37] Even when there is no real difference between one-step and two-step procedures to achieve the same end, the emotional impact may be very different.

(5) Similarly, the emotional impact of disjunctive beliefs has a com-plex relation to the emotions that would be triggered by the disjuncts. The disjunction of two beliefs, one of which has to be true and each of which will trigger emotion X, need not trigger emotion X.[38] Sup-pose that the public believes that an airplane explosion must be due either to mechanical malfunctioning or to sabotage. Suppose, more-over, that if the accident was shown to be due to malfunctioning the public would be angry at the airline for failing to take precautions and afraid of using that airline again. Suppose, finally, that the same emotions of anger and fear would be triggered if the explosion was shown to be the result of sabotage. My suggestion is that as long as the uncertainty remains unresolved, there will be less anger and fear than if it is resolved one way or another. (Or perhaps the anger will be directed at the agencies who are responsible for identifying the cause.[39]) The difference in reactions to the 1996 TWA explosion and the 1988 Pan-American explosion might seem to support this conjecture.

More generally, the abstract belief that you have been harmed by some unknown person or persons is unlikely to generate the same emotion as the concrete belief that you have been harmed by a specific person. To the extent that this is the case, the "truth commissions" that have been established in a number of countries that have undergone the transition from authoritarian to democratic rule may have the opposite effect of what was intended. Rather than inducing healing or catharsis, the knowledge of the identity of the person who killed your father or husband may serve to trigger and focus your anger and your desire for revenge.

In these cases, the disjunctive belief triggers a weaker emotion than would either disjunct. In the case of jealousy, the opposite is the case.

---

37. For an explicit recognition of this fact of political life, see Serck-Hanssen (1972). Since there is a paucity of other written sources, I have also relied on verbal com-munications from Hilde Bojer and Jens Chr. Andvig. For similar reasons, "farmers in West Germany favor a subsidy through price over a direct subsidy of income although this involves astronomical dead-weight losses and will certainly turn against them since it cannot be maintained" (Schlicht 1985).
38. The idea is related to the findings by Tversky and Shafir (1992) discussed in I.6.
39. Jonathan Cole (personal communication).

As we saw in II.3, the resolution of uncertainty with respect to *whether* one's lover is being unfaithful may exacerbate the jealousy – or kill it. In Proust's analyses of jealousy, the resolution of uncertainty with respect to the *identity* of the third party tends to calm the emotion. Thus when Swann begs Odette to tell him the name of the woman with whom she has had a homosexual relation, he says that "to be able to form a representation of the person will prevent me from having to think about it again . . . To be able to form a representation of things is so calming. What is horrible, is what one cannot imagine."[40]

According to Hume, what happens in such cases is that the primary emotion (the one which would be triggered by each of the disjuncts) is augmented and amplified by *fear*:

Let one be told by a person, whose veracity he cannot doubt of, that one of his sons is suddenly kill'd, 'tis evident the passion this event wou'd occasion, wou'd not settle into pure grief, till he got certain information, which of his sons he had lost. Here there is an evil certain, but the kind of it uncertain: Consequently the fear we feel on this occasion is without the least mixture of joy, and arises merely from the fluctuation of the fancy betwixt its objects. And tho' each side of the question produces here the same passion, yet that passion cannot settle, but receives from the imagination a tremulous and unsteady motion.[41]

Whatever we think about this particular account, the phenomenon reflects the general mechanism pattern that I discussed in Chapter I. On some occasions, uncertainty about the cause of an accident, about the identity of a perpetrator or a victim, or about the third party in an adulterous affair generates stronger negative emotions than when one knows exactly what happened. On other occasions, ignorance is (relative) bliss.

(6) As mentioned in II.1, human emotions differ from animals emotions by the complexity of the beliefs that may trigger them. In particular, their cognitive antecedents include

- Beliefs (including mistaken beliefs) about one's own emotions
- Beliefs about other people's emotions
- Beliefs about other people's motivations
- Beliefs about other people's beliefs
- Probabilistic beliefs

40. Proust (1954), vol. I, p. 365; also Grimaldi (1993), pp. 57–8.
41. Hume (1960), p. 445.

- Counterfactual and subjunctive beliefs
- "As-if" beliefs

Also, it is a unique feature of human beliefs that they may be *self-fulfilling* by a causal path that involves the emotions they generate. Below, I discuss each of these categories of beliefs and the emotions they may generate.

(7) An important set of cognitive antecedents are beliefs about one's own emotions. I refer to emotions that are consciously acknowledged as *proper emotions*. Their psychological and social implications are much broader than those of the proto-emotions that do not reach the stage of consciousness. If I know that I am experiencing a certain emotion, that cognition may serve to trigger further emotions, or *meta-emotions*. Unacknowledged proto-emotions, by contrast, cannot trigger meta-emotions. I have given several examples of meta-emotions induced by cognitions about lower-order emotions. Figure II.1 illustrates the process by which the perception of envy triggers shame or guilt. The Princess of Clèves felt guilt when she became aware of her love for the Duc de Nemours. The feminist and traditionalist mothers discussed by Hochschild might feel shame and guilt over, respectively, their guilt and lack of guilt about child care. As we shall see, Nico Frijda argues that American blacks may feel guilt about their anger. In these cases, the meta-emotion is either shame or guilt. Other emotions that can appear as meta-emotions include joy ("I'm so happy that I'm able to feel love again"), anger ("It's so stupid for me to feel guilty about this insignificant incident"), and fear ("I'm scared by the strength of my hatred for him"). As suggested by some of these examples, what triggers the meta-emotion can be the perception of an emotional disposition rather than of an occurrent emotion. When people go into therapy, it is often because they have persistent emotional patterns that worry them emotionally.

(8) Although people can and do form beliefs about their own emotions, they may also be unaware of them. In II.3 I distinguished between *strong proto-emotions* that the person might become aware of even though he or she currently isn't, and *weak proto-emotions* that the person cannot acknowledge because his or her culture lacks the relevant concept. A third category, to be illustrated below, is what we may call *semistrong proto-emotions* – emotions that the individual does not and cannot acknowledge even though the concept of that emotion exists in his culture and people around him can acknowledge that he has it. In illustrating these ideas, I rely on studies of four specific

emotions: depression, guilt, boredom, and romantic love. Although I conjecture that the claims I make generalize to other emotions, I have no evidence to this effect.

The basic idea is that a person can show many of the behavioral manifestations of an emotion – physiological arousal, physiological expressions, action tendencies, and valence – and yet not be aware of the emotion. In II.3 I noted that a person may be in love without being aware of it. Love can manifest itself simply as constant attention to the other person, happiness when being with him or her, frustration or grief when the other seems unresponsive, and so on. The same, I argued, is often true of anger, and no doubt of other emotions, too. Envy, for instance, can manifest itself in a sharpness of tone and a tendency to adopt a derogatory slant that are obvious to observers but not to the subject. In our society, this would be a case of a strong proto-emotion. What is lacking in all these cases is the putting together of all these behavioral manifestations of an emotion into a conscious recognition of its existence. Although this awareness may exist at an unconscious level before it reaches conscious awareness, there is no reason to assume that it always does so. From the fact that we experience an emotion of which we are not consciously aware, we cannot infer that we must be aware of it at an unconscious level. In fact, if the emotion exists only as a weak proto-emotion, the person *cannot* have an unconscious awareness of it. This being said, self-deception about one's own emotions – *motivated* ignorance – is a common phenomenon, as we saw in Chapter II.

A different kind of case is offered by Michael Lewis: "I had a patient named John who received the news that a very dear aunt had died. At first, he reported experiencing great sadness at the loss. But then his sadness seemed to dissipate. Several weeks later, he felt agitated and experienced some trouble eating and sleeping. When I asked John how he felt, he replied that he felt tired. When I asked him whether he was depressed, he said that he did not feel depressed."[42] Lewis suggests two mechanisms that might explain why John did not acknowledge the fact that he was depressed: self-deception and socialization. The latter is spelled out as follows. "As a child, John may have exhibited certain behaviors in situations of loss. When he did, his parents informed him that these behaviors means that he was tired, not sad. In other words, past experience may be capable of shaping people's self-awareness about an emotion, even to the extent

42. Lewis (1992), pp. 15–16.

of producing an awareness that is idiosyncratic in relation to the actual emotional state."[43] This amounts to what I called a semistrong proto-emotion.

John's unawareness of his depression was idiosyncratic in the sense that it deviated from the norm in his culture. He was not and could not become aware of his depression, but other members of his society could see that he was indeed depressed. But we also have information about a society in which depression existed only as a weak proto-emotion. Here, unawareness of depression and its misdescription as mere fatigue, far from being idiosyncratic, were shared by the culture as a whole. Robert Levy observes in fact that among the Tahitians, the subjective impact of loss is described as illness rather than depression. When one Tahitian,

feeling strange after being separated from his *vahine*, interprets his feelings as illness and in so doing accepts a pervasive cultural pattern of playing down feelings of loss, it is evident that in some way and at some level he must know that he has suffered a significant loss. That is why his separation from his *vahine* made him feel sick or strange in the first place. That is, one "feels" considerably more than cultural forms may make consciously accessible.[44]

In III.2 I also cited guilt in ancient Greece as an example of a weak proto-emotion. Although the literary sources provide descriptions of behavioral patterns that fit our concept of guilt, the Greeks themselves tended to conceptualize moral judgments in terms of shame. I believe, in fact, that the cluster of behaviors mentioned by Williams – indignation, forgiveness, reparations – are likely to be observed in all human societies, yet it is quite possible that only a minority of them has brought them together under a separate conceptual heading.

A third example can be taken from the history of *boredom*. It seems extremely likely that people always and everywhere have been bored and listless, in the sense of sometimes not knowing how to fill their days. In earlier times and in many contemporary societies, most people no doubt were too preoccupied with survival to have time to be bored. Yet in social structures that create large amounts of free time, such as the medieval monasteries of the West, the problem of boredom could arise in an acute form. A fourth-century preacher and

43. *Ibid.*, p. 17. Analogous phenomena exist in addiction. Patients who are dismissed from hospital after treatment with morphine may be unaware that what they are experiencing is withdrawal.
44. Levy (1973), p. 324; see also Levy (1984).

monk, Evagrius Ponticus, coined the phrase "the demon at noontime" to describe the temptations of boredom generated by the enforced inactivity of monastic life.[45] At the most trivial level, it was a matter of trying not to fall asleep in church.[46] At a more consequential level, boredom might suggest to the monk that his religious fervor might perhaps be better deployed elsewhere, inducing him to leave the monastery altogether.[47]

Yet boredom was not conceptualized as such. It was subsumed under the general heading of *acedia* or sloth, included on the list of the deadly sins until Gregory the Great rearranged it. *Acedia* included not only boredom, but laziness. For us, these are very different phenomena. For the medieval theologians, however, they were aspects of the same sin, betraying lack of devotion and of concentration on God. Boredom was not an involuntary psychological state. As Patricia Meyer Spacks writes, "The world that did not know boredom as boredom would necessarily have been one whose inhabitants believed in, lived by, a notion of personal responsibility."[48] When people – perhaps some time in the eighteenth century – did acquire the conceptual possibility to describe themselves as (involuntarily) bored, they might still have preferred another description: "If only because it seems more dignified, many people would rather suffer ennui than boredom, despite its presumably greater misery. Given that ennui and boredom exist by virtue of interpretation (*if we labeled our experience differently we would feel it differently*), a person's self-construction as *ennuyé* carries crucial meaning."[49] The sentence that I have italicized should not be understood as saying that boredom is a mere social construction. On the contrary: To say that awareness of an emotion can transform it presupposes that there is something to be transformed in the first place. In my language, Spack asserts that before the eighteenth century boredom existed as a weak proto-emotion. People were sometimes bored but never said to themselves, "God, I'm bored!" They could and did say, "He bores me!" but that is also different from saying that one is in a state of chronic boredom.

As a final example we may consider the idea put forward by C. S. Lewis and Denis de Rougemont that love remained (at most) a weak proto-emotion until the writings of the Troubadours in the eleventh

45. Wenzel (1967), pp. 4–5.
46. *Ibid.*, p. 84.
47. *Ibid.*, p. 5.
48. Spacks (1995), p. 11.
49. *Ibid.*, pp. 12–13.

century.[50] According to Lewis, "a glance at classical antiquity or at the Dark Ages at once show us that what we took for 'nature' is really a special state of affairs, which will probably have an end, and which certainly had a beginning in eleventh-century Provence." Later, he notes that the direction of causality could go either way: "If the feeling came first a literary convention would soon arise to express it: if the convention came first it would soon teach those who practised it a new feeling."[51] The two views could of course be combined, in a process of mutual reinforcement.

I wonder, though, if Lewis and Rougemont do not go too far when they argue that love as it emerged in the eleventh century was an entirely new emotion, rather than a proto-emotion that became conscious of itself. Lewis asserts, for instance, that in antiquity "love seldom rises above the levels of merry sensuality or domestic comfort, except to be treated as a tragic madness."[52] The only evidence he cites, however, is the writings of philosophers and poets, who could hardly be expected to describe an emotion for which their culture had no concept. I strongly suspect – but cannot prove – that in antiquity love did exist as a proto-emotion, manifested by a consuming interest in the other person, an intense desire to be with him or her, jealousy induced by third-party rivalry, grief at the loss of the other person – in short, all the behaviors shown by Mme. de Rênal before she discovered that she was in love. These are signs of love, not of merry sensuality or madness. Once the idea of love had been coined, it not only provided a unifying framework for all these phenomena, but also allowed further elaborations that had previously been absent. Today, people *expect* to fall in love, and question themselves if they don't. As noted in II.4, Emma Woodhouse illustrates not only the culturally induced expectation that it was time for her to fall in love, but also the culturally induced reluctance to recognize her symptoms for what they really were – signs of boredom.

Whether emotions are universal and invariant, cross-culturally and transhistorically, is a difficult question.[53] There is a camp of universalists and a camp of particularists, extreme forms of which are represented by Edmund Leach and Clifford Geertz respectively.[54] My inclination is to believe that proto-emotions are universal. They can

50. Lewis (1936); de Rougemont (1983).
51. Lewis (1936), pp. 3, 22.
52. *Ibid.*, p. 5.
53. Wierzbicka (1992) is a good discussion; see also Griffiths (1997).
54. See Levy (1984, pp. 216–7) for a summary.

be identified behaviorally and reliably by external observers or by historians in all cultures. By contrast, what we may call *proper emotions* are not universal. These are the subset of proto-emotions that are actual or potential objects of cognition by the persons who experience them and by other members of their society. If I am right, it follows that there are no emotions in any society that are "nothing but" social constructions, that is, entirely dissociated from universal features of the human condition. Yet I cannot back my conjecture by strong evidence. It would probably require a lifetime to make the case for it convincingly. It might also take a lifetime to make a strong case against it. As I have construed the universalist thesis, one cannot disprove it merely by pointing to the lack of the concept of a putatively universal emotion. There may be societies that lack the concept of agency, but that doesn't mean that their members don't act. To disprove the thesis, one would have to look at physiological and behavioral evidence that might not be easy to collect and interpret.

(9) Even when people do form beliefs about their emotions, they can be wrong. We encounter this idea several times in II.4. Orestes says that he "mistook" his love for hate. The Princess of Clèves "felt she almost hated [the Duc de Nemours], so much did the idea of guilty love pain her." Emma Woodhouse mistook her state of boredom for love. These misattributions are somewhat different from those reported in famous experiments by Stanley Schachter and Jerome Singer.[55] In their findings, arousal induced by injection of epinephrine (an artificial form of adrenaline) together with cues that might suggest anger or happiness did indeed induce these emotions unless the subjects were told that they could expect to feel heart flutters and the like as a result of the injection. Along similar lines, suppose that Emma Woodhouse, rather than being bored, had had loose bowel movements or suffered sleeplessness. Knowing that these are common effects of being infatuated, she might have told herself, "I'm in love!" As in the Schachter–Singer experiments, this would not be a case of mistaking one emotion for another, but of mistaking a nonemotional arousal for an emotional one. (Note that this is the converse of Levy's Tahitians, who mistook emotional arousal for a nonemotional one.)

---

55. Schachter and Singer (1962). Frijda (1986, pp. 222–3) asserts that attempts to replicate their findings have been partly unsuccessful, and that when they have been successful, other interpretations of the findings may be more plausible. For a conceptual criticism of their findings, see Gordon (1987, pp. 96–109).

Just as unawareness of one's emotions can be motivated, so can mistakes about them be. Orestes may well have been motivated to mistake his love for hate (see IV.3). In the case of Emma, her boredom itself provides a motivation for misinterpreting it as love. But people may also genuinely mistake one emotion for another. Given that the cognitive antecedents of regret and disappointment may overlap – a bad outcome might have been better both if the agent had acted differently and if a different chance event had been realized – a person may not be quite sure which of these subtly different negative emotions he is experiencing.[56] He might of course experience both, but he might also have only one of them and mistake it for the other.

(10) Beliefs about other people's emotions, including beliefs about their emotional dispositions, can serve as cognitive antecedents for what we may call *second-party emotions*.[57] Loving someone and believing that the love is not requited can induce despair (or hatred); believing that he or she loves someone else can induce jealousy. As we see in II.3, Ego's perception of Alter's love for Ego may enhance Ego's love for Alter (Hermione in *Andromaque*) or destroy it (Julien Sorel and Mathilde de la Mole in *Le Rouge et Le Noir*). As we have also seen, these mutually dependent emotions can be quite complex. Resentment at envy-enjoyment, for instance, involves two emotions in one party that are mediated by an emotion in another party.

We must distinguish between the emotions that are triggered by beliefs about the emotions and those that are triggered by beliefs about the observable manifestations of the emotions. This distinction is especially important in the case of shame and contempt. As I argued in III.2, shame is not induced by the belief that the other is withholding some benefit from me, but from the belief that he does so out of contempt. Also, if I notice that another person is angry, the belief that he is about to hit me will cause me to feel fear. But I might also feel contempt at the anger itself, as evidence of irrationality or lack of self-control. Or suppose a child has been given a beating by one parent and is then comforted by the other. The child might well believe that the comforting parent sympathizes with his feeling of humiliation, whereas in reality the feeling of sympathy is only directed toward his pain. As this example shows, beliefs about other people's emotions

---

56. On regret and disappointment, see Bell (1982, 1985) and Baron (1995), pp. 367–72.
57. This phenomenon differs from that of emotional contagion, as discussed by Hatfield et al. (1994). Sometimes, however, these writers appear to confuse the two phenomena, for example on pp. 5, 87, 198.

can easily be wrong. As with beliefs about one's own emotions, the mistakes can be (emotionally) motivated as well as unmotivated.

For an emotion to generate either meta-emotions or second-party emotions, it has to be consciously acknowledged by the agent or by observers. Unless it belongs to the conceptual repertoire of the culture, it cannot be consciously acknowledged. Culture therefore acts as a modifier – whether as amplifier or as brake – of the emotions. When an emotion is conceptualized and acknowledged, it may become more strongly and more widely felt. This is probably the case of boredom, and perhaps with depression. These are emotions that can feed on themselves by self-awareness and be contained within limits by lack of awareness. At the same time, awareness of emotions such as envy and irrational anger may induce repression, preemption, or transmutation.

(11) Beliefs about other people's motivations can be powerful triggers of emotions. If you buy a car that is fancier than mine, I may be envious. If I also believe that you enjoy my envy, it may turn into resentment. If I believe that you bought the car in order to make me envious, it may become murderous. In the first case, the emotion is triggered by (my belief about) your action; in the second case, by (my belief about) your emotion; in the third case, by (my belief about) the motivation behind your action. Such motivation-dependent emotions are very common. A gift may be met with gratitude or with resentment, depending on the motivation that the recipient imputes to the donor.[58] "An income distribution that could be tolerable as an accidental or random event ... might lead to violent revolt if seen to be the result of conscious choice on the part of another economic agent."[59] As noted in III.2, an expression of contempt may induce shame if seen as spontaneous but cause anger if seen as intended to induce shame.

Often the motivation for an action cannot be read off the action itself, but sometimes it can. Thus Matthew Rabin argues that in some cases of strategic interaction the motivation can be inferred from the action and induce an emotional response by another actor. Among his examples is the game of chicken, represented in Figure IV.2.

Relying on the notion of a "fairness equilibrium," in which each player does what is fair given the behavior of the other, Rabin comments: "Consider the Nash equilibrium (dare, chicken), where

58. Miller (1993), Chapter 1.
59. Hirshleifer (1987), p. 317.

Player 2

	Dare	Chicken
Dare	-2X, - 2X	2X, 0
Chicken	0, 2X	X, X

Player 1

Figure IV.2.

player 1 'dares' and player 2 'chickens out.' Is it a fairness equilibrium? In this outcome, it is common knowledge that *player 1 is hurting player 2 to help himself.* If X is small enough, player 2 would therefore deviate by playing dare, thus hurting both player 1 and himself. Thus, for small X, (dare, chicken) is not a fairness equilibrium."[60]

(12) As we have seen repeatedly in other chapters, beliefs about other people's beliefs can play a crucial role in generating emotions, independently of any emotions that those beliefs might trigger in these others. As Lovejoy says, man is "an animal which has an urgent desire for a thought of a thought,"[61] that is, the belief that others think well of him. If I believe that others believe – falsely or correctly – that I have committed some misdeed, I will get upset. Higher-order beliefs also occur. In II.4, we saw that the jealousy of the Prince de Clèves was based on his belief that his wife believed that the Duc de Nemours would believe that her refusal to see him was a sign of her love for him. In III.2 I argued that in the struggle for glory, an important determinant of the pride felt by the winner is the belief that his rival believes that third parties believe him to be superior.

(13) Some emotions are triggered only by beliefs that are held in the mode of certainty. Triumphant pride requires more than merely a high probability that one is or will be the winner: Absolute certainty is needed. Other emotions can be induced by beliefs held either in the mode of certainty or in a more probabilistic mode. Thus if the evidence strongly suggests that I have been unfairly bypassed in

60. Rabin (1993), p. 1290; my italics.
61. Lovejoy (1961), p. 92.

a promotion, my indignation may be less than if the mistreatment were known for certain but not a qualitatively different emotion. Still other emotions arise only when the relevant beliefs fall short of certainty. This is most obviously true of hope and fear. If a dreaded event is certain to occur, I feel despair rather than fear. According to Stendhal and Dorothy Tennov, love withers away both when one is certain that it is reciprocated and when one is certain that it is not. Although the case of jealousy may be more complicated, as we have seen, this emotion is also nurtured by doubt, suspicion, and uncertainty.

(14) Emotions can also be triggered by beliefs about imaginary states of affairs. Although subjunctive beliefs – for instance in the form of daydreaming about the future – might seem hard to distinguish from low-probability beliefs, I believe that the associated emotions are quite different. An event that is somehow viewed as "really possible," however remotely, may generate hope. Thus Tocqueville wrote that

In a country where it is not impossible that a poor man may come to the highest offices of the State, it is much easier to continue excluding the poor from any share of control over the government, than in those countries where all hope of rising to a higher rank is denied them. The idea of the imaginary grandeur to which he may one day be called, places itself continuously between the poor man and the contemplation of his real miseries. It is a game of chance, where the enormous possible gain lays hold of the mind in spite of the almost certainty of loss. He is charmed with aristocracy as with the lottery.[62]

By contrast, the daydream described in Dorothy Parker's short story "The Standard of Living" – how to spend a million dollars if a total stranger suddenly decided to leave one this sum in his will – does not involve hope that this event might actually come to pass.[63] Rather, it generates emotions of vicarious consumption together with the aesthetic emotion from a well-constructed daydream. One can tell oneself a story about the big prize in the lottery: Someone has to win it – why not me? By contrast, one cannot tell oneself a plausible story about bequests from total strangers.[64]

62. Tocqueville (1836), p. 150.
63. See Elster (in press a, section III.2) for a discussion of this story.
64. Tennov (1979, pp. 74–75) emphasizes that subjunctive fantasies about the consummation and reciprocation of love are also subject to plausibility constraints: "As

As I noted when discussing shame and envy in previous chapters, these emotions may involve counterfactual beliefs about what could have happened but didn't. Again, there is a plausibility constraint. For the emotion to be poignant, one has to be able to tell oneself, plausibly, "it could have been me" or, more generally, "it could have happened this way." Essentially, the rules of plausibility are those of constructing a novel – minimizing coincidence and reliance on other exceptional events.[65] Perceived control over the counterfactual event is also important.[66] In the important case of traumatic events, it is a question of finding the "closest possible world" in which the event did not happen.[67] If I hit a pedestrian when driving, I will feel guilt if the closest of the nonaccident worlds is one in which I paid more attention, and anger if it is one in which *he* paid more attention. Yet given the highly charged nature of these situations, it is somewhat unlikely that the counterfactual belief will be formed by dispassionate causal reasoning. There will be a pressure for the agent to come up with a belief that exonerates him and allows him to be angry with someone else rather than feeling guilty.[68] Observers may be more even-handed. Whereas the agent may have a tendency to shop around, as it were, for a belief that lets him off the hook,[69]

beautiful as a scene on a Caribbean island may be with you and [the person you love] dancing together in the moonlight, the scene brings the glow of bliss only when you are able to fill in the gaps, as it were, between present circumstances and the desired event." By contrast, as she notes, sexual fantasies are not subject to the plausibility constraint.

65. Kahneman and Tversky (1982); Kahneman and Miller (1986); Elster (in press a, section III.4).
66. Thus Markman et al. (1995, p. 593) found that in a gambling experiment the counterfactual undoing of the subjects "was drawn toward their own wheel when they had control over the spin and toward the other wheel when they controlled the choice of wheel."
67. Lewis (1973).
68. An alternative mechanism for "motivated counterfactual thinking" relies on the idea that people may choose upward or downward counterfactuals – possible outcomes that are better or worse than the actual outcome – for purely pragmatic reasons. Thus "people can strategically use downward counterfactuals to make themselves feel better and upward . . . counterfactuals to improve performance" (Roese 1994, p. 805; see also Markman et al. 1993, Roese and Olson 1995). Yet here, too, we would expect there to be plausibility constraints (Parducci 1995, p. 177). I conjecture that counterfactuals motivated by the agent's need to make himself feel better by a pure contrast effect are less important than those that are motivated by his need to absolve himself from blame.
69. This formulation assumes a multistep process somewhat similar to the one described in Fig. II.1. First, the person forms a belief that he was at fault. Second, the guilt induced by this belief induces him to rewrite the script so as to locate the fault in another person, with guilt being replaced by anger or whatever other emotion

neutral observers may decide on the relevant counterfactuals before they go on to allocate the blame.[70]

(15) A closely related category of beliefs are the "as-if" beliefs generated by novels or films. In the case of literature, to which I limit myself here, Robert Yanal notes that we are faced with the apparent paradox that all the following propositions appear to be true, yet at least one of them has to be false:

1. We feel emotion towards the characters and situations of some works of fiction.
2. We feel these emotions even though we believe that such characters and situations are fictional and not real.
3. We feel emotions towards characters or situations only when we believe them to be real and not fictional.[71]

The issue is related to one I raised in the discussion of Aristotle in II.2: Do emotions require full-fledged beliefs, that is, beliefs that something is the case in the actual world, or can they be generated by more shadowy cognitive entities? If – as seems clear – counterfactual and subjunctive beliefs can induce emotions, I cannot see why fictional beliefs could not have the same effect. As Yanal comments, "If there is a paradox forthcoming from feeling emotions towards fictions, then there is a closely related paradox generated from feeling emotions towards possibilities."[72] As he also argues, intuition (3) is the one to be discarded. From introspection, it seems that the emotion

might be appropriate in the rewritten script. As opposed to this self-deceptive mechanism, however, we might also observe the one-step process of wishful thinking. Observing that something bad happened, the person immediately concludes that someone else could have acted differently, without first forming and then repressing the belief that the closest world is the one in which he acted differently.

70. Most studies are concerned with the beliefs of observers; see notably Miller and McFarland (1986), Turley et al. (1995), and Branscombe et al. (1996). A study by Davis et al. (1995) is unusual both in studying the beliefs of agents and in dealing with real-life events rather than with hypothetical scenarios. Among the forty-two parents of car accidents victims who engaged in counterfactual thinking, 55% tried mentally to undo their own behavior, whereas the remainder tried to undo that of the deceased person. "Interestingly, not one person reported trying to undo the other driver's behavior, even though in most cases the other driver was negligent or allegedly under the influence of drugs or alcohol at the time of the accident" (p. 114). Because the parents knew that they were not in any way to blame, however, the study does not address the "agent bias" stipulated in the text.

71. Yanal (1994), pp. 54–55.

72. *Ibid.*, p. 60.

I feel when a character in a television play is making a fool of himself in public is very similar or even identical to the vicarious shame I feel when a friend is doing the same in a real-life situation. I cringe and want to stop watching or to leave.[73]

(16) Emotions can also rest on self-fulfilling beliefs. Even when the initial belief has little or no objective foundation, it may generate emotions whose observable expressions induce emotions or behaviors in another person that justify the original belief. Suppose I am afraid because I believe, wrongly, that a dog is about to attack me. In my fear I secrete adrenaline, which the dog takes for an expression of anger, these two emotions having the same chemical expression. Believing or perceiving that I am angry it attacks me, thus justifying my original belief. Or suppose, following Stendhal's analysis of love (II.4), that I fall in love with you because I believe, without much factual support, that you are in love with me. Observing my behavior, you form the belief that I love you – and that is all it takes for you to fall in love with me and thus verify my original belief. As a contrast to this virtuous cycle, we may consider the vicious spiral of jealousy. As Proust noted, "once the jealousy has been discovered, the person who is its object views it as a challenge that authorizes the infidelity."[74] As we saw in III.4, the general tendency in feuding societies to suspect the worst may have similar self-fulfilling properties, as also noted by Richard Nisbett and Dov Cohen in their analysis of the culture of honor in the Southern states of the United States:

In a culture where honor is so important, arguments lead to affronts that demand retribution. The availability of guns increases the chance that the retribution may be deadly. In addiction, the knowledge that the other person may be armed and may begin acting violently may lead to preemptive first strikes. Once conflicts escalate, a man may be more apt to take a first strike

---

73. Walton (1990, p. 202) argues that the tendency to walk out on the television play should not be confused with the action tendencies inherent in the emotions themselves. When people leave a movie depicting an attack by a horrible slime, their emotion is "fear of the depiction of the slime, not of the slime depicted." I wonder whether an account in terms of empathy may not be more convincing. To use another example, when I close my eyes before some horrible event on the screen it seems very similar or even identical to what I do when I close my eyes before a horrible real-life event that I am unable to influence.

74. Proust (1954), vol. 3, p. 150; see also Grimaldi (1993), p. 42. The mechanism involved here may be that of psychological reactance (Brehm 1966). The object of jealousy feels that the suspicion is a threat to his freedom of action and hence tries to reestablish the freedom by doing exactly what the jealous person fears, even if he would otherwise never have thought of being unfaithful.

as a matter of self-protection before he himself gets shot. At a cultural level, the occurrence of hundreds of these violent self-fulfilling prophecies creates a milieu where the threat of violence keeps individuals vigilant (perhaps hypervigilant) in their own defense.[75]

These self-fulfilling beliefs are one important mechanism in generating what we may call, following Paul Ekman, "emotional wildfires."[76] In IV.3 I consider another mechanism of emotional escalation that does not rely on social interaction, but rather on what I called "counterwishful thinking."

Not all emotions have cognitive antecedents. As Joseph LeDoux has shown, fear arises in two different pathways from the sensory apparatus in the thalamus to the amygdala, the part of the brain that causes visceral as well as behavioral emotional responses. In accordance with the traditional view that emotions are always preceded and triggered by a cognition, one pathway goes from the thalamus to the neocortex, the thinking part of the brain, and from the neocortex on to the amygdala. The organism receives a signal, forms a belief about what it means, and then reacts emotionally. There is also, however, a direct pathway from the thalamus to the amygdala that bypasses the thinking part of the brain entirely. Compared to the first pathway, the second is "quick and dirty." On the one hand, it is faster. "In a rat it takes about twelve milliseconds (twelve one-thousandths of a second) for an acoustic stimulus to reach the amygdala through the thalamic pathway, and almost twice as long through the cortical pathway."[77] On the other hand, the second pathway differentiates less finely among incoming signals. Whereas the cortex can figure out that a slender curved shape on a path through the wood is a curved stick rather than a snake, the amygdala cannot make this distinction. "If it is a snake, the amygdala is ahead of the game. From the point of view of survival, it is better to respond to potentially dangerous events as if they were in fact the real thing than to fail to respond. The cost of treating a stick as a snake is less, in the long run, than the cost of treating a snake as a stick."[78]

For the present purposes, this finding has two main aspects. First and crucially, rather than the cognitive representation of the dangerous object being a cause of the emotional reaction, they are both

75. Nisbett and Cohen (1996), p. 38.
76. Ekman (1992b), p. 172.
77. LeDoux (1996), p. 163.
78. *Ibid.*, p. 165.

caused by the same external event impinging on the organism. Second and less importantly, rather than the cognitive effect preceding the emotional one, it occurs at a later point in time. Even if the second statement had not been true, the first would have been sufficient to disprove the claim of "appraisal theorists" that cognition is a necessary condition for emotion.[79] (But if the second had not been true it would have been harder to establish the first.) Thus we find that neurophysiology confirms Descartes's intuition that surprise or astonishment (his word is "admiration," which had a different meaning in his time) "can happen before we know in the least whether this object is suitable to us or not" (PA §53).

Appraisal theorists might respond by saying that a state of the organism does not count as an emotion unless it has an intentional object. To be afraid is to be afraid *of something*, a condition that is not satisfied by the organism that goes into a freeze twelve milliseconds before the relevant cognition is formed. Emotions presuppose cognition because they presuppose intentionality, which presupposes cognition. But this reply might not be good enough. Phobics, according to LeDoux, are "consciously afraid of their phobic stimuli. This means that they also have an explicit conscious memory, formed through their temporal lobe memory system, that reminds them that they are afraid of snakes, heights, or whatever. This memory might be established during the initial traumatic learning situation, but some phobics do not recall such a learning experience, possibly because of a stress-induced memory loss."[80] For phobics in the latter category, the panic attack is triggered by the *perception* of an object of a certain kind, without a concomitant *cognition* that it is dangerous. The occurrent panic attack has an intentional object, but no cognitive antecedent. We simply have to accept that "[o]ur emotions are sometimes irrational in the sense that we know that the judgment upon which the emotion would be based if it *were* based on a judgment is untrue, and yet we cannot shake the emotion."[81]

Although striking, these findings are not centrally important in the context of the present work. In the first place, it is not known

---

79. Lazarus (1991).
80. LeDoux (1996), p. 255. As he emphasizes elsewhere (p. 244) it is not really a question of a memory *loss*. Rather, the stress involved in a traumatic experience might, by a specific neurophysiological mechanism, prevent any memory from being formed at all. As he also notes (p. 246), this account provides a clear alternative to Freud's theory of memory suppression.
81. Roberts (1984), p. 398.

whether they generalize from fear to other emotions. In the second place, in the complex human situations that mainly concern me here, a delay of twelve milliseconds is not likely to be that significant. In the third place, my focus is not on extreme emotional states such as phobias, panics, and post–traumatic stress disorders, but on the ordinary emotions that are the stuff of everyday life. Although the distinction is obviously not a hard-and-fast one, I believe that for some emotions in all situations and all emotions in most situations, a cognitive antecedent is in fact needed.

Romantic love may seem to provide a more relevant counterexample than instinctive, reflexive, or pathological fears. In II.3 I suggested a contrast between Pascal's cognitive approach to love and Shakespeare's "love is not love which alters when it alteration finds." More generally, Alan Soble argues that in what he calls the "agapic" tradition, x's love for y is not "dependent on what x believes about, or perceives in, y."[82] By its reference to perception, this idea is actually stronger than what we need here. A counterexample to the proposition that all emotions have cognitive antecedents might be a case in which love was based merely on perception of the other person's beauty, without any propositional beliefs about him or her at all. To take Pascal's categories in *Pensée* 567, cited in II.3, the other person's *beauty* is the object of the senses but his or her *judgment* is an object of the judgment. As Merleau-Ponty says somewhere, "I see that he sees" differs from "I think that he thinks." But before we conclude that mere beauty without any cognition can trigger love, we should remember Stendhal's claim (II.4) that love requires the belief that the other person may love oneself, a view that is consistent with the idea that love does not require beliefs about any particular *monadic* properties of the other.

Within the aesthetic domain there are many emotions that lack cognitive antecedents. The emotions of joy or grief generated by music, in particular, cannot by any stretch of the imagination be made to fit the appraisal theory of the emotions. Nor do rapturous emotions experienced in the contemplation of mountains or sunsets have a cognitive antecedent. (I bypass the question of whether and how emotions generated by natural beauty differ from those generated by man-made beauty.) Emotions generated by fiction do not, however,

---

82. Soble (1990), p. 6. On the alternative or "erosic" view defended by Pascal, "x loves y *because* y has S or because x perceives or believes that y has S" (*ibid.*, p. 4).

form a counterexample, assuming we are willing to include fictional beliefs among the cognitive states that can trigger emotions.

Emotional contagion may provide a final category of emotions that arise without a prior cognitive antecedent. Elaine Hatfield, John Cacioppo, and Richard Rapson argue that emotional contagion is based on mimicry of the emotional expression of others and feedback from the expressions that are mimicked to the emotions themselves.[83] In the Schachter–Singer experiments, people interpreted physiological arousal as an emotional experience when they were primed by the presence of confederates who appeared to be happy or angry. Yet these cases may not provide hard counterexamples, given that the artificially induced emotions are typically triggered by genuine emotions in others.

INTENTIONAL OBJECTS

Emotions are "about" something; they have intentional objects. Other attitudes such as desires and beliefs also have intentional objects, but there is a difference. The objects of beliefs and desires are always propositions: I believe that p, I desire that p. The objects of emotions can be propositions but need not be so. I have repeatedly distinguished between the emotions that are triggered by a belief about an *action* by oneself or another and those that are triggered by a belief about one's own or another's *character*. The former can have an intentional object of a propositional form: I am angry that he insulted me, I am proud that I won the first prize. The latter is directed at a person rather than at a state of affairs: I hate informers (Aristotle's example), I am ashamed of myself, and so forth.

Although I believe the distinction is valid, it is not always easy to keep it in mind. Much marital therapy involves learning to direct hostility caused by what the other does towards these actions rather than towards his or her person, presumably because the latter reaction is so common.[84] Rather than "I am angry that he insulted me," it may be more natural to say "I am angry with him for insulting me." The emotion of anger may be attached to a personal or to a propositional object. Yet in the case of hatred or love, the emotion can *only* be stated with a personal object. When we love, we love a person, whether or

83. Hatfield et al. (1994).
84. Lewis (1992), p. 181.

not we also love for a reason.[85] Envy, too, is always directed at a person. There are several entries in the *Oxford English Dictionary* for "I am indignant that ..." (*and* for "I am indignant with ...") but none for "I am envious that ...." I conclude, therefore, that whereas all social emotions *can* be stated with a personal object, some *must* have a personal object. The view that all emotions can be rendered "S emotes that p," on an analogy with "S believes that p," cannot be defended.[86]

Not all emotions have intentional objects. Specifically, it is often argued that emotions do not have an object when they take the form of moods. Moods, according to some theorists, are "nonintentional mental phenomena."[87] Above, I listed some twenty-odd states, ranging from joy to guilt, that must unambiguously be classified as emotions. Of these, some – joy, grief, sadness, anger – also exist in the form of moods. In addition, "free-floating anxiety" seems to be a sui generis mood, rather than a special mode of existence of an emotion that also exists in non-mood states. I wonder, however, whether moods might not rather be heightened dispositions to have occurrent emotions.[88] "He is in a happy mood" may either refer to an uninterrupted state of well-being or to an enhanced tendency to experience pangs of well-being. Reasoning from first principles suggests that the latter may be the more plausible idea. The life of the mind is a succession of events, not an enduring state. On this understanding, the reason why moods appear to lack an object or a target is simply that the object is constantly changing. Be this as it may, moods – whether they are states or dispositions – should be distinguished from the durable dispositions that we attach to a person's character rather than to the transient circumstances in which he finds himself. You

---

85. When discussing Hume's propositional theory of pride, Davidson (1980, p. 278) notes that "if Hume's theory is to cope with the other indirect passions a propositional form must be found for each of them" and then adds, "Thus Hume seems to explain loving *for a reason* rather than simply loving." This argument seems to confuse the question of cognitive versus perceptual antecedents of emotion with the question of propositional versus nonpropositional objects of emotion.
86. Gordon (1987) provides a clear exposition of this view.
87. Frijda (1993), p. 381. In his further discussion, Frijda oscillates between saying that moods have no object and that they have unstable, fleeting objects, without noting that the latter description (which corresponds to the view I suggest in the text) restores the intentionality to moods.
88. Relying on his "contextual theory of happiness," Parducci (1995, p. 174, n. 11) suggests that "bad moods might reflect a generalized disposition to add extreme upper endpoints to a great variety of contexts," thus devaluing actual experiences through a contrast effect.

do not have to be an irascible person to be in an angry mood, and neither is a necessary condition for being angry.

A more decisive counterexample is provided by emotions in music. As Malcolm Budd writes,

in the case of the musical expression of emotion, the emotion you are moved by is ... both abstract and, as it were, disembodied: the emotion is not about any definite state of affairs and it is not experienced by someone of definite characteristics (age, race, sex, and so on). If the emotion is triumph, it will be triumph whose object is not specified, and it will be the triumphant feeling, not of a particular individual, but only of an indeterminate persona, defined only by the nature of the emotion .... The emotion lacks both a definite object and a definite subject.[89]

AROUSAL

Emotions go together with some form of physiological change that, in many cases, may be appropriately referred to as arousal. Actually, as shown by Nico Frijda's exhaustive discussion, the range of physiological changes that accompany the emotions is very large. "Descriptively, at least four kinds of 'arousal,' of sources of activity of some sort, should be kept separate: sympathetic (or autonomic) arousal; attentional arousal or 'increased capacity for perceptual analysis'; behavioral activation; and electrocortical arousal."[90] There is some covariation among these components of physiological change, but it is very rough. The changes do not always vary together in magnitude or even in direction. In the terminology of Chapter I, both type A and type B mechanisms are observed. An instance of the former is the unpredictable tendency for threatening events to trigger either white or red anger, as manifested in pallor and blushing respectively.[91] An instance of the latter is that "sham rage causes increase of blood sugar level in cats; transsection of the spinal cord leads to a drop in that level; subsequent cutting of the vagal nerve again abolishes this drop, which demonstrates that it had been a parasympathetic response ordinarily masked by the sympathetic one."[92] The overall picture is complicated and does not lend itself to easy summary.

89. Budd (1995), p. 149.
90. Frijda (1986), pp. 170–1.
91. *Ibid.*, pp. 130–1.
92. *Ibid.*, p. 158. Sham rage is the phenomenon that minor stimuli can evoke violent anger responses in animals whose cerebral cortex has been removed (*ibid.*, p. 380).

Let me return to the distinction introduced in III.4 between the two kinds of fear. As Robert Gordon observes, the visceral *state of fear* may not induce the behavior required on the belief–desire model of fear: In fact, it may cause one to act in the very opposite manner. "I *flee* from the dog out of fear: but if I stand my ground and stare, I probably do not do so out of fear, even if I do so for fear that (because I am afraid that) otherwise the dog would attack me."[93] It would be thoroughly confusing and misleading to treat both kinds of fear as instances of emotion. I cannot agree entirely, therefore, with Frijda when he writes,

> Emotions may be said to be more intense the more persistent the intentions, the longer these remain, and the more varied the structures are. It is this kind of intensity that is of social relevance, rather than the intensity of momentary response, the loudness of the voice, the number of tears spent. Who ... is more afraid of nuclear war: he whose heart beats violently upon some news item, or bites his lips and reads with a contorted face, or he who, when considering the risks of nuclear war, modifies his life plans, enters politics, or loses his interest in life?[94]

If loss of interest in life is understood as depression, that *is* an emotional reaction. By contrast, I cannot see why somebody who enters politics to reduce the chances of nuclear war has to be emotionally involved in any way. In many cases, such behavior can be fully explained by the desire–belief model. Thwarted desires, to be sure, often generate emotions, but that is no reason for saying that the desire *is* an emotion. Consider someone who says he loves freedom. If he claimed to have heart flutterings whenever he thought of freedom, I might dismiss his emotion as *Schwärmerei*. If attacks on freedom tend to make him angry, that would still not amount to love of freedom. If attacks on freedom make him take action to defend it, whether or not he also is angered, we might conclude that he values freedom highly, but evaluations are not emotions. Although Frijda may be right in that deep commitments have more social relevance than arousal per se (but see below for some counterexamples), that is neither here nor there if what we want to study (as I do) is the social relevance *of the emotions*.

93. Gordon (1987), p. 77. Standing one's ground is *intentional* (non-)behavior, although behaviorally indistinguishable from "freezing," which is not.
94. Frijda (1986), p. 100.

What Gordon calls "fear-motivated action" need not go together with any arousal, although it might in the case that he envisages. When arousal is present, it need not influence behavior: As in Gordon's example, I may stand my ground even if I'm afraid. When arousal does influence behavior – as when my fear causes me to flee – it takes us beyond the belief–desire model. Frijda writes that "[e]motional action . . . is not usually guided by a prior goal representation."[95] For instance, "panicky flight is directed, not toward a place of safety, but away from the state of danger."[96] Also, "anecdotes abound about being unable to move or think when confronted with danger, or about ineffectual fumbling with oxygen masks and escape hatches, or about the last match extinguished by the trembling of one's fingers."[97] Emotion can induce ineffectual action such as fleeing from the fire into the frying pan; it can also block action altogether and substitute mere physical movement such as trembling of the hands. As in a famous example offered by Donald Davidson, the behavior caused by arousal may be indistinguishable from the action that is required by the beliefs and desires of the subject. "A climber might want to rid himself of the weight and danger of holding another man on a rope, and he might know that by loosening his hold on the rope he could rid himself of the weight and the danger. This belief and want might so unnerve him as to cause him to lose his hold, and yet it might be the case that he never *chose* to loosen his hold, nor did he do it intentionally."[98]

According to Ortony, Clore, and Collins, high arousal may occur even when the occurrence or nonoccurrence of an event is a matter of indifference to us, that is, if the event has both attractive and unattractive features that exactly cancel out. "The overall subjective importance of an event can probably best be thought of in terms of the sum of the (unsigned) [absolute] values of desirability and undesirability . . . It seems reasonable to suppose that physiological arousal is determined primarily by the subjective importance of the event so defined."[99] An emotional state might affect behavior qua mere nervous energy, even if the content of that state has no implications for behavior. The example from Tesser cited in I.6 illustrates this point.

95. *Ibid.*, p. 75.
96. *Ibid.*, p. 81.
97. *Ibid.*, p. 115.
98. Davidson (1980), p. 79.
99. Ortony et al. (1988), p. 51.

If large numbers of persons are regularly exposed to conditions that generate emotions with strong arousal effects, the "social relevance" may be considerable. Thus Frijda refers to "the higher habitual diastolic pressure levels of black male subjects whose coping style is that of suppressed hostility ('anger in' plus guilt feelings about anger)."[100] This may explain why blacks tend to need kidney transplantation at higher rates than whites.[101] Hypertension, a main cause of renal disease, is much more frequent in the black population, a fact that may be due to "psychosocial stress caused by darker skin color" in lower socioeconomic groups.[102] According to Frijda it is not the arousal as such but the need to contain it that has these psychosomatic effects. Similarly, patients with breast cancer who suppress their emotional reactions to the illness may have worse prognoses than others.[103] As women are often trained to suppress their anger,[104] this fate may not be uncommon. Other (non–subgroup-specific) studies have found that both occurrent episodes of anger[105] and chronic irascibility[106] increase the risk of coronary heart disease. Although there are many methodological pitfalls in these analyses, notably the problem of distinguishing true causation from mere correlation, their overall impact is to suggest that the arousal component of emotions has considerable medical and social consequences.

Not all emotions are accompanied by arousal. Frijda argues that sometimes "there are no signs of autonomic arousal while subjects say they are, or feel, happy or anxious or angry. It is as well to take such subjects at their word, as long as their behavior does not contradict them."[107] Another counterexample is provided by emotions generated by works of art. Although horror movies may generate arousal, the Goldberg Variations are less likely to do so.

---

100. Frijda (1986), p. 129.
101. Dennis (1995), pp. 136–9.
102. Klag et al. (1991). The authors mention, however, that another interpretation is also possible: The hypertension might be due to an interaction between some environmental factor (stress or diet) caused by socioeconomic disadvantage (shared by blacks and low-income whites) and a gene that has higher prevalence among blacks with darker skin color. On both hypotheses, *being a disadvantaged black* explains the hypertension, but only on the first is the explanation in terms of stress that is caused by this double disadvantage.
103. See Barraclough (1994, pp. 94–100) and Dubovsky (1997, pp. 333–7) for surveys of the literature.
104. Ekman (1980), p. 87.
105. Mittleman et al. (1995).
106. Kawachi et al. (1996).
107. Frijda (1986), p. 173.

PHYSIOLOGICAL EXPRESSION

Emotions have characteristic expressions. They include bodily posture, voice pitch, flushing and blushing, smiling and baring one's teeth, laughing and frowning, weeping and crying. Although, as Frijda says, "a thin line divides expression from true emotional actions,"[108] the distinction can usually be made. Also, many expressions are very closely related to the physiological responses I have just discussed, but some are not.

Many expressions are directly functional, parts of an action pattern that helps the organism cope with the situation that generates the emotion. "The prime example is the expression of disgust; it reduces sensory contact with distasteful substances in the mouth cavity and tends towards expelling those substances.... Expressions or eagerness, desire and reluctance are incipient actions of approach and shrinking back."[109] Similarly, "the oblique eyebrows and resulting vertical frown which are part of the expression universally recognized as one of fear ... may well result from an impulse to protectively close the eyes while simultaneously keeping them open, in order to keep track of the fearful object."[110] Other expressions are by-products of action patterns rather than functional parts of them. Loudness of voice or compression of the lips do not directly enhance coping but follow from the general mobilization of the organism against danger. Although these expressions do not themselves serve a function, they owe their existence to a functional system of which they are indissociably part.

Expressions of emotions that arise in social interaction may serve as signals to others, whether or not they owe their origin to the signaling function.[111] As the expressions described in the preceding paragraph are visible to others, they may have a signaling effect that does not enter into the explanation of their origin. By contrast, behaviors such as stamping one's foot are unlearned expressions of anger that "are not easily understood as preparations for attack or for bracing oneself against oncoming attack.... They are intimidating demonstrations

108. *Ibid.*, p. 12.
109. *Ibid.*, p. 11.
110. *Ibid.*, p. 16.
111. This presupposes that the relation between emotions and their expressions is one–one or one–many. To the extent that it is many–one or many–many (III.4), the signaling function is obscured.

of power."[112] These signaling expressions are to varying degrees under the control of the will. It is possible to imitate facial expressions and bodily postures that signal fear, anger, and joy, although most people can't do it; to compensate, most people can't discriminate between imperfect imitations and the real thing. In cultures in which words are usually accompanied by vivid movements of the hand, lying can often be detected by the absence of these gestures, because the concentration required for a convincing lie interferes with the spontaneous gesturing. Not many people are capable of such detection, however.[113]

Some expressions of emotion are purely learned, or conventional. In Albania, for instance, passing someone a cup of coffee under one's left arm is to express contempt for him.[114] These expressions are obvious targets of social norms, as we saw in III.2. Social norms ("display rules") can also regulate nonconventional expressions such as smiling or crying. In many situations, people are expected to smile politely, which is not to say that they have to appear to be sincere. In "the performance of such display rules ... errors are usually overlooked. An example of this type of display rule is that at beauty contests a winner may cry but not the losers. At funerals, one can note almost a 'pecking order' of grief expressions based on the rights to mourn. A man's secretary cannot look sadder than his wife unless she intends to state something quite different about the true nature of their relationship."[115] Sometimes, however, mistakes are not overlooked. Flight attendants and people in other service professions are subject to the norm of appearing to smile sincerely.[116]

Not all emotions have observable expressions; again the aesthetic emotions may provide the best example. Frijda argues that some forms of grief and sadness also lack well-defined expressions: "[P]assive sadness is not a response: It is nonbehavior.... Variants of sadness are primarily such as to turn this null state into withdrawal, or nonbehavior into behavior."[117]

---

112. Frijda (1986), p. 26.
113. Ekman (1992a).
114. Hasluck (1954), pp. 231–2.
115. Ekman (1980), p. 87.
116. Hochschild (1983).
117. Frijda (1986), p. 22.

VALENCE

Psychologists use this word to refer to the fact that emotions are experienced as pleasant or painful, desirable or undesirable, making for happiness or unhappiness. For affluent twentieth-century city dwellers, this is the most important aspect of the emotions. Although they may have originated as part of the defensive and offensive action systems of the organism and still exhibit that aspect under stressful circumstances, their hedonic aspect is much more important in everyday living. The feeling of shame can be unbearably painful, as shown by the suicide of a Navy admiral who was about to be exposed as not entitled to some of the medals he was wearing. Conversely, the radiant love of Anne Elliott at the end of *Persuasion* is unsurpassable happiness. Some emotions are intensely worth striving or wishing for, others intensely worth avoiding. In between, there are many emotions that are less intensely desirable or undesirable. I believe this is pretty much all one can say about interemotion comparisons of intensity.

The only known way of making cardinal measures of welfare is the von Neumann–Morgenstern procedure. One could imagine extending it to the case of emotional experiences, by asking people whether they would prefer to experience emotion X to a lottery that would give them extremes of (say) love and shame with probabilities p and $1 - p$ respectively. The value of p that renders them indifferent between the emotion and the lottery could then be used as a measure of its strength. The idea sounds absurd, and it is. The von Neumann procedure is both invalid in general and unreliable in the case of the emotions. It is invalid in general because it captures both the intrinsic desirability of the options and people's attitudes towards risk; moreover, there is no way to disentangle these two components from each other. Applied to the emotions the procedure is unreliable, because there is no reason to think that intuitions in this matter would be robust and trustworthy. The best one can do is produce a partial ordinal ranking of emotional experiences – some experiences are better than others, although one cannot say by how much, whereas other pairs do not lend themselves to comparison at all. When asked whether they would rather be caught cheating on an exam or suffer the break-up of a relationship, most people would probably be at a loss for what to say. Also, the nature of the former act would make it hard to admit, even to themselves, that they would rather feel shame than grief.

Valence and arousal are two different aspects of emotional *intensity*. Often, these go together; and even when they do not they are easily confused with one another.[118] They are nevertheless distinct, conceptually as well as empirically. First, as we have seen several times, mixed emotions may involve strong arousal while being hedonically neutral. Second, some emotions are high in arousal, low in valence. Thus Michael Lewis asserts that the feeling of embarrassment is "slightly negative, but intense."[119] Third, some emotions are low in arousal, high in unpleasantness. Thus by many measures boredom matches fear and distress with respect to unpleasantness, while being close to drowsiness and sleepiness as far as arousal is concerned.[120] These states are puzzling, because of their ambiguous relation to behavior. They may induce blushing or fidgeting, but not any form of goal-directed action. Perhaps the urge to act requires that both arousal and valence be above some threshold. Finally, to the extent that arousal is a multidimensional concept, the very idea of arousal and valence waxing and waning together is ill defined.

Valence enters doubly into the analysis of emotions. First, having the emotion can be painful or pleasurable. Second, if the action tendency of the emotion includes a desire for the world to be different, the pursuit and satisfaction of this desire may induce pleasurable emotions, the nature of which depends on the original emotion. As we saw in II.2, these secondary emotions may, by anticipation, arise more or less simultaneously with the primary emotion. The pain of being offended blends, for instance, with the pleasure of anticipated revenge. Yet the emotional rewards for actual revenge are likely to be much higher.[121] Guilt may trigger a desire for reparation or confession that, when satisfied, induces a strong feeling of relief or liberation from a burden.

In general, the net effect of the initial negative emotion and the positive emotion resulting from pursuing and satisfying the desire it generates is indeterminate. The pleasure from revenge might dominate the suffering that triggered the revenge; the feeling of relief from guilt may fail to offset the guilt. There is a partial analogy here to the opponent-process mechanism (I.2). In both cases, we are dealing

---

118. The discussion in Ben-Ze'ev (1992) about the "intensity" of envy seems to conflate arousal and valence.
119. Lewis (1992), p. 88.
120. Russell (1980).
121. Frijda (1994, p. 282) enumerates five dimensions of satisfaction derived from revenge.

with mechanisms of type B_2. In both cases, there is a process that has to run its course before the subject returns to a baseline state. And in both, we can observe a negative state triggering a positive one. There also are obvious differences. An initial positive emotion does not induce desires that, when satisfied, generate negative emotions. Also, the presently discussed case does not have the between-episode dynamics illustrated by the difference between the upper and lower parts of Fig. I.2. Finally, the opponent-process mechanism is purely psychic and does not require any action by the subject. The comparison is useful, nevertheless, in drawing attention to the fact that much of life may best be understood as *a succession of episodes* – deviating from and then returning to a baseline – rather than as a succession of punctual events.[122]

Not all emotions have positive or negative valence. Some emotional experiences may be neutral, in the sense that we are indifferent between having them and not having them. (The obstacles to comparing the intensity of emotional experiences obviously arise for such comparisons as well.) The most obvious examples are provided by composite emotional experiences. Bittersweet nostalgia – reflecting an endowment effect and a contrast effect that exactly offset each other (I.6) – is one illustration. Similarly, a friend's success may, all things considered, leave us indifferent (but not unaroused). Also, the mixed emotion that consists of anger together with the pleasurable anticipation of revenge may, on balance, be hedonically neutral. (Here, the obstacles to comparison are very obvious.) A more difficult question is whether elementary emotions can have zero valence. Introspection suggests that they cannot.

ACTION TENDENCIES

As defined by Frijda, these are "states of readiness to execute a given kind of action. . . . Action tendencies have the character of urges or impulses."[123] They are "virtual actions," as Thomas Aquinas said with respect to the destructive urge in envy.[124] The immediate impulse

---

122. Hence the idea that well-being is a sum or integral over time of momentaneous states of pleasure and pain (Kahneman, in press) may fail to capture important aspects of the phenomenon. People may attach value to episodes as a whole rather than to their individual constituents.
123. Frijda (1986), pp. 70, 78.
124. *Summa* IIae, qu.36, third article.

of the envious person is in fact to destroy the object of his envy or, if that is impossible, to destroy its owner. The action tendency of shame is to hide or disappear; that of guilt, to make atonements or to confess; that of love, to approach and touch the other person. According to Aristotle (II.2), anger and hatred differ in that the action tendency of the former is to make its object suffer, that of the latter to make it disappear. Fear, as noted in I.2, has two action tendencies: fight or flight.

Although roughly accurate, this standard account requires some modification. As noted in the discussion of envy (III.3), we may distinguish between an action tendency and a wish or desire for a certain state of affairs to obtain. In wrath, what matters is not simply that the other suffer: To restore my self-esteem and sense of agency it is necessary that *I* make him suffer.[125] In *hybris*, too, the humiliation of the other has to come about by my agency. In hatred, by contrast, what matters is that the hated person disappear from the face of the earth, not that *I* make him disappear. In envy, similarly, what matters is that the other not have the possession I envy him, not that he loses it by my agency. Although a strong desire may seem almost indissociable from the tendency to realize it by action, the case of envy, in which the most preferred state is that the other lose what he has but *not* by my agency, shows that they are conceptually distinct.

Action tendencies usually go together with inhibitory tendencies. Some inhibitions arise simultaneously with the action tendency they inhibit (mechanisms of type B_1) whereas others are triggered by it (type B_2).[126] An example of the former is when the sympathetic and parasympathetic nervous systems are activated simultaneously, the one producing the action tendency and the other a tendency to restraint or energy conservation.[127] The latter category includes not only self-control and control via social norms but also purely physiological mechanisms.

In this connection, we may cite an important observation by Frijda:

It may . . . be that emotional impulse as evoked by relevant stimuli potentially always is of maximal intensity, regardless of realistic or moralistic considerations; this impulse is toned down by inhibition, as a permanent stabilizing counterforce governed by reality and morality. Sham rage, Mark and Ervin's observations on unrestrained anger, enhancement of startle response

125. Frijda (1994), p. 276.
126. Frijda (1986), p. 392.
127. *Ibid.*, pp. 155–61.

after septal damage and hippocampectomy and when a stimulus is unexpected, ..., Freudian reflections, irritability after stress and under alcohol – all suggest that such maximal impulse propensity lurks behind inhibitory control.[128]

As an illustration, let us suppose that the desire for revenge is a spontaneous impulse of this kind. In modern societies, this desire is usually inhibited by social norms that become internalized at an early age. In feuding societies, the impulse is magnified and focused by strong social norms, as we have seen. I suggest, tentatively, that the ancient Greeks displayed *revenge behavior neither inhibited nor magnified by social norms*, that is, the presocial urge for revenge in something like its pure form.[129] To the extent that this conjecture is correct, attempts to interpret ancient Greek society by relying on studies of modern Mediterranean cultures may be somewhat off the mark.[130]

Not all emotions have action tendencies. Hume asserts, plausibly, that "pride and humility are pure emotions in the soul, unattended with any desire, and not immediately exciting us to action."[131] Also, relief, regret, disappointment, sadness, grief, and most of the aesthetic emotions do not seem to suggest any specific actions. Although small children sometimes want to get on the stage to save the actor from an impending danger, most works of art do not induce any action tendency in readers, listeners, or viewers. In fact, it has been suggested that the aesthetic emotions have an exceptional purity that is due to their dissociation from action.[132]

IV.3. RATIONALITY AND THE EMOTIONS

The relations between rationality and the emotions form an intricate web. One may distinguish among three partly overlapping sets of issues. First, we may try to determine the impact of emotions on the

128. *Ibid.*, p. 408; references deleted.
129. This is not to deny that the Greeks disapproved of those who failed to avenge themselves. It is clear from Demosthenes's speech against Meidias that he felt he had to explain why he had not retaliated immediately when the latter slapped him in public. Yet I do not think we need to stipulate anything like a code of honor to explain the disapproval of failures to take revenge. The disapproval might be as spontaneous as the urge to revenge itself.
130. Cohen (1991) is an example.
131. Hume (1960), p. 367.
132. Fry (1921), p. 13; also Budd (1995), p. 77.

rationality of decision making and belief formation. Second, we may ask whether the emotions themselves can be assessed as more or less rational, independently of their impact on choice and belief formation. And third, we may ask whether emotions can be the object of rational choice, that is, whether people can and do engage in rational deliberation about which emotions to induce in themselves or in other people.

Concerning the first set of issues, the traditional view is that emotions interfere with rational choice. They are, as it were, sand in the machinery of action. More recently, several writers have argued for the revisionist view that emotions, far from interfering with rational decision making, may actually promote it. Thus one may argue that emotions help us make decisions by acting as tie-breakers in cases of indeterminacy and, more generally, improve the quality of decision making by enabling us to focus on salient features of the situation. Another revisionist idea is that rational belief formation is incompatible with emotional well-being (the "sadder but wiser" hypothesis). Others have taken positions that go against the traditional as well as the revisionist views, by claiming that emotions merely affect the parameters of choice without affecting the rationality of choice itself. On this view, emotions enter into decisions as costs and benefits associated with the various options but not as psychic forces capable of shaping or distorting the mechanisms of choice.

Concerning the second set of issues, there are a number of arguments to the effect that emotions themselves can be assessed with a view to their rationality. One may argue that occurrent emotions are actions and hence can be assessed by the usual criteria of rational choice. Also, one may argue emotions are rational if they are appropriate or adequate to the cognitive appraisals that trigger them. Moreover, one may argue that emotions are rational if those appraisals themselves are rational. Finally, one may argue that rational emotional dispositions are those which make one happy. In considering these ideas I shall rely on a notion of rationality that is subjective through and through.[133] I shall not discuss, in other words, whether emotions are objectively useful or adaptive and, if they are, whether their usefulness explains why they exist.[134]

133. Elster (in press b), Ch. 3.3.
134. A good discussion of this issue is in Frijda (1986, pp. 475–9). Elsewhere (Elster in press a, section I.5) I consider a view not discussed by Frijda, namely that emotions are useful self-binding devices in strategic interaction.

Table IV.1.

	Occurrent emotions or their absence	Emotional dispositions
Induced by self	Schafer Solomon Backer	Character planning
Induced by others	Oratory (V.3) "Shaming" (III.2)	Backer Kandel and Lazear

Concerning the third set of issues, different approaches can be distinguished along two dimensions. First, we may ask whether the object of choice is an occurrent emotion or an emotional disposition; second, whether the choice is made by the person in whom the emotion occurs or by somebody else. The ensuing combinations are indicated by Table IV.1. Whereas examples in the lower left-hand case are discussed in other chapters, the remaining cases are considered here.

THE TRADITIONAL VIEW

Subjectively, rational choice involves three optimizing operations.[135] The action that is chosen must be optimal, given the desires and beliefs of the agent. The beliefs must be optimal, given the information available to the agent. The amount of resources allocated to the acquisition of information must be optimal, given the desires of the agent and his beliefs about the expected costs and benefits of information. Given this definition, rationality can fail in two ways: By indeterminacy or by irrationality. Later, I discuss a possible positive role of the emotions in cases of indeterminacy. Here, I discuss how, on the traditional view, emotions might be a cause of irrationality in decision making. They can do so, obviously, by subverting the rationality of action, of belief formation, and of information acquisition.

In his discussion of emotionally induced irrationality, Frijda considers a number of phenomena that may be classified as follows.[136] (i) Emotions affect "probability and credibility estimates" concerning

135. For fuller expositions see Elster (1989b, Chapter I); Elster (in press b, Ch. 3.3).
136. Frijda (1986), pp. 118–21.

events outside one's control. (ii) They "cause some measure of belief in the efficacy of actions one would not believe in under other conditions." (iii) They induce fantasy behavior, as when a widow for many years after the death of her husband sets the table for two each day. (iv) They induce various forms of "painful fantasies that, however painful, are yet sought by the subject himself." Othello's jealousy is cited as an example. (v) They cause irrational behavior, such as "anger at some deed that cannot be undone by the angry aggression, nor its recurrence prevented," or "desirous pursuit of someone whom one knows does not want to be pursued." He notes that in trying to account for these phenomena, "two kinds of explanation can be advanced that are advanced for unrealistic behavior generally, the one motivational, the other in terms of general strategic principles." The former explanation appeals to the tendency of the mind to seek immediate gratification by illusions and magical actions, at the expense of long-term gain. The latter rests on the premise that reactions that are subjectively irrational when considered as occurrent emotions may be manifestations of a more general disposition that, on average and in the long term, is objectively adaptive. He concludes that "both kinds of mechanism no doubt apply." The motivational explanation is the one that is relevant here.

Of Frijda's categories, the first three (in my classification) involve irrational belief formation, largely of the wishful-thinking variety. The importance of this phenomenon is obvious. It does not, however, exhaust the category of emotionally induced belief irrationality. Later in this section, and more extensively in V.2, I discuss how meta-emotions can induce belief changes that in turn generate new first-order emotions. The phenomena in category (iv) illustrate the mechanism of counterwishful thinking, briefly discussed in I.6 and II.3 and further discussed below. Those in category (v) illustrate irrationality at the level of action. Although Frijda does not mention that emotions may subvert the process of information acquisition, the fact that passion can make us jump to conclusions is too obvious to need stressing. What should be stressed, however, is that this does not occur only in the face of threatening events, when the expected opportunity costs of gathering information are so high that delays would be irrational. *Any* strong emotion creates a tendency to act immediately, even if nothing would be lost and something might be gained by pausing to find out more about the situation. The urge of a guilty person to seek relief by making atonement may be so strong that he does not take the time to find out what form of atonement might be in the victim's best interest. A person in love may be too impatient to find out whether the love object might have some unknown and perhaps less-than-wonderful qualities.

In the philosophical literature, the subversive influences of passion are usually described under the headings of self-deception (or wishful thinking) and weakness of the will.[137] The latter phenomenon can take several forms: Acting without regard for the consequences of one's behavior, and acting against one's own better judgment. Frijda's irrational anger might fit the first case, the irrational pursuit the second. Macbeth's behavior is also a good example of the second – "vaulting ambition" (1.7.27) making him do what he believes he should not. I believe the lack of regard for consequences – including the lack of concern for more information – is the most important mechanism by which emotion can subvert rationality. It can work in two ways, directly or indirectly. A person may simply be so caught up in visceral anger, fear, envy, shame, infatuation, or *hybris* that he fails to think more than one step ahead. (I return to this idea below.) Alternatively, he may be subject to social norms according to which a visible concern for consequences is dishonorable (III.4). In this case, fear of shame – rather than occurrent shame itself – will motivate him to act *as if* he had no regard for the consequences.

GUT FEELINGS

Ronald de Sousa and Antonio Damasio argue that emotions, rather than being sand in the machinery of action, can actually promote rational behavior in situations of indeterminacy. Their argument is not – or not only – that a person without emotions would make irrational decisions. They also claim – and I believe this is their key idea – that in many situations this person would make no decision at all or delay it for very long, and that such abstention or procrastination could be irrational. ("Deciding well also means deciding expeditiously, especially when time is of the essence."[138]) As stated, the claim does not imply that emotions have a causal role in reaching a decision or in reaching it sooner rather than later. Emotional flatness and indecisiveness could simply be correlated as joint effects of a common cause that is necessary for the former and sufficient for

137. Elster (1998b), section I.2.
138. Damasio (1994), p. 169.

the latter or vice versa. It is clear, however, that both writers want to argue for the stronger thesis that emotions are causally involved in rational decision making.

Indeterminacy, in general, can take the form either of indifference or incommensurability. Writing R for weak preference ("a is at least as good as b"), indifference obtains when both aRb and bRa and incommensurability when neither aRb nor bRa. Thus indeterminacy of choice arises when two options are equally and maximally good, or when each of two options is strongly preferred to all other options but neither is weakly preferred to the other. De Sousa argues that emotions can serve as a tie-breaker in cases of indifference:

> For suppose you are considering whether to take a fair bet. By definition, from the Bayesian point of view, a fair bet is equivalent to no bet at all: its expected desirability is zero. Yet there is clearly a significant option between the choice to minimize the greatest possible losses (maximin) and the choice to maximize the greatest possible gains (maximax).... And the choice between maximin and maximax strategies is obviously associated with such emotional and character traits as boldness or timidity.[139]

Indifference is a knife-edge property, rarely observed in nontrivial real-life situations. Incommensurability is, I believe, a vastly more important source of indeterminacy. Consider for instance a customer who cannot make up his mind whether to buy car brand A or brand B. If he were indifferent, a one dollar discount on A should make him decisively prefer A. If he still cannot make up his mind, as will typically be the case, the two brands must be incommensurate. To choose, he may flip a coin – or consult his "gut feelings."

Before I proceed to discuss how these feelings enter into the decision-making process, let me use some passages from Boswell's *Life of Dr. Johnson* to distinguish between two cases:

> Life is not too long, and too much of it must not be spent in idle deliberation how it shall be spent: deliberation, which those who begin it by prudence,

---

139. De Sousa (1987), p. 194. The example is somewhat defective, because in this case not making a decision is equivalent to making the decision not to gamble. It could be improved by stipulating that the agent is indifferent between two risky options, each of which has a higher minimum than the status quo. It is also defective for a different reason. The idea of a "fair bet" is usually defined in monetary terms rather than in utility terms. If the agent is indifferent between making the fair bet and not making it, the utility function must be linear in the relevant interval. Given the way cardinal utility functions are constructed, however, the presence of timidity or boldness would typically cause nonlinearity.

and continue with subtlety, must after long expence of thought, conclude by chance. To prefer one future mode of life to another, upon just reasons, requires faculties which it has not pleased our Creator to give us.[140]

We talked about the education of children; and I asked him what he thought was best to teach them first. JOHNSON. 'Sir, it is no matter what you teach them first, any more than what leg you shall put into your breeches first. Sir, you may stand disputing which is best to put in first, but in the mean time your breech is bare. Sir, while you are considering which of two things you should teach your child first, another boy has learnt them both."[141]

He did not approve of late marriages, observing that more was lost in point of time, than compensated for by any possible advantages. Even ill assorted marriages were preferable to cheerless celibacy.[142]

The first passage illustrates the case (i) of pure incommensurability, in which one could not conceivably gather enough information to make an informed choice. In such cases, a person who could not make up his mind unless he had "just reasons" to go one way or another would simply be paralyzed. The other passages illustrate the case (iia) in which one might gather enough information to make an informed choice, although the opportunity costs of doing so would be prohibitively high. In a more important and realistic variety (iib) of this case, the costs of gathering information *might* – rather than *would* – be too high. I might meet the perfect spouse by waiting a bit longer – but then again I might not. When I know that the expected costs of gathering more information would exceed the benefits, the choice is easy: I just flip a coin or consult my gut feelings. When I do not know – and do not know whether it would be worthwhile to find out – we are dealing with a more radical form of indeterminacy.[143]

De Sousa writes that the "role of emotion is to supply the insufficiency of reason . . . For a variable but always limited time, an emotion limits the range of information that the organism will take into

---

140. Boswell, *The Life of Dr.Johnson*, Ætat. 57. By contrast, "Darwin [apparently] suggested that [what] one should do if one wanted to choose the right person to marry" was to "write down all the options and their myriad unfolding scenarios, and consequences, and so forth" (Damasio 1994, p. 172).
141. Boswell, *The Life of Dr. Johnson*, Ætat. 54. Johnson, being a Shakespeare scholar, may have had in mind the King's remark in *Hamlet* (3.3): "[L]ike a man to double business bound I stand in pause where I shall first begin, and both neglect."
142. Boswell, *The Life of Dr. Johnson*, Ætat. 61.
143. For discussions of the infinite-regress problem that gives rise to indeterminacy in such cases, see Winter (1964) and Elster (1984, section II.4).

account, the inferences actually drawn from a potential infinity, and the set of live options from which it will choose."[144] It is not clear which of (i), (iia), or (iib) he has in mind. A reference to work by Daniel Dennett on information retrieval may suggest that he is mainly interested in (iib), but it is hard to tell. The standard view, in any case, is that the urgency of the emotions helps us make optimal decisions in case (iia). Because of their limited rationality, people always use rules of thumb to make short-cuts to a decision. "Emotion may well enhance utilization of these heuristics, in view of the desirability of rapid action or, more generally, the restriction of range of cue utilization."[145]

What we may observe here, however, is not emotion doing what reason cannot do, but rather emotion doing what reason could also do, only differently. De Sousa and others who argue along similar lines consistently present a strawman of rational-choice theory, according to which a rational agent would always take account of all possible outcomes of all possible options. According to LeDoux, if you were a small animal faced with a bobcat and "had to make a deliberate decision about what to do, you would have to consider the likelihood of each possible choice succeeding or failing and could get so bogged down in decision making that you would be eaten before you made the choice."[146] What Philip Johnson-Laird and Keith Oatley call "impeccable rationality" enables "the organism to decide which goals to pursue at any point in time, and to decide at each choice the best course of action in pursuit of these goals. No contingency is unanticipated, and performance is invariably optimal."[147] Below, I cite a passage from Damasio to the same effect.

These authors all assume that rationality amounts to what I have called elsewhere an *addiction to reason*.[148] Some people do indeed have a craving to make all decisions on the basis of "just" or sufficient reasons. That, however, makes them irrational rather than rational. A rational person would know that under certain conditions it is better

---

144. De Sousa (1987), p. 195. Along similar lines, Johnson-Laird and Oatley (1992) argue that because the ideal of "impeccable rationality" assumes that "there are no surprises, no misunderstandings, no irresolvable conflicts," it cannot guide action in situations that are characterized by these features. Instead, "emotions enable social species to co-ordinate their behaviour, to respond to emergencies, to prioritise goals, to prepare for appropriate actions, and to make progress towards goals . . . even though individuals have only limited abilities to cogitate."
145. Frijda (1986), p. 121; see also p. 116.
146. LeDoux (1996), p. 176.
147. Johnson-Laird and Oatley (1992), pp. 204–5.
148. Elster (1989d), pp. 117–22.

to follow a simple mechanical decision rule than to use more elaborate procedures with higher opportunity costs.[149] If we disregard cases in which the twelve-millisecond delay of the cortex could be crucial, the organism might cope perfectly well by adopting and following mechanical decision rules, such as "when you hear a sound you cannot identify, stand still" or "when food tastes bitter, spit it out." In reality, of course, that's not how we cope with novelty or bitter-tasting food – not because the program is unfeasible but because natural selection has wired us differently. It is somewhat misleading, therefore, to assert that emotions are a "supplemental" principle that "fills the gap" between reflex-like behavior and fully rational action.[150]

We can take this argument one step further. If we do not and cannot respond to emergencies by following a mechanical decision rule, it may be because our cognitive faculties are temporarily clouded by the emotional arousal caused by the emergency. The emotion serves as *a functional equivalent for the rational faculties it suspends*, by inducing the very behavior that is rationally required and that reason, if left undisturbed, could have come up with by itself. The emotions do solve problems – but problems that are to some extent of their own making. The capacity for the emotions to supplement and enhance rationality would not exist if they did not also undermine it.

In his (independently developed) argument for the rationality of the emotions, Damasio draws on findings from patients with specific brain lesions. Some patients who have suffered damage in their frontal lobes become emotionally flat and lose their ability to make decisions, while retaining their cognitive powers. Patients who have suffered damage to their somatosensory cortices display similar symptoms, although in their case there is also severe cognitive malfunctioning. From his analysis of these patients, and drawing on general neurophysiological data, Damasio concludes that their defective decision-making capacity is due to their lack of emotion. Not knowing much about the brain I cannot do full justice to his

149. Thaler (1980) argues that neglect of opportunity costs and excessive focus on out-of-pocket expenses is a frequent source of cognitive irrationality. The neglect of the opportunity costs that are created by the fact that *decision making takes time* is also an important and pervasive source of irrationality.
150. For such claims, see De Sousa (1987), p. 194; Johnson-Laird and Oatley (1992), p. 206. The point I am making is well stated by LeDoux (1996, p. 175): "In responding first with its most-likely-to-succeed behavior, the brain buys time. This is not to say that the brain responds automatically for the purpose of buying time. The automatic responses came first, in the evolutionary sense, and cannot exist for the purpose of serving responses that came later" (LeDoux 1996, p. 175).

argument, but I hope I can present and discuss some key aspects without distorting it too much.

The claim that the patients lack emotions has both inferential and evidential support. On the one hand, some of them engage in behavior that is strongly contrary to prevailing social norms. With respect to the nineteenth-century patient in whom the frontal-lobe syndrome was first observed, Damasio remarks, "We can infer at least that he lacked the feeling of embarrassment, given his use of foul language and his parading of self-misery."[151] This inference from the patient's behavior is in accordance with the argument made in III.2, that social norms are sustained by the emotions of agents (and observers[152]) rather than by material sanctions.[153] On the other hand Damasio offers direct behavioral and physiological evidence that the brain-damaged patients are emotionally flat. They rarely, and then only within a limited repertoire, show signs of emotion. They can discuss their own tragic situation without appearing to be in the least affected by it. When confronted with disturbing pictures or when engaged in gambling experiments they do not have the skin conductance responses of normal individuals.

Damasio also offers behavioral evidence for the lack of decision-making rationality of his patients. They spend inordinate amounts of time on trivial tasks. Damasio says about one of his patients that "the particular task ... was actually being carried out *too* well, and at the expense of the overall purpose."[154] About another of his patients he tells two strongly contrasting stories. On one day, his lack of "gut reactions" was highly advantageous when driving on an icy road, where most people tend to hit the brakes when they skid rather than gently pulling away from the tailspin. On the next day, Damasio

---

151. Damasio (1994), p. 51; see also pp. 55–56 for reports on similar behavior in another patient.
152. Davidson (1995, p. 364) argues that "the perception of emotion and the experience or expression of emotion" are likely to be based on different neutral control systems. Hence an alternative explanation of the behavior of the foul-language patient might be that he was unable to detect the emotional reactions of others to his behavior.
153. This view presupposes that the emotions of shame and embarrassment would not exist in the absence of the norms. It is confusing, therefore, to see Damasio (1994, pp. 124–25) arguing that "the perils preempted by [social conventions and ethical rules] may be immediate and direct (physical or mental harm), or remote and indirect (future loss, embarrassment)," as if the emotions could exist independently of the norms.
154. Damasio (1994), p. 37.

was discussing with the same patient when his next visit to the laboratory should take place. I suggested two alternative dates, both in the coming month and just a few days apart from each other. The patient pulled out his appointment book and began consulting the calendar.... For the better part of a half-hour, the patient enumerated reasons for and against each of the two dates: Previous engagements, proximity to other engagements, possible meteorological conditions, virtually anything that one could reasonably think about concerning a simple date. Just as calmly as he had driven over the ice, and recounted that episode, he was now walking us through a tiresome cost-benefit analysis, an endless outlining and fruitless comparison of options and possible consequences. [We] finally did tell him, quietly, that he should come on the second of the alternative dates. His response was equally calm and prompt. He simply said: "That's fine."[155]

In the gambling experiment, the brain-damaged patients consistently did worse than others. (This is the only case Damasio discusses in which the patient's failure was to make bad decisions rather than delaying them.) The game required subjects to draw cards from one of four decks. Each time the subjects drew a card from decks A and B they received a large sum of play money, and a smaller sum when they drew from decks C and D. When taking a card from A and B, they also sometimes had to pay back a very large amount of money. As they learn about the structure of the game, normal subjects mostly take cards from C and D and usually end up ahead. Brain-damaged subjects, by contrast, stick to decks A and B even though they regularly go bankrupt halfway through the game. Damasio's explanation is that these patients suffered from an inability to be motivated by mental representations of future states. Although they had normal skin conductance reactions to monetary loss, they differed from normal subjects in having no *anticipatory* responses in the period immediately preceding their selection of a card from a bad deck.[156]

Brain-damaged patients, then, tend to be emotionally flat and to have defective decision-making capacities. It remains to characterize the relation between these two features. Damasio's strong causal claim is that *"Reduction in emotion may constitute an ... important*

---

155. *Ibid.*, pp. 193–94.
156. In a recent experiment (Bechara et al. 1997) it is also shown that normal subjects "began to generate anticipatory skin conductance responses (SCRs) whenever they pondered a choice that turned out to be risky, before they knew explicitly that it was risky, whereas patients [with prefrontal damage] never developed anticipatory SCRs, although some eventually realized which choices were risky." In other words, conscious awareness of costs and benefits is neither a necessary nor a sufficient condition for rational choice.

source of irrational behavior."[157] Elsewhere, he makes the weaker claim that "The powers of reason and the experience of emotion decline together."[158] This is to assert correlation, but not causation. To support the strong claim he first describes a decision-making problem that the owner of a business might confront, "faced with the prospect of meeting or not with a possible client who can bring valuable business but also happens to be the archenemy of your best friend, and proceeding or not with a particular deal. The brain of a normal, intelligent, and educated adult reacts to the situation by rapidly creating scenarios of possible response options *and* related outcomes."[159] He then argues that (what he takes to be) the rational-choice approach to this problem would involve impossibly complex calculations. The decision would take an "inordinately long time" or might never be made at all. Because we are, as a matter of fact, able to make such decisions quite rapidly and efficiently, something else must be going on:

Consider again the scenarios that I outlined. The key components unfold in our minds instantly, sketchily, and virtually simultaneously, too fast for the details to be clearly defined. But now imagine that *before* you apply any kind of cost/benefit analysis to the problem, something quite important happens: When the bad outcome connected with a given response option comes into mind, however fleetingly, you experience an unpleasant gut feeling. Because the feeling is about the body, I gave the phenomenon the technical term *somatic* state . . .; and because it marks an image, I called it a *marker*.

[The] somatic marker . . . forces attention on the negative outcome to which a given action may lead, and functions as an automated alarm signal which says: Beware of danger ahead if you choose the option which leads to this outcome. The signal may lead you to reject *immediately*, the negative course of action and thus make you choose among other alternatives. The automated signal protects you against future losses, without further ado, and then allows you *to choose from among fewer alternatives*. There is

157. Damasio (1994), p. 53; italics in original.
158. *Ibid.*, p. 54. We may note, for future reference, that this claim about the covariation of emotion and reason differs from another, perhaps more dubious claim that he also makes. Referring to the contrast between sadness and happiness or, in extreme cases, between depression and mania, he writes that "because both the signal of the body state (positive or negative) and the style and efficiency of cognition were triggered from the same system, they tend to be concordant" (*ibid.*, p. 147). Depressive states go together with slow and inefficient mental functioning, and elated states with fast but not necessary efficient functioning. The theory of "depressive realism" discussed below seems to go against this view.
159. *Ibid.*, p. 170.

still room for using a cost/benefit analysis and proper deductive competence, but only *after* the automated step drastically reduces the number of
options.[160]

Once again, going by one's gut feelings is not the only way to cut
through the maze of a complex decision problem. One can also, for
instance, flip a coin. Damasio might counter that this procedure is
inferior to going by gut feelings, which enable one not only to make
swifter decisions but also better ones. But the coin-tossing heuristic
is only the most simple of many rules of thumb that are used in complex decision-making problems. The best-known is perhaps Herbert
Simon's idea of *satisficing*, embodied in such sayings as "never change
a winning team" and "if it ain't broke, don't fix it."[161] Also, medical
diagnoses and prognoses can be very efficiently done by mechanical point systems that rely on a small number of variables. In fact,
such methods almost invariably tend to perform better than intuition
based on "gut feeling."[162] In opposing gut feelings to hyperrational
cost–benefit calculation Damasio is simply setting up a strawman.

This objection does not, however, affect Damasio's claim that in
most complex decisions people do, as a matter of fact, consult their
gut feelings. When confronted with a novel challenge for which no
rule of thumb is available, some people procrastinate more or less
indefinitely, while others, for better or for worse, make a snap decision based on some salient feature of the situation. Damasio claims
(i) that more often than not this feature has great predictive value for
making a good choice or at least avoiding a bad one, and (ii) that
its salience is signaled by an occurrent emotion. Concerning (i), he
appeals to a regular reinforcement process, although he does not use
that term. "Somatic markers are . . . emotions and feelings [which]
have been connected, by learning, to predicted future outcomes of
certain scenarios."[163] On the basis of what I know of reinforcement
theory it seems implausible that this mechanism could guide the decision whether to deal with a businessman who is the enemy of one's
best friend. For reinforcement to establish behavior, it should ideally

---

160. *Ibid.*, p. 173; italics in original. Elsewhere (*ibid.*, pp. 175, 187) Damasio also
    acknowledges positive somatic markers that lead to the pursuit of specific options
    rather than their elimination.
161. See for instance Simon (1954) and, for a striking application, Nelson and Winter
    (1982).
162. Dawes et al. (1989).
163. Damasio (1994), p. 174; italics deleted.

occur *soon* after the behavior in question, occur *invariably* when the behavior is chosen, and the behavior itself should be one that is chosen *frequently*. None of these conditions is even approximately satisfied in the example.

Concerning (ii), Damasio acknowledges that some somatic markers may operate unconsciously, as when "worker bumblebees 'decide' on which flowers they should land."[164] In this case, no emotions are involved. From introspection, some hunches involve no occurrent emotion at all. Sometimes I play a game with myself in which I try to estimate how much time has passed since the last time I looked at my watch. In doing so, I try out various estimates, letting each of them sink in for a while, until I hit upon one that seems just right. It's like a little click in my mind, as when something falls into place. Usually, I do pretty well, to within a minute or two on half-hour intervals. My guess – another hunch! – is that those who do well on the stock market do so because they are good at similar, although vastly more complex mental calibrations, not because they consult their emotions.[165] Reinforcement is too crude a mechanism for shaping these decisions.

Other decisions do involve emotions. Coming back from holiday and opening my mail, I have to decide in which order to reply to my correspondents. In doing so, what floats before my mind is not a large number of scenarios and their consequences, but a small number of rules of thumb. The most recent letters can wait; letters from friends are more important than letters from colleagues; unpleasant matters should be dealt with at once; bills have to be paid on time. In deciding which of these rules should take precedence when they point in different directions, emotional tugs and pulls certainly play a role. I do not think, though, that the emotions work by providing information about the likely consequences of the various options; nor is emotional urgency the only mechanism at work. The reason I give priority to an unpleasant matter is that I want to have it over and done with, much as I might want to schedule an appointment with the dentist for the earliest possible date.

---

164. *Ibid.*, p. 185.
165. Damasio (1994, p. 43) reports that one of his brain-damaged patients performed normally when the task was "to generate an acceptable estimate based on bits and pieces of unrelated knowledge," an example being to estimate how many giraffes there are in New York City. In this case, the estimate was not a simple hunch but based on a rough knowledge of the number of zoos in the city and the number of giraffes in each zoo. I wonder how the patient would have performed on the time-guessing task.

Although paying bills on time is certainly important in consequential terms, I do not need my emotions to tell me that it should take priority.

Rather than telling more of my own counteranecdotes, let me try to address Damasio's argument and evidence more directly. He argues plausibly that (i) lack of emotionality causes (ii) defective social behavior, and that (iii) lack of ability to be motivated by the representation of absent events causes (iv) defective decision making. He makes a plausible argument, moreover, that (i) and (iv) tend to go together.[166] It remains to be shown that (i) is the cause, or a cause, of (iv). His argument seems to be that (i) is the cause, or a cause, of (iii). Future events gain motivational significance through the somatic, emotional markers attached to their representation. Although nothing in the data he presents excludes this counterintuitive hypothesis, I cannot see that they exclude the alternative view that the same brain damage that induces (i) also causes (iii) and thereby (iv). There is correlation, but for the time being we cannot tell whether there is also causation. Moreover, the causal mechanism – reinforcement – that is supposed to link emotions to decisions seems too coarse for the range of cases it is supposed to explain.

Damasio's theory may be contrasted with the view put forward by Robert Frank in *Passions within Reason*.[167] Both assert that criminal behavior can be explained by some emotional deficiency. Moreover, both stipulate a link between emotions and the ability to be motivated by the future. Yet their arguments are very different. Damasio claims that the behavior of at least some "developmental sociopaths or psychopaths" fits the general pattern he is describing. While being "the very picture of the cool head we were told to keep in order to do the right thing," they also act "to everybody's disadvantage, including their own. . . . They are, in fact, yet another example of a pathological state in which a decline in rationality is accompanied by diminution or absence of feeling."[168] They lack, presumably, the emotional markers that enable them to be motivated by the future. (Here I go beyond what Damasio says, but the imputation seems plausible.)

Frank, too, finds the key to criminal behavior in the inability to be motivated by future consequences of present behavior. His

---

166. In one of the cases he describes (Phileas Gage), it is not clear whether the maladjustment of the patient is due to (i) or to (iv).
167. Frank (1988); see also Elster (in press a, section I.5) for some comments.
168. Damasio (1994), p. 178.

mechanism, however, is entirely different. In most of us emotions such as guilt weigh in as *current representatives of the future payoffs* and thus impart greater motivational force to the latter. "If the psychological reward mechanism is constrained to emphasize rewards in the present moment, the simplest counter to a [short-term] reward from cheating is to have a current feeling that tugs in the opposite direction."[169] Damasio would assent to Frank's proposition that "the widespread and chronic impulsiveness of criminal offenders may ... be interpreted as support for the claim that emotional competencies underlie moral behavior,"[170] but for entirely different reasons. When the data are in Damasio may turn out to be right, but for the time being I find Frank's view more plausible.[171] Yet the discussion would be incomplete if we ignored that many emotions have the opposite effect – they tend to reduce our ability to take account of the future consequences of present action, not to enhance it. As Bacon said, "affection beholds principally the good which is present; reason looks beyond and beholds likewise the future and sum of all."[172]

SADDER BUT WISER

Mania and depression, in the clinical sense, are extreme versions of the more ordinary emotions of exultation and sadness. These, in turn, are stronger versions of contentment and lowspiritedness. As we move inward in this way, away from the extremes, we presumably reach a ground state with a neutral emotional tonality. A natural working assumption is that this would also be the cognitive ground state, the state, that is, in which belief formation is unaffected by motivational bias. This assumption would fit well with two other assumptions that we routinely make, that depressed people tend to believe that things are worse than they in fact are and that those in more exuberant moods tend to believe they are better.

169. Frank (1988), p. 82.
170. *Ibid.*, p. 162.
171. Brothers (1995, p. 1112) objects to Damasio that he "considered the somatic portion of a social experience simply to signal reward or punishment," whereas "evidence from amygdala stimulation is in favor of specific and variegated emotional states (e.g., guilt, feeling ostracized) rather than simply reward or punishment." I have no competence to judge who is right; my objections to Damasio's theory are of a more elementary nature.
172. "On the dignity and advance of learning" in Bacon (1875), vol. IV, p. 457.

The second of these routine assumptions is, I believe, valid. Let me illustrate it by a personal example. For about fifteen years, from 1968 to 1984, I worked on a book on Karl Marx, and eventually felt I got to know him quite well. He was, very obviously, a very emotional person. Moreover, his emotions equally obviously distorted his thinking, both in what he wrote about the communist society and about the process of getting there. His mind seems to have been shaped by two implicit assumptions: Whatever is desirable is feasible, and whatever is desirable and feasible is inevitable. The first shows up in his refusal to consider trade-offs between values, and in his beliefs that all good things go together. The second underlies his unwavering belief in the imminent and immanently necessary communist revolution.

These observations, although true, provide only part of the truth. The other side of the coin is that the emotions of rage, indignation, and hope provided the indispensable motivation for Marx's political and theoretical work. They kept him going through years of exile and misery in London and sustained his enormous scholarly labors no less than his tireless organizational work. It would seem absurd and unrealistic to wish that he had the same level of motivation without the correlative cognitive distortions. The motivation for achievement may interfere, as it did in his case, with the efficacy of achievement. The emotions that provided him with a meaning and a sense of direction to life also prevented him from going steadily in that direction. Again, not all good things go together. To achieve much, one has to believe one can achieve more than one can.[173]

The first of the routine assumptions, by contrast, is probably wrong. One of the more striking psychological findings over the past fifteen years is that *the emotional ground state may not be the cognitive ground state*. Rather, the only persons who are capable of taking an unbiased view of the world are the depressed. They are "sadder but wiser."[174] The results are far from final. The effects may not be as strong in real-life settings.[175] In some contexts, the polarization described in the

---

173. See Elster (1983b, pp. 157–61) for a number of examples. The relation between expected and actual achievements is not, however, monotonic: "Pride goes before a fall" (see I.3 and Baumeister 1993, p. 180).
174. The important article by Alloy and Abramson (1979) that launched this line of research used this phrase in the title.
175. Dunning and Story (1991).

previous paragraphs is in fact observed.[176] Nevertheless, most of the numerous experiments made to test the hypothesis tend to confirm it.

I shall cite some typical findings from a survey article by two of the originators of "depressive realism" theory, Lauren Alloy and Lyn Abramson.[177] In experiments designed to test subjects' understanding of their control in situations with imperfect correlation between their responses and an observable outcome, nondepressives exhibit an "illusion of control" whereas depressed subjects judge their degree of control accurately. Moreover, nondepressives show an "illusion of no control" when the outcome is associated with failure. Furthermore, depressed subjects accurately assess their chances in dice-rolling experiments, whereas the nondepressed tend to overestimate their chances. Depressed subjects tend to be more evenhanded in their causal attribution of credit and blame, whereas nondepressives typically attribute negative events to others and positive events to their own intervention. Nondepressive subjects see themselves more positively than they do others with the same objective characteristics, whereas the depressed are not subject to this self-serving bias, nor to the opposite, self-deprecating bias. Depressed subjects have an accurate idea of how other people perceive them, whereas nondepressives exaggerate the good impressions they make on others.

If people are emotionally excited, they often get things wrong, but this is only a sufficient condition, not a necessary one. To get it right, one has to sink into depression. Of course, the depressed are not very motivated to do anything. The reason why there is no sand in *their* machinery of action is that the engine is idling. Whenever there is a motivation to act, to get on with the business of living, we find sand in the machinery, but that is not the fault of the emotions because, to repeat, one does not have to be emotionally aroused to get it wrong. To wish for an emotional state in which one got it right would be to wish for a state in which one didn't *care* about getting it right, or about anything else. There is an analogy between this predicament and a much-discussed moral problem. According to Bernard Williams,

such things as deep attachments to other persons . . . cannot at the same time embody the impartial view, and they also run the risk of offending against it. They run that risk if they are to exist at all; yet unless such things exist, there will not be enough substance or conviction in a man's life to compel

176. Vasquez (1987).
177. Alloy and Abramson (1988).

his allegiance to life itself. Life has to have substance if anything is to have sense, including adherence to the impartial system; but if it has substance, then it cannot grant supreme importance to the impartial system, and that system's hold on it will be, at the limit, insecure.[178]

Similarly, we may have to accept that cognitive rationality can only be achieved at the cost of lacking anything we want to be rational *about*.

EMOTIONS AS PSYCHIC COSTS AND BENEFITS

To the extent that economists consider the role of emotions in behavior,[179] they tend to view them simply as a source of preferences. The most typical approach is to assume that a given action may have emotional costs and benefits as well as material costs and benefits.[180] In choosing among various options, the agent maximizes an inclusive utility function in which all costs and benefits are considered together. On some occasions, the material benefits associated with one option may be large enough to offset any negative emotions that it might induce; on other occasions the emotional costs may be decisive; in the general case some compromise between material and emotional satisfaction will be sought. When emotions are viewed in this way, the standard apparatus of indifference curves and trade-offs automatically applies. Well-known analyses of emotions by Gary Becker, Robert Frank, and Jack Hirshleifer all rely on this approach.[181]

There are two ways in which the pleasure and pain associated with the emotions may enter into the utility function. To illustrate them, let me refer to Gary Becker's analysis of guilt (see below for a fuller discussion). First, the guilt itself is a cost. Even if I do not have any money with me, I may cross the street to avoid coming face-to-face with a beggar whose visible misery would induce the unpleasant feeling of guilt. Second, the guilt may induce behavior that is costly

178. Williams (1981), Chapter 1.
179. See Elster (1998a) for a survey.
180. For reasons of space, I limit myself to the relation between emotion and material self-interest. Similar issues arise for the relation between emotions and impartial motivations. For instance, a wealthy liberal might on impartial grounds prefer to send his children to a public school, but his emotional attachment to the children might induce a preference for a better-quality private education.
181. For Becker, see subsequent text. For discussions of Frank (1988) and Hirshleifer (1987), see Elster (in press a), section I.5.

in the material sense. If I do have money with me, I know that if I come face-to-face with the beggar I would give him something to alleviate my guilt. More accurately, I would give up to the point at which the marginal utility of money in alleviating my guilt equals its marginal utility for other purposes. (If crossing the street is costly, this would also have to be taken into account.)

In many other analyses, the encounters that trigger the emotion are taken for given and not subject to choice. The question of choice arises only because the agent has to weigh emotional satisfaction against other satisfactions, as in the choice of how much to give to the beggar. In modeling envy, we may assume that the agent is willing to invest resources in making his rival worse off up to the point at which he derives more utility from making himself better off. In modeling altruism, we can make a similar assumption. Economic analyses of regret also assume that agents weigh satisfaction from actual outcomes and emotions generated by counterfactual beliefs. Strictly speaking, none of these analyses need to rely on valence, in the sense of subjective feelings of pleasure and pain. All that is needed is that we can draw indifference curves that reflect the trade-offs involved. We may think of emotional valence as the underlying mechanism behind these trade-offs, but it need not be directly reflected in the formal analysis. In a modeling perspective, "emotional altruism" is indistinguishable from "reason-based altruism."

To assess the validity of the cost–benefit model of the emotion, we may consider the case of guilt. Assume that a person is tempted to steal a book from the library. If he feels guilty about doing it, he may abstain. If he steals the book and then feels guilt, he may return the book to the library. On the assumption that guilt is to be modeled as a cost, both the abstention from stealing and the return of the book would be explained by a simple cost–benefit analysis. This approach has the great advantage that it allows us to account for the undeniable existence of a trade-off between moral emotions and self-interest. The world is not made up of two exclusive and exhaustive categories, those who would always steal a book whenever there was no risk of detection and those who would never do so. Many people would go ahead and steal the book if but only if its value to them was sufficiently high and/or its value to others sufficiently small. To model such behavior, we can talk "as if" guilt and interest add up to an inclusive utility, with the marginal disutility from guilt being an increasing function of (say) the number of people on the waiting list for the book and the marginal utility from interest a decreasing function of (say) the time the agent expects to use the book.

Independently of its predictive adequacy, I submit that this model is conceptually flawed. If guilt were nothing but an anticipated or experienced cost, an agent whose guilt deters him from stealing or retaining the book should be willing to buy a guilt-erasing pill if it was sufficiently cheap. *I submit that no person who is capable of being deterred by guilt would buy the pill.* In fact, he would feel guilty about buying it. For him, taking the pill in order to escape guilt and be able to steal the book would be as morally bad as just stealing it. He would not see any morally relevant difference between stealing the book in a two-step operation (taking the pill to steal the book) and stealing it in a one-step operation. There is a strict analogy between this argument and a point that I have made elsewhere, namely that a person who discounts the future very highly would not be motivated to buy a pill that would reduce his rate of time discounting.[182] To want to be motivated by remote consequences of present behavior *is* to be motivated by remote consequences of present behavior. Similarly, to want to be immoral *is* to be immoral. A person willing to take the guilt-erasing pill would not need it.

We need, therefore, a model that can account for the trade-off between guilt and interest and yet does not imply that a reluctant agent would buy the guilt-erasing pill. I conjecture that the model would involve some kind of nonintentional psychic causality rather than deliberate choice. The catastrophe model discussed in I.8 can serve as an example. Suppose that the agent is initially unwilling to steal the book, but that as its value to him increases he finally decides to do so.[183] Suppose conversely that the agent has stolen the book, but that as its value to others increases he finally returns it to the library. In the first case, suppose that its value to others is 10 and that he decides to steal it just when its value to him reaches 15. In the second case, suppose that its initial value to him is 15 and the initial value to others is 6. On the cost–benefit model, he would return it when its value to others reaches 10. On the catastrophe model, he might not do so

---

182. Elster (1997).
183. Technically, the dependent value has to be continuous rather than the dichotomous choice between stealing the book and not stealing or returning it. We can assume, therefore, that the dependent variable is a propensity to steal the book and that the agent proceeds to steal it once the propensity reaches a certain level. Alternatively, we could use an example in which the choice variable is continuous, such as the amount to give to the beggar in the street.

until its value to others reached 15. The reason for this asymmetry is found in the mechanism of dissonance reduction. An individual who is subject to several motivations that point in different directions will feel an unpleasant feeling of tension. When on balance he favors one action, he will try to reduce the tension by looking for cognitions that support it; when he favors another, he will look for cognitions that stack the balance of arguments in favor of that action. Thus the timing of the switch in behavior will be path-dependent.

Dissonance theory is more realistic than the cost–benefit model in that it views individuals as making hard choices on the basis of *reasons* rather than on the basis of introspections about how they feel. Although the person who has stolen the book but feels guilty about it may try to alleviate his guilt, he would do so by coming up with additional reasons that justify his behavior rather than by accepting a guilt-erasing pill. It is a fundamental feature of human beings that they have an image of themselves as *acting for a reason* (see also V.2). Guilt, in this perspective, acts not as a cost but as a psychic force that induces the individual to rationalize his behavior. Beyond a certain point, when the arguments on the other side become too strong and the rationalization breaks down, a switch in behavior occurs. Although we may well say that the switch occurs when the guilt becomes unbearable, we should add that the point at which it becomes unbearable is itself influenced and in fact *delayed by the guilt*.

What this example suggests is that emotions can have a dual role in behavior, by affecting the rewards that are traded off against each other as well as the shape of the trade-off itself. In Chapter III I made somewhat similar arguments about the role of shame and envy in behavior. When one is suffering from intense shame, it is hard to imagine that the state will not last forever. The overwhelming desire is for immediate release. Shame has a causal effect on the evaluation and perception of other rewards *over and above its own role as a (negative) reward*. In the case of envy, the urgent wish for the destruction of the envied object or its possessor may induce destructive behavior that leaves the agent worse off rather than better off. These cases – guilt, shame, and envy – are not at all similar. There is no particular reason to expect all emotions to interact with interest in the same way. Yet the cases all support the claim that the simple cost–benefit model is *too* simple.

Some of the remarks I have made about shame and guilt suggest that emotions could be modeled as *temporary preferences*. The person who sees a beggar in the street and feels an urge to give him money, or the person who is in the grip of shame and feels an urge to kill himself, may be viewed as undergoing a short-term change of preferences. It is in fact an important feature of many occurrent emotions that they have a relatively short duration. Anger, for instance, tends to "spend itself" quickly.[184] Aristotle comments that "men become calm when they have spent their anger on someone else. This happened in the case of Ergophilus: Though the people were more irritated against him than against Callisthenes, they acquitted him because they had condemned Callisthenes to death the day before" (*Rhetoric* $1380^b 11-13$). In trials of collaborators in German-occupied countries after World War II, those who were tried later generally received milder sentences even when the crimes were similar.[185]

Yet some emotions have a more durable character. In Becker's analysis of love (see below), the reason why a prudent man would take care to avoid low-income women is presumably that he might contract a life-long disposition to share his income. One might question, perhaps, whether the relationship between spouses typically involves emotions in the full sense of the term. Marital love may involve concern for the welfare of one's spouse, but not the strong arousal and action tendencies that we associate with "limerence" (II.4). In her study of this emotion, Dorothy Tennov found that the typical duration of an episode was from eighteen months to three years, with some episodes lasting only a few weeks and others a whole lifetime. Revenge behavior provides another counterexample to the idea that emotions can be modeled as momentary preferences. In societies where blood feuds are common, revenge can be a lifetime obsession (III.4). The "prejudice emotions," contempt and hatred, can also be very durable and frequently all-consuming.

These "standing" emotions shape preferences in a durable manner. When they are all-consuming, we can best model them by a lexicographic preference ordering. For the person who is in a state of limerence or in pursuit of revenge, there is no trade-off between satisfaction of the emotion and material interest. Ordinary economic activities are pursued only to the extent that they promote – or do not come at the expense of – the emotional goal of the agent. Unlike the person who is in the grip of an acute emotion of shame or

184. Frijda (1986), p. 43.
185. Tamm (1984), Chapter 7; Andenæs (1978), p. 229; Mason (1952), p. 187, n. 36. The most thorough discussion is in Huyse and Dhondt (1993, p. 231), who consider and reject the hypothesis that the trend is an artifact of the most serious crimes having been tried first. See also Elster (1998b).

anger, people who are subject to an all-consuming durable passion are perfectly capable of acting in an instrumentally rational fashion. As Aristotle noted, the angry man is irrational whereas the man animated by hatred is not. The emotion may be grounded in an irrational belief, but that is another matter.

We may conclude, therefore, that the interaction between emotion and interest cannot be modeled in terms of competing costs and benefits. Concerning the short-lived emotions, the model correctly predicts that there will be a trade-off between emotional rewards and other rewards, but it fails to incorporate the fact that the trade-off itself may be shaped by emotion. Concerning the durable emotions, the model ignores that the pursuit of emotional satisfaction may be so fundamental to a person's life that all other considerations become secondary. In brief summary, the short-lived passions undermine the theory of the rational actor, whereas the durable ones undermine the theory of *homo economicus*.

ACTIONS OR PASSIONS?

The traditional view rests on the premise that emotions are involuntary, suffered in a passive mode (whence "passion") rather than chosen in an active mode.[186] From Sartre onwards, a number of writers have denied this assumption.[187] Here I discuss the two authors who have produced the most sustained arguments for the view that emotions are *chosen* rather than *undergone*, Roy Schafer and Robert C. Solomon. Although they do not claim that emotions are invariably rational, it follows from their views that emotions, being actions, are at least capable of being assessed as rational or irrational. Schafer does not acknowledge this implication,[188] but Solomon does.

Schafer set out to create "a new language for psychoanalysis," in which we would refer to emotions by verbs and adverbs – "action language" – rather than by nouns. As part of this project, he wanted to show that emotions are "enacted" rather than "undergone." Because of the psychoanalytic framework, much of what he has to say

---

186. See Dodds (1951) for discussions of this idea in early Greek thinking. Gordon (1987) is an excellent modern defense of the traditional view.
187. Sartre (1936), Schafer (1976), Hochschild (1983), Ainslie (1992), Solomon (1993).
188. Schafer does not even say explicitly that emotions are *chosen* (his favorite verb is "enacted") but the idea seems to follow from the general tenor of his discussion (notably Schafer 1976, pp. 103, 336).

is opaque, at least to me. I shall try, however, to extricate some arguments from his analysis that can be discussed independently of that framework.

To refute the idea that emotions occur involuntarily, Schafer begins by stating a paradox that we encountered in IV.2: "Even when we hold ourselves accountable for our emotions (e.g., 'I hate myself for feeling so envious!'), we usually go on believing that we are in fact finding or encountering our own emotions, thereby taking the paradoxical position of being responsible for what we cannot help feeling."[189] Now, there is a long tradition for arguing that one can be responsible for what one cannot help. Aristotle argued, for instance, that "to the unjust and to the self-indulgent man it was open at the beginning not to become men of this kind, and so they are such voluntarily; but now that they have become so it is not possible for them not to be so."[190] The same argument applies to the emotions.[191] Yet it seems implausible to assume that when people feel guilty about their emotions it is because they believe there is something they could have done at some earlier time to develop different emotional dispositions. I may feel guilty about my inappropriate mirth at a funeral or my lack of happiness on my wedding day without knowing *what* I could have done to develop a disposition to react differently, or even without believing *that* there was something I could have done to develop it.[192]

The fact that we do blame ourselves for our occurrent emotions (or lack of them) is a prima facie argument in favor of Schafer's thesis. Yet in blaming ourselves we might merely be misguided, just as Schafer argues that we are misguided in thinking that emotions occur involuntarily. The meta-emotion of guilt triggered by our first-order emotions or lack of them might simply be irrational or inappropriate, in a sense to be discussed shortly. The idea, admittedly, is speculative and does not provide a compelling refutation of his argument. To supplement it, I shall try to refute two of his other arguments and later argue directly against the thesis itself.

Schafer is concerned with refuting the idea of a lawlike connection between triggering conditions and emotions. "Should this apparently

---

189. Schafer (1976), p. 333.
190. *Nicomachean Ethics* 1114a.
191. Sankowski (1977).
192. Sabini and Silver (1987) comment that they "do believe that some people at some moments have been responsible for their emotions – although perhaps this responsibility is iatrogenic, limited to those who have studied Aristotle's theory."

lawlike behavior stand up to examination, we should have to accept a passive conception of emotional experience; for then we could attribute activity legitimately only to a person's getting into, staying in, or putting an end to those situations that *must* engender one emotion or another."[193] Although I agree that the proper causal framework is that of mechanisms rather than lawlike regularities, I do not think this issue is related to that of activity versus passivity of the emotions. Schafer's argument implies the absurd conclusion that the rational consumer is entirely passive, as we can predict his behavior with lawlike regularity: When prices go up, he buys less. A proponent of the view that emotions are actions might argue that agents *predictably choose* to have the emotion that will best promote their ends.

Schafer does not claim that the nonlawlike character of the emotions implies that emotions are chosen, only that their lawlike character would exclude that conclusion. To show that emotions are indeed chosen he relies on the fact that an individual can choose how to perceive the situation that triggers the emotion. Discussing the variety of responses to the extreme circumstances that the Nazis created for their victims, he writes that "in circumstances that seem identical to us as independent observers, some people conduct themselves more reasonably, resourcefully, patiently, boldly, or decently than others," because "at least in some important respects the 'stronger' ones have defined their circumstances differently."[194] Although the statement is not entirely clear, it can be read as asserting that people choose their emotions by deciding how to perceive the situation. I would use the belief–emotion connection to argue for the very opposite conclusion: It is precisely because people cannot "decide to believe"[195] that they cannot decide which emotions to have.

Over the past twenty years Robert C. Solomon has developed the view that emotions are actions.[196] "The Myth of the Passions has so thoroughly indoctrinated us with its notion of passivity that we are no longer capable of seeing what we ourselves are doing. Once the Myth is exploded, however, it is obvious that we make ourselves

193. Schafer (1976), p. 334.
194. *Ibid.*, p. 336.
195. Williams (1973); Elster (1983b), pp. 57–8; Elster (1984), pp. 49–54.
196. He first developed his theory of emotion as action in Solomon (1973). In Solomon (1976), which I cite in the revised edition of Solomon (1993), he modified some of the more outrageous claims from the article while still upholding the central argument. An explicit enumeration of the theses from the article that are abandoned in the book appears in the appendix to Solomon (1980), a reprint of Solomon (1973).

angry, make ourselves depressed, make ourselves fall in love."[197]
He claims, moreover, that emotions are always intelligible and often
rational.[198] "Every emotion is a subjective strategy for the maximization of personal dignity and self-esteem."[199] Like Schafer, he
acknowledges that emotions are experienced as if "they happen to
us," but argues that this way of perceiving them is itself a matter
of choice – "a vehicle of irresponsibility, a way of absolving oneself
from those fits of sensitivity and foolishness that constitute the most
important moments of our lives."[200] The influence of Sartre, here as
elsewhere, is evident. Another strong influence, as will be evident
from the next paragraph, is Nietzsche.

Solomon's claim about the rationality of emotions is probably best
conveyed by some examples.[201] Anger promotes self-esteem because
it is always tinged with self-righteousness, except when it is directed
against oneself, as in guilt.[202] The latter emotion contributes to self-
esteem because "the ability to admit and atone for our mistakes is . . .
essential to wisdom and personal dignity." Anxiety promotes self-
esteem by virtue of being a "perverted form of self-aggrandizement."
Contempt does so by making oneself appear superior. Depression
does so (at least in intention) by "a Cartesian method: Doubt everything until you find at least one value or task that remains un-
challengeable." Despair contributes to self-esteem by encouraging
self-indulgence and self-pity. Dread makes its contribution by virtue
of being "an apt excuse for paralyzing curiosity." Duty and morality
"can be used as weapons against obviously superior forces." Embarrassment allows one to be the center of attention, "even at the
expense of dignity (but to the benefit of self-esteem)." Envy, in sym-
biotic alliance with resentment, "seeks to rob the superior man of his
virtues and possessions" in an ideologically justified way. Fear may
involve "protection of a self-image." Gratitude "places oneself in the
dignified position of passively receiving." Hate, which presupposes
self-esteem, seeks to expand it by confrontation with powerful and
evil opponents.

197. Solomon (1993), p. 132.
198. Solomon (1993, p. 188) distinguishes between two senses of rationality. The first
     corresponds roughly to the idea of intentionality, the second, although left un-
     defined, seems to correspond more or less to the idea of rationality used here.
199. Solomon (1993), p. 222.
200. Solomon (1993), pp. 130, 131–2.
201. From Solomon (1993), Chapter 8.
202. Solomon defines as guilt what I have defined as shame and vice versa. The
     reference in the text uses my terminology.

My résumé of the catalogue stops here, about halfway through Solomon's alphabetical list of some thirty-odd emotions. It ought to be clear even from this condensed sample that his approach is both insightful and arbitrary. Many of his Nietzschean statements about how emotional states serve some further psychic purpose illustrate the "alchemies of the mind" further discussed in V.2. The vignette of "a woman [who] continues to patronize a shop which she knows has cheated her [because] her small losses are more than compensated for by the self-righteous satisfaction of her continuing indignation"[203] rings true enough. Rather than supporting his theoretical argument, however, the story directly undermines it. It suggests that the woman chooses to get into a certain situation because it predictably – that is, *independently* of her will – generates the gratifying emotion of indignation. Alternatively, the emotional gratification might act as a reinforcer on her behavior. On the basis of this and similar examples, one could interpret Solomon as arguing that people choose situations because of the emotional gratification they provide, which is of course different from his official view that they choose the emotions themselves.

Even on that more plausible interpretation, however, Solomon's claim that *all* emotions *always* exist to promote self-esteem and personal dignity, and that they even maximize these values, cannot be taken seriously. The statement that all emotional reactions can be explained by their contribution to self-esteem is a reckless generalization from a few selected cases. Most depressions are *not* vehicles for self-esteem; most cases of grief and sadness are *not* occasions for self-pity; and so on. The idea that an agent, faced with a given external situation, screens all possible emotional reactions and then selects the one that maximizes self-esteem and dignity is nothing short of absurd.

To be sure, someone steeped in the hermeneutics of suspicion can always come up with a story in which any emotional reaction can be seen as an ultrasubtle self-serving strategy. "Most emotions involve...strategies for the maximization of self-esteem that would shame a professional confidence man and a prereflexive awareness of psychological intrigue that would impress even Dr. Freud."[204] Yet in my opinion, the ingenuity is all Solomon's. He offers no evidence whatsoever for the mind's capacity to engage in these strategic calculations. In fact, it is hard to square his views about the

203. Solomon (1993), p. 222.
204. *Ibid.*, p. 181.

strategic nature of the emotions with two other views that he asserts, namely that the emotions are "undeliberated, unarticulated, and unreflective,"[205] and that they are myopic because the purposes they serve tend to be short-sighted.[206] Nor does Solomon offer any evidence for the supremacy of self-esteem over all other values or, more generally, for the idea that emotions exist to serve some psychic purpose.

Now, one cannot refute a conclusion by showing that arguments that have been made for it do not work. Turning now to a more direct approach, I can offer the following arguments in favor of the view that emotions are, by and large, passively undergone rather than actively chosen or enacted. (i) Those who see emotions as actions either have to argue that this view applies to nonhuman organisms and small children as well as to adult humans or to argue for a radical discontinuity. In my opinion, both horns of the dilemma are highly unattractive. (ii) Even in adult humans, there is very strong evidence that "[b]ecause emotions can occur with rapid onset, through automatic appraisal, with little awareness, and with involuntary response changes in expression and physiology, we often experience emotions as happening to, not chosen by us. One can not simply elect when to have which emotion."[207] (iii) If we can choose our emotions without any costs and constraints, why do we not choose always to be happy? (iv) If there are costs and constraints on which emotion can be chosen, what are they and where do they come from? Also, would not these constraints and costs precisely reflect the involuntary nature of the emotions? (v) Most emotions are triggered by beliefs, which cannot be chosen. (vi) Emotions that are not triggered by beliefs, such as panics and phobias, are even less plausibly viewed as chosen for the purpose of maximizing self-esteem.

In my opinion, therefore, the views of Schafer and Solomon are not only counterintuitive: They are false. There is, nevertheless, an element of truth in the view that the emotions are under our voluntary control. When an emotion arises from some external stimulus, we can "let it happen," amplify it by giving full rein to its expression, or try to limit it, for example by directing attention elsewhere.[208] We can also create emotions without any external stimulus. Within limits

205. *Ibid.*, p. 131.
206. R. C. Solomon (1980), p. 265. This claim is not among those that are repudiated in the appendix.
207. Ekman (1992b), p. 189.
208. Frijda (1986), Chapter 8.

it is possible to stimulate emotions deliberately by remembering (or imagining) situations in which they arose (or would arise) spontaneously. Arlie Hochschild, for instance, tells how one air stewardess handles angry passengers without getting angry herself: "I pretend something traumatic has happened in their lives. Once I had an irate that was complaining about me, cursing at me, threatening to get my name and report me to the company. I later found out that his son had just died. Now when I meet an irate I think of that man."[209] Yet as Hochschild also observes, this technique is parasitic on genuine emotion: "[T]o remember experiences emotively, he or she must first experience them in that way too."[210] By exploiting the feedback from emotional expressions to the emotions themselves, we can elicit an emotion by performing the verbal and nonverbal behaviors that normally express it. As Montaigne noted, professional orators and professional mourners may end up experiencing the emotions they are paid to express (*Essays* p. 944). Yet these cases, too, are parasitic on the normal or spontaneous occurrences. The traditional view that occurrent emotions are undergone rather than chosen is, I believe, basically sound.

APPROPRIATE EMOTIONS

Rather than viewing emotions as actions, one might view them as analogous to beliefs (although not *as* beliefs). Beliefs are rational if they are adequate or appropriate, given the available evidence. Similarly, one might argue that emotions can be appropriate or adequate, given the beliefs that elicit them.[211] In this sense, an emotion can be rational even if it is based on irrational beliefs, and irrational even if based on rational beliefs. Although I have argued against "moral-

---

209. Hochschild (1983), p. 25.
210. *Ibid.*, p. 41.
211. Greenspan (1989, p. 88) stipulates that "an emotion will count as appropriate where it is keyed to a *significant subset* of the perceptual evidence available." In my terminology, she relates emotions to information rather than to beliefs. Elsewhere (p. 106) she restates the criterion as the claim that an emotion is appropriate "as long as it rests on evidence that, if recognized, would yield prima facie warrant for the corresponding belief." I might feel mildly afraid of someone on the basis of subliminal cues that in the past have been regularly associated with lack of trustworthiness. Were these cues to become consciously recognized, they might justify a belief that the person does indeed have qualities that justify the fear. In that case, the emotion is appropriate even if the belief is not actually formed.

ized definitions" of the emotions (IV.2), *moralized assessments* are not vulnerable to the same objections.

Let me recall the main examples cited here and in previous chapters of putatively irrational emotions:

1. Anger at those whom we have harmed
2. Anger at those who have helped us
3. Love of those whom we have helped
4. Love of those who have harmed us
5. Anger at those whom we bore
6. Hating those who fail to requite our love
7. Anger at a person who has proved us to be wrong
8. Anger at those who frustrate our goals even if they did not and could not have been expected to foresee the consequences of their actions
9. Guilt for emotions, thoughts, or events outside our control
10. Shame for emotions, thoughts, events, or character traits outside our control
11. Pride for events outside our control
12. Contempt for features of a target individual that are outside his control
13. Admiration for features of a target individual that are outside his control
14. Agapic love, that is, love which lacks cognitive support
15. Panics or phobias that lack cognitive support
16. Jealousy, which is always irrational, because it presupposes cognitive antecedents that undermine the love which is a condition for the jealousy itself

With the exception of (4), (14), and (16), these seem all to be reasonably well-established phenomena. In cases (1), (2), (5), (6), and (7), *damage to our self-esteem* induces a hostile emotion towards another person. Without denying its reality, I find case (3) more opaque. In cases (8) through (13) an emotion is triggered by a *truncated cognition*, which focuses on a favorable or unfavorable outcome without any concern for its causal history. Cases (9) and (10) are especially puzzling. These emotions are not only inappropriate but painful. Whereas irrational anger is induced by the need to repair damage to our self-esteem and irrational pride actually enhances it, irrational guilt and shame seem to be sources of pointless suffering. One person feel ashamed when he goes bald or starts losing his sense of hearing and tries to hide it from others. Another feels guilty when he learns that a friend has died in a car accident and realizes that he could have prevented it by calling him up and delaying his departure by a few minutes. We may well wonder, What's in it for them? Case (15) is somewhat different from the others, in that people subject to these fears usually know they are unfounded.

In many of these cases, the irrational emotion goes together with irrational belief formation. Because our self-esteem may not allow us to harbor emotions that we cannot defend to ourselves and to others, we invent some kind of story to justify even the most irrational reactions. Cases (1) and (8) can yield especially virulent examples of this mechanism. Arguing from first principles, the process must have four stages. First, the emotion occurs. Second, there is an unconscious recognition that it is unjustified. Third, the recognition causes some kind of mental discomfort or dissonance. Finally, there is the invention of a justification to reduce the discomfort. In practice, we only observe the first and the last stage, which may occur almost simultaneously. I return to the interaction between emotion and cognition below and then again in V.2.

It remains to determine the criteria for an emotion being "appropriate" or "rational." To some extent, this may be a cultural matter. For the Greeks, cases (9), (12), and (13) were not instances of irrationality. In our own society, many may not view case (13) as an irrational emotion. I doubt, however, that culture can provide the whole explanation. I conjecture that there are no societies in which cases (1) and (8) are not seen as inappropriate by the agent and those around him. Case (1), in particular, seems recalcitrant to a purely cultural explanation. All societies have norms for what constitutes justified harm. The norms may vary across societies, but there are no societies that do not have some norm of this kind. It follows that in all societies there will be cases in which people hurt others without being justified in doing so. If they get angry with a person when and because they have hurt him without justification, they are irrational. Although case (1) is instantiated in all societies, it will have different instantiations in different societies. By contrast, there may be some societies in which, say, case (12) is never instantiated, not because individuals do not feel contempt towards the ugly or disabled, but because they experience no discomfort in doing so. These are difficult issues, and I am far from confident that I've gotten hold of the right end of the stick.

IRRATIONAL EMOTIONS AND BELIEF-IRRATIONALITY

One might also argue that emotions are irrational if their cognitive antecedents embody some form of belief irrationality. This proposal can be spelled out in a number of ways, which capture different varieties of irrational emotions. The most important case, of which I shall distinguish three subcases, is that of irrational emotions caused by emotionally induced belief irrationality.

Consider first, however, cases of belief formation by cold irrationality, due to defective cognitive processing of various kinds.[212] During the Second World War, Londoners were persuaded that the Germans systematically concentrated their bombing in certain parts of their city, because the bombs fell in clusters. This invalid inference, which reflected a lack of understanding of the statistical principle that random processes tend to generate clustering,[213] probably made the Londoners living in those areas more fearful than they would otherwise have been. One might say, therefore, that their fear was irrational or irrationally strong. Conversely, the idea that lightning never strikes twice in the same place may induce an irrational *lack* of fear.

In the case just discussed the process that results in this irrational emotion does not itself originate in an emotion. Even if it does, emotionally caused beliefs need not be instances of motivated irrationality. Emotions may affect belief formation qua sheer arousal, regardless of their content and direction. It is difficult to make correct inferences when one is in the throes of a strong passion. Assume, for instance, that a salesman is unable to add up sums correctly because he is constantly distracted by thoughts about a woman he just met. Sometimes the errors in the sum might benefit the customer, sometimes himself: There is no reason to expect a pattern either way.[214] If his trembling arithmetical hand leads him to believe that the customer owes him a great deal of money, any elation that might ensue would be irrational because grounded in an irrational belief.

A third variety arises when an emotion affects belief formation – and thereby generates another emotion – by virtue of its content rather than by virtue of its arousal properties. Consider the following generic tragic scenario. Emma loves Henry, who spurns her. The jealous

212. For a survey see Nisbett and Ross (1980).
213. Feller (1968), p. 161.
214. We may note in passing that this case shows the need to distinguish between "hot" and "motivated" irrationality – two categories that have been treated as synonymous by several writers, including myself (see Rosen 1996, p. 48, n. 25).

Emma tells Henry's best friend Paul, who loves Emma, a lie to the effect that Henry has behaved dishonorably towards her. The infatuated Paul, believing Emma in the face of strong evidence to the contrary, kills Henry in anger. Later, Paul discovers that Emma had lied and kills her. In one phrase: Paul's *love* for Emma induces the irrational *belief* in him that Henry has behaved badly towards her, and this belief, together with Paul's *love* for Emma (which thus enters doubly into the story), induces the *anger* that makes him kill Henry. Although nothing as simple as this scenario is found in Shakespeare or Racine, their plays do turn on the basic mechanisms of emotion-induced beliefs and belief-induced emotions.

A final variety occurs when an emotion generates a meta-emotion that induces a subsequent belief change. This is a central theme in the present book as a whole and is discussed in some detail in V.2. In one variation on this theme, the new belief induces a new emotion. This case is illustrated by the transmutation of envy into righteous indignation, as shown in Fig. II.1. In another subvariety, an irrational emotion generates a pressure to invent a belief that would justify it. If irrational anger is caused by a truncated cognition, the agent may supplement the belief by providing a causal story that justifies the anger. In a third subvariety, the agent may replace the original belief with another, more serviceable one. In II.3 I cited an example from Montaigne, in which the angry Piso invented a new reason for being angry when his original reason turned out to be unfounded. In II.4 I cited a similar episode from *Middlemarch*, in which Mrs. Farebrother, learning that Lydgate is not the natural son of Bulstrode, suggests that "[t]he report may be true of some other son."[215]

The formation of a belief that justifies a feeling of anger occurs, to put it crudely, to make one feel good. Although irrational, the phenomenon is fully intelligible. The more puzzling case is that of Othello, whose jealousy makes him believe Iago even though the evidence for Iago's claims is exceedingly slight, he has no emotional

215. These cases of substitution do not represent displacement of affect in the Freudian sense. Displacement of anger from one object to another is one of the defense mechanisms (V.2) and supposedly motivated by the need to ward off unavowable impulses. Substitution, by contrast, is caused by the disappearance of the original object and the need for a new one. Thus substitution also differs from what happens when "emotional experience motivates search for causes explaining that experience ... Why this angry mood? or what, precisely, in the other's action made one white with anger?" (Frijda 1986, pp. 255–56.) The goal of substitution, by contrast, is to create an object for the emotion, not to discover it.

attachment to Iago that makes him want to believe him (unlike the case of Paul discussed above), and believing Iago will make him feel bad. Although his perceptions of a racial prejudice may enter into his willingness to believe the worst, they cannot fully account for it – and in any case there are many other instances of irrational jealousy in which there is no such prejudice at work. It is enough to cite the extensive analyses of jealousy in *A la recherche du temps perdu*.[216]

A more mundane illustration of the same mechanism is the following. Walking through a wood at night, we suddenly hear a faint sound and become worried that it might represent a danger. Our incipient fear leads us to interpret all sorts of other innocent sounds as ominous signs, until we start running in full-fledged panic. "In such an emotional inferno one cannot be reassured; that is not what one seeks. One acts to intensify whatever emotion is felt, turning fear into terror, anger into fury, disgust into revulsion, distress into anguish."[217] This is the phenomenon of *counterwishful thinking*, which I have discussed in various sections (I.6, II.3, III.3). The mechanism seems mysterious, and yet it is hard to deny that it exists. As in irrational anger, an initial emotion induces a belief that justifies and even strengthens it, generating an "emotional wildfire." The difference with anger, to repeat, is that it's hard to see what's in it for the organism. In that respect, irrational jealousy and fear may be classified with irrational guilt and shame.

RATIONAL EMOTIONS AND THE GOOD LIFE

I have discussed whether and in which sense occurrent emotions can be rational. A different issue is whether emotional dispositions can be rational. With respect to this question one might argue that rational emotions are those that make ones life go as well as it could, given external circumstances. This idea can be spelled out in two ways. On the one hand, we can ask which set of emotional dispositions it would be optimal to *have*. On the other hand, we can ask which dispositions it would be optimal to *develop*. Although one cannot acquire an emotional disposition in the way in which one can raise one's arm, by just doing it, one can engage in various actions that will, more or less predictably, produce it.

216. See notably Grimaldi (1993), p. 49.
217. Ekman (1992a), p. 172.

Here I only address the latter question, which allows us to connect the idea of the rationality of emotions with that of choice of emotions – an idea that, as we have seen, makes little sense for the occurrent emotions. Note that one cannot assume the rationality of an effort to undertake a disposition that, once acquired, would make one's life go better. The costs of that effort also have to be taken into account. I might be better off with my moderate propensity to irrational guilt than if I were to pay a psychoanalyst large sums of money to get rid of it. It may not be worth while to spend ten years in Buddhist training in order to obtain the peace of mind that will enable me to get by on three hours of sleep a night. Moreover, as these examples suggest, there might be some uncertainty about the causal efficacy of the various techniques of character planning. I return to that point below.

I shall assume, in a somewhat simplistic fashion, that the maximand for character planning is subjective welfare, which is made up of hedonic as well as emotional satisfaction. (By this assumption I exclude, for instance, the desire to become moral.) I also assume, in a somewhat unrealistic fashion, that the contributions of emotional experiences to welfare can be measured and compared. I assume, finally, that all satisfaction derives from encounters with the world and the further outcomes, if any, of such encounters. (This implies the exclusion of daydreams as a source of welfare.) The stream of encounters and their outcomes depend partly on our own choices, partly on the choices made by actual or potential interaction partners, and partly on external or parametric factors, ranging from one's genetic make-up through the weather to the state of the national economy.

We can now state the problem at hand somewhat more precisely. Welfare over time is a function of two variables. On one hand it depends on the stream of encounters and their further outcomes. On the other hand, it depends on the hedonic and emotional dispositions that determine the satisfaction provided by these encounters and their outcomes. To illustrate, a wine-tasting contest may be one such encounter and the prize for winning the contest a possible outcome. By participating in the contest I may gain the hedonic satisfaction from the wine, the emotional satisfaction from winning the contest, and a monetary prize that will enhance my ability to have future emotional and hedonic experiences. In addition, the encounter and its outcome may be a source of utility from memory and anticipation.[218]

218. Elster and Loewenstein (1992).

Encounters (and their outcomes) and dispositions are not independent of each other. Encounters with the world are the most effective way of acquiring a disposition or changing it. Meditation and inner exhortation, by themselves, have limited force. Stendhal observed, "Everything can be acquired in solitude, except character"; also, "To have a strong character one must have experienced the effect produced by others upon oneself; therefore we need the others" (*il faut les autres*).[219] Aristotle, too, argued that dispositions or habits are acquired by action: "[B]y doing the acts that we do in our transactions with other men we become just or unjust, and by doing the acts that we do in the presence of danger, and being habituated to feel fear or confidence, we become brave or cowardly. The same is true for appetites and feelings of anger; some men become temperate and good-tempered, others self-indulgent or irascible, by behaving in one way or the other in the appropriate circumstances. Thus, in one word, states arise out of like activities."[220]

Conversely my dispositions may affect the number of my encounters with others and shape the outcomes of such encounters in a direction that is more or less favorable to me. If others know that I am irascible, they will not deal with me if they can avoid it. (A benevolent disposition, on the other hand, may cause others to seek me out.) If they cannot avoid it, their fear of my temper will induce them to make concessions they would not otherwise have made. (A benevolent disposition, on the other hand, may induce me to make concessions I would not otherwise have made.) The net result of these two opposing effects is, in general, indeterminate.[221] Irascible (and benevolent) people may or may not benefit materially from their disposition.

Given these preliminaries, the problem at hand can be defined as follows: In a parametric environment, which actions will bring about the encounters, outcomes, and dispositions that maximize net expected welfare over time? Although it is intuitively obvious that this question has no answer, it may be instructive to understand exactly why life could never be the solution to a maximization problem. Two main obstacles are, I submit, those of *uncertainty* and of *by-products*. Moreover, the emotions themselves can get in the way.

---

219. Stendhal (1980), fragments 1, 92.
220. *Nicomachean Ethics* 1103^{b}12–20. The word translated as "state" is "hexis," sometimes rendered as "disposition."
221. In Elster (in press a, section I.5). I criticize Robert Frank and Jack Hirshleifer for their exclusive focus on the benefits of a disposition to be angry.

On the one hand, the intellectual and pragmatic bankruptcy of psychoanalysis and most other forms of therapy shows that we simply do not know enough about the workings of the mind to be able to change its course predictably and reliably.[222] If read as a guide to planned character change, Aristotle's remarks are too simplistic. A person with no settled disposition either way may perhaps mold himself by his actions, but it is far from obvious that an irascible person can change his disposition by controlling outward expressions of anger.[223] Moreover, for some dispositions the Aristotelian recipe will not work even in the former case. To become compassionate, it is not enough to behave compassionately. One has to have suffered oneself to understand the sufferings of others.

On the other hand, certain dispositions may be intrinsically unamenable to conscious planning. They can only arise as by-products of activities that are undertaken for other ends.[224] Compassion, again, provides an example. A person who felt insufficiently compassionate could not develop that disposition by voluntarily exposing himself to suffering. To take a trivial example, one cannot bring oneself to understand what it means to fail at an important examination by deliberately flunking an examination oneself, because failing means trying and not succeeding rather than not trying. The by-product problem also arises with regard to the intentional production of occurrent emotional states. I cannot make myself laugh by telling a joke to myself or tickling myself. I may feel proud of my achievements, but I will not achieve much if I am moved only by the desire to feel pride. More generally, people cannot plan the surprise that will enhance their emotions.

To the extent that my encounters with the world are both independent of my actions and unpredictable, I may not know what to plan *for*. A set of emotional dispositions that is useful in one state of affairs may be counterproductive in another. A stoic attitude may be useful if one goes bankrupt but might otherwise be a killjoy. Montaigne observed, "If you say that the convenience of having our senses chilled and blunted when tasting evil pains must entail the consequential inconvenience of rendering us less

---

222. For the pragmatic issue, which is the most relevant one here, see Dawes (1994).
223. See for instance Izard (1991), pp. 251–2.
224. See Chapter II of Elster (1983b) for the idea of states that are essentially by-products.

keenly appreciative of the joys of good pleasures, I agree. But the wretchedness of our human condition means that we have less to relish than to banish" (*Essays*, p. 548). In the turbulent times in which he lived, this was perhaps a correct appreciation, but in general I do not think one can defend the claim that the benefits of feeling pain less acutely offset the cost of a less keen sense of pleasure.

Finally, the emotions themselves may serve as an obstacle to emotional planning. Making contingency plans for dealing with unpleasant emotions in the future is a source of unpleasant emotions in the present. "Making a list of worries before embarking on a trip seems like a reasonable cognitive coping strategy. But nobody likes to worry; thus, we 'forget' to act on such advice.... Relatively few people can plan for tomorrow's emotional distress."[225] Although such avoidance behavior may be irrational,[226] it need not be. Thus towards the end of his life Montaigne found that he had been wrong earlier when he had argued that we should keep death constantly in our mind in order to reduce the fear of death. In doing so, "we prepare ourselves against our preparations for death! Philosophy first commands us to have death ever before our eyes, to anticipate it and to consider it beforehand, and then she gives us rules and caveats in order to forestall our being hurt by our reflections and our foresight" (*Essays*, p. 1191).

BECKER'S THEORY OF THE EMOTIONS

Although the idea of rational planning of one's own emotional dispositions may be chimerical, could one have more success in planning those of others? Over the past twenty years Gary Becker has moved towards a position of this kind. In most of his work, Becker has taken emotional dispositions for given and tried to incorporate them into economic models. In his most recent writings he goes beyond this approach, by trying to endogenize emotions. More specifically, he tries to show that emotional dispositions as well as occurrent emotions (or

---

225. Vaillant (1993), p. 71.
226. "No wonder that [ordinary people] often get caught in a trap. You can frighten them simply by mentioning death; and since it is mentioned in wills, never expect them to draw one up before the doctor has pronounced the death-sentence. And then, in the midst of pain and terror, God only knows what shape their good judgement kneads it into!" (Montaigne 1991, p. 93).

their absence) can be the result of rational choice by the emotional subject or by others.[227]

Becker's writings on altruism view this emotion as an externality in the utility function, a person's utility being a function of his or her own consumption, the consumption of spouse, and the consumption of children. In some applications, the utility of the altruistic member is assumed to depend on the utility rather than on the consumption of other family members. Applying this idea within the context of a family, Becker shows that the presence of a genuinely altruistic person in a household may induce selfish or even envious members of the household to act as if they, too, were altruistic. Modeling envy as another utility externality, he shows that if the head of the family is envious, selfish family members act as if they, too, were envious. As these results are well known and do not involve emotions in more than a minimal sense, I shall not discuss them further.

In various places Becker extends the analysis to cover parental preferences over what he calls "merit goods,"[228] or "particular traits or behavior [sic] of children that parents care about."[229] These include emotional dispositions such as envy, other dispositions such as laziness, and behavioral patterns such as gambling and excessive drinking. Parents, typically, do not want their children to be lazy or envious, or to waste their money on gambling and liquor. Conversely, they might have a preference for positive merit goods, such as working hard or being obedient. In conjunction with his writings on altruism and envy, Becker's theory of merit goods suggests that parents have preferences over their children's utility, their consumption, their behavior, and their character traits. Although he briefly mentions the possibility of parents who are envious of their children[230] or who take a sadistic pleasure in making them worse off,[231] he mainly

---

227. In his various references to emotions, Becker discusses altruism (1976, Chapters 12, 13; 1991, Chapter 11), respect (1976, pp. 258–9), envy (1976, pp. 259–60, 278–80; 1991, pp. 288–92), guilt (1996, pp. 152–5, 232–3), and love (1991, pp. 326–8; 1996, pp. 233–6). Indirectly, Becker (1996, Chapter 11) also refers to shame in his discussion of social norms. As these references indicate, the discussions of altruism are by far the most extensive. Although Becker (1976, pp. 278–80) also refers briefly to hatred, this is for him simply a synonym of envy. This cavalier use of terminology reflects the fact that Becker seems entirely unaware of the psychological literature on the emotions, at least as far as one can judge from his written work.

228. Becker (1976), pp. 275–7; Becker (1991), pp. 10–3, 290, 298.

229. Becker (1991), p. 10.

230. Becker (1991), p. 210.

231. Becker (1996), p. 157.

assumes that their preferences reflects a concern for what they believe to be good for the children, whether or not that is also what the children prefer.

By and large, preferences over merit goods take second place to preferences over consumption or utility. In his discussion of envy in the family, for instance, Becker analyzes the behavior of an altruistic father with a daughter Jane and an envious son Tom, assuming that the utility of the father "depends positively on his own consumption, the utility of Tom, and the utility of a selfish Jane."[232] Under this assumption, "a shift of Tom's utility function toward greater envy would reduce his father's contribution to Jane; indeed, if Tom became sufficiently envious, the contribution to Jane might be reduced to zero." The assumption seems to be that, for the father, a utile is a utile is a utile, independent of the motivation that underlies it. If Tom's envy makes him suffer intensely from Jane's well-being, their father will take income away from Jane to assuage his envy. In fact, "Tom might benefit from actions that harmed Jane sufficiently to reduce family income, because his father might not reduce his contribution to Tom by much." At this point Becker seems to notice the somewhat surreal nature of the argument, for he adds, "Of course, the father's utility function might depend only on Tom's consumption and not on Tom's utility if the father *disapproved* of envy between his children." Sometimes, utiles are indeed not interchangeable. Yet this brief appearance of common sense is only a momentary one. In the continuation of the discussion, Becker argues that the victims of envy would "want to lower the envy income of the envier and harm him because he would then make them better off."[233] More plausibly, in my opinion, they might harm him because of the *anger* induced by their perception of the envious motivation. As I noted in IV.2, beliefs about other people's motivations can trigger powerful emotional reactions.

Before I proceed to the more interesting case of endogenous emotions, let me note a curious feature of Becker's discussion of envy and altruism. In *A Treatise on the Family* from 1991, envy is treated together with altruism as respectively negative and positive externalities in the utility function. In a 1974 article, "A Theory of Social Interaction,"[234] envy is paired with respect rather than with altruism. The general idea is that a person might maximize utility by

232. Becker (1991), p. 289.
233. *Ibid.*, p. 291.
234. Reprinted in Becker (1976) and Becker (1996).

allocating some of his income to activities that affect others rather than to his own consumption. Thus he might seek to achieve "distinction" by investing in activities that will gain him the respect and approval of others. Alternatively, he might seek to enhance his well-being by investing in activities that will detract from the income or prestige of others.[235] Envy is contrasted, that is, both with the desire to make others better off and with the desire to make others think well of oneself. The latter two motivations would seem to be very different from each other. In his application of his theory to the issue of charitable contributions, Becker notes that "apparent 'charitable behavior' can . . . be motivated by a desire to avoid the scorn of others or to receive social acclaim," but adds nevertheless that "not much generality is sacrificed . . . by only considering charity motivated by a desire to improve well-being."[236] Although there may be analytical purposes for which it makes no difference whether people donate to charities to make themselves better off or to make others better off, there are contexts in which that distinction may be important. Some people, for instance, prefer to donate anonymously.

In his recent work, Becker tries to explain the emotions rather than taking them for given. True to his general program, he aims at giving a rational-choice explanation. As indicated in Table IV.1, he focuses on preventing occurrent emotions from arising in oneself and on inculcating emotional dispositions in others.[237]

The idea of emotional self-management is a relatively undeveloped category, represented only by a brief note in Becker's most recent book.[238] The idea is that people have an incentive to avoid situations that might trigger certain emotions they do not want to have, an idea that is applied first to guilt and then to love. Except for those who enjoy meeting beggars because it make them "feel superior or lucky,"[239] people avoid beggars because they want to avoid the feelings of guilt triggered by the encounters. It is not clear from Becker's discussion whether the root cause is the negative valence of the emotion or the monetary loss associated with the giving which is the action tendency of guilt. When he asserts that "people do not want to

235. Becker (1976), pp. 255–60.
236. Becker (1976), p. 273.
237. Chapter 1 of Becker (1996) also discusses character planning, but mainly with regard to time preferences and not at all with regard to emotional dispositions (see Elster 1997 for a critical review).
238. Becker (1996), Chapter 12.
239. *Ibid.*, p. 232.

encounter beggars, *even though* they may contribute handsomely after an encounter,"[240] the phrase that I have italicized suggests the first
reading. On the second reading, we would expect "because" rather
than "even though."

If the case of guilt is supposed to be analogous to that of love, however, the second reading must be chosen. Here, Becker's argument is
that high-income individuals stay away from low-income individuals of the opposite sex, because they know that they might fall in love
with them and that if they do they will want to share their income
with them. In this case the emotion itself has positive valence but is
avoided because of the loss of income that will be predictably induced
by the associated action tendency. Because guilt as well as love may
induce generous feeling and because generosity is costly, individuals
who care about their income stay away from occasions that might
trigger these emotions. I offer a somewhat similar argument in V.2,
when discussing the transmutation of interest into passion. Here I
shall only note that this avoidance behavior might have costs of its
own. If the set of partners is very restricted, one might not meet *anyone* who triggers the emotion. The plot of *Pride and Prejudice* would
not have gotten off the ground if Darcy had acted in accordance with
Becker's analysis.

In *Accounting for Taste*, Becker offers two analyses of the inculcation
of emotions in others. One is parental inculcation of guilt in children,
the other is upper-class inculcation of religion in the lower classes.
Although religion is not an emotion, it is sustained by social norms
that are, in turned, sustained by feeling of shame. Although this is a
borderline case, I discuss it here because it suggests some interesting
perspectives on inculcation more generally.

In both cases, the inculcation is done for the benefit of the incul-
cator rather than for the benefit of the persons who are inculcated.
Becker's analysis of guilt differs, therefore, from Frank's. Yet Becker
does not imply that parents care only for themselves. Because they
also care for their children, they want them to be well off; hence they
will invest in their education. At the same time, they want to be well
off themselves in their old age. They can achieve this end by reducing
the amount of bequests they leave to their children, or by investing
in actions that induce guilt in the children, so that they will take care
of their parents when they grow old. Because of their altruism, the
parents suffer when their children feel guilty. They also suffer when

240. *Ibid.*, p. 233.

the children, to relieve their guilt, transfer income to the parents and thereby make themselves worse off. Given these various interconnections, optimal investments by parents in the education and guilt of their children, as well as optimal bequests, are then determined by the appropriate marginal balancing.

Note that the analysis refers to the negative valence of guilt as well as to the action tendency induced by the emotion. On the one hand, the guilt of the children is costly to the parents, because they care about the welfare of their children. On the other hand, it is beneficial to the parents, because it induces the children to support them in old age. Becker also assumes, however, that "children feel less guilty when they contribute more."[241] If the parents anticipate that effect – as they should – the cost to them of their children's guilt should also be reduced. As far as I can judge from Becker's compact treatment, he does not take into account this implication. In calculating the cost of the children's guilt to the parents, he considers the pretransfer situation rather than the more relevant post-transfer situation.

Although Becker does not specify what he means by "investment in guilt," it could be spelled out as follows. In raising children, example tends to work better than prescription or manipulation. "Do as I say, not as I do" is notoriously ineffective. To ensure that the children will feel guilty enough to support them, parents may have to incur the cost of supporting their own parents. Yet what is missing in this analysis is that children also feel love for their parents, not only guilt when they fail to support them. (In fact, one reason they love their parents may be that they observe how loving the latter are towards *their* parents.) There is an unjustified asymmetry in assuming that parents transfer income to the children because they love them and want them to be better off, whereas children transfer income to their parents only to reduce their own guilt. Why assume that what matters for the children is the amount they transfer to their parents rather than the post-transfer income of the parents? I think many children support their parents because they love them. Moreover, I do not think this love is a result of any previous parental investment in filial love. Were Becker to make that argument, we would have to ask him whether the parents' love for their children could not also be result of the children investing in parental love (by "playing cute" and so forth).

I have two further objections to this analysis. First, parental investment in guilt might not be rational if, as is plausible, the guilt

241. *Ibid.*, p. 159.

is largely an effect of social norms to the maintenance of which any given parent can only make a tiny contribution. Second, if the inculcation of guilt were motivated mainly by a desire to profit from it, the targets would not feel guilty. Rather as I have argued repeatedly in the case of shame, they would be angry. The guilt-inducing intention is *incoherent*, in the sense defined in III.2. Becker overlooks the important role of motivations in triggering behavior. At the very least, he would have to assume that the parents successfully hide their inculcating motivations, that they misrepresent their self-interest as a concern for the welfare of their children. Yet, as I argue in V.3, misrepresentation of motivations is subject to severe constraints that can make it difficult to carry out in practice.

Although the strategy of hiding the self-interested motivation from one's children is especially unlikely to be successful in the intimate atmosphere of the family, it might seem more likely to succeed in the impersonal atmosphere of the firm, which has been the object of a similar analysis by Eugene Kandel and Edward Lazear.[242] This article makes the interesting point that investments by employers in creating respectively guilt and shame in their employees differ in their temporal structure. Whereas guilt requires a heavy one-shot investment, shame requires continuous low-level investments in monitoring. Yet their argument, too, suffers from the problem of internal incoherence. Employees are not like children. If employers try to manipulate them into feelings of guilt and shame, they are likely to notice it and get angry instead. If they are unionized, this outcome is extremely likely.

In an essay on norms and the formation of preferences, Becker argues that the upper class can inculcate religious beliefs in the lower class as an alternative to buying protection against the predatory behavior of the latter.[243] To allow themselves to become indoctrinated, the lower classes must receive some form of compensation. Although Becker does not explain what forms this could take, he observes that in order to prevent free riding the compensation would have to be produced jointly with the belief inculcation. Thus the rich could subsidize the building of churches and the payment of clergy, while also offering (say) cheap day care for regular church goers. It would seem to follow from Becker's analysis – although he does not draw this implication – that compensation would only be necessary in the

242. Kandel and Lazear (1992).
243. Becker (1996)., Chapter 11.

start-up phase. Once the poor are "hooked" on religion, the compensation can be withdrawn because by now churchgoing is supported by social norms among the poor. These norms do not simply tell you to go to church and to behave in certain ways (the ways desired by the rich in the first place), but also to punish those of your fellow poor who do not follow the norms.

I find this analysis intrinsically implausible and devoid of empirical support. Had Becker looked at the historical literature, such as the chapter on the transforming power of the cross in E.P. Thompson's *The Making of the English Working Class*, he would have found that for religious indoctrination to work the indoctrinators have to believe in the religion themselves.[244] Self-consciously manipulative attempts to inculcate religious and political ideologies tend to fail, for reasons well understood by social psychologists.[245] Becker might respond that for his purposes he only needs to assume the existence of some preachers who already believe in the religion. The rich could then subsidize them in secret, on the condition that the preachers also offer the congregation the selective benefits needed to draw initial nonbelievers into the churches, to get them hooked. Again, I do not know of any empirical evidence that might support this claim.

APPENDIX: THE PLACE OF EMOTIONS IN THE EXPLANATION OF BEHAVIOR

If nothing else, I believe I have shown that the place of the emotions in the explanation of behavior is very complex. Let me try to summarize and illustrate some of the main strands of the discussion in the previous three chapters. The cases do not exhaust all the ways in which emotions can affect behavior or even all the ways I have mentioned, but I believe they capture the main thrust of my analysis.

In the list given below, cases (1) and (2) refer to behavior undertaken now in order to generate or avoid *emotional experiences in the future*. Cases (3) and (4) refer to behavior undertaken now in order to generate *emotional dispositions*. Cases (5) and (6) refer to behavior that follows from the *action tendencies* of an emotion. Case (7)

244. Thompson (1968).
245. Brehm (1966).

refers to behavior that is *inseparable from the emotion* itself. Case (8) refers to behavior caused by the *desire to maintain or change a situation* that generates positive or negative emotions. Case (9) refers to behavior *against one's own better judgment* ("weakness of will") under the influence of emotions. Cases (10) and (11) refer to emotions that can induce *myopic* and *farsighted* behaviors respectively. Cases (12) through (14) refer to behavior generated on the basis of emotionally induced *beliefs*. Cases (15) and (16) refer to behavior induced by emotions that are triggered by the perception or anticipation of the *emotions of others*. Case (17) refers to behavior triggered by *irrational emotions*. Case (18) refers to behavior in situations in which the emotions serve as *tie-breakers*. Cases (19) and (20) refer to *avoidance and undoing behavior* induced by negative emotions. The hodge-podge nature of this list is obvious. Although I believe it reflects the complexity of the facts, others might wish for a more parsimonious and coherent account.

(1) Emotional experiences with positive valence ("positive emotions," for short) may serve as the goal of behavior. The link between behavior and outcome may be provided either by intentional choice or by the reinforcement properties of the experience. *Example*: Solomon's case of a woman who was willing to take a financial loss in order to get the pleasant feeling of righteous indignation.

(2) Future occasions that would generate negative emotions may steer behavior away from those occasions. The link between behavior and outcome may be provided either by intentional choice or by the reinforcement properties of the experience. *Example*: not going to a party at which we might meet a person towards whom we have behaved badly.

(3) We may engage in activity A for the purpose of changing or acquiring emotional dispositions in ways that will enhance the value of activity B. *Example*: seeing a psychotherapist to get rid of feelings of guilt about sex.

(4) We may engage in activity A for the purpose of acquiring emotional dispositions that will prevent us from engaging in activity C. *Example*: imitating moral behavior in order to become moral (Aristotle).

(5) Emotions may orient behavior in the present, by virtue of the associated action tendencies. *Example*: striking someone in anger.

(6) Emotions may also play a role in determining whether these tendencies are expressed or inhibited. *Example*: striking A when

angry at him because the shame one would feel towards B if one didn't outweighs the shame one will feel towards C if one does.

(7) Emotions may affect the likelihood of behavior to which they are intrinsically linked. *Example*: hybristic or sadistic behavior, which is indissociable from the pleasure of humiliating or hurting others.

(8) Emotions may affect behavior in the present by inducing a desire to maintain or change the situation that triggered the emotion. *Example*: jealousy inducing one to talk badly about one's rival in the hope of tipping the balance in one's favor.

(9) Emotions may affect behavior in the present by virtue of the associated arousal (viscerality) that makes one act against one's own better judgment. *Example*: marital infidelity.

(10) More specifically, emotions may affect behavior by inducing a drastic shortening of the time perspective. *Example*: the tendency to take revenge immediately even when it could be done more efficiently and at lower risk by delaying it.

(11) Conversely, emotions may enhance the ability to take account of long-term consequences, by acting as current motivational proxies (Frank) or as current cognitive signals (Damasio). *Example*: shame that may help me resist an urge to cancel my appointment with the dentist.

(12) Emotions may affect beliefs and, through them, behavior. *Example*: a person in a highly elated state acts on exaggerated, emotionally induced beliefs about the personal efficacy of behavior.

(13) Emotions may affect beliefs and, through them, emotions and, through them, behavior in one of the ways already mentioned. *Example*: Paul's love for Emma may induce him to believe her implausible statement that Henry has behaved badly towards her, thus making Paul angry enough at Henry to hurt him.

(14) Emotions may affect emotions and, through them, beliefs and, through them, emotions and, through them, behavior in one of the ways already mentioned. *Example*: Envy causes shame which induces a belief that the situation is one that justifies righteous indignation and subsequent punishment of the target person (see Fig. II.1).

(15) The emotions of others, when perceived, may induce emotions in the agent and, through them, behavior in one of the ways already mentioned. *Example*: The perception of another's envy-enjoyment may transform envy into anger and permit aggressive behavior that otherwise would have been kept in check by shame.

(16) Emotions of others, when anticipated, may induce anticipation of emotions in the agent and, through them, behavior in one of the

ways already mentioned. *Example*: a small child fighting at school to avoid the shame he would feel if his father expressed disgust at him for being a sissy.

(17) By virtue of ill-understood psychic mechanisms, beliefs may induce emotions that are, in some ill-understood sense, inadequate or inappropriate. These emotions, in turn, may induce behavior in one of the ways already mentioned. *Example*: My guilt for the bad weather while my guests are visiting may induce me to do more for them than I would otherwise have done (although the causal chain could also go in the opposite direction).

(18) By serving as tie-breakers in situations of indeterminacy, occurrent emotions may help us choose more decisively and perhaps more wisely than we would otherwise have done. *Example*: When I am trying to decide whether to propose marriage to A or to B, gut feelings about who is more suitable enable me to avoid procrastination and perhaps to choose the one that is more suitable.

(19) Occurrent emotions with negative valence may induce behavior intended to blunt their impact. *Example*: an alcoholic who drinks to escape the guilt induced by the knowledge that he is ruining his life by drinking.

(20) Occurrent emotions with negative valence may induce behavior intended to harm the person who triggered them, even if that person is no longer in a position to do harm. *Example*: victims of torture who seek out their torturers to bring them to justice.

Chapter V

Alchemies of the Mind: Transmutation and Misrepresentation

V.1. INTRODUCTION

The present chapter offers a number of applications of the ideas introduced in II.3 and IV.3. The basic argument is simple. When acting, people can have any number of motivations. Often, these motivations can be ranked in terms of how acceptable they are to the actor or to other people. In III.4, for instance, I suggested that among the Greeks justice, revenge, interest, and envy were ranked in that order. To act on a motivation that the actor finds unacceptable is painful. To act on a motivation that other people condemn is also painful. Typically, perhaps, the former pain is that of guilt, the latter that of shame. (Yet as we saw in III.2, people's emotions can make them feel ashamed as well as guilty.) To avoid pain, the actor has an incentive to *transform* the motivation from a less acceptable to a more acceptable one. The words "transform" and "transformation" are used here as general terms for two distinct species. On the one hand, a motivation may be *transmuted* into another that is more acceptable to the agent. This is an unconscious mechanism, operating "behind the back" of the person. On the other hand, the agent may consciously *misrepresent* his motivation to others. These two phenomena are the topics of V.2 and V.3 respectively.

Let me begin with a simple example, which only involves misrepresentation. In the Melian dialogue as recounted by Thucydides, the Athenians make the following statement to the Melians:

For ourselves, we shall not trouble you with specious pretenses – either of how we have a right to our empire because we overthrew the Mede, or are now attacking you because of wrong that you have done us – and make a long speech which would not be believed; and in return we hope that you, instead of thinking to influence us by saying that you did not join the Spartans, although their colonists, or that you have done us no wrong, will aim at what is feasible, holding in view the real sentiments of us both; since you know as well as we do that right, as the world goes, is only in question between equals in power, while the strong do what they can and the weak suffer what they must. (5.89)

Here, the Athenians very explicitly claim that they will *not* try to misrepresent their real motives. Commenting on this and other passages, A.H.M. Jones writes, "If these speeches are intended to reproduce the actual tenor of Athenian public utterances, it must be admitted that the Athenians of the fifth century were ... a very remarkable, if not unique, people in admitting openly that their policy was guided purely by selfish considerations and that they had no regard for political morality." In fact, he finds the speeches so implausible that he concludes that "Thucydides, in order to point his moral, put into the mouths of Athenian spokesmen what he considered to be their real sentiments, stripped of rhetorical claptrap."[1] Even the notoriously frank Greeks, in other words, would not be that frank. In other cultures, presumably, the pressure towards misrepresentation would be even stronger.

A more complex example involves both transmutation and misrepresentation, as well as the relation between them. In a society with progressive taxation, those with high incomes have a strong interest in low taxes. In defending this system, however, they cannot simply appeal to their interest. They cannot say, publicly, "Taxes should be low because that's good for me." By appealing to trickle-down effects or supply-side considerations they can claim that *everybody* will be better off if the rich get a tax break. If they make this argument in public, repeatedly, they may end up believing it themselves. *Most people do not like to think of themselves as liars or cynics.* To say one thing and think another is a source of tension and discomfort that can be removed by aligning one's thought on one's utterances. In fact, that tension need not even arise. *Most people do not like to think of themselves as motivated only by self-interest.* They will, therefore, gravitate spontaneously towards a world-view that suggests a coincidence between

1. Jones (1957), pp. 66, 67.

their special interest and the public interest.[2] This example suggests not only that people have the options both of misrepresentation and of transmutation, but that if the former is chosen it may induce the latter.

To classify and analyze phenomena of transmutation and misrepresentation, I use La Bruyère's trichotomous division of motivations into *passion*, *interest*, and *reason*. As we shall see, these motivations enter processes of transformation in three different ways. First, they exist as raw material to be transformed. Second, they provide the need or incentive for transformation. Third, they exist as the outcomes of these processes. Figure II.1 illustrates the case in which passion serves all three functions. In the more general case, interest and reason can also appear as input, engine, or output of transformation. If we classify the cases by input–output combinations, there are nine possible forms of transmutation and nine of misrepresentation.

In each case, the transformation might be induced by any one of the three motives. In theory, therefore, we might have to consider a somewhat mind-boggling fifty-four cases. Some of these, however, are logically incoherent. As engine of misrepresentation, for instance, reason can only work on itself as input. As input to the same process, reason can only be transformed by reason itself. In transmutation, only passion (*amore-propre*) can serve as engine. Other combinations, although perhaps conceivable, seem less important empirically. Although I shall argue that there may be cases of transmutation of reason into interest, I cannot cite or even imagine an instance of reason being transmuted into passion. With regard to the transmutation of interest into passion, I can imagine illustrations but not actually cite real or fictional examples. Because the case seems interesting, I shall allow myself to discuss it using made-up examples; in all other cases, however, I try to show that the phenomena do exist in reality or in fiction. As in II.4, I regard fictional examples as legitimate provided that they are not made up to fit my argument and that their authors are independently credible.

I am concerned only with cases of *motivated* transformations, but not with all such cases. To be specific, I consider only cases of conscious

---

2. Similarly, Marx asserted that *ideology* could be understood as the tendency to assert the special interest of one class as the general interest of society (Elster 1985, pp. 482–6). In Marxist writings there is a tradition for asserting that the ideological as well as the political expressions of class interest are subject to what I shall call the "imperfection constraint": The interests of the economically dominant class are best served by a regime that does not try to promote them on each and every occasion (*ibid.*, pp. 407, 422, 472–3).

and deliberate misrepresentation and unconscious but motivated transmutation. The idea of unconscious misrepresentation is incoherent, at least as I use these words. Misrepresentation is a form of lying and presupposes awareness that one is lying.[3] Conscious transmutation, although not an incoherent idea, is important only to the extent that it is accompanied by misrepresentation. As further discussed in V.3, a speaker may try to work himself into a state of passion in order to have a greater impact on his audience, but he will succeed only if they believe his passion to be spontaneous rather than willed.

The sharp dichotomy of unconscious transmutation and conscious misrepresentation is doubly problematic. First, as I argued in II.3, deception may, by a variety of mechanisms, collapse into self-deception. Alternatively, deception may be preempted by self-deception. As Tocqueville said, "party politicians ... are often accused of acting without conviction; but my experience goes to show that this is much less frequent than is supposed. It is just that they have a faculty, which is precious and indeed sometimes necessary in politics, of creating ephemeral convictions in accordance with the feelings and interests of the moment."[4] For either reason, durable and consciously hypocritical or cynical stances are probably quite rare.

I largely ignore this complication, however. I assume, that is, that people are capable of keeping their private beliefs and their publicly professed ones in separate compartments. I also largely ignore some further complications that arise from that assumption. Suppose we observe a person arguing for some policy by appealing to a notion of fairness, although it is also clear that the policy promotes his interest very well. In the first place, we cannot infer from this fact alone that he is "really" motivated by his interest. Because in general any given position will correspond to somebody's interest, this inference, if valid, would allow us to conclude that rational consensus

3. Saarni and Lewis (1993, p. 11) claim that "[w]e can deceive others and not be aware that we are doing so." They give three examples. The first, multiple personality disorders, is too exotic to be decisive. The second is that "one can compliment another on that person's look or what that person said and not mean it, but be unaware of it." That may or may not be so. It doesn't ring true to me: What's the evidence? And would such cases really be deception, with an intention to be believed? The third example is "the husband who deceives his wife about an extramarital affair and does so because he feels that to tell her would hurt her feelings. In some sense he knows that he is deceiving his wife, yet he deceives himself into thinking that the reason why he is deceiving her is for her own good." But this is not an example of what it is supposed to instantiate: He knows *that* he is deceiving her but fools himself (not her!) about *why* he does it.
4. Tocqueville (1990), p. 84.

is impossible, which is manifestly false. In the second place, even if we have grounds for thinking that he is "really" motivated by interest, perhaps because of his behavior in other contexts, we may not be able to tell whether he is deceiving himself or others. Many of the examples given below should be read with these qualifications in mind. For some readers, what I cite as examples of transmutation may be more plausibly understood as misrepresentation, and vice versa.[5]

Second, what I describe as black or white – misrepresentation *or* transmutation – may often be more accurately characterized as nuances in gray. Neither philosophy nor social science is of much help in explaining how we may believe partly or weakly in the ideas that we present ourselves to others as believing fully and strongly. The comments in III.2 on the "culture of hypocrisy" in the former USSR and in China, for instance, were perhaps too simplistic in this respect. The constant need to assert one's belief in communism in public probably induced *some kind* of mental assent. This process cannot be understood as a form of dissonance reduction. According to dissonance theory (V.2), the strong punishments imposed on anyone who spoke out against the system provided enough justification for the hypocritical behavior to obviate any need for belief adjustment. Rather, I conjecture that people "believed" in communism because there was nothing else to believe in. This being said, I do not know how to characterize the difference between belief and "belief."

The three motivations that can serve as inputs, engines, and outputs of transformation have often been contrasted with one another in a pairwise manner. The opposition between *reason and passion* is very ancient, as is the claim that reason in general offers very little resistance to the passions. Albert Hirschman has shown that in the eighteenth century *passion and interest* were frequently held up against each other, the latter being thought capable of holding at bay the more destructive aspects of the former. Hence the dominance of

5. A further complication, which I also ignore, is that the motivation that is misrepresented may itself be the outcome of transmutation. Any motivation must pass through two filters before one can profess it to others. First, it has to be acceptable for the person himself; second, any motivation that passes that hurdle has also to be acceptable to others. Montaigne (1991, p. 953) claimed that any motivation that passes the first filter should also pass the second: "Let us not be ashamed to say whatever we are not ashamed to think." Now, what "we are not ashamed to think" may result from transmutation of something we were ashamed to think. In that case, a person who violates Montaigne's rule – as surely many do – would *misrepresent a transmuted motivation.*

interest over passion in a commercial society constituted "a political argument for capitalism before its triumph."[6] Finally, many discussions of political institutions and political change have been guided by the contrast between *reason and interest*. In analyses of the Federal Constitutional Convention in Philadelphia, for instance, these two principles are often assumed to exhaust the motives of the framers.[7]

We get a broader picture of human behavior, however, by considering all three motivations in their relation to each other. To my knowledge, the first to do this explicitly was La Bruyère in a passage cited in II.3: "Nothing is easier for passion than to overcome reason, but the greatest triumph is to conquer a man's own interest." One of the tasks I set myself below is to spell out what could be meant by phrases such as "overcome" and "conquer." It could mean that under the influence of passion I act against my own better judgment, whether the latter is an intention to promote my private interest or the public good. (See also the discussion of weakness of will in IV.3.) In that case there would be a double psychological conflict: first because the different motives that animate me suggest different courses of action, and second because the motive that wins out is not the one that, all things considered, I believe to be the most weighty. The phrase could also mean that passion does away with the second conflict, by inducing beliefs that justify my priority. I could mean, finally, that passion does away with the first conflict, by inducing me to adopt a conception of my private interest or the public good in which they coincide perfectly (or optimally: see below) with what my passion tells me to do. In V.2 I explore this last approach, in a generalized form. But first let me define my terms more carefully.

My conception of *reason* relies on work by Jürgen Habermas and Brian Barry. Habermas argues that an agent who aims at *understanding* rather than *success* is committed to three "validity claims": propositional truth, normative rightness, and sincerity or truthfulness.[8] He must be open to rational argument and willing to change his view as the result of such argument. It follows that a speaker who wants to *appear* – to himself or others – as aiming at understanding must also appear to be committed to these claims. It is this secondary or

---

6. Hirschman (1977).
7. Jillson (1988) pp. 193–4 (citing Madison, Hamilton, and Tocqueville to the same effect) and *passim*; Rakove (1987).
8. Habermas (1984/87).

derived concern that is my main topic here. I do not try to explore in any detail the conceptual implications of the claims; rather, I consider what agents must do to appear to be committed to them and what happens if this appearance breaks down. My argument rests on the empirical assumption that people do in fact have a strong desire to appear in this way. Barry puts the point very well:

The desire to be able to justify our actions to ourselves and others on a basis capable of eliciting free agreement is, as common experience attests, widely shared and deeply grounded. We find the same desire manifesting itself when people defend institutions from which they benefit. It is indeed a curious and striking illustration of the strength of this desire that the beneficiaries of such institutions as slavery and racial discrimination seldom defend their position as a frankly unjustifiable assertion of superior power, with the implication that, if the tables were turned, they would have nothing to say against their new position of inferiority except that they didn't like it and would overthrow it if they could. Rather, we find elaborate defenses in terms suggesting, however implausibly, that even those on the losing end would, if they understood the position aright, find it reasonable to accept their status. Granted that this is a perversion of the intellect, it still seems to me significant that it occurs at all.[9]

The present chapter is to a considerable extent an exploration of such perversions of the intellect. As we shall see, however, the desire to appear as impartial is not the only motive that can induce these mental contortions.

Returning now to the three claims made by Habermas, the first is straightforward: In any communication about factual issues the parties share the assumption that there is *a fact of the matter* by virtue of which what they say is either true or false. In V.3 I argue that by virtue of its objectivity truth can serve as a strategic resource: By restating a threat as a warning, a speaker may present an interest-based claim in the language of reason. The second claim is more controversial. Rather than identifying the normative variety of reason with a particular conception of justice, I shall count any impartial, disinterested, and dispassionate motive as a reasonable one. In order to be viewed by oneself or others as having a morally or socially acceptable motivation, what matters is to be seen as moved by *some* impartial conception, not by any particular one. The third claim imposes, as we

9. Barry (1990), p. 284. For a book-length discussion of impartiality, see also Barry (1995).

shall see, constraints of how the second claim can be met. An impartial conception that corresponds too closely to the speaker's interest, for instance, may not be seen as fully sincere.

Let me say a bit more about normative impartiality, which is the most important aspect of reason to be discussed below. Impartiality as such is not a conception of justice, but a necessary feature of any view that wants to be taken seriously as a conception of justice. It is a constraint on justice, not itself a conception of justice. Utilitarianism, for instance, is impartial in its insistence that in the calculus of welfare "each is to count for one and nobody for more than one." Rights-based theories are impartial to the extent that rights are assigned universally rather than selectively. Equal-distribution theories are impartial, as are theories advocating distribution according to need, merit, or contribution. John Rawls's theory of justice is impartial by construction, being presented as the theory that rational individuals would choose behind a veil of ignorance.

For my purposes, two closely related features of impartial justice will prove especially important. First, as just noted, there are *many* conceptions of justice that satisfy the constraint of impartiality. As a consequence, claims that are motivated by interest or emotion will often be able to find an *impartial equivalent*, an impartial argument converging to the same conclusion.[10] Second, impartial intent does not imply impartial effect. The law, in many contexts, allows rules that have "disparate effect" on different categories of individuals, while prohibiting those that embody "disparate intent." Thus a court might strike down a layoff rule that explicitly favors men over women or white over blacks, while allowing rules based on seniority, which because of the more recent entry of women and blacks into the labor force, have the same effect.[11] If one could prove that seniority was adopted in order to produce that effect, it would be struck down. Yet because it is hard to prove intention *and* because seniority is prima facie fair, courts tend to respect the principle.

10. In wage bargaining, for instance, "[t]aking account of all possible permutations, the number of plausible-sounding norms is certainly well into three figures. It would be a particularly unfortunate or inept group that did not find some norm to justify *its* claim to a larger share" (Elster 1989b, p. 233). Cp. also the description of American democracy in Tocqueville (1969, p. 177): "[I]n the United States a politician first tries to see what his own interest is and who have analogous interests which can be grouped around his own; he is next concerned to discover whether by chance there may not be somewhere in the world a doctrine or a principle that could conveniently be placed at the head of the new association."
11. Romm (1995).

Impartiality, being both disinterested and dispassionate, has two antonyms: interested dispassionate behavior and passionate disinterested behavior. By *interest* I mean any motive, common to the members of some proper subgroup of society, that aims at improving the situation of that subgroup in some respect such as pleasure, wealth, fame, status, or power.[12] Subgroups made up of one individual form an important special case. For larger subgroups, interest will not be causally efficacious unless individual group members are motivated to embrace it. A politician may identify with his party because if he doesn't he won't get renominated. A worker may identify with his fellow workers because he views their welfare as part of his. A doctor may identify with his patients because of his professional norms. Interest by definition is partial, as it does not extend beyond the subgroup. I shall assume that in the pursuit of their interest people follow the canons of instrumental rationality.

By *passion* I mainly understand emotion in the sense explained in IV.2. Occasionally, however, I shall use the term in a broader sense that also includes sexual desire and states of intoxication. When misrepresentation takes the form of offering excuses for what one has done, "I was drunk" may do as well as "I was angry." Some might argue that passion, rather than being a separate motivation, is an aspect of other motivations. We often pursue reason or interest in a passionate way and may experience fear, hope, regret, disappointment, or relief at various stages of that pursuit. But if these emotions make us do things that we would not otherwise have done, they do form a separate motivation; if not, they are not relevant for the present purposes.

Transmutation and misrepresentation are more specific mechanisms than the general phenomenon of lying to oneself or to others. Most cases of self-deception and wishful thinking involve changes of beliefs about the world, not changes in beliefs about one's own motivation. Paradigm cases of self-deception and wishful thinking occur when (i) a person's desire for X to be the case causes him to believe that X is the case. Transmutation, by contrast, occurs when (ii) a wish to be motivated by X causes a belief that one desires Y out of X rather than out of one's real motivation Z. Similarly, most cases of deception involve professing beliefs about the world that one does not hold, the paradigm being (iii) "if I profess belief or desire X others will

---

12. Thus I follow La Rochefoucauld (II.3) in stipulating that the need for self-esteem does not count as an interest.

punish me, therefore I will profess belief or desire Z." The paradigm of misrepresentation, by contrast, is (iv) "if I profess motivation Z for desiring Y others will punish me, therefore I will profess motivation X for desiring Y."[13] The distinctions between (i) and (ii) or between (iii) and (iv) are not absolute, however. If they were, transmutation and misrepresentation would have no real effects because they would not induce any change in overt behavior. Because of the *constraints on transformation* considered below, however, these processes do have real effects. They are, as we shall see, doubly deceptive: Motivation X for professing Y is transformed into motivation Z for professing W. They are not simply ex post rationalizations of behaviors that can be fully explained by the untransformed motives. Some of these real effects, further discussed in the conclusion to V.3, are due to what I call *the civilizing force of hypocrisy*.

V.2. TRANSMUTATION

The metaphors of alchemy and transmutation are not uncommon in the study of human behavior and motivations. As we saw in III.3, Nietzsche referred to the process of "transmuting weakness into merit." William Lee Miller, writing on the debates over slavery in the American Congress before the Civil War, observes that "the slavery *interest* had transmuted into the glorious Southern *cause*."[14] The defenders of slavery sincerely believed that they were arguing the cause of civilization, not of barbarism. On the one hand, they argued, slavery "was not an evil, but a great good – a blessing, making a better life for the African."[15] On the other hand, they attacked the Northerners

---

13. There is little overlap, therefore, between the present analysis and that offered in Kuran (1995); see also the comments at the end of the present chapter.

14. Miller (1996), p. 184. The Southerners, although not of course recognizing this process in themselves, had no difficulty seeing it at work in the Northerners, as shown by the following extract from a speech by Waddy Thompson, a representative from South Carolina: "As long as the slave trade was profitable and tolerated, it had no horrors in their sight ... they had no sympathies with the poor Indians until they had literally exterminated all the tribes by whom their fathers, flying from another land, were kindly and hospitably received ... Now, when they are no longer incommoded by the vicinity of the savage, their circumstances are not with their brethren, circumstanced as their fathers were. *Their philanthropy and their selfish interests are never opposed.* I like not your courtesan turned prude, after ability to be vicious has ceased" (*ibid.*, p. 245; my italics). Note the tell-tale recognition, by the reference to vice, of the weakness of his own position.

15. *Ibid.*, p. 249.

for putting their lives in danger: "The safety of our wives and children is endangered by their mischievous and incendiary attempts to produce a servile insurrection among our slaves."[16] To fear those whom one has harmed is rational enough. To argue that the harm is not a harm but a blessing, and that only malicious third parties could make the victim believe he has been harmed, is evidence of transmutation (see also the quote from Barry above).

In the opening pages of a book on ego defenses, George Vaillant resorts several times to these metaphors. Defensive self-deception is a form of "psychic alchemy [that] helps to explain the resilience of individuals who are abused and disadvantaged during the first decade of life." Later, he asserts that "choice of defense may evolve throughout adult life and may transmutate irritating grains of sand into pearls." He also refers to "the capacity of the ego's self-deception to turn life's leaden moments into gold."[17] As these quotations illustrate, Vaillant sees the defensive mechanisms and the transmutations they induce as potentially valuable and positive. Although recognizing that the defenses can take both psychotic and neurotic forms, he claims that "they are more often healthy than pathological."[18] The turning of lead into gold – of being content with what one has, even if it isn't what one had hoped for – can indeed be a healthy form of adjustment.[19] When, however, it goes together with turning gold into lead, as with the fox and the sour grapes, it can be far from healthy.[20]

16. *Ibid.*, p. 60.
17. Vaillant (1993), pp. 1, 3, 4.
18. *Ibid.*, p. 17.
19. Whether the behaviors recommended as healthy are defense mechanisms in a technical sense is a different matter. If we assume (Elster 1983a, pp. 71–2) that the unconscious is incapable of long-term planning, for example of suffering anticipatory grief now in order to reduce acute grief later (see IV.3), we may ask whether the following two statements can both be true. (i) "Defenses, by necessity, are 'unconscious.' By this I do not mean that the defensive behavior itself is invisible to the user, only that the user does not recognize the defense *as* a defense" (Vaillant 1993, p. 19). (ii) "Defenses should be oriented toward the long term, not the short term" (*ibid.*, p. 104). If the second statement had "are" instead of "should be," there would be no problem. The normative phrasing suggests, however, an intentional origin of the defense mechanisms that is hard to square with their being both unconscious and long-term–oriented.
20. This ubiquitous tendency is nowhere listed among the defense mechanisms of the ego. None of the approximately forty defense mechanisms listed in appendices 1 through 5 in Vaillant (1992) captures the simple idea that people devalue what they do not have or cannot have. In the original Freudian formulation, in which all defenses were directed against sexual or aggressive impulses and their associated affects, this omission is understandable. In the modern formulations in which defenses are tools for managing psychic conflicts quite generally (Vaillant 1993, p. 98 and *passim*), it is astonishing.

TRANSMUTATION OF INTEREST INTO REASON

"Self-interest speaks all manner of tongues and plays all manner of parts, even that of disinterestedness" (M39). This observation by La Rochefoucauld has very wide application. First, however, let me warn against applying it too widely. As I have noted, the fact that a person argues for a policy that serves his interest does not allow us to conclude that he argues out of interest.[21] The emancipation of women provides a good example. When women argued for female suffrage, they were arguing for a change that was certainly in their interest, and some of them may well have argued out of interest. Yet I believe that many, perhaps most women were motivated by what they saw as a matter of simple justice. To be deterred from pursuing justice simply because one might benefit from it would seem perverse. To avoid suspicion, one might try to rig the cards so that one would not benefit personally were the proposal adopted. When Mirabeau opposed the ban on choosing ministers from within the first French constituent assembly, he ironically proposed to limit this exclusion to himself so that he could not be suspected of self-interested motives.[22] He didn't succeed, however, and in general this is not likely to be a plausible way of deflecting suspicion.

Instances of "self-serving conceptions of impartiality" are numerous. Some turn upon outcome-oriented considerations, others on considerations of fairness. In conflicts over child custody, each parent is often convinced that he or she will be the better custodial parent, that is, will bring about the best outcome for the child whose welfare is supposed to be the impartial value promoted by society. "I only want what is best for the child, and it just so happens that it will be best for the child to stay with me." It follows that each parent will tend to think, at least under the "best-interest" standard, that he or she is more likely to be granted custody by the court in case of litigation; hence more litigation will be undertaken than if the parents had non–self-serving conceptions of what the interest of the child requires. Below I cite experimental evidence that supports these implications.

In collective bargaining, the use of self-serving conceptions of fairness is very common. The choice of a reference group compared to which one's wages can be argued to be unfairly low, for instance, is

21. Similarly, Veyne (1976, p. 469) notes that "there are so many ... intellectuals who take positions that go against those of their class that one might well credit those who don't with an equally disinterested attitude."
22. Castaldo (1989), p. 170.

highly subject to self-serving manipulations.[23] Because everything is a little bit like everything else and because intuitions about fairness are sensitive to a great variety of factors, one can usually identify a better-paid group that is similar in some normatively relevant respect. Thus in wage bargaining between a teachers' union and a school board, the union would tend to view neighboring high-wage districts, and the board to view low-wage districts, as comparable.[24] These are cases of "hedonic framing" (I.8), although in a somewhat unusual sense. If the purpose of the hedonic framing was to make one feel good, one would compare oneself with low-wage workers (III.3). Choosing a high-wage group as the reference point would rather tend to make one feel bad. Although the comparison may be useful for achieving the long-term goal of higher wages, I doubt whether the unconscious is capable of choosing behavior that involves short-term sacrifice for the sake of long-term gain. The appeal to reference groups is probably one of those half-sincere, half-hypocritical behaviors – partly transmutation, partly misrepresentation – that elude precise analysis.[25]

In "local justice" the use of seniority as a criterion for layoffs is perhaps the most clearcut case of self-serving conceptions of fairness.[26] When unions advocate this principle, they often refer to ideas of desert and merit. As the senior workers have "given the best years of their life" to the firm, it is only fair that they should be retained over new hires. The argument is weak (what else should they have done with their life?) and often a mere dressing-up for self-interest. As long as the workers have reason to believe that the firm will never lay off more than half of them, the workers with the greatest seniority will vote for the principle out of self-interest.[27] Yet this motivation is very likely to be transmuted into a genuine belief that seniority is more fair. There is also a widespread belief, and not only among the elderly,

23. Elster (1989a), Chapter VI.
24. Babcock and Olson (1992); see also Babcock et al. (1995).
25. Thus Babcock et al. (1992, p. 18) raise the possibility that "in advocating a particular set of comparables to the other side during negotiations, the parties lose track of the fact that they have selected them strategically and come to view them as fair." This illustrates the idea that misrepresentation may induce transmutation.
26. Elster (1992); Romm (1995).
27. One might think that a similar argument could be made to explain why the younger half of the workforce would vote for inverse seniority. Although the younger workers are indeed likely to have this preference, it will be weaker than that of older workers for straightforward seniority. The younger workers will, after all, get older; the older will never grow any younger.

that old people should be given priority in various contexts, because of "what they have done for society." The idea that entitlements are generated by the mere passage of time has wide and strong appeal.[28] When it coincides and fuses with self-interest, it may be irresistible.

In constitution-making processes, one regularly observes that the interests of different groups are defended in impartial language. At the Federal Convention in Philadelphia, this tendency was strikingly illustrated in the debates between the small and the large states over their respective representation in the Senate.[29] The small states systematically argued for equality of representation, the large states for proportionality. Although this confrontation involved some threats of force, impartially phrased argument had a more central place. Both sides, in fact, were able to defend their views by appeals to fairness and justice. There were obvious arguments from equality – equal representation of the states versus equal representation of individuals.[30] Also, there were opposing arguments based on the nature of contracts. According to Sherman the time had now come to undo the inequality created at the birth of the republic. "That the great states acceded to the confederation, and that they in the hour of danger, made a sacrifice of their interest to the lesser states is true. Like the wisdom of Solomon in adjudging the child to its true mother, from tenderness to it, the greater states well knew that the loss of a limb was fatal to the confederation – they too, through tenderness sacrificed their dearest rights to sacrifice the whole. But the time is come, when justice will be done to their claims."[31] Paterson turned the argument on its head. "It was observed ... that the larger State gave up its point, not because it was right, but because the circumstances of the moment urged the concession. Be it so. Are they for that reason at liberty to take it back? Can the donor resume his gift without the consent of the donee."[32] For Paterson, justice required contracts

---

28. Zajac (1995, pp. 121–2), who cites as a "striking example of status quo property or equity rights ... the attempt to 'vintage' utility rates, that is, to charge 'old' customers a different, usually lower rate than 'new' ones." See also the passage from Aristotle's *Rhetoric* 1387^{a}15–16 cited in II.2; also Weber (1968, p. 326): "The mere fact of the regular occurrence of certain events somehow confers on them the dignity of oughtness."

29. Elster (1996b).

30. See for instance Madison (Farrand 1966, vol. 1, p. 151) versus Dickinson (*ibid.*, vol. 1, p. 159).

31. *Ibid.*, vol. 1, p. 348. The argument rests on the idea that *urgency tends to equalize bargaining power*, further developed in Elster (1996b).

32. Farrand (1966), vol. 1, pp. 250–1.

to be binding even if they are unfair. For Sherman, justice required contracts to be undone if they are unfair.

In other constitution-making contexts, we find some actors dressing up their interests in consequentialist garbs, while others appeal to nonconsequentialist values. In the recent transitions to democracy in Eastern Europe, for instance, most parties and groupings favored the electoral laws that favored them.[33] Small parties favored proportionality (with low thresholds), large parties favored majority elections in single-member districts (or proportionality with high thresholds). The former tended to defend their views in terms of democratic values, the latter in terms of the need for an efficient and stable government. Similar self-serving biases were observed in the design of the presidency. If a group has a strong candidate for this position, its interest is to have a strong presidency and that of the opposition to have a weak one. The corresponding impartial arguments tend to be, for the former, that the difficult period of transition to democracy requires a strong leadership and, for the latter, that a strong man at the head of the state might recreate an authoritarian regime.

There is also experimental evidence that people tend to choose judgments of fairness that favor themselves. Linda Babcock, George Loewenstein, and their collaborators have carried out laboratory experiments in which subjects are assigned to the role either of plaintiff or of defendant in a tort case and asked to negotiate a settlement.[34] They are also asked to predict the award of the judge and to assess what they considered a fair out-of-court settlement for the plaintiff. The investigators found that plaintiffs predicted higher awards and assessed higher fair-settlement amounts than defendants, and that pairs of subjects who reached more similar predictions and assessments were more likely to settle than those who reached very different assessments. The first finding is clear evidence of a self-serving bias in conceptions of fairness. The second finding suggests (but does not prove: see below) that the overall effect of self-serving biases may work against the interest of the parties. Let me pursue that idea for a moment.

Paul Veyne suggests, as a general maxim, that beliefs born of passion serve passion badly.[35] Similarly, the second finding just cited

33. Elster (1993b). Vaclav Havel's preference for proportional representation in Czechoslovakia was a notable exception (Elster 1995).
34. Loewenstein et al. (1993); Babcock et al. (1995); Babcock and Loewenstein (1997).
35. Veyne (1976), p. 667; also Elster (1983b), p. 156.

might seem to show that beliefs born of interest serve interest badly. Yet the *probability* of settlement is only one of the factors that affect the expected outcome of the parties. The *amount* of settlement, in cases where an agreement is reached, also matters. If a biased perception of fairness reduces the probability, it also tends to increase the amount. "For every dollar's increase in the defendant's perceived fair-settlement value, actual settlements rose, on average, by 50 cents," or, to put it the other way around, when the parties settled the defendant paid less the greater his bias.[36] As the authors note, "these benefits of a sense of entitlement have to be weighed against the increased risk of not settling."[37] We are dealing, that is, with a type B mechanism in which the net effect, in general, is indeterminate.[38] Beliefs born of interest may serve interest – or not.

I conclude this discussion of the transmutation of interest into reason by introducing a proviso that will prove important throughout the rest of the chapter. Even assuming a self-serving bias, we should not assume that it will always induce the conception of impartiality that is optimal from the point of view of self-interest. The selection of a conception of fairness is subject to *constraints* that prevent us from picking and choosing conceptions of fairness à la carte according to what best serves our interest. I consider two such constraints, the *consistency constraint* and the *imperfection constraint*. Although the consistency constraint certainly applies to transmutation as well as to misrepresentation and the imperfection constraint no less certainly applies to misrepresentation, I am less confident about the role of the imperfection constraint in transmutation.

The consistency constraint arises because the impartial conception adopted on a specific occasion has to be consistent with impartial conceptions adopted on earlier occasions. If it is not – if the agent opportunistically adjusts his idea of impartiality to what serves his interest on any given occasion – it will be psychologically difficult for

36. Loewenstein et al (1993), pp. 152–3. They add, "Curiously, however, plaintiff's predictions and fairness values did not have a significant effect on settlement values."
37. *Ibid.*, p. 153, n. 42.
38. Elster (1989b, pp. 86–94) discusses cases in which prebargaining behaviors of the parties have a negative impact on the probability of agreement and a positive impact on the amount agreed upon, as well as cases in which they increase the share of the total while reducing the size of the total to be shared. These behaviors are, however, intentionally chosen and would presumably not be undertaken unless the expected net effect was positive. The fairness bias, although shaped by interest, is not similarly guided by interest.

him to maintain the belief that he is not motivated by self-interest. Some people may be capable of this feat of self-deception, but most are not. An impartial conception, once adopted, is perceived as binding and objectively valid in a way that constrains frictionless adjustment to new situations. *The same need for self-esteem that caused us to justify self-interested behavior by impartial considerations in the first place may also prevent us from changing our conception of impartiality when it no longer works in our favor.* In character development, therefore, much would seem to depend on the accidental order in which we are exposed to circumstances in which judgments of fairness or other impartial arguments might arise (path-dependence). By the interacting mechanisms of self-serving bias and the need for consistency people may get locked into a conception of impartiality that bears no recognizable relation to their overall interest later in life.

The work by Babcock, Loewenstein, and co-authors cited above also offers evidence that consistency serves as a constraint on self-serving biases. Their findings do not by themselves show that failure to reach agreement is *caused* by the self-serving conceptions of fairness with which they are correlated. "Perhaps an unmeasured factor, such as variation in the character trait of the negotiators, caused the same people to exhibit the self-serving bias to negotiate in a manner that impeded settlement."[39] To test this possibility, they ran a variant of the experiment in which the subjects had to make their assessments of fairness *before* they knew whether they were going to take the role of the plaintiff or the defendant in the negotiation process. They found that "there were four times as many disagreements when bargainers knew their roles initially than (*sic*) when they did not know their roles."[40] The idea of a consistency constraint seems to make sense of this result: Once the bargainers have decided behind "the veil of ignorance" what would be a fair settlement, they are stuck with that assessment and less likely to make opportunistic adjustments when they find out where their interest lies. Matthew Rabin refers to this phenomenon as *moral priming*.[41]

Conceptions of impartiality are not entirely irreversible. They may change under the pressure of changing interest, but the impact is often delayed. In the 1930s, wages of Swedish metal workers lagged behind

39. Babcock et al. (1995), p. 1338.
40. *Ibid.*, p. 1339.
41. Rabin (1995).

those of construction workers. The strong dissatisfaction of the metal workers with the existing wage differentials was a major cause of the move towards centralized bargaining with its greater emphasis on interindustry wage equality.[42] Later, when the metal workers became the high-wage outliers, they were bound by their past appeals to solidarity. As early as "at the beginning of the war, they were already some who thought that Metall had blundered by becoming the standard bearer for the idea of solidaristic wage policy in 1936. Certainly, it had been the underdog then, but now that they were better off, it gave them the moral obligation to show solidarity even when it was to their disadvantage."[43] It took fifty years for the norm of equality to lose its grip on the metal workers' union.[44]

The imperfection constraint arises because a *perfect* coincidence between self-interest and the impartial argument would often be too transparently opportunistic. To be credible to oneself or to others, the impartial argument has to deviate somewhat from the policy that, if adopted, would promote one's interest maximally. It should not deviate too much, of course, because then it might not promote one's interest at all. The optimal policy, therefore, has to strike a balance between interest and the appearance of disinterestedness. As La Rochefoucauld said, "What passes for generosity is often merely ambition in disguise, scorning petty interests so as to make for greater" (M246). This constraint is certainly important in misrepresentation of interest, as I argue in V.3. I suspect that it is also important in transmutation. In the local-justice cases that I cite in V.3 to illustrate the imperfection constraint on transformation, for instance, transmutation may also be at work. Yet direct evidence for the imperfection constraint in transmutation is hard to come by. Below, I suggest how a variant of the Ultimatum Game might be used to test the idea of an imperfection constraint on transmutation, and other experiments are also conceivable.[45]

---

42. Swenson (1988), pp. 43–5.
43. Gösta Rehn, cited after Swenson (1988), p. 60.
44. Elster (1989b), p. 241. For other examples of the role of consistency arguments in wage bargaining, see *ibid.*, pp. 239–40.
45. One could, for instance, offer subjects the choice among several maxims of fairness and see whether they choose one that corresponds moderately to their interest or one that offers a perfect fit. To induce transmutation rather than misrepresentation, one could tell them that actual allocations would be made by applying an average of the fairness proposals made by different subjects, and (nonveridically) that no one would know who chose which maxim.

TRANSMUTATION OF PASSION INTO REASON

Because Mr. Casaubon (in *Middlemarch*) was jealous towards Will Ladislaw, he wanted to bind his wife Dorothea so that she might not marry Will when he died. Yet, George Eliot writes, "Mr Casaubon, we know, had a sense of rectitude and an honourable pride in satisfying the requirements of honour, which compelled him to find other reasons for his conduct than those of jealousy and vindictiveness" (Chapter 42). As this example shows, an induced concern for duty and morality need not be self-serving in the sense of promoting one's *interest*, as I have defined it. Once dead, Mr. Casaubon has nothing to gain from preventing Dorothea's marriage. The driving forces that induce the transmutation are an emotion, jealousy, and a meta-emotion, shame at his jealousy.

Many transmutations take the form of rewriting the triggering situation as a violation of some impartial standard of fairness, justice, or entitlement. Often, these are also cases of transmutation of passion into passion, mediated by reason. Consider first the case of envy. In III.3, I discussed an example from Tocqueville that shows how people get rid of their feelings of inferiority by explaining the success of others in terms of dishonest behavior. A very similar analysis occurs in Netanyahu's analysis of the persecution of the Jewish *conversos* by the Spanish Inquisition.

That [the distinction between pure blood and the polluted blood of the Jews] was capable of attracting many an old Christian to the racial theory is manifest for other reasons, too. It flattered his ego and raised him automatically, without requiring any effort on his part, to a higher level than that of any converso, however, famous and successful. The phenomenal rise of the conversos in all spheres puzzled these groups no less than it dismayed them. How did it happen, they inevitably asked themselves, that they who were yesterday despised Jews, and most of them, upon their conversion, destitute, became overnight so rich and influential? That this happened largely as a result of the freedom the conversos were given to exercise their powers – and that, in addition, it was due to their industry, their learning, their ingenuity, their frugality, their driving force and, perhaps above all, their talents, was an answer which these groups refused to accept. To accept it would mean to ascribe their low condition to their lack of the qualities that make for success. It would mean an admission of the conversos' superiority, or, even worse, of their own inferiority – an admission which their self-respect could not permit. Consequently, they looked for another explanation, one that could heal their wounded pride and restore their shaken faith in themselves.

Such an explanation were offered them by the racists, according to whose theories the attainment of the conversos were not due to any virtues, which they never owned, but to the vices and defects which they had in abundance. Above all, it was due to their falsehood and deception, which enabled them quickly to obtain by fraud what no honest man could attain by fair means.[46]

What drives this process is the first-order pain of envy, a burning feeling of inferiority. In other words, envy serves both as input to the process and as its engine.[47] As in Tocqueville's analysis, the output of the process is the belief that the envied individuals have succeeded through immoral behavior. And as with Tocqueville, Netanyahu describes a process of preemption rather than transmutation of envy. It serves to eliminate the feeling of inferiority rather than to justify the physical elimination of the superior. The distinction might seem tenuous, because once the envied person has been singled out as immoral the urge to eliminate him arises naturally. Other preemptive strategies, such as the belief that beautiful blondes are dumb (III.3), do not have similar implications for behavior. It remains true, nevertheless, that the cognitive rewriting is not *initially* caused by the need to justify behavior that would otherwise be too shameful. The transmutation of emotion occurs as a mere by-product of cognitive reframing.

In other cases, the operative motive is the need to avoid the second-order pain of envy. In David Lodge's *Small World*, Morris Zapp receives a letter from his friend and academic rival Philip Swallow, informing him that he has met a wonderful woman and asking Zapp to reserve a room for them at the Jerusalem Hilton. "The letter reads like the effusion of some infatuated teenager. Morris *will not admit to himself that there may be a trace of envy* in his harsh assessment. He prefers to identify his response as righteous indignation at being more or less compelled to collude in the deception of Hilary [Swallow's wife]. For a man who claims to believe in the morally improving effects of reading great literature, Philip Swallow (it seems to Morris) takes his marriage vows pretty lightly."[48] The phrase that I have italicized

---

46. Netanyahu (1995), p. 989.
47. In theory, this can be the case for all emotions with negative valence. Guilt can induce a rewriting of the script to justify the behavior that induced the guilt. Regret for missed opportunities may induce one to rewrite the past so as to eliminate grounds for regret (Landman 1993, Chapter 8). Disappointment, too, may be eliminated by telling oneself some appropriate story. Note, however, that unlike rewriting motivated by envy cognitive reframing in these cases does not usually trigger new emotions that might in turn find behavioral expressions.
48. Lodge (1984), pp. 281–2.

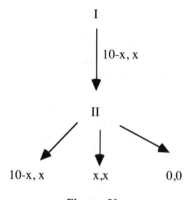

Figure V.1.

clearly identifies the second-order shame or guilt at feeling envious as origin of the transmutation. This mechanism may also have been involved in the cases discussed by Tocqueville and Netanyahu. In practice, the first-order and second-order pains of envy are likely to fuse together into a single negative emotion, except when the social disapproval of envy is too weak to induce the second-order pain.

Along these lines, one can imagine the following variant of the Ultimatum Game.[49] As shown in Fig. V.1, player I first proposes a division of $10 between player II and himself, with x for II and $10 - x$ for himself. Player II then is offered the choice among three responses: accepting the proposal, taking what was offered and leaving I with the same amount (an option available only if $x \leq 5$), and ruining the transaction so that neither gets anything.

If subjects in position II choose (0,0) rather than (x,x) in retaliation against a low proposal, it would be inconsistent with envy as a conscious motivation but consistent with the idea that an initial envy is suppressed and replaced by righteous indignation. This choice would also be consistent, however, with the idea that player II was motivated by righteous indignation from the beginning and simply wanted to punish I severely for his unfair proposal. To assess this idea, one could tell player I that the game structure is as in Fig. V.1 minus the middle branch, and player II that it is as in Fig. V.1 minus the left branch but that player I believes it is as in Fig. V.1 minus the middle branch. If player II is genuinely motivated by righteous indignation, we should expect him to choose (0,0) rather than (x,x),

49. Guth et al. (1982); see also Roth (1995) for a survey.

because this is the only way he can punish player I.[50] If instead we find player II tending to choose (x,x), the original motivation is more likely to be envy.

In these cases, to repeat, we observe first-order and second-order pains of envy, followed by a cognitive reframing in terms of unfairness, followed or accompanied by some other emotion such as righteous anger or righteous indignation. This scenario must be distinguished from direct transmutation of one passion into another, unmediated by cognitive rewriting. Although this idea is important in the Freudian theory of defense mechanisms, I doubt that it occurs frequently or at all. I return to this question below.

Some cases of transmutation of passion into reason do not lead to any modification of the initial passion. Irrational anger, as we saw in IV.3, often invents a story to justify itself. For many people, to be angry without a good reason is incompatible with their self-image. At the same, admitting they were wrong may also be an unacceptable blow to their self-esteem. The only solution that satisfies their *amour-propre* is to persuade themselves that their anger was in fact justified by something the other had done. As in the phrase from Seneca quoted in II.3, "Reason wishes the decision that it gives to be just; anger wishes to have the decision which it has given seem the just decision." Or as he also says in telling the story about Piso (cited from Montaigne's retelling in II.3), "how clever is anger in devising excuses for its madness."[51] Iago's anger at Othello (II.4) is a case in point.

Prejudice, too, is a form of passion that can be dressed up as reason. Those who harbor what Allport calls "prejudice with compunction"[52] may be relieved if they can find an impartial reason to act on their bias. In a study of attitudes towards blacks and affirmative action, Paul Sniderman and coauthors discuss two views of the relation between passion, reason, and policy preference in the area of affirmative action.[53] The commonsense view is that people who *either* have a favorable (unfavorable) emotional attitude towards blacks *or* believe that the problems of blacks are due to factors outside (within) their control, are induced to adopt policy preferences in favor of (against)

---

50. I am assuming, perhaps controversially, that what matters for II is the actual punishment of I by reducing his payoff below what it would otherwise have been, rather than acting in a way that leads I to *believe* he has been punished.
51. *On Anger* I.xviii.
52. Allport (1979), Chapter 20.
53. Sniderman et al. (1991), Chapter 6.

affirmative action. This view, however, is not confirmed empirically. Rather the data suggest that people go from their emotional attitude towards blacks directly to the policy conclusion and then go backward to adopt the view of internal versus external control that justifies the preferred policy. "I don't like blacks; therefore, they should not receive assistance; therefore, they do not deserve assistance." Reason is the handmaid of passion.

In a discussion of public attitudes towards AIDS and homosexuality, the same authors formulate and test the following hypothesis:

> Some fraction of the public is prejudiced against homosexuals. All the same, they feel some inhibition against openly expressing or acting on their homophobia ... But AIDS provides a socially acceptable cloak, to dress up and disguise prejudice against homosexuals. Or, more exactly, people may express hostility against gays legitimately – hostility they would otherwise be under pressure to suppress – if the issue of AIDS is suitably framed as a need for mandatory testing and other "preventive" measures in order to prevent the disease from spreading and protect public health.[54]

The authors find that the data do *not* support this hypothesis. They suggest, however, that the future might be different. As the magnitude of the AIDS problem increases, "it is difficult ... to be confident that the public will persist in its support for gay rights and the rights of persons with AIDS – partly because fear and intolerance are bound to be excited, difficult still more fundamentally because the value of tolerance, in addition to being vulnerable to the intolerance promoted by fear, is vulnerable as well to the altogether legitimate value of public health."[55] They fear, in other words, that prejudice and fear may ally themselves with the impartial value of public health to defeat another impartial value, namely civil liberties.

A final example may be taken from the war trials in countries that had been occupied by Germany during World War II. The immediate reaction after liberation was invariably to demand very heavy sentences for collaborators and informers. In several countries, the death sentence was reintroduced into the penal code. Many of those who advocated these measures no doubt thought of themselves as motivated by the wish that justice be done. In many individuals, however, this is likely to have been due to a transmutation of emotion, triggered by an intense passion for revenge together with a belief that revenge

54. *Ibid.*, pp. 49–50.
55. *Ibid.*, pp. 52–3.

is a form of uncivilized behavior characteristic of the very regime they had been fighting.[56] Evidence that their ultimate motivation was the passion for revenge rather than a wish for justice is found in the fact, cited in Chapter IV, that the severity of sentences declined radically after a few years. On grounds both of absolute and relative justice, many of those who had been judged immediately after the war were then pardoned or released early from prison. These measures did not always, however, help small criminals who might already have served their full sentence,[57] nor big ones who might already have been executed for crimes that a few years later would at most have gotten them twenty years of prison.[58]

TRANSMUTATION OF INTEREST INTO PASSION

The transmutation of an interest in some object A into a passion for A may be illustrated by the phenomenon of marrying for money. Because there is something incongruous and shameful about this procedure, at least in modern societies, those who engage in it will sometimes find a way to persuade themselves that they are really marrying for love. The love thus generated will fall short of Stendhal's "amour-passion" (II.4), which is characterized by reckless disregard of interest, and coincide more closely with his "amour-goût," which never goes against interest. Yet for all that it may still be passion of a sort, unlike Lucy Steele's switch of what she calls her "affections" from Edward to Robert Ferrars in *Sense and Sensibility*. In some cases "amour-goût," rather than being interest transmuted into love, is love constrained by interest. Rather than first seeking out the richest potential spouse available and then persuading oneself of being in love, one may simply eliminate from consideration all partners below a certain level of wealth and then let one's affections settle where they may (see also the discussion of Becker in IV.3). In that case, there could be "amour-passion" and not merely "amour-goût."

The latter scenario could also, however, be due to the imperfection constraint: It is harder to persuade oneself that one is marrying for

---

56. For references to the importance of this attitude ("we are not like them"), see Andenæs (1978, p. 62); Lottman (1986, pp. 50, 109, 186); and Huyse and Dhondt (1993, p. 100).

57. Huyse and Dhondt (1993), p. 170; Tamm, (1984), p. 446. In Denmark, some of those who (i) received short sentences and (ii) were tried early actually served longer than those who had been sentenced to longer sentences (*ibid.*, p. 449).

58. Huyse and Dhondt (1993), p. 125.

love if the chosen person is *the very richest* among all who might be available. The consistency constraint may also operate in such cases. Whereas Lucy Steele had no difficulty transferring her affections to one brother when the other was disinherited, someone who genuinely falls in love with a person who was originally singled out on grounds of interest may not be able to fall out of love when interest dictates that course of action. In a person who has internalized the idea that love is not love which alters when it alteration finds, self-respect may win out over self-interest. As in the case of fairness, there is an asymmetry between adopting an attitude when and because it serves one's interest and giving it up when and because it no longer does. In a speculative vein, we may stipulate that in *King Lear* both Burgundy and France love Cordelia because of her prospects, but that only the former cares so little about his self-image that he is able to shed the emotion when it no longer coincides with his interest.

In modern democracies, political office is not supposed to be sought for its own sake. Naked ambition, therefore, is easily self-defeating. Disguised ambition is more likely to succeed. Although politicians sometimes disguise their ambitions to others only, the strain of living a lie may cause them to deceive themselves as well. Their interest in holding office is transmuted into passion for a cause that may best be served, or so they tell themselves, by holding office. Here, the interest in A is transmuted into a passion for B rather than, as in the case of love, a passion for A. This transmutation is illustrated in the career of Robert Moses. In an early idealist stage, he haughtily refused to use any dishonorable means.[59] In the middle stage, the end came to justify the means.[60] In the final, most corrupt stage, the means came to justify the end.[61] Any cause that allowed him to retain power and exercise it was capable of exciting his passion.

Murder may be undertaken out of interest, which is then transmuted into passion, as illustrated by the following generic plot of many crime novels. A son in need of money suddenly has the thought that all his problems would be solved if his father died. Although he first recoils in horror at the thought, he then begins to ask himself why his father could not help him out of his gambling debts, one more time. It is not as if the old man needs the money, so the refusal

59. Caro (1974), Chapter 5, notably pp. 79–86.
60. *Ibid.*, part 4, notably pp. 275–6.
61. *Ibid.*, Chapter 35, notably pp. 833–4.

to support him can only be due to a spiteful and malicious desire to keep him down. Following Montaigne, he might tell himself that "[i]t is right that [a father] should let [his children] use what Nature deprives him of: Otherwise there is certainly an element of malice and envy."[62] The thought that another is deliberately and maliciously holding one down is intensely aversive and capable of triggering strong destructive urges. The murder, when it happens, takes place in anger and the outcome is seen as simply getting what one is entitled to. In this scenario, the shame felt at the thought of killing one's father for gain is the engine behind the transmutation of interest into passion. An alternative scenario is one in which the frustration of the son's interest causes him to feel irrational anger, which he then transmutes into justified anger by the story that his father is keeping him down.

TRANSMUTATION OF PASSION INTO INTEREST

We may also observe the converse transmutation, that of passion into interest.[63] This is especially likely to happen in contexts, such as

---

62. Montaigne (1991), p. 439.
63. Frank (1988, p. 209) suggests that what looks like transmutation may also occur as a result of *self-misinterpretation*. Assuming that the brain is a system of modules that have only limited access to each other, one module may come up with the wrong interpretation of behavior generated by another module. Even though people may marry for love, they may be unaware of their reasons and interpret their behavior in terms of interest: "[I]f forces beyond awareness do in fact play a major role in binding partners together, we should not be surprised that the reasons people give for pairing bear little relation to their true motives. . . . In a culture that places a premium on rationality and the pursuit of self-interest, it seems hardly surprising that the explanations we hear are often of the rationalist mold." In a footnote to the same page he suggests that a similar mechanism may account for what I have called transmutation of interest into reason: "[B]ecause people know that society encourages altruistic behavior, their language modules may contrive altruistic explanations for behaviors that were in fact prompted by self-interest." Frank argues, in other words, that these phenomena are based on wishful thinking rather than on self-deception. There is no need to assume (as I have done) that people are aware of their original motivation and then suppress it by transmuting it into another which they find more acceptable. Rather, because lack of communication between different parts of the brain prevents them from being aware of the original motivation that was responsible for their behavior, they simply interpret their actions in terms of whatever motivation they find most pleasing. Frank's analysis may well account for some cases of discrepancy between a person's real motivation and his belief about what motivates him. Yet because the latter belief always arises *after* the behavior, Frank cannot account for cases in which the transmutation affects behavior.

357

market competition, in which adherence to the canons of instrumental rationality is vital. To act against a business rival out of envy or a desire for revenge is rarely profitable. Both motives go together with disregard for consequences, in the form of a willingness to suffer a net loss, as long as the other also suffers or suffers more. Price cutting may be an effective form of revenge against a competitor, but the firm practicing it may drive itself out of business as well. One member of a cartel may be so envious of the large profits made by another member that he triggers the breakup of the cartel by lowering prices. When passion, as in these cases, induces actions against one's interest there may be a tendency to persuade oneself that they do in fact promote it. Initiation of a price war may be reconceptualized as an instrumentally rational response to the behavior of the other firm. The head of the firm that breaks out of the cartel may persuade himself that the short-term superprofits will offset the long-term losses.

Although I have not seen any evidence that envy and revenge – dressed up as profit maximization – actually serve as motives in business transactions, I do not think the idea can be excluded. When two motives – interest and passion – point in different directions, the tension may be reduced by one of the motives aligning itself with the other. The examples cited above of passion aligning itself on interest seem quite plausible. The presently cited examples of interest aligning itself on passion, although not totally implausible, are clearly more conjectural. Yet the general idea of interest as the output of transmutation may be somewhat more robust, as the following discussion shows.

TRANSMUTATION OF REASON INTO INTEREST

The most common phenomenon of transmutation is to represent oneself to oneself as in some sense better – more just, virtuous, and reasonable, less motivated by self-interest – than one actually is. For the moralists who first introduced this line of reasoning, it was close to self-evident that when the mind fooled itself, it was to present baser motivations in the guise of reason. Although this is no doubt the most common form of transmutation, it is not the only one. Some people have and value an image of themselves as aggressively motivated by interest and ambition. They would be embarrassed to think of themselves as do-gooders or as concerned with anyone's welfare but their own. At the same time, they may have a tendency – of genetic origin, or inculcated into them by social-ization – to promote the good of others. To reconcile this tendency with their self-image, they tell themselves a story in which the other-regarding behavior is made to appear as based on mere enlightened self-interest.

To illustrate this case, I cite two passages from *Democracy in America*:

The Americans ... enjoy explaining almost every act of their lives on the principle of self-interest properly understood. It gives them pleasure to point out how an enlightened self-love continually leads them to help one another and disposes them freely to give part of their time and wealth for the good of the state. I think that in this way they often do themselves less than justice, for sometimes in the United States, as elsewhere, one sees people carried away by the disinterested, spontaneous impulses natural to man. But the Americans are *hardly prepared to admit that they give way to emotions* of this sort. They prefer to give the credit to their philosophy rather than to themselves. (DA, p. 526; my italics).

I have known zealous Christians who constantly forgot themselves to labor more ardently for the happiness of others, and I have heard them claim that they did this only for the sake of rewards in the next world. But I cannot get it out of my head that they were deceiving themselves. I respect them too much to believe them. Christianity does, it is true, teach that we must prefer others to ourselves in order to (*pour*) gain heaven. But Christianity also teaches that we must do good to our fellows for (*par*) love of God. (DA, p. 429)[64]

Tocqueville was a very acute observer. I believe his claims carry some weight. In contemporary America, an instance of what he describes may occur when people boast that their charitable and philanthropic contributions are tax-exempt – as if this could prove them to be truly hard-headed! Within the dominant pattern of interest transmuted into reason, there may be a subpattern that takes the opposite form.

---

64. In this passage, Tocqueville is not only asserting that the Christians who believe that they do good for the purpose of getting to heaven are deceiving themselves, but also that they could not get there if this were in fact their true motive. Promoting the happiness of others is a causal condition for salvation, but only if you do it out of love for God; hence "pour" must be taken in the causal rather than in the intentional sense.

TRANSMUTATION OF PASSION INTO PASSION

This phenomenon can take three forms. First, emotion A towards intentional object X may be transmuted into emotion A for object Y. Second, it may be transmuted into emotion B for X. And third, it may be transmuted into emotion B for Y. The Freudian defense mechanisms that I discuss below include all three varieties. Here, I briefly discuss an example of the first kind and then more extensively one of the second kind.

The first example is taken from Montaigne's discussion of the fear of death. He notes first that people claim that what they fear is not death but the pain which goes before it and then adds that the claim is self-deceptive: "[I]t is our inability to suffer the thought of dying which makes us unable to suffer the pain of it . . . As reason condemns our cowardice in fearing something so momentary, so unavoidable, so incapable of being felt as death is, we seize upon a more pardonable pretext" (*Essays*, p. 58). Schematically, a first-order emotion (fear of death) triggers a second-order emotion (shame or guilt), which induces a first-order emotion (fear of pain) that is more consistent with my self-image as a rational individual. Fear of death, for Montaigne as for the Stoics, was an irrational emotion. "Why should we fear to lose something which, once lost, cannot be regretted?" (*Essays*, p. 102). Fear of pain, by contrast, is a "natural" emotion (*Essays*, p. 1195).

The second example is the transmutation of love into hate in Stendhal's *Le Rouge et le Noir*. In this novel, the daughter of a wealthy and high-placed aristocrat, Mathilde de la Mole, falls in love with Julien Sorel, the son of a carpenter and her father's secretary. Initially, she tells herself that it "shows a high heart and a daring spirit to love a man so far beneath [her] in social position" (II.xi). She views her love for him as something heroic and out of the ordinary. "If, while still poor, Julien had been noble, my loving him would be nothing more than a vulgar act of folly, a commonplace misalliance; I wouldn't want such a thing; it would have nothing of what characterizes a grand passion – the enormous obstacles to be overcome, the dark uncertainty of the outcome" (II.xii). Her love for a social inferior, at this stage, is a source of pride rather than shame because she frames his situation as one of *extraordinary* inferiority rather than of extraordinary *inferiority*.

Giving in to this contrived or artificially heightened passion, Mathilde writes a letter to Julien expressing her love, and then regrets it bitterly: "She was writing *first* (what a terrible word) to a man in the lowest rank of society. This circumstance, were it to be discovered, ensured her everlasting disgrace. Which of the women who came to see her mother would dare to take her side? What tactful phrase could be found for them to say to soften the blow inflicted by the frightful contempt of the drawing-rooms?" (II.xiv). Yet even this acute feeling of social shame is swept away when Julien, playing hard to get, refuses to respond unambiguously to her overture. She summons him to find a ladder and climb into her room. He obeys; she receives him; but almost immediately has second thoughts:

I've given myself a master, so Mademoiselle de la Mole was saying to herself, plunged into the most doleful grief. He may be the soul of honour, well and good: but if I provoke his vanity to extremes, he will revenge himself by making the nature of our relations known. Mathilde had never had a lover before, and at that moment in life which gives even the hardest hearts some soft illusions, she was tormented by the most bitter reflections
He has tremendous power over me, since he rules by terror and can inflict a frightful punishment on me if I try him too far. This idea was enough of itself to incline Mathilde to insult him, for courage was the prime quality of her character. Nothing could stir her in any way or cure her of an underlying feeling of boredom (*ennui*) constantly springing to life again, except the idea that she was putting her whole existence at hazard. (II.xvii)[65]

At this stage, the two lovers are "unconsciously animated by the keenest hatred towards each other" (II.xvii). When after various vicissitudes they reunite, Mathilde once again breaks with Julien:

Remorseful virtue and resentful pride made her, that morning, equally unhappy. She was in some sort shattered by the dreadful idea of having given certain rights over herself to a mere humble priest, who was a peasant's son. It's almost, she said to herself, as if I had to reproach myself with a partiality for one of the footmen. With proud and daring characters, there is only one step from anger against oneself to fury with other people, transports of rage

65. Cp. also the following description of Marguerite de Valois that Stendhal cites as an apt description of Mathilde de la Mole: "An *itch for excitement*, such was the character of my aunt, the beautiful Marguerite de Valois.... A need for hazardous sport (*le besoin de jouer*) was the whole secret of this amiable's princess's character; from thence came her quarrels and her reconciliations with her brothers, from the age of sixteen. Now what can a young woman hazard? All that she has most precious: her honour, her lifelong reputation" (II.xii). All of this harks back to Pascal and the need to gamble as distraction from *ennui* (Elster, in press c).

afford one intense delight in such circumstances ... Mathilde ... found it an exquisite satisfaction for her pride in punishing in this way both herself and him for the adoration she had felt a few days before. (II.xx)

For the Princess of Clèves, the emotion caused by her love is indeed very close to "remorseful virtue." Mathilde's reactions are more complicated. In her meta-emotions there may be an element of remorse or guilt, but there is above all social shame and the anger or "resentful pride" triggered by "having a master." Although her uncompromising character will accept nothing short of absolute love, which for her is defined as total subjugation to Julien, it also makes her rebel against the thought of actually having him as her master. When Julien in his misery makes the fatal mistake of pleading for himself, he offers her only a pretext for punishing him. At the very beginning of their relationship, she told herself that "at the first sign of weakness I see in him, I'll give him up" (II.xi). What now transpires is the opposite: She justifies her desire to give him up by the weakness he displays when she makes it known to him. She delights in the feeling of righteous anger and the catharsis of revenge.

MECHANISMS

The phenomena I have discussed are not all equally robust. The transmutation of interest and passion into reason are well-documented phenomena, the transmutation of interest and passion into one another less so. Transmutations of passion clearly occur, although not all of us have experienced them as dramatically as Mathilde de la Mole and Julien Sorel. Yet whatever doubt one might cast on the importance of this or that class of cases, the general idea is, I believe, hard to deny. By contrast, the mechanisms behind the phenomena are not at all well understood. *Exactly how* does it happen that people fool themselves into thinking that they do what they do for other motivations than those which really animate them?

In *Middlemarch*, George Eliot says that "Bulstrode shrank from a direct lie with an intensity disproportionate to his more indirect misdeeds. But many of these misdeeds were like the subtle muscular movements which are not taken account of in the consciousness, though they bring about the end that we fix our mind on and desire"

(Chapter 68). La Rochefoucauld observes that "The virtues lose themselves in self-interest like rivers in the sea,"[66] anticipating Sartre's idea that "one falls into self-deception (*mauvaise foi*) like one falls asleep."[67] Another commonly used metaphor is that of "gravitating" towards the conception of fairness that serves one's interest.[68] A more specific analogy is with a sleeping person who tosses around and adjusts his position until he finds one that is acceptable. Although the final position is explained by the fact that it is comfortable, it is not true that he *chose* it because it was comfortable.[69] A transmuted motive might arise by a similar process of random, unconscious search combined with a deterministic selection criterion.

However suggestive, these are metaphors, not theories or even mechanisms. What is needed is a theory or a mechanism-generating framework that can explain the role of the various motivations as inputs, engines, and outputs of transmutation. *But there is no such theory or framework.* Neither of the two dominant theories of motivated attitudinal change, Festinger's theory of cognitive dissonance and Freud's theory of defense mechanisms, addresses the issues I have identified, although each of them touches on closely related questions. Moreover, Freud's theory is, I believe, implausible even with regard to the issues that it does address.

Each of the two theories is internally complex, and the relation between them correspondingly hard to fathom. To convey a rough idea of the different predictions yielded by the two theories when confronted with the same independent variable, consider a person who believes he might have homosexual tendencies that he values negatively.[70] According to the theory of cognitive dissonance, he might resolve the psychic conflict by finding similar tendencies in others whom he likes, thus making homosexuality a less undesirable trait. According to psychoanalytic theory, he might react by denying the tendency in himself, finding it in others ("projection"), and, moreover, developing a dislike of them. As will be clear from this brief contrast, dissonance theory has an intuitive appeal that is lacking in the psychoanalytic account, which leaves us puzzled as

66. Maxim 171.
67. Sartre (1943), p. 109.
68. Rabin (1995).
69. Elster (1983a), pp. 61–3.
70. The example is taken from the comparison of the two theories in Wicklund and Brehm (1976, pp. 201–11).

to *why* projection of the tendency to others would help resolve the tension.[71]

Cognitive dissonance is stipulated to arise when a person holds two or more "cognitions" that are inconsistent with one another. Here, cognitions include not only ordinary factual beliefs but also consciously held values as well as mental representations of the choices or behaviors of the subject. Even emotions may be cognitions, if they have developed beyond the stage of proto-emotions. The notion of inconsistency is not that of logical contradiction, but a somewhat looser idea that can be characterized, perhaps, by saying that A and B are inconsistent when the presence of A induces an expectation of the absence of B. Thus if a person has just bought a car of brand X, the expectation is that he will not believe brand Y to be better. Or to take another famous paradigm of dissonance research, if a subject is opposed to abortion we would not expect him to write an essay favoring it.

Dissonance reduction (or avoidance) takes place by changing or blocking some of the dissonant cognitions, and sometimes by adding new ones. In spite of certain ambiguities in Festinger's original formulations, the process has to be thought of as unconscious. In the car example for instance, dissonance can be reduced by reading ads for the car one has just bought and avoiding reading ads for other brands. These behaviors cannot proceed from conscious choices for the purpose of reducing dissonance, for if one *knew* that the ads were read or avoided to bolster one's confidence in the choice one had just made, no bolstering could take place.[72] Somehow, one "just gravitates" towards the behaviors that confirm the wisdom of the choice one has made. The dissonance-reducing change in the essay-writing example is even more obviously constrained to be unconscious. When subjects are asked to write to an essay favoring the view they oppose and are unable to tell themselves that the behavior is justified by their lack of any choice in the matter or by strong inducements (reward or punishment), they reduce their dissonance by adopting a more

---

71. A reviewer comments that in this special case projection may in fact have the kind of intuitive plausibility I am requiring: "Since I hate gays so much, I can't possibly be one myself." I do not think, however, that similar intuitions underlie all other cases of alleged projection. The case of a woman who projects her own desires for children and beautiful clothes upon others in a form of "altruistic surrender" (Freud 1935, pp. 123–7), and of "Harry Hughes" who as an adolescent in boarding school "tried to demonstrate that it was the school authorities, not himself, who were afraid of sex" (Vaillant 1993, p. 113), do not fit this pattern.
72. Elster (1984), pp. 178–9.

favorable attitude towards the view they defend. As mentioned in the beginning of this chapter, misrepresentation may induce transmutation.

Dissonance involves physiological arousal, as measured for instance by the capacity to perform simple tasks (which is enhanced by arousal) or the capacity to perform complex tasks (which is reduced by arousal).[73] In the cognitive-dissonance literature it is rarely suggested that the arousal associated with dissonance could be linked to *emotion*.[74] Rather, the arousal is put on a par with nonemotional visceral factors such as hunger, thirst, or pain.[75] Emotion is simply not mentioned in descriptions of the dynamic forces that induce dissonance reduction.[76] Even in discussions of how unjustified aggression may induce derogation of the victim ("quos laeserunt et oderunt"), shame at one's own behavior is not mentioned as a motive force.[77] The reason may be that, unlike psychoanalytic theory, dissonance theory places the "emphasis on the individual's concept of *what he is* rather than his concept of *what he should be* (superego)."[78] I can see no reason, though, for this restriction. If a belief about what he should be enters among the cognitions of the individual, it has the same dissonance-creating potential as any other cognition.

In a development of dissonance theory ("self-discrepancy theory") Tory Higgins has taken the further step of classifying states of

---

73. Pallak and Pittman (1972).
74. Even if the theory does not have a place for emotions as a motive for dissonance reduction, they can enter into an explanation of why the dissonance arose in the first place. Thus Festinger argued that if a person experiences a strong emotion without being able to produce a reason for it, he will suffer dissonance and be motivated to tell himself a story that justifies the emotion: "[B]eing afraid, and knowing one is afraid, leads to a tendency to acquire cognition consonant with this fear" (Festinger 1957, p. 236).
75. Aronson (1995), pp. 235–6; Wicklund and Brehm (1976), pp. 95–6; Eagly and Chaiken (1993), pp. 547–51.
76. In an article that is explicitly devoted to the role of emotion in attitude change, Breckler (1993, pp. 468–9) devotes one page to dissonance arousal and attitude change. He first discusses the hypothesis that people "change their attitudes in an effort to reduce *arousal* (regardless of its hedonic value)" and then the hypothesis that they "are motivated to reduce *negative affect* (regardless of degree of arousal)," and he finds confirmation of the second but not of the first. In the findings that corroborate the second finding, however, affect is operationalized as "tension," that is, as a state lacking both in cognitive antecedents and intentional object.
77. Wicklund and Brehm (1976), pp. 196–8. They note that guilt can act as an "energizer" of dissonance (*ibid.*, pp. 94–5), without allowing it to be a source of dissonance in its own right.
78. Festinger and Bramel (1962), p. 271.

365

dissonance according to the emotions they arouse.[79] Thus a discrepancy between what you think you are and what you would ideally like to be generates disappointment; a discrepancy between what you think you are and what you think you ought to be generates guilt; a discrepancy between what you think you are and what others think you should ideally be generates shame in the subject (and an expectation of disappointment in others); and a discrepancy between what you think you are and what others think you ought to be generates fear in the subject (and an expectation of anger in others). Although an important development of dissonance theory, self-discrepancy theory also falls short of its predecessor in that it does not try to account for the *reduction* of dissonance (or discrepancy). The dependent variable is discrepancy-induced emotion, not emotion-induced discrepancy reduction. Also, Higgins does not include (nor exclude) *motivations* among the attributes of the person that are the object of assessment by self or others. These are not intrinsic limitations of his theory, simply issues that it has not addressed.

The Freudian theory of defense mechanisms allows a much more important place for the emotions, both as targets and as motive forces for transmutation. Concerning the second aspect, Otto Fenichel enumerates guilt, disgust, and shame as possible motives of defense, guilt being the most important.[80] Concerning the first aspect, Anna Freud argued, in the original statement of the theory, that the defense mechanisms are primarily directed against sexual and aggressive impulses, and only secondarily against emotions. Moreover, they target emotions only when and because these are associated with unacceptable impulses.[81] She added, however, that "[e]ven if owing to the repression of an instinct the ego is impelled by anxiety and a sense of guilt to defend itself against the accompanying affect ... it is all the more ready to ward off affects associated with prohibited sexual impulses if these affects happen to be distressing, e.g. pain, longing, mourning."[82] Thus although emotions with negative valence cannot by themselves trigger the defense mechanisms, they can reinforce the defense against the impulses with which they are associated. But this seems arbitrary, unless it is assumed, implausibly, that all negative emotions are associated with sexual or aggressive impulses. Later

79. Higgins (1987).
80. Fenichel (1945), Chapter VIII.
81. Freud (1935), pp. 32, 61.
82. *Ibid.*, p. 62.

formulations of the theory do not give the same priority to impulses over emotions, however, but treat them on a par as potential threats to the individual. Even these do not, as far as I know, address the issues of emotional transmutation discussed above, of envy into indignation or of irrational anger into justified anger. Even less do they raise the possibility that the defensive mechanisms might transmute emotion into interest or vice versa.

In any case, I believe that the theory is too obscure to be useful. Although claims have been made that defense mechanisms can be validated by interobserver agreement,[83] there is an obvious risk of *pseudointersubjectivity* – "of imposing on the material idiosyncratic views of the judging group or at times of its leader."[84] The within-group agreements that are sometimes reported stand in stark contrast to the massive between-group disagreements. George Vaillant, for instance, offers *a list of lists* of defense mechanisms. One author "reviewed 12 psychoanalytic authors, who among themselves had described 27 distinct mechanisms of defense, only 7 of which were noted by 11 of the 12 writers. [Another author] reviewed 17 psycho-analytically informed authors ... and identified 37 different terms for defense mechanisms. Only 5 of these 37 mechanisms ... were cited by 15 of [the] 17 authors, and only 14 of his 37 terms were cited by as many as 5 out of 17 authors."[85]

To be sure, this taxonomic chaos is matched by that of the emotions themselves. There is almost as little agreement on the number of distinct emotions as there is on the number of defense mechanisms. Also, the lack of agreement on how to generate the defense mechanisms from simpler conceptual structures[86] is equaled or surpassed by the lack of agreement on how to generate complex emotions from basic ones.[87] We have much stronger reasons, however, to believe

---

83. Vaillant (1992, 1993).
84. Knapp (1988), p. 111.
85. Vaillant (1992), p. 45.
86. For various (and very different) attempts of this kind, see Suppes and Warren (1982), Jackendoff (1988), and Plutchik (1993).
87. Another curious analogy between emotions and defense mechanisms is the following. We saw in IV.3 that there can be emotions in search of an object. Similarly, Freud argued (1937, p. 238) that we can observe defense mechanisms in search of a threat. "The adult's ego, with its increased strength, continues to defend itself against dangers which no longer exist in reality; indeed, it finds itself compelled to seek out those situations in reality which can serve as an approximate substitute for the original danger, so as to be able to justify, in relation to them, its maintaining its habitual modes of reaction." Thus defense mechanisms are not simply ways of justifying behavior: They may themselves need to be justified!

in the existence of the emotions than to believe in the existence of the Freudian defense mechanisms. The emotions are directly experienced, on a par with macroscopic everyday objects. We may be unsure about how to classify them and how to distinguish them from one another, but the reality of, say, anger and fear could not possibly be denied. Defense mechanisms, by contrast, cannot be directly observed. They must be inferred from their effects, like invisible planets[88] or subatomic particles.[89] Given the flexibility of the notions, and the possibility to stipulate the simultaneous operation of several defense mechanisms, one can always after the fact infer their existence from observed behavior, emotion, or cognition. But that is also true of the mechanisms assumed to be at work in astrology. By contrast, one cannot simply invent an emotion X and claim that it is typically triggered by the presence of, say, umbrellas.

With a few exceptions, the defense mechanisms have no intuitive plausibility. Consider the transmutation of "I love him" into "he hates me," or of "my mother hates my father" into "I hate my brother."[90] It is entirely mysterious to me why the threat that may be posed by the first cognition in each pair is deflected by transmuting it into the second. To take another example, Ray Jackendoff suggests that the following "rule of irrational inference" may be at work in psychodynamic displacement:

Major premise (enduring attitude): 'X has characteristic Z' is bad, to be avoided.
Minor premise (particular situation): X has characteristic Z.
Conclusion: X does not have characteristic Z – someone else does.[91]

In the language of dissonance theory, the cognition that "someone else has Z" is neither consonant nor dissonant with the two premises. It is simply irrelevant and thus cannot contribute anything to the resolution of inner conflict.[92] One could argue, perhaps, that the displacement process is a "blindly" causal mechanism and that there is no presumption that it will *solve*, even partially and temporarily, the conflict that *causes* it. That would be, however, to go against the grain of all writings on the defense mechanisms from Freud onward. "The

88. Vaillant (1993), p. 100.
89. Vaillant (1992), p. 99.
90. Suppes and Warren (1982).
91. Jackendoff (1988), p. 215.
92. Wicklund and Brehm (1976), p. 4.

mechanisms of defence serve the purpose of keeping off dangers. It cannot be disputed that they are successful in this."[93] Or one might argue that people's reactions are governed by an implicit theory that the sum of (a given) affect in the universe is constant: If an emotion is denied in the subject, it has to be imputed to someone else. Hence, if tension is to be revolved by means of denial, it has to take the form of projection. Although the latter does not by itself resolve tension, it is an inevitable by-product of tension resolution. But I do not know of any evidence that people entertain this theory; it is a purely speculative notion.

Similar objections could be addressed, I believe, to most of the other mechanisms. Regarding projection, for instance, "attributing one's own unacknowledged feelings to others," it's not clear (to me at least) what kind of relief or satisfaction it can provide for the subject.[94] By contrast, projective identification, in which the subject "misattributes [affects or impulses] as justifiable reactions to the other person," is readily intelligible.[95] It is essentially a variant on Seneca's "quos laeserunt et oderunt," spelled out by saying that "the subject confuses the fact that it was he himself who originated the projected material, and, unlike simple projection, believes himself to be the just rather than the unjust victim." In the equally perennial mechanism of rationalization, "the individual deals with emotional conflicts, or internal or external stressors, by devising reassuring or self-serving but incorrect explanations for his or her own or others' behavior."[96] But we did not need psychoanalysis to tell us this. Where plausible, the theory offers truisms; where innovative, it is implausible.

A satisfactory theory of transmutation would have to incorporate two simple ideas. On the one hand, people have a strong desire to promote their material interests. On the other hand, they have a strong desire to maintain a positive self-image. For most people, the self-image includes a belief that they are not motivated only or even mainly by material interest. For some, it may include a belief that they are motivated only or mainly by interest. Sometimes, these two desires can be satisfied simultaneously without transmutation. When the oppressed fight for their liberation, interest and self-image are almost inseparable. For the aggressively amoral entrepreneur, too,

93. Freud (1937), p. 237.
94. The definition of projection is from Vaillant (1992, p. 244).
95. *Ibid.*, p. 255.
96. Vaillant (1992), pp. 255, 256.

there is no conflict between the two values. Most people, however, often find themselves in situations where the two suggest opposite courses of action. Sometimes, they may be able to accommodate both through a process of transmutation. The extent to which they succeed depends on the extent to which they are limited by the consistency and imperfection constraints. Also, some people may be intrinsically better than others at telling self-serving stories to themselves. In a passage immediately following one cited in V.1 on the need for self-deception in politics, Tocqueville claimed, for instance, that "unluckily I have never been able to illuminate my mind with such peculiar and contrived lights, or to persuade myself so easily that my advantage and the general weal conformed."[97]

V.3. MISREPRESENTATION

The self-deceptive practices discussed in the previous section may be contrasted with the less paradoxical phenomena of deception. Although a person may be fully aware that he is really animated by one motivation, that very same motivation may lead him to present a different motivation to others. (As indicated earlier, I shall mostly ignore the psychic strains and tensions that may be caused by this dual attitude and assume that the person successfully and costlessly maintains a double accounting system of his motivations.) Also, the person may be guided by two different aims: the desire to achieve a certain goal and the desire to be perceived in a certain way by others. Even if the first aim can be achieved without misrepresenting his motivation, the second might, if important enough, induce him to falsify it, at the expense of the first.

The target of misrepresentation may either be an interlocutor or a third-party audience. Consider for instance a husband and a wife bargaining over custody as well as over the property settlement. The husband may try to misrepresent himself to his wife as having a strong interest in custody, to get a favorable property settlement. If this is unfeasible, because it is common knowledge between him and his wife that he does not really want to take responsibility for the child, he may address a third party instead. In front of a judge, he may successfully misrepresent himself as having a strong interest in custody, because any statement by his wife to the contrary

97. Tocqueville (1990), p. 84.

will be discounted as motivated by *her* self-interest (or spite). Because it is often in people's interest to denounce others as motivated by interest, claims to that effect, even when true, may not be credible to third parties. In fact, the claim might backfire – C might think that when it is in A's interest to claim that B is arguing out of interest, A is probably not telling the truth, an implication being that B probably is.

Or consider a legislator arguing *to* other legislators *before* a national audience of voters. He may dress up his interest in impartial language in order to persuade his fellow legislators that his proposal is well founded. To the extent that legislators are indeed (i) willing to listen to "the mild voice of reason"[98] and (ii) unable to distinguish insincere from sincere appeals to reason, this stratagem may succeed. Even if neither (i) nor (ii) obtains, however, his interest in getting reelected may induce the legislator to couch his proposal in impartial terms, with a wink that is visible to his co-legislators but not to the public. As Richard Posner suggests, he may then adopt "Aesopian language,"[99] fearing that voters might punish representatives who explicitly present legislation as pieces of self-interested bargaining. I return to that issue below.

Before I proceed to examples of cases classified by input–output pairs, let me say a few words about the motivations behind the misrepresentation. Consider first *reason* as a motive. This motive can only, I believe, operate when reason itself is the input. An impartial aim may be so important that one is willing to misrepresent one's motivation in order to achieve it. This may seem inconsistent with my characterization of reason as "being open to rational argument and being willing to change one's view as the result of such argument" (V.1). Yet when a person motivated by reason interacts with others who are not so motivated, deviations from this first-best behavior may be allowed or even required. Against subterfuge, reason may itself have to adopt subterfuge.[100]

Consider next *interest* as a motive for deceiving others about one's real motivation. When this motive operates, it also tends to coincide with the motivation that is being misrepresented. Yet the opposite does not hold: The motivation for hiding one's interest may be

98. This phrase by Madison (from *The Federalist* no. 42) is also the title of Bessette (1994).
99. Posner (1982), p. 273.
100. Elster (1983b), pp. 24, 38–9.

passion rather than interest, for example if one feels shame at professing self-interested motives. Hence when the motive for misrepresentation is *passion*, the motive that is misrepresented need not itself be a passionate one. The coincidence may occur in this case too, however, as when the shame attached to envy induces a speaker to argue in terms of fairness. Note, however, that social norms may also induce misrepresentation via interest. A shameless person might care about the material sanctions through which others express their disapproval (III.2), even though he is unaffected by that disapproval itself.

A final preliminary comment concerns the behaviors by which one communicates or signals one's motivation to others. In most of the cases I discuss, this is done by describing one's motivation in words. In some cases, however, motivations can be revealed by nonverbal behavior, or by non–content-related aspects of verbal behavior. If I vote for candidate A over B, this usually allows others to infer something about my state of mind, namely that I prefer A over B. When I cast my vote, the motive of inducing that inference may in fact be uppermost in mind. If I argue passionately for a given policy, the audience may infer that my real motivation is not found in the arguments I am adducing, but in my passion. More generally, the theory of misrepresentation overlaps with the theory of signaling, including the theory of mimicry in animal and human behavior.[101]

MISREPRESENTATION OF INTEREST AS REASON

In many public debates many speakers are mainly motivated by some form of interest. In all public debates, all speakers represent themselves as being motivated by reason. The first statement is an empirical claim that would hardly be contested by anyone, although there may be disagreement about the exact importance of the interest motive. The second is close to a conceptual truth. One can, to be sure, try to anchor it empirically by appealing to norms against self-interested statements. James Coleman argues that if "members [of an assembly] appear hesitant to bring up self-interest and sometimes express disapproval when another member does so," it is because there is a social norm "that says that no one should take a position that cannot be justified in terms of benefits to the collectivity."[102] Although not

101. See Hauser (1996, section 7.4) for a discussion of deceptive animal practices.
102. Coleman (1990), p. 393.

false, this analysis fails to locate the essential problem of the appeal to self-interest. To say, in a public debate, "We should choose policy A because it is good for me," is to show a fundamental lack of understanding of what it *means* to offer an argument for something – or to make it clear that one is engaged in a process of bargaining rather than arguing.[103]

In theory, perhaps, the second of these statements is consistent with the first statement being *universally* true. Each and every instance of public reason-giving might represent self-interest in disguise. As noted by Perelman and Olbrechts-Tyteca, "there are those who claim that resort to argumentation is sometimes, *or even always*, a pretense." Yet, as they go on to say, "it is difficult to give a satisfactory explanation of the resort to the mechanism of argument ("la mise en branle de l'appareil argumentatif") if, at least in some cases, there is no real persuasion."[104] *Why bother to argue* if people are universally motivated by self-interest?

In response, one might imagine a society in which some members falsely believe that some (unknown) members are genuinely open to argument and offended by naked appeals to interest. Because the former do not know who the latter are, they may decide to use impartial language on all occasions, on the principle "can't hurt, might help" (see below, however, for ways in which the constraints on impartial language *may* hurt the speaker). Even a person in the third category – someone who neither is open to argument nor believes that anyone else is – might decide to use impartial language, reasoning as follows: "If I express my interest directly without impartial garbs, those who believe in the existence of members open to argument might punish me, because they fear that if they don't those whom they falsely believe to be open to argument might punish them for not punishing me."

This story, although implausible, illustrates an important point. We can change the story and assume that it is common knowledge

---

103. For a similar argument, see Perelman and Olbrechts-Tyteca (1969, p. 75). Cohen (1992, 1995) argues that a related inconsistency is at the heart of the theory of justice offered by Rawls (1971). Rawls argued that even in a perfectly just society some inequality of income may be necessary in order to provide the more skilled members of society with incentives to perform socially valuable work. But, Cohen objects, the skilled themselves cannot say that the inequalities are necessary, because they make them necessary. Any such insistence on their part is either incoherent, or bargaining dressed up as arguing. (I am grateful to Cohen for this formulation of his views.)

104. *Ibid.*, p. 56; my italics.

that some members of society, perhaps a small fraction, are genuinely open to argument, but that one cannot tell who they are. This knowledge might trigger the cascade of simulations just described. When A interacts with B before a public consisting of C, D, . . ., A has two reasons for misrepresenting his interest as an impartial appeal to reason. First, B might, for all A knows, be one of the genuinely impartial members of society. If A expresses his interest directly, he will both lose the chance of persuading B and run the risk of being punished by B.[105] Second, even if B does not belong to that subset, A knows that B will know that one of C, D . . . belongs to it. A knows that B knows that if B fails to punish A, one of C, D . . . will punish B, which gives B has an incentive to punish A for expressing purely self-interested concerns.[106] Hence, the known presence of *some* genuinely reasonable people in the population may induce others to mimic their behavior.[107]

In V.2 I gave some examples of self-serving appeals to reason to illustrate the mechanism of transmutation. Several of these might equally plausibly be understood as instances of misrepresentation. When large parties argue for majority voting in single member districts on the ground that this system favors the impartial values of governability and stability, their real and quite conscious motive is often to favor party interest, as their rivals will not fail to point out. When a parent argues for custody by citing the interest of the child, he or she may engage in self-conscious misrepresentation of a purely private interest, as the other parent will not fail to point out. When, in a Norwegian wage bargaining case from 1990, ambulance drivers cited bank functionaries as a "natural" reference group for wage comparisons, nobody believed they believed what they said.

A more general class of cases arises in legislatures. When an interest group obtains legislation that is passed for no other reason than the

---

105. I am assuming here that punishment takes a material form such as voting someone out of office rather than shame-inducing behavior (III.2). The shame case is discussed below.
106. There is no reason to go to a higher-order argument and assume that B might expect a purely self-interested C to punish him because if he doesn't one of D, E . . . will punish C for not punishing B. As the transaction between A and B takes place in full view of all other members of society, B knows that he will be punished by someone for not punishing A.
107. This is obviously a very rough and stylized argument. I doubt, though, that it could be made more rigorous without introducing artificial assumptions along the lines of those made by Kreps and Wilson (1982) to sustain a somewhat similar argument.

benefits created for the group, this fact is rarely stated. Instead, as Posner said, Aesopian language is used. A law requiring the licensing of shoe salesmen, for instance, might be justified on public-health grounds, by the need to limit the spread of athletes' foot.[108] Jonathan Macey argues that "special interest legislation is ... often drafted with a public-regarding gloss ... because this gloss raises the costs to the public and to rival groups of discovering the true effect of the legislation. This, in turn, minimizes the major cost to the legislator of supporting narrow interest group legislation – the loss of support from groups that are harmed by the legislation – and thus reduces the cost to special interest groups of persuading the legislature to vote for the special interest legislation."[109] The cost to the interest group of this public-regarding gloss is that courts will give statutes their public rather than their private meaning whenever the two diverge. Because legislative bargains will therefore be only imperfectly enforceable, fewer will be struck.

Another possible cost to the interest groups arises from the imperfection constraint. To fool the public they may have to accept legislation that is somewhat suboptimal from their points of view, provided it is superior to the status quo. Hence the wedge between the private and the public meanings would be present from the very beginning and presumably create even more opportunities for courts to favor the latter over the former. Before proceeding to give some examples, I make some general comments on the place of the consistency and imperfection constraints in conscious misrepresentation.

The need to satisfy these constraints follows from the more general need to prove one's sincerity, to show that one is not choosing impartial arguments à la carte in a purely opportunistic manner. To the extent that one is offering impartial arguments in order to *persuade* others, there is, strictly speaking, no need to prove sincerity. One can, in fact, assert something like the following without violating the norms of argument: "I do not believe in justice and fairness. I want this policy implemented simply because it is in my interest. I notice, however, that there are also purely impartial arguments for the same policy, which I offer to you in case you hadn't thought of them." Others are unlikely, however, to give serious considerations to arguments offered in this spirit. My attempt to persuade you is much more likely to succeed if I can make you believe that I believe

108. Posner (1982), p. 286.
109. Macey (1986), p. 251.

in the arguments I offer for your consideration. In any case, of course, impartial arguments intended to *deceive* others cannot succeed unless perceived as offered in a sincere spirit.

As noted above, coincidence between an impartial argument and the speaker's interest is not in itself proof of insincerity. To deflect the suspicion that will nevertheless tend to arise, the speaker may try to preempt criticism by pointing to other occasions on which he behaved in a counterinterested manner.[110] This is not a knock-down proof of sincerity, because the earlier counterinterested argument might have been induced by the need to be consistent with a still earlier occasion on which it did coincide with self-interest. Yet if the audience has a short memory, this objection may not occur to them. Counterinterested behavior is often seen as a good indicator of a disinterested attitude even though it may simply be an expression of the consistency constraint.

A speaker may also try to convey sincerity by playing the Devil's advocate rather than being an out-and-out proponent of his favored policy. "Everything that furnishes an argument against the thesis being defended by the speaker, including objections to his own hypothesis, becomes an indication of sincerity and straightforwardness and increases the hearer's confidence."[111] To the extent that the intention is to deceive the audience, to avoid being seen as acting on bad motives, this is a costless strategy. To the extent, however, that the intention is to persuade, pointing out the weaknesses in one's own position has two opposite effects. Although it makes the audience more disposed to examine the argument seriously, it could also make it aware of weaknesses that it might otherwise not have noticed. Rational self-interest would make the speaker lean over backwards, but not too far, in pointing out the weaknesses in his own argument.

Trying to prove one's sincerity by respecting the imperfection constraint creates a similar dilemma. The need for this constraint arises because perfect coincidences arouse suspicion. "Plebiscites and elections yielding results too favorable to the propositions or candidates of the government side have rarely been regarded as a sincere expression of the voters' opinion."[112] Stupid dictators get themselves reelected by a majority of 95%; smart dictators content themselves with 65%. Yet even that majority may be too high to fully deflect suspicion:

---

110. Perelman and Olbrechts-Tyteca (1969), p. 62.
111. *Ibid.*, p. 457.
112. *Ibid.*, p. 473.

Only loss of the election would be truly convincing. More generally, arguing for a position that deviates from one's first preference has two opposed effects. Although making the proposal more credible and thus more likely to be adopted, it also serves one's interest less well if it is adopted. If proposals can be varied continuously, there may exist a policy arguing for which maximizes expected utility – unless the audience is so skeptical that only counterinterested arguments will convince them. If proposals are naturally lumpy or discrete, the closest alternative to one's preferred policy may be so distant that the status quo is preferable. In that case, one is better off not proposing anything: One is damned if one does and damned if one doesn't.

I now offer four local-justice examples and a recent legal decision in which the success or failure of policy proposals based on interest turns on the extent to which they embody that interest imperfectly rather than perfectly. Among the local-justice cases, the first two illustrate negative discrimination, the last two positive discrimination. I do not claim that positive discrimination is always based on group interest, or even that this is invariably true in the two cases I discuss. Typically, I believe, coalitions behind affirmative action include some who believe that such policies are intrinsically fair and some who support them on the basis of group interest. For the first group, the misrepresentations that I discuss belong to the subsection on misrepresentation of reason as reason. For the second group, they belong here.

Consider first restrictions on the right to vote. In many societies, property has been used as a criterion for the suffrage. One may, to be sure, offer impartial arguments for this principle. At the Federal Convention, Madison argued that the stringent property qualifications for the Senate, rather than protecting the privileged against the people, were a device for protecting the people against itself.[113] But there is something inherently suspicious about such arguments. They coincide too well with the self-interest of the rich. It may then be useful to turn to literacy, as an impartial criterion that is *highly but imperfectly* correlated with property. At various stages in American history literacy has also served as a legitimizing proxy for other unspeakable goals, such as the desire to keep blacks or Catholics out of politics.[114] These cases are, as noted below, more accurately seen as misrepresentation of passion as reason.

113. Farrand (1966), vol. 1, pp. 421, 430.
114. Creppell (1989).

377

American immigration policy has also used literacy as a proxy for criteria that could not be stated publicly.[115] Proposals to screen immigrants by testing them for literacy in their native language were usually justified as a way of selecting on the basis of individual merit, a widely accepted impartial procedure. The real motivation of the advocates of literacy was, however, usually prejudice or group interest. Patrician nativists wanted to exclude the usually illiterate immigrants from Central and Southeastern Europe (passion or prejudice misrepresented as reason). Labor feared that an influx of unskilled workers might drive wages down (interest misrepresented as reason).

Turning now to positive discrimination, recent decades have seen conflict between the goal of favoring ethnic minorities in college admission and the principle of color-blind admission imposed by courts and state legislatures.[116] Although some colleges have tried to get around this problem by various forms of subterfuge,[117] the current trend is towards admitting minority students as part of a preferential admission of students from culturally or economically disadvantaged backgrounds. On the one hand, this policy will admit some students from (say) poor Irish families that would not have made it into college under the earlier system and deny admission to some middle- or upper-class minority students that would have been admitted under a race-based system of affirmative action. On the other hand, it will admit more minority applicants than under a purely merit-based system. By diluting the goal, it becomes more feasible to implement it.[118]

Consider, finally, the use of race as a criterion of allocating kidneys for transplantation.[119] Three facts conspire to make American blacks badly placed in this allocative process. First, they are overrepresented as patients, partly because of the hypertensive problems mentioned

---

115. The following draws on Mackie (1995).
116. The following draws on Conley (1995).
117. In their admission processes, some state colleges assign points for disadvantages of various kinds. As Conley (1995) explains, this process is sometimes backward-driven, in the sense that the weights are assigned so as to get a preset number of minority applicants admitted. For a similar manipulation of the Preliminary Scholastic Assessment Test see "College Board Revises Test to Improve Chances for Girls," *New York Times* (2 October 1996), section B 8.
118. Although a diluted goal would be legally feasible, the dilution would also have other consequences. According to a study by Thomas Kane, cited in *The New York Times* (27 February 1997), "in order to replicate the current level of nonwhite admission, elite colleges would have to grant preferences to six times as many low-income students."
119. The following simplified exposition draws on Dennis (1995).

378

in IV.2. Second, they are underrepresented as donors. Third, because of their unusual antigen patterns they are less likely to benefit from a kidney taken from a white person. To the extent that kidneys are allocated on the basis of antigen matching (an impartial criterion of efficiency), blacks do badly. To compensate for this form of medical bad luck, the United Network for Organ Sharing allows transplantation centers to use time on the waiting list (an impartial criterion of fairness) as an additional principle. This criterion is viewed as acceptable because it does not uniquely favor blacks, but also enhances the prospects of other individuals or groups with unusual antigen patterns.

A recent case in which legislation was struck down because it violated the imperfection constraint is provided by a decision of the New York Supreme Court.[120] In 1989, the New York legislature created a special program for handicapped children living in the village of Kiryas Joel, a religious enclave for practitioners of strict Judaism. Upon appeal, the law was struck down by the U.S. Supreme Court on the grounds that by targeting public funds to a religious organization it violated the Establishment Clause of the First Amendment. Eleven days after the decision, the state legislature passed a new law allowing the establishment of similar programs in all communities that meet certain facially neutral criteria. As a matter of fact, of the 1,546 existing municipalities in New York state, only Kiryas Joel meets all these criteria. Moreover, a spokesman for the legislature said in public that the law was basically a "trick." In 1996, the New York Supreme Court declared the new law invalid, saying that it was "unimpressed with defendants' claim of facial neutrality, buttressed by evidence that another municipality may at some time in the future become eligible." Citing from an earlier decision to the effect that "the Constitution 'nullifies sophisticated as well as simple-minded modes' of infringing on Constitutional protections," the Court would "not countenance indirect attempts to accomplish what cannot be accomplished directly." It is clear from the decision that the law would have been upheld if it had satisfied the imperfection constraint, by offering the right to special programs to religious and (existing) nonreligious communities alike.

The strength of the imperfection constraint varies. From Marx, Nietzsche, and Freud we have inherited what Paul Ricoeur called

---

120. *Grumet v Cuomo* 1996 NY App. Div. Lexis 8713. The decision was upheld with similar reasoning in *Grumet v Cuomo* 1997 NY Int. 69.

"the hermeneutics of suspicion" – a tendency to find hidden motives behind any appeal to the common good. In some cases, the suspicion may be so strong that only proposals manifestly contrary to the interest of the speaker will pass muster. (As noted in II.3, the suspicion may even extend to oneself.) That strategy, too, may invite suspicion. If sincerity is valued as a useful asset and the most effective way of persuading an audience of one's sincerity is to argue directly against one's interest, a second-order suspicion may develop: If somebody argues against his interest it is only to build a reputation for sincerity that he intends to exploit for self-interested purposes in the future. Readers of Machiavelli will recognize the idea.[121] The result may be to create an atmosphere of universal distrust, in which, as I said, one is damned if one does and damned if one doesn't.[122]

I have tried to show how strategic actors may find it in their interest to substitute an impartial argument for a direct statement of their interest. I shall now argue that they may also find it useful to substitute truth claims for credibility claims. Instead of making a *threat* whose efficacy depends on its perceived credibility, they may utter a *warning* that serves the same purpose and avoids the difficulties associated with threats. By "warnings" I mean utterances about events that are not within the control of the actors, and by "threat" utterances about those that are.[123] Threats are statements about what the speaker *will do*, warnings about what *will happen*, independently of any actions taken by the speaker. Thus understood, warnings are factual statements that are subject to the normal rules of truth-oriented communication. Disregarding a warning is more like disbelieving a statement about the past than it is like calling a bluff.

First, let me say a few words about credible threats. If a threat has to be carried out, it is ipso facto a sign that it has not worked. The event that the threat was supposed to prevent has already happened and cannot be undone by executing the threat. At the same time, executing it typically involves some risks or costs to the actor. A

---

121. Thus Montaigne (1991, p. 470) criticizes Guicciardini for seeing base motives everywhere: "It is impossible to conceive that among the innumerable actions on which he makes a judgement there were not at least some produced by means of reason. No corruption can have infected everyone so totally that there was not some man or other who escaped the contagion. That leads me to fear that his own taste was somewhat corrupted: Perhaps he based his estimates of others on himself."
122. For a brilliant discussion of this predicament, see Perelman and Olbrechts-Tyteca (1969) §96.
123. For a further discussion of this distinction, see Elster (in press a, section I.4).

rational actor would not carry out an action that involves no benefits and some costs; if he believes others to be rational, and believes them to believe him to be rational, he will not, therefore, threaten to do so either. Following Schelling, many authors have discussed various ways of overcoming this problem.[124] Here I shall discuss strategies that amount to substituting warnings for the threats, thus making the issue one of truth rather than credibility.

The idea can be illustrated by wage negotiations. Sometimes, a union leader will say things like, "If you don't give us what we ask for, I won't be able to stop my members from going on strike," or, "If you don't give us what we ask for, the morale of my members will fall and productivity will suffer." Formally, these are warnings rather than threats. Needless to say, managers will not always take them at face value. They may suspect that the effects cited in the warnings are actually within the control of the union boss. At the same time they can't be sure that the leader doesn't have access to information that they lack. Perhaps his members are in fact as recalcitrant as he makes them out to be. Perhaps, indeed, he has made sure, before coming to the bargaining table, that they are so heated up that he won't be able to stop them, turning them in effect into a doomsday machine. Note the difference between the latter strategy and other prebargaining ploys. Often, unions invest in the *credibility of threats*, for example by building up a strike fund. Alternatively, they can invest in the *truth of warnings*, for example by irreversibly stirring up discontent among the members.[125]

Let me give some examples from two constituent assemblies, those of Philadelphia in 1787 and Paris in 1789 through 1791. In the debate over the representation of the states in the upper house at the Federal Convention, delegates from both the large and the small states appealed to the fairness of the proposal they favored, as we have seen. In addition, they played deliberately on the ambiguity between threats and warnings. On June 30, Bedford asserted that "[t]he Large States dare not dissolve the confederation. If they do the small ones will find some foreign ally of more honor and good faith, who will take them by the hand and do them justice. He did not mean by this to intimidate or alarm. It was a natural consequence; which ought to be avoided by enlarging the federal powers not annihilating the

---

124. Dixit and Nalebuff (1991) is a recent survey.
125. Schelling (1960), p. 27.

federal system."[126] The statement is most plausibly seen as a threat, with the reference to the "natural consequence" serving to underline its credibility.

On July 5, Gouverneur Morris counterattacked:

Let us suppose that the larger States shall agree; and the smaller refuse: and let us trace the consequences. The opponents of the system in the smaller States will no doubt make a party and noise for some time, but the ties of interest, of kindred & common habits which connect them with the other States will be too strong to be easily broken. In N.Jersey particularly he was sure a great many would follow the sentiments of Pena. & N.York. This Country must be united. If persuasion does not unite it, the sword will. He begged that this consideration might have its due weight. The scenes of horror attending civil commotion can not be described, and the conclusion of them will be worse than the term of their continuance. The stronger party will then make traytors of the weaker; and the Gallows and Halter will finish the work of the sword. How far foreign powers would be ready to take part in the confusion he would not say. Threats that they will be invited have it seems been thrown out.[127]

Here Morris states that he had understood Bedford's statement as a threat. His own reference to the sword and the gallows is more ambiguous. It can be taken as a threat or as a mere warning. Some of the other delegates undoubtedly took it as a threat, as indicated by the following retreat by Williamson on his behalf: He "did not conceive that Mr. Govr. Morris meant that the sword ought to be drawn agst. the smaller states. He only pointed out the probable consequences of anarchy in the U.S."[128] In other words, Williamson sought to make it clear that Morris had been uttering a warning, not making a threat.

On the same day, Bedford also retreated, by making it clear that

he did not mean that the small States would court the aid & interposition of foreign powers. He meant that they would not consider the federal compact as dissolved until it should be so by the acts of the large States. In this case the consequence of the breach of faith on their part, and the readiness of the small States to fulfill their engagements, would be that foreign nations having demands on this Country would find it in their interest to take the small States by the hand, in order to do themselves justice.[129]

126. Farrand (1966), vol. 1, p. 492.
127. *Ibid.*, p. 530.
128. *Ibid.*, p. 532.
129. *Ibid.*, p. 531.

Again, what was initially made (or understood) as a threat is restated as a warning. I shall shortly discuss the reasons speakers may have for making such restatements. First, however, I want to look at an example from the French context. When considering it one should keep in mind that whereas the delegates to the Federal Convention deliberated in perfect isolation from the larger society around them, the Assemblée Constituante was suspended between the King's troops at Versailles and the crowds in Paris. Both extraparliamentary actors came to play an important role in the proceedings of the assembly, as the basis for threats or warnings. The simultaneous presence of soldiers and crowds is in fact a frequent feature of constituent assemblies, as illustrated also by the Paris assembly of 1848, the Frankfurt Assembly of 1848 and 1849, the Weimar assembly of 1919, and the quasiconstitutional Round Table Talks in Eastern Europe in 1989.

In the first days of July 1789 the King reinforced the presence of troops near Versailles. The implied threat to the assembly escaped nobody. In his replies to the King's challenge, Mirabeau played on the threat–warning ambiguity. In his first speech on the subject he limited himself to a warning: "How could the people not become upset when their only remaining hope [the Assembly] is in danger?"[130] In his second speech he became more specific. The troops "may forget that they are soldiers by contract, and remember that by nature they are men."[131] The implied threat to help nature along by stirring fermentation among the troops is clear. Furthermore, the assembly cannot even trust itself to act responsibly: "Passionate movements are contagious: We are only men (*nous ne sommes que des hommes*); our fear of appearing to be weak may carry us too far in the opposite direction."[132] In this argument, Mirabeau presents himself and his fellow delegates as subject to a psychic causality not within their own control. If the King provokes them, they might respond irrationally and violently. Formally, this is a mere warning. In reality, nobody could ignore that it could be a threat.[133]

There are two reasons why a speaker might find it to his advantage to substitute warnings for threats. First, as emphasized above, he does not have to worry so much about credibility. Even though

---

130. *Archives Parlementaires*, vol. 8, p. 209.
131. *Ibid.*, p. 213.
132. *Ibid.*
133. In some cases, however, predictions about one's own future behavior may be uttered as genuine warnings. See Frank (1988, p. 55 and *passim*).

his adversaries know that the events referred to in the warning may in fact be within his control, they must also take account of the possibility that he may have access to relevant private information. It is not unreasonable to think that the union leader knows more than the management about the state of mind of his members. Similarly, Mirabeau might be expected to know more than the King about the psychology of the delegates to the Assembly.

Second, warnings belong to the realm of argument and hence enable the speaker to avoid the opprobrium associated with naked appeals to bargaining power. As observed by Perelman and Olbrechts-Tyteca, "Too explicit use of some arguments is contrary to good taste, dangerous or even prohibited. There are arguments that can be referred to only by insinuation or allusion, or by a threat to use them. *The threat may actually be one of these forbidden arguments.*"[134] At the Federal Convention, the restatement of threats as warnings allowed the proceedings to stay within the rules of the debating game. Similarly, Mirabeau could warn the King about his soldiers without risking the accusations of seditious talk that would have been made had he threatened to stir up unrest among the troops.[135]

MISREPRESENTATION OF INTEREST AS PASSION

The strategic misrepresentation of interest as passion can occur when a speaker wants to plead diminished responsibility for some past action; when the agent can gain a strategic advantage if others believe that he is blind or deaf to consequences; when he wants to deflect suspicions of being motivated by gain; and when he believes that others are more likely to be persuaded by a passionate appeal than by an appeal to reason. In some cases the speaker may try to induce (genuine) passion in himself rather than fake it.[136] This is a case of conscious transmutation, but with the particular feature that it has to

134. Perelman and Olbrechts-Tyteca (1969), p. 487; my italics.
135. We may note at this point the possibility of self-fulfilling warnings, which are, in this respect, intermediate between ordinary warnings and threats. By publicly telling the King that his troops were unreliable, Mirabeau may in fact have ensured the truth of that statement. For another example, see O'Brien (1992, p. 125).
136. Thus upon the announcement on July 2, 1938, of a British emissary, "Hitler started up and said: '*Gott im Himmel!* Don't let him in yet. I'm still in a good humor.' He then proceeded, in front of his staff, to work himself up until his face darkened, he was breathing heavily, and his eyes were glazed" (Bullock 1991, p. 571).

be presented as spontaneous rather than whipped-up on command. It is, to that extent, a form of misrepresentation. I now discuss these cases in turn.

In some legal systems "crimes passionnels" – such as killing's one spouse and the spouse's lover when catching them in flagranti – incur mild sentences and may even bring acquittal. In all legal systems there are similar distinctions between premeditated violence "in cold blood" and violence undertaken in the heat of the moment.[137] There is, therefore, an obvious incentive to present one's crime as rooted in passion, and a correlative incentive for the prosecution to show that it was in fact rooted in interest. A passage from Stephen Wilson's book on Corsican feuding illustrates both phenomena: "The man from Silvareccio who killed his wife in 1832 when he found her in the house with another man was sentenced only to a fine of ten francs, an indication that his action was believed to have been justified. Giudici Giudicelli, a miller from Porta, was convicted in 1852 of killing his wife in similar circumstances and was sentenced to five years' imprisonment, still a fairly lenient sentence. He claimed to have found her *in flagrante delicto*, but there was a previous history of disputes and separations of which the court took account."[138]

This misrepresentation may be purely verbal and ex post or also affect behavior ex ante. If a man knows he will be acquitted if the court believes his killing of his adulterous wife to have occurred in a fit of passion, he has an incentive to stage the crime before a public who can swear to the incendiary nature of the situation. If he knows, however, that a successful plea on grounds of passion will only get him off with (say) five rather than twenty years in prison, his main incentive is to avoid being caught altogether. If he is apprehended in spite of having taken precautions and then claims to have acted out of passion, these very precautions will, if detected, count against the claim. The misrepresentation is less likely to work if it does not satisfy the consistency constraint.

A threat is noncredible when it would not be in the interest of the speaker to carry it out. Because it is known that passion can induce people to act against their interest, the speaker has an interest in presenting himself as moved by passion rather than by interest. Others may then be deterred by the threat because they believe he

137. Sass (1983) gives a good psychological and legal analysis.
138. Wilson (1988), p. 121; see also Sass (1983, pp. 567–9) for thirteen reasons why a claim to have committed a crime out of passion might lack credibility.

would actually carry it out. Conversely, a speaker may find it in his interest to appear as moved by passion in order to make others believe that he will not be deterred by a threat that would be effective when directed against a person moved by rational self-interest.[139] "A seeming madman, therefore, may be a superior strategist, because his threats are more readily believed. Could Colonel Ghadafi and Ayatollah Khomeini have understood this principle better than the cool, rational leaders of Western nations trying to deal with them?"[140] Hitler, apparently, was a master of this form of deception.[141] Richard Nixon deliberately cultivated an appearance of erratic behavior, in order to persuade the Soviets that he could not be counted on to react rationally to a first strike.[142] He even, paradoxically, boasted of the fact.[143]

The consistency and imperfection constraints impose sharp limits on this strategy, however. To convey a believable impression that one is irrational, occasional grandstanding is not enough. "Hypocrisy is the most difficult vice to pursue. It cannot be practiced at spare moments: It's a full time occupation."[144] One has to engage in seemingly emotional behavior on numerous occasions, important as well as unimportant, to create the impression that the irrationality is a character trait rather than a mask. Also, one has to show in practice that one is willing to suffer considerable losses because of one's emotional disposition. Someone who gets out of control when and only when he would gain *on that occasion* by having others believe

139. Schelling (1960, p. 143) mentions both these cases, with the difference that he emphasizes conscious transmutation rather than misrepresentation.
140. Dixit and Nalebuff (1991), pp. 165–6.
141. "Hitler never said anything, even when he appeared to have lost his temper, without calculating the effect both on those present and on those to whom they would recount it" (Bullock 1991, p. 571).
142. Isaacson (1993), pp. 163–4, 181–2.
143. *Ibid.*, p. 294. It is probably a mere accident that this episode occurred just one year before the publication in *The New Yorker* of a drawing that shows a disgruntled-looking man selling pencils on the street with a whip in his hand and a sign around his neck saying, "Irrational." Frank (1988, p. 55) reproduces this drawing and adds that "the sign round the man's neck is not the only, or even a very good signal that he is not fully rational. On the contrary, that he seems to have realized the sign might serve his purposes can only detract from its ability to do so." Isaacson, by contrast, characterizes Nixon's boasting of his irrationality as "disarming and alarming." My hunch is that Isaacson is right: As a rational man would understand that boasting of his irrationality is self-defeating, doing so is actually self-confirming. The argument could of course, be taken one step further and so on ad infinitum, leaving the issue essentially indeterminate, which may have been enough for Nixon's purpose.
144. The phrase is from Somerset-Maugham, but I have been unable to locate it.

him irrational will find it difficult to build a reputation for being dangerously emotional. In particular, he will not be credible if he backs off in encounters with other emotional persons. In the language of game-theoretic biology, such behavior will reveal him to be a "Bluffer" rather than a "Hawk."[145] Again, there is a trade-off: Complete credibility is not desirable if the losses you have to incur in order to be seen as emotional are greater than the gains you can expect from being seen as emotional.[146]

In classical Athens, there were "sycophants" or professional accusers who initiated public lawsuits (*graphe*) for private gain, either because they could hope for a share of the fine or because they hoped that even innocent plaintiffs would settle in private rather than taking the risk of litigation. As sycophants were regarded with deep suspicion, it was important for them to misrepresent their motivation. As explained by Mogens Herman Hansen, it was more effective to disguise their interest as passion than to try to pass themselves off as motivated by impartial motives: "When a citizen appeared in court as a public accuser his first anxiety was . . . to dispel any suspicion that he was a sycophant. He could stress his public-spiritedness, but that tends to make ordinary folk even more suspicious, and usually there was a much more cogent argument to deploy: He could declare that the accused was his personal enemy and that he was using his citizen right to prosecute for revenge and not for gain."[147]

In the cases canvassed above the agent who simulates passion counts on the rationality of his interlocutors. A different "strategic use of passion" is to simulate emotion in order to generate and manipulate emotions in others, perhaps to the point of making them disregard their interest. I do not have in mind cases (important though they may be) in which A fakes anger at B in order to induce fear of A in B. Rather, I am thinking of cases in which A fakes being angry with C in order to make B angry with C. According to Aristotle, this rhetorical strategy can work only when B's interest is not at stake. Appeals to emotion can be effective in legal debates, when pleading before members of a jury who are deciding "other people's affairs," but not in political oratory where "the man who is forming a judgment is making

145. Maynard-Smith (1982), Chapter 9.
146. Thus after the invasion of Cambodia in 1970, "Nixon's 'madman' strategy was backfiring on him: He was coming across as unhinged in the eyes of his own nation. As a result, the Cambodian invasion would turn into the greatest victory for Hanoi since it lost the 1968 Tet offensive" (Isaacson 1993, p. 270).
147. Hansen (1991), p. 195; see also Ober (1989, p. 212) for a similar comment.

a decision about his own vital interests."[148] Now, Aristotle certainly thought people capable of acting against their own interest under the sway of emotions, notably anger.[149] Yet it makes sense to assume that emotions induced by oratory tend to be weaker than those that arise in face-to-face interaction, and thus less capable of overriding interest.

Is a speaker more likely to persuade his audience if he shares the emotion he is trying to communicate, or is faking the emotion more effective? According to Montaigne,

> The orator (says Rhetoric) when acting out his case will be moved by the sound of his own voice and by is own feigned indignation; he will allow himself to be taken in by the emotion he is portraying. By acting out his part in a play he will stamp on himself the essence of true grief and then transmit it to the judges (who are even less involved in the case than he is); it is like those mourners who are rented for funerals and who sell their tears and grief by weight and measure: for even though they only borrow their signs of grief, it is nevertheless certain that by habitually adopting the right countenance they get often carried away and find room inside themselves for real melancholy. (*Essays*, p. 944; see also p. 638)

Along similar lines, Frijda writes that "a speech meant to be inciting may well be more effective if the speaker is indignant: Turns of phrase and tone of voice come naturally in that mood, whereas these have to be constructed with effort when one is cool."[150] As Paul Ekman has shown, it is hard to fake emotions.[151] True, he has also shown that most people find it hard to detect faking in others.[152] Yet I conjecture that imperfectly faked emotions will have less of an emotional impact on others, even when they are unaware of the faking. If Hatfield, Cacioppo, and Rapson are right in their argument that emotional contagion is based on mimicry of the emotional expression of others and feedback from the expressions that are mimicked to the emotions themselves, we would expect this process to be less effective if the expressions are only partly realized.

Yet there is also an argument to be made for the opposite view. When in the grip of genuine passion, a speaker may lose the ability to

---

148. *Rhetoric* 1354^b–1355^a. Analogously, in his analyses of the debates at the Federal Convention Jillson (1988, p. 16) argues that the speakers were swayed by *reason* only when their interest was not at stake.
149. *Nicomachean Ethics* 1202b.
150. Frijda (1986), p. 114.
151. Ekman (1992a); Ekman and Frank (1994).
152. Ekman (1992a), pp. 85–7.

calculate the effect of his words on the audience. In *On Anger*, Seneca makes a general argument that the alleged instrumental benefits of anger are quite spurious, for "when once the mind has been aroused and shaken, it becomes the slave of the disturbing agent."[153] This also applies to oratory:

'The orator,' you say, 'at times does better when he is angry.' Not so, but when he pretends to be angry. For the actor likewise stirs an audience by his declamation not when he is angry, but when he plays well the role of the angry man; consequently before a jury, in the popular assembly, and wherever we have to force our will upon the minds of other people, we must pretend now anger, now fear, now pity, in order that we may inspire others with the same, and often the feigning of an emotion produces an effect which would not be produced by genuine emotion.[154]

Perelman and Olbrechts-Tyteca argue for a similar view:

The great orator, the one with a hold on his listener, seems animated by the very mind of his audience. This is not the case for the ardent enthusiast (*l'homme passionné*) whose sole concern is with what he himself considers important. A speaker of this kind may have an effect on suggestible persons, but generally speaking his speech will strike the audience as unreasonable.... The man swayed by passion argues without taking sufficiently into account the audience he is addressing: carried away by his enthusiasm, he imagines his audience to be susceptible to the same arguments that persuaded him.[155]

If we assume a rigid dichotomy between genuine and faked emotions, each line of argument seems compelling. On the one hand, feigned emotions may fail to produce much of an effect, because the tell-tale bodily expressions that mediate between the emotions of the speaker and those of the audience are absent. On the other hand, genuine emotions in the speaker may produce the wrong effect, because he may be too carried away to monitor the reactions of the audience and adjust his speech accordingly. Thus the phrase by Nietzsche cited by Alan Bullock in his analysis of Hitler's oratory, "Men believe in the truth of all that is seen to be strongly believed in,"[156] cannot be literally true. Bullock himself emphasizes Hitler's "flair for divining

---

153. *On Anger* I.vii.
154. *Ibid.*, II.xviii.
155. Perelman and Olbrechts-Tyteca (1969), p. 24.
156. Bullock (1991), p. 72.

what was hidden in the minds of his audiences,"[157] combined with "the gift he possessed of concealing his exploitation of this power and convincing the audience that the fanaticism he conveyed was the proof of his sincerity."[158] Great orators are those who somehow manage to have it both ways, to enjoy the benefits of sincerity *and* those of misrepresentation. Their emotions belong to what I referred to above as the gray area between transmutation and misrepresentation; they are neither fully genuine nor entirely feigned. Although I cannot offer anything like a conceptual analysis of this phenomenon, I am convinced that it exists.

MISREPRESENTATION OF INTEREST AS INTEREST

Voting as well as bargaining may be represented in the following schematic form. First, the citizens or bargainers express their preferences over certain options. These preferences are used as inputs to a decision-making mechanism, which then renders a judgment as to "what shall be done." In the case of voting, the inputs may be the top-ranked preferences of the citizens with regard to a set of candidates or policies, and the output the selection of one candidate or policy. In the case of bargaining, the inputs may be the von Neumann–Morgenstern utilities of the bargainers associated with the various ways of dividing a sum of money among them, and the outcome may be the choice of one particular division.[159] In both cases, the following problem may arise. Suppose that an agent states his preferences truthfully; other agents state theirs; and as the result an outcome X is produced. The agent may then ask himself whether he could have achieved an outcome that he prefers to X by stating another set of preferences. In that case, he has an incentive to misrepresent his preferences. Equivalently, it is in his (real) interest to *say* that his interest lies elsewhere than it really does. These are not hypothetical or unlikely examples, but pervasive and fundamental features of voting and bargaining procedures.[160] Note that in this case, interest serves all three functions: as input, output, and engine of misrepresentation.

157. *Ibid.*, p. 351.
158. *Ibid.*, p. 146.
159. This "cooperative" model of bargaining is perhaps better thought of as a model of fair arbitration.
160. For voting, see Gibbard (1973). For bargaining, see Crawford and Varian (1979) and Sobel (1981).

In the case of voting, two effects may be at work. On the one hand, there is *the pure effect of strategic voting* that obtains even when the voting is secret. In this case, the person is not really representing anything to others. On the other hand, there is the *presentation effect* that obtains when, first, voting is public so that others can draw inferences about his motivation and, second, he cares about which inferences they draw. Sometimes, these two effects may point in opposite directions. Imagine a Communist voting for a Nazi Chancellor in the Weimar parliament, to prevent a Social Democrat from being elected. Under conditions of publicity, such behavior may earn him a reputation of deviousness and unscrupulosity that he might want to avoid. In other cases, the two effects may reinforce each other. By voting for his second-ranked rather than his top-ranked proposal, a person may both promote his real preferences, by enabling the choice of his second-ranked over his third-ranked proposal, *and* earn a useful reputation for moderation and impartiality.

The latter case has a snag, however. If other people know how his interest ranks the different options *and* are able to figure out that by voting for his second-ranked option he promotes his interest better than by sincere voting, they will not draw the desirable inference about his impartial motivations. They will, on the contrary, assume that he is simply motivated by interest. The imperfection constraint may then induce him to vote for his third-ranked proposal, to prevent the bottom-ranked proposal from being adopted. (I assume that his vote is pivotal in the choice between the second-ranked and the third-ranked proposal.) He has to vote, that is, both against the proposal that, were it adopted, would best realize his interest and against the proposal that, given the expected votes of others, will best realize his interest. He will do so, however, only if the utility gain from a reputation of disinterestedness outweighs the utility difference between the second-ranked and the third-ranked proposal.

MISREPRESENTATION OF PASSION AS REASON

Given the impulsive nature of many emotional reactions, it would seem that an agent thus motivated would be too caught up in the situation to have the detachment of mind required to misrepresent his motivation. Yet there are at least two classes of cases in which this seems to happen quite frequently. In the first place, the agent may explain his *past* emotional behavior as really motivated by reason (or some other motivation). In the second place, he may be subject to a *standing passion* or prejudice that does not interfere with the capacity for strategic misrepresentation. Here, I illustrate the second case by the misrepresentation of passion as reason. Below, I illustrate the first case by indicating how agents may misrepresent their past emotional behavior as motivated *by another emotion* than the one that was actually at work.

The cases I consider turn on the misrepresentation of *prejudice*. Above I mentioned how the literacy test for voting or immigration has served as an impartial pretext for discrimination on ethnic and religious grounds. Another striking example is the policy adopted by Yale College in the 1920s to limit the admission of Jews. Following a recent scandal at Harvard, Yale did not want to use explicit quotas. Instead Yale adopted a policy of geographical diversity, ostensibly as a goal in its own right, but in reality to reduce the number of Jewish students. "Though many individual Jews (concentrated in the northeast region from which Yale received most of its applications) would be affected by this principle, it was not an innately anti-Jewish principle. A geographical policy applied without regard for religion that would help an individual Milwaukee Jew or Duluth Catholic as much as it would hurt a New York atheist or Hoboken Protestant could not appropriately be termed religiously biased."[161] The policy, in other words, satisfied the imperfection constraint, the impartial criterion of geographical diversity serving as a diluted and therefore more acceptable equivalent of ethnicity.

In the United States of the 1990s, racial prejudice can be presented much more simply as an impartially grounded objection to affirmative action. The situation is somewhat similar to the issue of prejudice towards blacks or AIDS patients discussed in V.2. In that case, prejudice allied itself with an outcome-oriented impartial theory emphasizing public health against a rights-based impartial theory emphasizing protection of civil liberties. Here, prejudice allies itself with a conception of impartiality as color-blindness against a veil-of-ignorance conception of impartiality that requires compensation for disadvantages due to color. I am not saying that all advocates of color-blindness are prejudiced, nor can I point to clear cases in which this advocacy is a mere pretext. Yet I believe that those who hold the color-blind view on genuinely impartial grounds would agree that they often find themselves with strange bedfellows; in fact, if they

161. Oren (1985), p. 198; see also Conley (1995).

didn't I would suspect their impartiality. Glenn Loury, a black conservative critic of affirmative action, certainly agrees when he writes that "selling these positions within the black community is made infinitely more difficult when my black critics are able to say: 'But your argument plays into the hands of those who are looking for an excuse to abandon the black poor'; and I am unable to contradict them credibly."[162] I mentioned earlier that reason and interest may form coalitions *for* affirmative action; similarly, reason and passion may form coalitions *against* it.

The recent constitutions in Central and Eastern Europe contain impartially worded clauses whose origin is unambiguously found in ethnic prejudice. All the constitutions in the region include clauses that ban (negative) discrimination on grounds of race, nationality, ethnicity, sex, religion, and many similar grounds. Only three constitutions – those of Bulgaria, Romania, and Slovakia – also contain explicit bans on reverse or positive discrimination, that is, affirmative action. These are also the countries in the region with the largest minority populations[163] and the strongest history of ethnic conflict. In the Romanian document, the ban only covers reverse discrimination on ethnic grounds. Bulgaria and Slovakia did at least try to satisfy the imperfection constraint by extending the ban on positive discrimination to *all* the criteria that are enumerated in the bans on negative discrimination. Yet in these countries, too, the clauses are due to the prejudices of an ethnic majority in the constituent assembly against various minorities. The biases against ethnic minorities would have been even stronger had not delegates from the Council of Europe intervened in the constitution-making processes. The first draft of the Romanian constitution, for instance, contained an impartially worded ban on ethnically based parties that was directly aimed at the large Hungarian minority.

MISREPRESENTATION OF PASSION AS PASSION

Certain emotions are more objectionable than others. Because different emotions may give rise to similar behaviors, people may have an incentive to substitute a more acceptable emotion for the one that

162. Loury (1995), p. 21.
163. The percentages are: Albania, 2%; Bulgaria, 15%; the Czech Republic, 5.5% (not counting Moravians); Hungary, 8.6%; Poland, 2%; Romania, 10.5%; Slovakia, 14.4%. Source: Bugajski (1994).

actually moved them to act. I illustrate this idea by some examples from politics in ancient Greece, where the unavowability of envy and *hybris* induced commoners as well as kings to present actions thus motivated in a different light.

In "On Envy and Hate," Plutarch writes that "men deny that they envy ... and if you show that they do, they allege any number of excuses and say they are angry with the fellow or hate him, cloaking and concealing their envy with whatever other name occurs to them for their passion." In classical Athens, this tendency was revealed by the practice of denouncing others, who claimed to act for the sake of revenge, as being really motivated by envy. In David Cohen's summary, the orator Lysias "argues that his opponent will falsely claim that he brings the prosecution out of enmity so as to get revenge, but in fact it is only out of envy because the speaker is a better citizen. ... The desire for revenge apparently would be seen by the judges as a legitimate reason for prosecuting, so the speaker must deny that this is the case. Meanspirited envy, on the other hand, reflects badly upon the accuser's character and indicates that the suit is unreliable."[164]

In ancient Greece, as we saw in III.4, *hybris* was a punishable offense and, moreover, a strongly disapproved form of behavior. Against accusations of *hybris* therefore, it was expedient to represent one's behavior as motivated by a more acceptable urge. In the *Politics*, Aristotle tells a story about a tyrant, Archelaus, who was killed (among other reasons) because one of his boyfriends decided that their association had been based on "*hybris* not on erotic desire" (1311^b20). Aristotle then offers the advice to tyrants who want to stay in power, that in their acquaintances with youth, they should appear to be acting from desire rather than from *hybris*.[165] In other contexts, those accused of *hybris* represent their behavior as motivated by revenge. Although there may have been truth in their allegations of having been wronged, they might still be guilty of *hybris* if the revenge was disproportionate to the offense.[166]

One could also try to deflect accusations of *hybris* by arguing that one had been drunk, or even get drunk so as to be able to insult an enemy without laying oneself open to the charge of *hybris*. Hoping that readers will find it as fascinating as I do, I quote an extended discussion of the issue from N. R. E. Fisher's treatise:

164. D. Cohen (1995), pp. 82–3.
165. 1315^a23; see also D. Cohen (1995), p. 145 and Fisher (1992), p. 30–1.
166. Fisher (1992), p. 509 (summarizing analyses from earlier chapters, notably Chapter XI).

One "ideal type" of *hybris* is an act like that of Meidias in the theatre, where no excuse of drink, sudden onrush of hatred or anger, or pressure from intense competition or conflict could mitigate the outrage, or suggest that he did not reveal a cold, premeditated, intention to insult Demosthenes, for the pleasure it would give him to display his ability to so act. But other cases are imaginable, where some of these mitigating elements are present, yet the act is still *hybris*; and the [speech against] Meidias in fact offers a useful selection of possibilities. ... First, Euaion killed Boiotos when angered and dishonoured by the blow from Boiotos and by the *hybris* which he felt accompanied it; but Boiotos was drunk and they were at a dinner party (21.7 1 ff.). The same possibility was felt by the jury to be relevant to the whipping by Ctesicles of his enemy at the festival procession (21.180); but the feeling was that he had acted 'in *hybris* and not in wine'; the same phrase is used of Meidias in contrast with Boiotos; and presumably Boiotos therefore could be said in some way to have acted "in wine." But in fact each case is different, and that of Boiotos less serious than either that of Ctesicles and that of Meidias. Boiotos and Ctesicles were both drunk, and both assaulted and insulted another. But one can distinguish between cases of drunken assault: some may be cases where the drink and the occasion might have induced any ordinary man to engage in fighting and insults; cases where the drink greatly exacerbated an existing tendency to insult others; and cases where the drink was little more than a cover to hide a deliberate decision to insult an enemy. Ctesicles was held by the jury to fall into the last category, and *hybris* was the main cause of his act, and the drink contributed little or nothing. Boiotos may have been thought by Euaion to fall into that category but the neutral observers would place him in the second, or even the first.[167]

In modern legal systems, passion can only be an extenuating circumstance, never (to my knowledge) an aggravating one. For the Greeks, it could be either. Because revenge was attenuating, it could be used as an excuse. Because *hybris* was aggravating, it had to be excused away, by appeals to revenge, sexual desire, or drunkenness.

MISREPRESENTATION OF PASSION AS INTEREST

In some cases, the more acceptable misrepresentation of an emotion may be interest rather than another emotion. An example that comes to mind is the misrepresentation of fear as prudence. In many societies fear in the face of danger is seen as dishonorable. One can

167. Fisher (1992), pp. 57–8.

imagine two reasons why this might be so. First, to the extent that we are dealing with genuine fear rather than the kind of fear that is merely a complex of beliefs and desires (III.4), it is dishonorable because it shows a lack of self-control. Second, either variety of fear might be subject to social disapproval because it testifies to an excessive concern with mere survival and a corresponding lack of concern with honor. In cultures of honor, an agent has nothing to gain from misrepresenting his fear as a form of prudential behavior. On the contrary, such behavior is interpreted as a sign of cowardice. In other societies, however, an agent might be motivated to present an image of himself as someone who flees danger out of rational prudence rather than out of panic.

Prejudice, too, may be dressed up as interest. Thus when prejudiced members of a racial or ethnic majority argue against affirmative action favoring minorities, they may take the low road of interest rather than the high road of reason. In societies that are both permeated by interest groups and dominated by egalitarian ideologies, there certainly attaches less opprobrium to interest than to prejudice. Being for oneself is more legitimate than being against others. Moreover, by defending their views in terms of interest rather than reason, groups can avoid the costs that arise from the consistency and imperfection constraints. In ethnic conflicts, this mechanism may coexist with that described in the previous paragraph. An ethnic group may misrepresent behavior that is really caused by fear as grounded in rational prudence, while also claiming that the conflict is generated by a conflict of interest over scarce territorial resources rather than by hatred or prejudice.

MISREPRESENTATION OF REASON AS INTEREST

A person who is genuinely motivated by impartial concerns may find it expedient to argue in terms of self-interest, for one of two reasons. In the first place, he may try to persuade an interlocutor to adopt his proposal by arguing that it is in the interest of both. In the second place, he may appeal to interest if the society in question penalizes appeals to reason. I discuss these cases in turn.

Several writers have argued that a just social order is that which would be chosen by rational, self-interested individuals behind a hypothetical veil of ignorance. This basic idea can be spelled out in different ways, to support utilitarian theories no less than the theories of John Rawls and Ronald Dworkin.[168] In none of these versions does it amount to a claim that justice can be deduced from rationality alone. The veil of ignorance, in these theories, is itself derived from prior normative conceptions of what features of individuals count as "morally arbitrary." If we consider actual rather than hypothetical veils, however, mere self-interest may be sufficient to generate consensus on basic constitutional issues, if the relevant outcomes lies so far into the future that nobody can tell how they and their descendants will be affected. This is the structure of a veil-of-ignorance argument that was used repeatedly at the Federal Convention, most strikingly in an intervention by George Mason:

We ought to attend to the rights of every class of people. He had often wondered at the indifference of the superior classes of society to this dictate of humanity & policy, considering that however affluent their circumstances, or elevated their situations, might be, the course of a few years, not only might but certainly would distribute their posteriority through the lowest classes of Society. Every selfish motive therefore, every family attachment, ought to recommend such as system of policy as would provide no less carefully for the rights and happiness of the lowest than of the highest orders of Citizens.[169]

Veil-of-ignorance arguments were also used in other contexts. Thus Gouverneur Morris argued that "State attachments, and State importance have been the bane of this Country. We cannot annihilate; but we may perhaps take out the teeth of the serpents. He wished our ideas to be enlarged to the true interest of man, instead of being circumscribed within the narrow compass of a particular spot. And after all how little can be the motive yielded by selfishness for such a policy. Who can say whether he himself, much less whether his children, will the next year be an inhabitant of this or that state."[170] This argument refers to the thirteen states then in existence, but it was also used to cover the accession of future states. Against Gerry's proposal to "limit the number of new states to be admitted into the Union, in such a manner, that they should never be able to outnumber the Atlantic States,"[171] Sherman replied that

168. Rawls (1971) and utilitarians such as Harsanyi (1955) have in common the assumption of a very thick veil of ignorance, but they differ with respect to the principles of choice they impute to rational individuals behind the veil. Dworkin (1981) differs from either in stipulating a thinner veil.
169. Farrand (1966), vol. 1, p. 49.
170. *Ibid.*, p. 530.
171. *Ibid.*, vol. 2, p. 3.

"we are providing for our posterity, for our children and grand children, who would be as likely to be citizens of new Western states as of the old states."[172] These arguments should not be confused with genuine appeals to impartiality, as in Mason's argument for granting new states equal status: "Strong objections have been drawn from the danger to the Atlantic interests from new Western states. Ought we to sacrifice what we know to be right in itself, lest it should prove favorable to states which are not yet in existence. If the Western states are to be admitted into the Union as they arise, they must, he would repeat, be treated as equals, and subjected to no degrading discrimination."[173]

I have mentioned that a speaker who is motivated only by interest might, *without hiding his real motives*, offer impartial arguments for his proposal in the hope of persuading others. Conversely, a speaker might offer interest-based arguments that mimic impartiality without trying to hide that he is in fact genuinely motivated by impartial concerns. Alternatively, he might misrepresent himself as having the same motive as the one he appeals to in others. That course of action has the advantage that he does not present himself as superior to his interlocutors and hence does not risk offending their *amour-propre*. Although it violates the Habermasian norm of truthfulness or sincerity, that norm may not hold outside the ideal speech situation in which *all* speakers are motivated by the ideal of impartiality.

An impartially minded speaker may also choose to hide his motivation in order to avoid the disapproval of others rather than their resentment. Although most societies have norms that enjoin the citizens to take an interest in public affairs, not all do; some, in fact, have norms *against* public-spirited behavior. In Edward Banfield's study of the Italian village Montegrano (not its real name), he found that he could make sense of the observed behavior by assuming that "the Montegranesi act as if they were following this rule: Maximize the material, short-run advantage of the nuclear family; assume that all others will do likewise."[174] One implication he draws from this assumption, and which he finds confirmed by observation, is that "for a private citizen to take a serious interest in a public problem will be regarded as abnormal and even improper," and "the claim of

172. *Ibid.*
173. *Ibid.*, vol. 1, p. 578.
174. Banfield (1958), p. 83.

any person or institution to be inspired for zeal for public rather than private advantage will be regarded as fraud."[175] Banfield also cites from an earlier work on Calabria: "Speaking of all below the upper classes, I should say that disinterested benevolence is apt to surpass their comprehension, a goodnatured person being regarded as weak in the head. Has this man, then, no family, that he should benefit strangers?"[176] Although Banfield's work has been severely criticized, this particular set of claims ring true enough.

In this society, impartial motivations cannot be stated publicly. A person thus motivated would, to be effective, have to misrepresent himself as animated by the same private, familial concerns as everybody else. Banfield gives no examples of such behavior from Montegrano, but casual evidence leads me to believe it must be quite common. In "cultures of suspicion," a man who professes impartial motives will not be trusted. Others will suspect that he is hiding a private and possibly sinister motive and refuse to deal with him. Frank confessions of interest, by contrast, can be taken at face value.

MISREPRESENTATION OF REASON AS REASON

It may happen, in a given society, that *specific* impartial arguments – rather than, as in Montegrano, impartial arguments in general – become suspect. In that case, impartially minded speakers may have an incentive to substitute another impartial argument for the one that has fallen into disrespect. There are two possibilities, depending on whether the speakers do or do not believe in the substitute argument. I shall discuss these two cases in turn.

To illustrate the first case, I can report from a recent public meeting in New York City at which I heard a black law professor discuss affirmative action policies with considerable anguish. Although he was clearly in favor of such policies, on grounds of fairness, he also reported that in the current political climate, explicit advocacy of affirmative action generated so much "toxicity" that he would make this argument only if all else failed. For the time being he found it more expedient, he said, to make a substitute impartial argument in terms of support for the economically and culturally disadvantaged more

175. *Ibid.*, pp. 85, 95.
176. Douglas (1915), p. 124; cited in Banfield (1958), p. 110.

generally. From what he said I inferred that he also believed in the justice of this policy. Although he obviously thought that members of racial and ethnic minorities had *stronger* claims than disadvantaged members of the majority, he admitted that the latter, too, had some claims on society.

I illustrate the second case with a debate from October and November 1789 in the French Assemblée Constituante. At that early stage of the revolution, the delegates had not yet adopted the ruthlessly consequentialist attitude that came to dominate them in later stages, memorably enshrined in the Comité du Salut Public. It was far from being generally accepted that established rights could be overridden for the sake of the common good; in fact, any such argument was sure to meet with disapproval. Utilitarian or efficiency-oriented framers, therefore, were constrained to frame their arguments in terms of rights. This is what happened in the debates in the Assemblée Constituante over the confiscation of Church property.

In their attempts to justify the confiscation of the Church goods, both the opportunistic Mirabeau and the hypocritical Talleyrand argued that these goods in reality belonged to the nation, instead of simply saying that the acute financial crisis made this measure necessary. The argument, unbelievably bad it was, went as follows.[177] If the Church had not, on the basis of its income and property, provided religious services and assistance to the poor, the State would have had to do so. Therefore, the State is the real owner of that property and no rights would be violated by turning it over to the State. The best reply to this specious argument came from Clermont-Tonnerre, based on a deep and modern understanding of the rights of corporate actors.[178] But we can also follow Camus and proceed by analogy.[179] A father has the obligation to provide a dowry for his daughter. Assume that a friend or a relative is willing to provide it instead, thereby discharging the father of his obligation. Should we imply that he thereby becomes the owner of the dowry offered to his daughter? Although I find it hard to believe that anyone in the assembly believed that those who made the rights-based arguments for confiscation believed in what they were saying, the proposal was adopted.

---

177. For the most explicit statements, see *Archives Parlementaires*, vol. 9, pp. 639 ff., 649 ff.
178. *Ibid.*, p. 496.
179. *Ibid.*, p. 416.

MOTIVATIONS, CONSTRAINTS, COSTS, AND CONSEQUENCES

The reasons for disavowing a certain motivation may be intrinsic or extrinsic. On the one hand, if the motive was known it might induce disgust and contempt in others that in turn would induce feelings of shame in oneself. The disguise of fear as prudence, or of envy as anger, illustrates this case. On the other hand, public knowledge of one's motivation might be counterproductive in terms of that motivation itself. The disguise of interest as reason or passion, of passion as reason, or of reason as interest illustrates this case.

In all cases, the misrepresentation is subject to the consistency and imperfection constraints. Both constraints impose costs, in the sense of forcing us to act or argue against our interest. The consistency constraint also imposes the purely mental costs involved in keeping track of one's lies. Montaigne wrote, "My wit is not supple enough to dodge a sudden question and to escape down some sideroad, nor to pretend that something is true. My memory is not good enough to remember that pretence nor reliable enough to maintain it: so I act the brave out of weakness. I therefore entrust myself to simplicity, always saying what I think."[180]

Montaigne's scenario is not the only one. Often, the pressure for misrepresentation and the penalties for speaking one's mind are strong enough to make people willing to bear the costs of dissembling. For many, this is unambiguously undesirable. Timur Kuran and Glenn Loury, for instance, argue that misrepresentation or preference falsification has a divisive and polarizing effect on society. Loury is particularly explicit on this count:

In economics, Gresham's law holds that when two types of currency circulate and one is intrinsically more valuable (say, gold instead of silver, despite an equivalent face value) people hoard the good money and make purchases with the bad. Soon only the bad money remains in circulation. Similarly, people with extreme views can drive moderates, who want to avoid the reputational devaluation of being mistaken as zealots, out of a conversation. In effect, the moderates "hoard" their opinions; hence, the public discourse on some issues (perhaps abortion, for example) can be more polarized than is the actual distribution of public opinion.[181]

180. Montaigne (1991), p. 737.
181. Loury (1995), p. 154; see also Kuran (1995), p. 56.

The Kuran-Loury analysis is not fully comparable with mine. Their concern is with the pressure to argue for substantive *policies* (e.g., affirmative action or legal abortions) that one does not really support. My concern is with the pressure to present one's genuinely preferred policy as grounded in *motivations* that one does not really hold. Yet as I remarked at the end of V.1, the latter pressure may also induce a shift in the policy itself, because of the consistency and imperfection constraints. I believe that these induced policy shifts are more likely to be benign and desirable than the ones discussed by Kuran and Loury. The pressure to present oneself as motivated by impartial concerns rather than interest can force the strong to pull their punches. To promote the public good, a system of arguing in public may be preferable to bargaining in private.

To be sure, one may think of exceptions to this claim. If the initial endowments of two bargainers, although unequal, have a clean pedigree, there is nothing objectionable in an unequal outcome of bargaining. Even if the result of bargaining is exploitation, in the technical Marxist sense, it need not be unjust.[182] It follows that if the better-endowed are forced by the public setting to adopt an impartial argument, they may get less than their fair share. Also, arguing in public may be severely inefficient, if both parties to a debate appeal to principles so as to make it more difficult for themselves to back down, or if the need to please the public forces them into a process of overbidding.

I believe, however, that in most actual cases greater initial endowments are due to luck or unfair exploitation rather than to hard work, saving, or risk-taking. Also, bargaining has inefficiencies of its own, due to misrepresentation of preferences, strategic precommitment, and other mechanisms.[183] If we take account of equity effects as well as efficiency effects, arguing in public is probably a superior form of collective decision making than bargaining in private. Needless to say, this is not a statement for which proof can be offered. It is based on a rough overall assessment of historical trends, not on quantifiable analysis. To the extent that it is true, the *civilizing force of hypocrisy* creates the opposite of Gresham's effect, with the good motives driving out the bad.

---

182. Roemer (1985b).
183. For a survey, see Elster (1989b), pp. 94–6.

Coda

As will by now be obvious to the reader, the present book is not organized as a systematic treatise. The individual chapters could, to some extent, stand on their own. At the same time, the numerous cross-references across chapters do make for greater coherence than a mere collection of essays. I now try to pull these cross-references together, by singling out for separate discussion a number of themes that have been recurrent strands throughout the book. I shall also go beyond mere summing up, indicating where more work might be needed or where emphasis might most usefully be placed.

WHY EMOTIONS MATTER

Most simply, emotions matter because if we did not have them nothing else would matter. Creatures without emotion would have no reason for living nor, for that matter, for committing suicide. Emotions are the stuff of life.

Subjectively, emotions matter because we feel them so strongly, and because they can be intensely pleasant as well as intensely unpleasant. Because of these properties, emotions can have a compelling urgency that is lacking in most other aspects of human life. To be sure, the euphoria or dysphoria induced by cocaine or abstention from it, and the aversiveness of intense thirst or pain, are as overwhelmingly urgent as any emotional experience can be. Yet these visceral experiences are not to the same degree part of the fabric of social life. Emotions are the most important bond or glue that links us to others. Even hatred is a bond, in the minimal sense that it can make another person an intensely important part of one's own life. From the point of view of interest, other people are essentially fungible. In an emotional perspective, they are not.

Objectively, emotions matter because many forms of human behavior would be unintelligible if we did not see them through the prism of emotion. The recent civil wars in the former Yugoslavia or in Africa may to some extent be explained in terms of rational preemption, but that is a very incomplete explanation and a very impoverished account. To fully explain the mass slaughters we must take account of emotions of fear, anger, contempt, hatred, and resentment. The key to recent Albanian politics is that Albanians are furiously *angry* with the pyramid schemes that made each of them on average lose about four hundred dollars – an anger compounded by disappointment and general resentment. When people kill themselves out of shame, it is not because they have rationally reached the conclusion that the discounted present value of life is negative. Being in the horribly painful state of shame that blots out all other considerations, they reach for the only solution that will give them peace.

HOW DO WE KNOW WHAT WE KNOW ABOUT THE EMOTIONS?

Human emotions can be very subtle and powerful phenomena. Because of their subtlety, there are limits to what we can learn from studies of animal behavior. Animals are by and large incapable of forming the complex beliefs that play a large part in many human emotions. Because of the power of many emotions, there are limits to what we can learn from studies of human behavior under controlled conditions. Inducing strong emotions of love, shame, and hatred in the laboratory would not only be blatantly unethical but unfeasible. And there is no presumption that what we can learn from studying the milder forms of these emotions – liking, embarrassment, or disliking – will generalize to the more urgent or virulent forms.

Yet the glass can be viewed as half full as well as half empty. There are emotions that humans share with other animals, and that can fruitfully be studied with animal experiments. The neurobiology of fear, for instance, has now been unraveled with results that may require a rethinking of the psychoanalytic theory of suppressed trauma. More generally, physiological studies have taught us a great deal about the mechanisms of physiological arousal that are a central aspect of the emotions. Laboratory experiments with human subjects have enabled psychologists to purify and test hypotheses that can then be confronted with more unwieldy historical and anthropological data. Once controlled studies have isolated a given mechanism, we may be able to identify it in other contexts as well.

This being said, I believe the most important sources for our understanding of the emotions lie outside the laboratory: in history, anthropology, fiction, and philosophy. Even casual observation, newspaper readings, and introspection can be crucial for exploring the mechanisms of emotional life. Only in these wider contexts can we observe emotions in the wild, as it were – with their raw motivating power, embedded in complex social networks. Although there is some interaction between psychologists and anthropologists, there should be much more of it. And the virtually nonexistent field of historical psychology ought to become a cornerstone of the social sciences.

EMOTIONS AND THE ARTS

Novels and plays may be invaluable sources for the understanding of human emotions, but this is not the only way in which the arts are relevant for the study of emotion. The experience of a work of art may trigger emotional experiences in the reader, viewer, or listener. The work may generate emotional experiences that are similar to those we may have in the ordinary walks of life, although both weaker (because nothing is at stake) and stronger (because more concentrated and purified). Moreover, the formal properties of a work of art are capable of generating specifically aesthetic emotions such as wonder or surprise.

The capacity of works of art to generate emotions has important conceptual implications. The widely held view that emotions are invariably triggered by a prior cognitive assessment is invalidated by the fact that music can generate emotions even though no beliefs are involved. Similarly, emotions induced by works of art may be unaccompanied by arousal, specific physiological expressions, intentional objects, and action tendencies. In the case of music, we seem to experience emotion in something like a pure state, a qualitatively unique experience similar to a unique shade of red.

THE ROLE OF EMOTIONS IN SCIENTIFIC EXPLANATION

Emotions can be studied as effects or as causes – as explananda or as explanantia. First, we can try to explain the emotions themselves, by identifying the conditions under which they tend to arise. The link between the triggering situation and the emotion has been viewed as largely conceptual, as causal and deterministic, or as causal but partly indeterminate. To illustrate the last approach, which is the one I've been taking here: When the suspicion that one's lover is unfaithful is transformed into certainty, the effect may either be to exacerbate the jealousy or to kill it. Second, we can appeal to emotions in order to explain other phenomena. These include other mental states – beliefs and other emotions – as well as behaviors that are triggered either directly by the emotions or indirectly, through these other mental states.

Laboratory studies of human subjects have by and large focused on explaining the emotions. Given the methodological limitations of such studies this bias is understandable, but also regrettable. I do not want to say that the scientific importance of the emotions lies exclusively in their power to explain other phenomena. Because emotions are among the main sources of pleasure and pain, it can be important to identify the conditions under which they arise. The emotional value of art provides an example: Public funding of investment in museums or opera houses must ultimately be justified by the emotional experiences they can provide. Public support of sport can use a similar justification, among others.

The example of support for the sports also points to an intrinsic difficulty with this kind of justification. In an ex post assessment of the value of the 1994 Winter Olympics for the Norwegian population, the sheer emotional exuberance generated by the Norwegian winners should be a major item on the income side of the balance sheet. I am firmly convinced that these emotional gains by themselves were large enough to justify the huge construction expenses. Yet because this experience could not have been planned, the expenses may not have been justified ex ante. The point is not simply that nobody could count on the Norwegians being so successful: It is that if their victories *had* been predictable, they would have generated much less excitement. If the actual emotional satisfaction from Norwegian success in the Games was a decreasing function f(p) of the ex ante probability p of Norwegian success, the expected emotional satisfaction p · f(p) may have been too small to justify the investment. When an emotional experience is heavily dependent on surprise, it may not lend itself to planning.

Yet although there is a case to be made for giving some place to the emotions in welfare economics, their central importance for the social sciences lies perhaps in their positive, explanatory role. Some might think that emotions fall in the category of friction or noise, inducing random irregularities of behavior about which nothing general can be asserted and which in any event will cancel out in aggregate. I believe, however, that emotions do have large-scale, systematic effects. Because of the phenomenon of emotional contagion, emotions cannot be treated as random, independent events. The occurrence of one emotional event may increase the likelihood of another. Also, emotional events may occur in a systematic way because they have a common cause. Thus after the broadcast of Orson Welles's *War of the Worlds* in 1938, thousands of panic-stricken listeners took to the streets. Finally, emotions have a systematic effect on behavior through their role in sustaining social norms. In a given case, as in the recent civil wars in the former Yugoslavia, all three mechanisms may operate.

EFFECTS OF EMOTION

Emotions exercise some of their effects merely by virtue of their arousal properties. Although the emotion itself may be transient, the physiological changes leave traces that may affect the person's life in a durable manner. Anger – or the suppression of anger – can have a number of somatic effects, including worse prognoses for cancer, hypertension and subsequent liver failure, and coronary heart disease. To the extent that occasions for anger – or the propensity to suppress it – are nonrandomly distributed in the population, this provides a further mechanism by which emotions can become incorporated into the social sciences. The mortality and morbidity rates of women and ethnic minorities may differ from those of white males because of emotionally relevant differences in their socialization and in the social environments to which they are exposed.

Other effects of emotion arise because of their pleasurable and painful aspects. There is an urge to eliminate painful states and maintain pleasurable ones. Painful emotions, in particular, can have strong effects. To the extent that emotions are triggered by specific beliefs, they can be rendered less painful by rewriting the script – redefining the situation so that the painful emotion is muted and perhaps even replaced by a pleasurable one. Given the fact that one cannot decide to believe, this cannot be a conscious operation. Somehow – we do not know how – the mind manages to come up with an interpretation of states or events that takes some of the emotional sting out of them. Alternatively, one may try to achieve the same end by acting upon the world itself rather than upon beliefs about it. If I feel angry because of an insult I may mute the emotion by viewing the other's behavior in a more favorable light – or I may hit him. If I feel envy because of another's greater fortune I may transmute the emotion into righteous indignation – or destroy his property.

EMOTION AND COGNITION

The relation between emotion and cognition is perhaps the central issue in the study of the emotions. It has (at least) three aspects: A cognition may trigger emotion, it may be influenced by emotion, and it may have an emotion as its intentional or propositional object.

Most emotional reactions have an immediate cognitive antecedent. First, we form a belief that the world is such and such; and then we react emotionally to that belief. (The belief may itself have been emotionally shaped, but that is another matter.) If I believe that your bumping into me was intentional or neglectful I get angry; if I believe that you were pushed yourself by a third party, I am less likely to be angry. As noted above, emotions induced by art offer an exception to the view that all emotions are triggered by a cognitive antecedent. From recent studies it now appears that certain primal emotions such as fear are also capable of arising without any cognitive processing. The perception of what looks like a snake on the path triggers a neural response that bypasses the thinking part of the brain entirely and makes me freeze while I wait for the brain to assess the object more carefully. It is possible that emotions directed toward other people – such as love or disgust – are similarly capable of being shaped by mere *perception* without any concomitant *cognition*. In other cases, perception can reinforce cognition – I give to the beggar in the street but I do not make charitable contributions to help others whom I know to be equally needy.

A subject that needs further exploration is how fine-grained differences in cognition can have large implications for the emotions they trigger. Emotions lack the property of *extensionality* – logically equivalent beliefs may trigger entirely different emotions. The glass that can be seen as both half full and half empty provides a simple example. More generally, the study of emotions could benefit from incorporating theories of *framing* from cognitive psychology. As the study of jealousy demonstrates, the various modalities of belief – that something is the case, is probably the case, might plausibly have been the case, or may conceivably be the case – can also make a considerable difference for the nature of the emotion.

The view that emotion may in turn affect cognition is an old one; it was in fact part of Aristotle's formal definition of emotion. In his discussion and in virtually all later analyses it has been assumed that the influence was a negative one. There is no doubt that cognitive rationality is often undercut by emotion – by wishful thinking, by a narrowing of the attention span so that fewer factors are taken into account, or by other mechanisms. Yet in recent psychological and physiological work it has been argued that the traditional view is one-sided. Some writers have explicitly argued that emotion can enhance cognition, by enabling us to choose the best option by "gut feelings" in situations that are too complex for explicit rational assessment. The support for the claim seems weak, however. A more robust argument – relying on the finding that those who are most likely to make unbiased cognitive assessments are the clinically depressed – is that the emotional price to pay for cognitive rationality may be too high.

Finally, people also have cognitions *about* their emotions and about those of other people. It does not go without saying that having an emotion is tantamount to being aware of it. Angry, infatuated, and envious people are often unaware of their emotion. Although they may show all the behavioral manifestations of the emotion and others are easily able to recognize it in them, they may not themselves conceptualize it as such. The lack of awareness may itself be a result of the emotion: In the heat of the moment the intensive focus on the target of the emotion prevents them from reflecting on themselves. Or the emotion may creep up on them so slowly that they fail to notice it. Or they may have been taught to see it as a nonemotional state, for example as fatigue rather than depression. And sometimes, the unawareness may be motivated or self-deceptive. An adulterous love, for instance, may be suppressed because it cannot be acknowledged. This being said, people are usually aware of the emotions they are experiencing. Self-deceptive ignorance presupposes, in fact, that the person is aware of the emotion at some level.

PROTO-EMOTIONS, META-EMOTIONS, AND SECOND-PARTY EMOTIONS

When a person is unaware of the emotion he or she is experiencing, I have referred to it as a "proto-emotion." Once an emotion reaches the level of consciousness, the corresponding second-order cognition may in turn trigger a new emotion, or a "meta-emotion." This meta-emotion may in turn induce a change in the first-order cognition that was the basis for original, first-order emotion. In the paradigm case that I have used, the first-order cognition is that another possesses an object I lack, the first-order emotion is that of envy, the second-order cognition is the awareness that I am envious, and the second-order emotion triggered by that cognition is shame, which in turn causes me to rewrite the original script so that the situation appears as one that justifies the more acceptable feeling of righteous indignation. Note that in this case, all three relations between cognition and emotion are observed.

We may also have cognitions about other people's emotions, which may trigger emotions in ourselves, "second-party emotions." I may fear the angry behavior of my neighbor but feel contempt for the anger itself. I may feel dejected when the person I love makes it clear that my love is not requited but feel jealousy when I discover that the person loves somebody else. This phenomenon differs both from that of vicarious emotions, as when we blush inwardly at the sight of a friend making a fool of himself in public, and from that of emotional contagion, as when we unconsciously mimic another person's emotional expressions and the feedback from expression to emotion then creates an analogous state in ourselves. In the vicarious emotion, the trigger is not what we believe the other person feels but what we believe *he would have felt* had he known how he appeared to others. In emotional contagion, it is not clear that there is any cognitive trigger at all.

EMOTIONAL DYNAMICS

Most studies of the emotions have a static character, in the sense that they aim at explaining how emotions arise or affect behavior in a one-shot situation. Because of the methodological difficulties of studying emotions under controlled conditions, this limitation is understandable. Yet studies of this kind do not help us understand how a given emotional event can set in motion an emotional chain or "wildfire" with consequences far beyond those of the initial episode. These emotional dynamics deserve, I believe, more intensive study than they have received so far.

Some emotions simply have to run their course once they are set in motion. Anger grows and then subsides, when it has "spent itself." Other emotions, such as fear or jealousy, have the more disturbing feature that they can escalate more or less indefinitely. Although initially without much cognitive support, the emotion feeds upon itself and builds to a frenzy. As the behavior of Othello shows, the consequences may be disastrous. In his case, the growing fury of his jealousy did not owe anything to changes in Desdemona's behavior. Being in the grip of causal mechanisms that we do not fully understand, he simply wished to believe the worst.

In other cases, the emotion gains in strength because it affects those against whom it is directed and causes them to behave in ways that justify the initially unfounded belief. This applies not only to jealousy, but also to feuding, revenge, and civil war. In these cases, too, the tendency to believe the worst is an important factor. Yet emotions can also escalate through wishful thinking. When people fall in love, it is sometimes because they pull each other up by the bootstraps, each of them acting on a belief that turns out to be justified because of the effects it has on the other.

In still other cases, we observe the phenomenon of emotional contagion. One person harbors and shows an emotion towards another person that is transmitted to a third party through some form of contagion. Again, the mechanisms involved are not fully understood. As explained, third-party emotions may arise through unconscious imitation followed by feedback. Alternatively, the first-party behavior may have a disinhibitory effect on the third party, by signaling to him that it is acceptable to give in to emotions which he normally would keep in check.

CULTURE AND EMOTION

Whereas all animals of a given species have pretty much the same emotions, human emotions vary heavily with local culture. (Here, "culture" is only shorthand for the shared beliefs and values held by individual members of a society or a subculture within the society, including the belief that these beliefs and values are widely shared.) The influence of culture is shown in three main ways: in the labeling of emotions, in the evaluation of emotions, and in the determination of the behaviors that tend to trigger specific emotions.

If a person is unaware of his emotion, it may be because he lives in a society that does not provide a unifying cognitive label for the behavioral and physiological expressions of that particular emotion. In some societies, our modern concepts of guilt, depression, boredom, or love may not exist, and individuals suffering these emotions may not describe their states the way we would do. As a consequence, these emotions cannot be the target of meta-emotions or second-party emotions. Although people in the Middle Ages could be blamed for behaving in ways that we associate with boredom, those who blamed them viewed the behavior as an instance of sloth, a general category of sinful, weak-willed behavior that also included laziness. There was no important difference between falling asleep in church and slowness in carrying out one's religious duties.

Culture also affects how emotions are experienced by placing positive or negative valuations on them. Wrath – the passion for vengeance – is viewed negatively in societies that teach the doctrine of turning the other cheek, but positively in societies that go by the Lex Talionis. Although most societies condemn envy, some do so more vigorously than others. A characteristic feature of bourgeois morality is the condemnation of regret: "Don't cry over spilt milk!" A given emotion may give rise to negative or positive meta-emotions and second-party emotions, depending on the culture. When the assessment is negative, there is a pressure to hide the emotion for oneself and others, perhaps by transforming it into one that is more acceptable.

Finally, culture affects emotional life in a more substantive way by defining the *behaviors* that are appropriately viewed as objects of contempt and shame. Many spontaneous actions that would pass unnoticed in some societies can trigger strong emotions in others. The impact of social norms is partly to induce people to perform these behaviors only when others cannot see them, partly to make them abstain from them altogether. This third category overlaps with the second, as some of the prescribed or proscribed behaviors concern the outward manifestation of the emotions themselves. In our societies, picking one's nose in public and laughing at a funeral are both shameful behaviors.

Coda

EMOTION AND INTEREST

People are often subject to several motivational forces that pull them in different directions. Emotions – including social norms sustained by emotions – may induce them to act recklessly or without regard for consequences. At the same time, their material interest and notably their interest in survival may pull them in a different direction. An envious or angry person who wishes to make another person worse off may find that he cannot do so without making himself worse off too. In duels, vendettas, and feuds, the concern for honor comes up against the interest in survival. And there is a general tendency for material interest and social norms – sustained by the emotions of shame and contempt – to prescribe different courses of action.

Although we do not know exactly how such conflicts are resolved, there are several possibilities. First, one of the motivations may be transmuted so as to align itself on the other. A man who would be ashamed of marrying for money may, as if by miracle, fall in love with the richest girl in town. A may feel less anger towards B than towards C even though B has hurt him more, if retaliating against B would be more costly. Second, we may view the negative emotions as costs that attach to action and simply subtract them from the material benefits. Economists, for instance, standardly treat envy and sympathy as externalities in the utility function, or they view shame and guilt as costs that may or may not offset expected monetary earnings from the same transactions. Although this approach has the great advantage of being manageable and may be quite useful for some purposes, it fails to capture the phenomenology of psychic conflict. If guilt was merely a cost that attached to actions, people should be willing to pay for a pill that would eliminate it – but I don't think they are. Third, therefore, we may look for causal mechanisms that capture the fact that people are in the *grip* of their emotions.

I do not claim that people are insensitive to incentives, only that the interaction between emotions and incentives is more complex than in a cost–benefit model. The role of emotions cannot be reduced to that of shaping the reward parameters for rational choice. It seems very likely that they also affect the ability to make rational choices within those parameters. This *dual role of the emotions* – shaping choices as well as rewards – has analogues in pain, addictive cravings, and other visceral factors. As in these other cases, the claim is not that the emotions fully determine choice, or that there is no trade-off

413

between emotional rewards and other rewards. Rather, it is that the trade-off itself is modified by one of the rewards that are being traded off against the others.

EMOTION AND CHOICE

Although we cannot choose our emotions, choice can affect emotional experiences in a number of ways. Obviously, choice may induce behaviors that trigger emotions through their unintended consequences – a notable feature of many tragic plays. More relevantly, people sometimes make choices with their expected impact on emotions firmly in mind – to avoid negative emotions or to produce positive ones. In going about this task, they can use either direct or indirect strategies.

Given that one cannot choose which emotions to have, the direct strategy amounts to acting on the situations that tend to induce them. In the case of negative emotions such as anger, one can try to avoid occasions that are likely to make one angry and avoid learning facts that will induce that emotion. The latter strategy sounds paradoxical, for wouldn't one have to *know* the fact in order to avoid learning it? The problem can be resolved by deciding to avoid learning a general category of facts, well ahead of any suspicion one might have on particular occasions. Marrying couples might take a vow not to read each other's diaries. In the case of positive emotions, another paradox arises. Many of the positive emotions we welcome most arise on occasions that take us by surprise – but as I noted about the Norwegian Olympics, you cannot plan for surprise. Yet the paradox is not always insurmountable. One may decide to have children because of the emotional enhancement they provide, knowing that they will produce a steady stream of surprises although not knowing exactly what those surprises will be.

The indirect strategy is to work on one's emotional dispositions, to become less irascible, less worried, less afraid of love, or less prone to crying over spilt milk. This much-recommended strategy may not work well in practice. We do not know how to bring about durable and profound character changes. Also, the impact of such changes on one's emotional experiences will depend heavily on external and sometimes unpredictable events. And even if we knew the technology for character planning and could predict the course of external events, the investment might not be justified in terms of its results.

Characters in Woody Allen movies evidently find psychoanalysis a good investment because it provides them with something to talk about, but that is another matter.

EMOTIONS AND THE SOCIAL SCIENCES

Relations among the various social sciences have tended to take one of two forms: division of labor and imperialism. There might be a natural division according to subject matter. Economists, for instance, may take preferences for given and let sociologists study the formation of preferences through socialization and peer pressure. Alternatively, one discipline might try to cast itself as the master discipline whose methodology and substantive assumptions are applied across the board of all social phenomena. For a while it looked as if psychology could become the master discipline. Today, many economists engage in relentlessly imperialistic behavior, arguing for instance that the process of preference formation is in fact guided by rational choice and thus falls within the domain of economics.

In the study of the emotions, we find a similar duality. Many believe that the social-scientific study of the emotions should rest on a division of labor. Some disciplines should specialize in developing theories of emotion. Other disciplines can then apply these theories to their specific subject matter. Thus political scientists should look to psychology for what they need to know about how emotions might make a difference for, say, presidential elections or popular attitudes toward affirmative action. At the same time, we can detect incipient imperialisms in this field as well. There is an economic imperialism and a cultural-studies imperialism. According to the first, emotions can ultimately be explained by the rational-choice paradigm, perhaps expanded to include the maximization of biological fitness. According to the second, emotions are endlessly malleable social constructions.

I would argue for a different conception. The basis for the study of emotions should be what I have called *historical psychology*, where "history" is taken in a broad sense that also includes anthropology and sociology. The contribution of psychology – taken in a broad sense that also includes neurobiology – is vital. Because emotions are in fact not endlessly malleable, the other social sciences need psychology to keep them honest. Yet because of the intrinsic limitations on what we can learn from laboratory experiments on animal and human subjects, psychology cannot be the master discipline in the study of the emotions. To understand the relation among emotion, cognition, and behavior in real-life situations, historical studies are indispensable. Yet these studies, too, have their limitations. Because of the nature of most archival records, they rarely allow us to probe the fine grain of the emotions. When the Catholic population of Spain supported the Inquisition's persecution of the Jews, we cannot really tell whether they did so on the basis of what I called the "first-order pain of envy" (the shame of feeling inferior), on the basis of the "second-order pain of envy" (the shame of feeling envious), or both.

To probe more deeply, we have to turn to fiction. The best novelists and playwrights are – almost by definition – those who understand human nature better than others. In their writings, emotions almost invariably have a central place. A small handful of philosophers and moralists – Aristotle, Montaigne, La Rochefoucauld, and perhaps others whom I have neglected here – can also assist us in building this *fine-grained understanding of real-life emotional phenomena* that is the aim of the study of the emotions.

SOME UNEXPLORED AND UNRESOLVED QUESTIONS

In the previous pages, I have singled out some topics that may need to be developed more fully. Let me summarize them briefly, and then add a couple more remarks.

It is sometimes said that there is a movement in current psychology away from the cognitive studies that have dominated the field for the past twenty years, and towards an approach that gives more importance to the emotions. Although a movement in this direction is to be welcomed, it would be a pity if it went too far. I believe that many of the insights of cognitive psychology have great potential for the study of the emotions. Theories of framing and of reference-point effects, in particular, are likely to be indispensable tools for an understanding of the emotions.

Concerning the impact of emotions on behavior, one outstanding unsolved problem is that of the relation between emotion and interest. It is a question not so much of determining the relative importance of these two motivations as of identifying the mechanism by which they interact. Although a simple additive model in which emotions are factored in as costs or benefits may be a useful first step, I believe it is also somewhat simplistic.

Another set of partly unresolved issues arise in the study of emotional dynamics, and notably in the analysis of emotional escalations or wildfires. From the point of view of the social sciences, the interpersonal mechanisms are the most important ones. When people interact, their mutually dependent beliefs, emotions, and behaviors generate patterns that, although complex, are not hopelessly indecipherable. We should first try to isolate the atomic mechanisms involved and then go on to identify molecular patterns that can be used in accounting for observed social phenomena.

Another important and largely unresolved issue concerns the universality of emotions. Although I have suggested that human beings in all times and places are subject to the same "proto-emotions," and that societies only differ in the extent to which these are explicitly acknowledged and labeled, I do not claim to have anything like a conclusive argument for this view. For progress to be made on this question, historians and anthropologists would have to focus their attention on the observable manifestations of the emotions, rather than on the language in which they are described.

A related unresolved issue is the vexed question of the *origin* of the predominant values and beliefs in a culture. A common answer is to explain such cultural items by looking at the functions they serve in society. More often than not, such answers are highly speculative. Also, they do not throw any light on the question of *change* – the rise and fall of specific labeling systems for the emotions and of the normative assessments associated with them. In this book I have ignored these dynamic issues, not because they are unimportant but because I find them too hard.

Finally, there is a need for analytical work on *amour-propre* – the need for esteem and for self-esteem. *Amour-propre* is the engine of the alchemies of the mind – emotional deception as well as self-deception – that are the topic of much of this book. Whereas deception is a relatively straightforward phenomenon, self-deceptive beliefs about emotion and the role of emotion in self-deception remain theoretical puzzles. An even more puzzling phenomenon is the tendency for the human mind to engage in counterwishful thinking, as in Othello's propensity to assume the worst, against all evidence.

References

Abreu, D. (1988), "On the theory of infinitely repeated games with discounting," *Econometrica* 56, 383–96.

Adkins, A. W. H. (1972), *Moral Values and Political Behaviour in Ancient Greece*, New York: Norton.

Ainslie, G. (1992), *Picoeconomics*, Cambridge University Press.

Akerlof, G. (1976), "The economics of caste and of the rat race and other woeful tales," *Quarterly Journal of Economics* 90, 599–617.

Akerlof, G. (1980), "A theory of social custom, of which unemployment may be one consequence," *Quarterly Journal of Economics* 94, 749–75.

Alloy, L., and Abramson, L. (1979), "Judgment of contingency in depressed and nondepressed students: Sadder but wiser?," *Journal of Experimental Psychology: General* 108, 441–85.

Alloy, L., and Abramson, L. (1988), "Depressive realism," in L. B. Alloy (ed.), *Cognitive Processes in Depression*, New York: Guilford Press, pp. 223–65.

Allport, G. (1979), *Prejudice*, Reading, Mass.: Addison-Wesley.

Andenæs, J. (1978), *Det vanskelige oppgjøret*, Oslo: Tanum.

American Psychiatric Association (1994), *Diagnostic and Statistical Manual of Mental Disorders*, 4th ed., Washington, D.C.: Author.

Aronson, E. (1995), *The Social Animal*, New York: Freeman.

Axelrod, R. (1986), "An evolutionary approach to norms," *American Political Science Review* 80, 1095–111.

Babcock, L., and Loewenstein, G. (1997), "Explaining bargaining impasse: The role of self-serving biases," *Journal of Economic Perspectives* 11, 109–26.

Babcock, L., and Olson, C. (1992), "The causes of impasses in bargaining," *Industrial Relations* 31, 348–60.

Babcock, L., Wang, X., and Loewenstein, G. (1992), "Choosing the wrong pond: Social comparisons in negotiations that reflect a self-serving bias," *Quarterly Journal of Economics* 111, 1–20.

Babcock, L., et al. (1995), "Biased judgments of fairness in bargaining," *American Economic Review* 85, 1337–43.

References

Bach, K. (1997), "Thinking and believing in self-deception" [comment on Mele (1997)], *Behavioral and Brain Sciences* 20, 105.

Bacon, F. (1875), *The Works of Francis Bacon*, London: Longman.

Banfield, E. (1958), *The Moral Basis of a Backward Society*, New York: The Free Press.

Baron, J. (1995), *Thinking and Deciding*, Cambridge University Press.

Barraclough, J. (1994), *Cancer and Emotion*, New York: Wiley.

Barry, B. (1990), *Theories of Justice*, Berkeley and Los Angeles: University of California Press.

Barry, B. (1995), *Justice as Impartiality*, Berkeley and Los Angeles: University of California Press.

Baumeister, R. F. (1993), "Lying to yourself: The enigma of self-deception," in M. Lewis and C. Saarni (eds.), *Lying and Deception in Everyday Life*, New York: The Guilford Press, pp. 166–83.

Baumeister, R. F., and Wotman, S. R. (1992), *Breaking Hearts: The Two Sides of Unrequited Love*, New York: Guilford Press.

Bechara, A., et al. (1997), "Deciding advantageously before knowing the advantageous strategy," *Science* 275, 1293–95.

Becker, G. (1962), "Irrational behavior and economic theory," reprinted as Chapter 8 in Becker (1976).

Becker, G. (1976), *The Economic Approach to Human Behavior*, Chicago: University of Chicago Press.

Becker, G. (1991), *A Treatise on the Family*, Cambridge, Mass.: Harvard University Press.

Becker, G. (1996), *Accounting for Tastes*, Cambridge, Mass.: Harvard University Press.

Belfiore, E. S. (1992), *Tragic Pleasures*, Princeton University Press.

Bell, D. (1982), "Regret in decision making under uncertainty," *Operations Research* 30, 961–81.

Bell, D. (1985), "Disappointment in decision making under uncertainty," *Operations Research* 33, 1–27.

Bénichou, P. (1948), *Morales du grand siècle*, Paris: Gallimard.

Ben-Ze'ev, A. (1992), "Envy and inequality," *Journal of Philosophy* 89, 551–81.

Bessette, J. R. (1994), *The Mild Voice of Reason: Deliberative Democracy and American National Government*, University of Chicago Press.

Billacois, F. (1986), *Le duel dans la société française des XVIe-XVIIe siècles*, Paris: Editions de l'Ecole des Hautes Etudes en Sciences Sociales.

Billacois, F. (1990), *The Duel*, New Haven, Conn.: Yale University Press.

Black-Michaud, J. (1975), *Cohesive Force: Feud in the Mediterranean and the Middle East*, New York: St. Martin's Press.

Boehm, C. (1984), *Blood Revenge: The Anthropology of Feuding in Montenegro and other Tribal Societies*, Lawrence: University of Kansas Press.

Bös, D., and Tillman, G. (1985), "An 'envy tax:' Theoretical principles and applications to the German surcharge on the rich," *Public Finance/Finances Publiques* 40, 35–63.

References

Boskin, M. J., and Sheshinski, M. E. (1978), "Optimal redistributive taxation when individual welfare depends on relative income," *Quarterly Journal of Economics* 92, 589–602.

Boudon, R. (1984), *La place du désordre*, Paris: Presses Universitaires de France.

Bourdieu, P. (1969), "The sentiment of honour in Kabyle society," in J. G. Peristiany (ed.), *Honour and Shame: The Values of Mediterranean Society*, Chicago: University of Chicago Press, pp. 191–241.

Boyer, P. (1996), "Admiral Boorda's war," *The New Yorker* (September 16).

Branscombe, N. R., et al. (1996), "Rape and accident counterfactuals: Who might have done otherwise and would it have changed the outcome?," *Journal of Applied Social Psychology* 26, 1042–67.

Breckler, S. J. (1993), "Emotion and attitude change," in M. Lewis and J. M. Haviland (eds.), *Handbook of Emotions*, New York: The Guilford Press, pp. 461–74.

Brehm, J. (1966), *A Theory of Psychological Reactance*, New York: Academic Press.

Brehm, S. S. (1988), "Passionate love," in R. J. Sternberg and M. L. Barnes (eds.), *The Psychology of Love*, New Haven: Yale University Press, pp. 232–63.

Brennan G. (1973), "Pareto desirable redistribution: The case of malice and envy," *Journal of Public Economics* 2, 173–83.

Bromiley, P., and Curley, S. P. (1992), "Individual differences in risk-taking," in J. F. Yates (ed.), *Risk-Taking Behavior*, New York: Wiley, pp. 87–132.

Brothers, L. (1995), "Neurophysiology of the perception of intentions by primates," in M. Gazzaniga (ed.), *The Cognitive Neurosciences*, Cambridge, Mass.: M.I.T. Press, pp. 1107–16.

Bryson, R. F. (1933), *Honor and Duel in Sixteenth-Century Italy*, Ph.D. Dissertation, Department of Romance Languages and Literature, University of Chicago.

Bryson, R. F. (1935), *The Point of Honor in Sixteenth-Century Italy*, New York: Publications of the Institute of French Studies, Columbia University.

Budd, M. (1985), *Music and the Emotions*, London: Routledge and Kegan Paul.

Budd, M. (1995), *Values of Art*, London: Allen Lane.

Bugajski, J. (1994), *Ethnic Politics in Eastern Europe*, Armonk, N.Y.: Sharpe.

Bullock, A. (1991), *Hitler and Stalin*, New York: Vintage Books.

Burnyeat, M. (1980), "Aristotle on learning to be good," in A. Rorty (ed.), *Essays on Aristotle's Ethics*, Cambridge University Press, pp. 69–92.

Busquet, J. (1920), *Le droit de vendetta et les paci corses*, Paris: Pedone.

Byrne, D., and Kurmen, S. K. (1988), "Maintaining loving relationships," in R. J. Sternberg and M. L. Barnes (eds.), *The Psychology of Love*, New Haven, Conn.: Yale University Press, pp. 293–310.

Cairncross, J. (trans.) (1967): *Jean Racine: Andromache and Other Plays*, London: Penguin Books.

Cairns, D. (1993), *Aidos: The Psychology and Ethics of Honour and Shame in Ancient Greek Literature*, Oxford University Press.

References

Cameron, L. (1995), "Raising the stakes in the Ultimatum Game: Experimental evidence from Indonesia," Working Paper # 345, Industrial Relations Section, Princeton University.

Caro, R. A. (1974), *The Power Broker: Robert Moses and the Fall of New York*, New York: Vintage Books.

Carroll, N. (1996), *Theorizing the Moving Image*, Cambridge University Press.

Cartwright, N. (1983), *Why the Laws of Physics Lie*, Oxford University Press.

Castaldo, A. (1989), *Les méthodes de travail de la Constituante*, Paris: Presses Universitaires de France.

Cohen, D. (1991), *Law, Sexuality and Society: The Enforcement of Morals in Classical Athens*, Cambridge, U.K.: Cambridge University Press.

Cohen, D. (1995), *Law, Violence and Community in Classical Athens*, Cambridge University Press.

Cohen, G. A. (1982), "Functional explanation, consequence explanation, and Marxism," *Inquiry* 25, 27–56.

Cohen, G. A. (1992), "Incentives, inequality, and community," in G. B. Peterson (ed.), *The Tanner Lectures on Human Values*, vol. 13, Salt Lake City: University of Utah Press, pp. 263–329.

Cohen, G. A. (1995), "The Pareto argument for inequality," *Social Philosophy and Policy* 12, 160–85.

Coleman, J. (1990) *Foundations of Social Theory*, Cambridge, Mass.: Harvard University Press.

Conley, P. (1995), "The allocation of college admissions," in J. Elster (ed.), *Local Justice in America*, New York: Russell Sage, pp. 25–80.

Cooper, J. (1993), "Rhetoric, dialectic, and the passions," in C. C. W. Taylor (ed.), *Oxford Studies in Ancient Philosophy XI*, Oxford University Press, pp. 175–98.

Cope, E. M. (1877), *The Rhetoric of Aristotle*, Cambridge University Press.

Cornish, D. B. (1978), *Gambling: A Review of the Literature and its Implications for Policy and Research*, London: Her Majesty's Stationery Office.

Crawford, V., and Varian, H. (1979), "Distortion of preferences and the Nash theory of bargaining," *Economic Letters* 3, 203–6.

Creppell, I. (1989), "Democracy and literacy: The role of culture in political life," *Archives Européennes de Sociologie* 30, 22–47.

Crouzet, M. (1990), *Stendhal*, Paris: Flammarion.

Crouzet, M. (1996), *Le roman Stendhalien*, Orléans: Paradigme.

Damasio, A. (1994), *Descartes' Error*, New York: Putnam.

Darwin, C. (1872), *The Expression of the Emotions in Man and Animals*, New York: Appleton.

Davidson, D. (1980), *Essays on Actions and Events*, Oxford University Press.

Davidson, R. J. (1995), "Cerebral asymmetry, emotion, and affective style," in R. J. Davidson and K. Hugdall (eds.), *Brain Asymmetry*, Cambridge, Mass.: M.I.T. Press, pp. 361–88.

References

Davis, C., et al. (1995), "The undoing of traumatic life events," *Personality and Social Psychology Bulletin* 21, 109–24.

Dawes, R. (1994), *House of Cards*, New York: The Free Press.

Dawes, R. M., Faust, D., and Meehl, P. E. (1989), "Clinical versus actuarial judgment," *Science* 243, 1668–74.

Dennis, M. (1995), "Scarce medical resources: Hemodialysis and kidney transplantation," in J. Elster (ed.), *Local Justice in America*, New York: Russell Sage, pp. 81–152.

Dixit, A., and Nalebuff, B. (1991), "Making strategies credible," in R. Zeckhauser (ed.), *Strategy and Choice*, Cambridge, Mass.: M.I.T. Press, pp. 161–84.

Dixon, N. F. (1976), *On the Psychology of Military Incompetence*, London: Futura.

Djilas, M. (1958), *Land Without Justice*, London: Methuen.

Dodds, E. R. (1951), *The Greeks and the Irrational*, Berkeley and Los Angeles: University of California Press.

Doubrovsky, S. (1980), *Parcours critique*, Paris: Editions Galilée.

Douglas, B. (1915), *Old Calabria*, Boston: Houghton Mifflin.

Dournon, J.-Y. (1993), *Le dictionnaire des proverbes et dictons de France*, Paris: Hachette.

Dover, K. (1994), *Greek Popular Morality*, Indianapolis: Hackett.

Dubovsky, S. L. (1997), *Mind-Body Deceptions*, New York: Norton.

Dunning, D. D., and Story, A. L. (1991), "Depression, realism, and the over-confidence effect: Are the sadder wiser when predicting future actions and events?" *Journal of Personality and Social Psychology* 61, 512–32.

Dworkin, R. (1981), "What is equality? Part 2: Equality of resources," *Philosophy and Public Affairs* 10, 283–345.

Eagly, A., and Chaiken, S. (1993), *The Psychology of Attitudes*, Orlando: Harcourt Brace.

Edgerton, R. (1985), *Rules, Exceptions and the Social Order*, Berkeley and Los Angeles: University of California Press.

Ekman, P. (1980), "Biological and cultural contributions to body and facial movement in the expression of the emotions," in A. Rorty (ed.), *Explaining the Emotions*, Berkeley and Los Angeles: University of California Press, pp. 73–102.

Ekman, P. (1992a), *Telling Lies*, New York: Norton.

Ekman, P. (1992b), "An argument for basic emotions," *Cognition and Emotion* 6, 169–200.

Ekman, P., and Davidson, R. (1994), *The Nature of Emotion*, Oxford University Press.

Ekman, P., and Frank, M. G. (1994), "Lies that fail," in M. Lewis and C. Saarni (eds.), *Lying and Deception in Everyday Life*, New York: The Guilford Press, pp. 184–200.

Elster, J. (1975), *Leibniz et la formation de l'esprit scientifique*, Paris: Aubier-Montaigne.

References

Elster (1976a), "Some conceptual problems in political theory," in B. Barry (ed.), *Power and Political Theory*, Chichester, U.K.: Wiley, pp. 245–70.

Elster, J. (1976b), "A note on hysteresis in the social sciences," *Synthese* 33, 371–91.

Elster, J. (1978), *Logic and Society*, Chichester, U.K.: Wiley.

Elster, J. (1983a), *Explaining Technical Change*, Cambridge University Press.

Elster, J. (1983b), *Sour Grapes*, Cambridge University Press.

Elster, J. (1984), *Ulysses and the Sirens*, rev. ed., Cambridge University Press.

Elster, J. (1985), *Making Sense of Marx*, Cambridge University Press.

Elster, J. (1989a), *Nuts and Bolts for the Social Sciences*, Cambridge University Press.

Elster, J. (1989b), *The Cement of Society*, Cambridge University Press.

Elster, J. (1989c), "Social norms and economic theory," *Journal of Economic Perspectives* 3, 99–117.

Elster, J. (1989d), *Solomonic Judgments*, Cambridge University Press.

Elster, J. (1990), "Norms of Revenge," *Ethics* 100, 862–85.

Elster, J. (1991), "Envy in social life," R. Zeckhauser (ed.), *Strategy and Choice*, Cambridge, Mass.: M.I.T. Press, pp. 49–82.

Elster, J. (1992), *Local Justice*, New York: Russell Sage.

Elster, J. (1993a), *Political Psychology*, Cambridge University Press.

Elster, J. (1993b), "Rebuilding the boat in the open sea: Constitution-making in Eastern Europe," *Public Administration* 71, 169–217.

Elster, J. (1995), "Transition, constitution-making and separation in Czechoslovakia," *Archives Européennes de Sociologie* 36, 105–34.

Elster, J. (1996a), Review of Kuran (1995), *Acta Sociologica* 39, 113–15.

Elster, J. (1996b): "Equal or proportional? Arguing and bargaining over the Senate at the Federal Convention," in J. Knight and I. Sened (eds.), *Explaining Social Institutions*, Ann Arbor: University of Michigan Press 1995, pp. 145–60.

Elster, J. (1997), Review of Becker (1996), *University of Chicago Law Review* 64, 749–64.

Elster, J. (1998a), "Emotions and economic theory," *Journal of Economic Literature* 36, 47–64.

Elster, J. (1998b), "Coming to terms with the past," *Archives Européennes de Sociologie* 39, 7–48.

Elster, J. (in press a), *Ulysses Unbound*, Cambridge University Press.

Elster, J. (in press b), *Strong Feelings*, Cambridge, Mass.: M.I.T. Press.

Elster. J. (in press c), "Addiction and gambling," in J. Elster and O.-J. Skog (eds.), *Getting Hooked*, Cambridge University Press.

Elster, J. (in press d), "Accountability in Athenian politics," in B. Manin, A. Przeworski, and S. Stokes (eds.), *Democracy, Accountability, and Representation*, Cambridge University Press.

Elster, J. (in press e), "Sagesse on science: Le rôle des proverbes dans la connaissance de l'homme et de la société," to be published in a *Festschrift* for Raymond Boudon.

References

Elster, J., and Loewenstein, G. (1992), "Utility from memory and anticipation," in G. Loewenstein and J. Elster (eds.), *Choice over Time*, New York: Russell Sage, pp. 213–34.

Farrand M. (ed.) (1966), *Records of the Federal Convention*, vols. I–III, New Haven, Conn.: Yale University Press.

Fearon, J., and Laitin, D. (1996), "Explaining interethnic cooperation," *American Political Science Review* 90, 715–35.

Feller, W. (1968), *An Introduction to Probability Theory and its Applications*, vol. 1, 3d ed., New York: Wiley.

Fenichel, O. (1945), *The Psychoanalytical Theory of Neurosis*, New York: Norton.

Fernandez, R. (1981), "La méthode de Balzac," in *Messages*, Paris: Grasset, pp. 54–69.

Festinger, L. (1957), *A Theory of Cognitive Dissonance*, Stanford University Press.

Festinger, L., and Bramel, D. (1962), "The reactions of humans to cognitive dissonance," in A. Bachrach (ed.), *The Experimental Foundations of Clinical Psychology*, New York: Basic Books, pp. 254–79.

Fisher, N. R. E. (1992), *Hybris*, Warminster, U.K.: Aris and Phillips.

Foley, D. K. (1967), "Resource allocation and the public sector," *Yale Economic Essays* 7, 45–198.

Fortenbaugh, W. W. (1970), "Aristotle's *Rhetoric* on emotions," cited after the reprint in J. Barnes, M. Schofield, and R. Sorabji (eds.), *Articles on Aristotle*, vol. 4: Psychology and Aesthetics, London: Duckworth, pp. 133–53.

Fortenbaugh, W. W. (1975), *Aristotle on Emotion*, London: Duckworth.

Foster, G. (1965), *Tzintzuntzan: Mexican Peasants in a Changing World*, Boston: Little, Brown.

Foster, G. (1972), "The anatomy of envy," *Current Anthropology* 13, 165–86.

Frank, R. (1988), *Passions Within Reason*, New York: Norton.

Frede, D. (1996), "Mixed feelings in Aristotle's *Rhetoric*," in A. O. Rorty (ed.), *Essays on Aristotle's Rhetoric*, Berkeley and Los Angeles: University of California Press, pp. 258–85.

Freud, A. (1935), *The Ego and the Mechanisms of Defense*, Madison: International Universities Press.

Freud, S. (1937, 1964), "Analysis terminable and interminable," in *The Complete Psychological Works of Sigmund Freud*, vol. 23, London: The Hogarth Press, pp. 216–53.

Frijda, N. (1986), *The Emotions*, Cambridge University Press.

Frijda, N. (1993), "Moods, emotion episodes, and emotions," in M. Lewis and J. M. Haviland (eds.), *Handbook of Emotions*, New York: The Guilford Press, pp. 381–404.

Frijda, N. (1994), "The Lex Talionis: On vengeance," in S. M. Goozen, N. E. van de Poll, and J. A. Sergeant (eds.), *Emotions: Essays on Emotion Theory*, Hillsdale, N.J.: Lawrence Erlbaum, pp. 263–90.

Fry, R. (1921), *Vision and Design*, New York: Brentano.

References

Gambetta, D. (1997), "Concatenations of mechanisms," in P. Hedström and R. Swedberg (eds.), *Social Mechanisms: An Analytical Approach to Social Theory*, Cambridge, U.K.: Cambridge University Press, pp. 102–24.

Gardner, E. (1997), "Brain reward mechanisms," in J. H. Lowinson, et al. (eds.), *Substance Abuse: A Comprehensive Handbook*, Baltimore: Williams and Wilkins, pp. 51–85.

Garapon, R. (ed.) (1990), *La Bruyère: Les Caractères*, Paris: Bordas

Geen, R. G. (1983), "The psychopathology of extraversion-intraversion," in J. T. Cacioppo and R. E. Petty (eds.), *Social Psychophysiology: A Sourcebook*, New York: Guilford Press, pp. 391–416.

Genette, G. (1969), "Vraisemblance et motivation," in *Figures II*, Paris: Seuil, pp. 71–100.

Gibbard, A. (1973), "Manipulation of voting schemes," *Econometrica* 41, 587–602.

Girard, R. (1961), *Mensonge romantique et vérité romanesque*, Paris: Grasset.

Gloor, P. (1986), "The role of the human limbic system in perception, memory and affect," in J. P. Aggleton (ed.), *The Amygdala*, New York: Wiley, 1992.

Goldhagen, D. (1996), *Hitler's Willing Executioners*, New York: Knopf.

Goldthorpe, J. H., et al. (1969), *The Affluent Worker*, Cambridge University Press.

Gordon, R. M. (1987), *The Structure of Emotions*, Cambridge University Press.

Gray, F. (1986), *La Bruyère: Amateur de caractères*, Paris: Nizet.

Gray, J. A. (1991), *The Psychology of Fear and Stress*, Cambridge University Press.

Greenberg, M. E., and Weiner, B. B. (1966), "Effects of reinforcement history upon risk-taking behavior," *Journal of Experimental Psychology* 71, 587–92.

Greenspan, P. (1989), *Emotions and Reasons*, London: Routledge.

Griffiths, P. (1997), *What Emotions Really Are*, University of Chicago Press.

Grimaldi, N. (1993), *La jalousie. Etude sur l'imaginaire proustien*, Arles: Actes Sud.

Gur, R. C., and Sackeim, H. A. (1979), "Self-deception: A concept in search of a phenomenon," *Journal of Personality and Social Psychology* 37, 147–69.

Guth, W., Schmittberger, R., and Schwartz, B. (1982), "An experimental analysis of ultimatum bargaining," *Journal of Economic Behavior and Organization* 3, 367–88.

Habermas, J. (1984/87), *The Theory of Communicative Action*, vols. I–II, Boston: Beacon Press.

Hammond, P. (1987), "Envy," in *The New Palgrave*, London: Macmillan.

Hansen, M. H. (1991), *The Athenian Democracy in the Age of Demosthenes*, Oxford: Blackwell.

Hardin, R. (1995), *One for All*, Princeton, N.J.: Princeton University Press.

Harsanyi, J. (1955), "Cardinal welfare, individualistic ethics, and interpersonal comparisons of utility," *Journal of Political Economy* 61, 309–21.

Hasluck, M. (1954), *The Unwritten Law in Albania*, Cambridge University Press.

References

Hatfield, E., Cacioppo, J., and Rapson, R. (1994), *Emotional Contagion*, Cambridge University Press.

Hauser, M. D. (1996), *The Evolution of Communication*, Cambridge, Mass.: M.I.T. Press.

Hegel, G. W. F. (1982), *The Phenomenology of Spirit*, Oxford University Press.

Heider, F. (1958), *The Psychology of Interpersonal Relations*, New York: Wiley.

Hempel, C. A. (1965), *Aspects of Scientific Explanation*, New York: Free Press.

Herrnstein, R., and Prelec, D. (1992), "Melioration," in G. Loewenstein and J. Elster (eds.), *Choice over Time*, New York: The Russell Sage Foundation, pp. 235–264.

Higgins, E. T. (1987), "Self-discrepancy: A theory relating self and affect," *Psychological Review* 94, 319–40.

Hippeau, L. (1978), *Essai sur la morale de la Rochefoucauld*, Paris: Nizet.

Hirschman, A. (1977). *The Passions and the Interests*, Princeton University Press.

Hirschman, A., and Rothschild, M. (1973), "The changing tolerance for income inequality," cited after the reprint in A. Hirschman (1981), *Essays in Trespassing*, Cambridge University Press, pp. 39–58.

Hirshleifer, J. (1987), "The emotions as guarantors of threats and promises," in J. Dupré (ed.), *The Latest on the Best*, Cambridge, Mass.: M.I.T. Press, pp. 307–26.

Hochschild, A. (1979), "Emotion work, feeling rules, and social structure," *American Journal of Sociology* 85, 551–75.

Hochschild, A. R. (1983), *The Managed Heart*, Berkeley, Calif.: University of California Press.

Holmes, S. (1993), "Tocqueville and democracy," in D. Copp, J. Hampton, and J. Roemer (eds.), *The Idea of Democracy*, Cambridge University Press, pp. 23–63.

Holmes, S. (1996), "Ordinary passions in Racine and Descartes," in B. Yack (ed.), *Liberalism Without Illusions*, University of Chicago Press, pp. 95–110.

Hume, D. (1960), *A Treatise of Human Nature*, in Selby-Bigge (ed.), Oxford University Press.

Hume, D. (1963), *Essays: Moral, Political and Literary*, Oxford University Press.

Hutson, S. (1971), "Social ranking in a French Alpine community," in F. Bailey (ed.), *Gifts and Poison*, Oxford: Blackwell, pp. 41–68.

Huyse, L., and Dhondt, S. (1993), *La répression des collaborations*, Bruxelles: CRISP.

Hyman, H. (1968), "Reference groups," in *The International Encyclopedia of the Social Sciences*, vol. 13, New York: Macmillan, pp. 353–61.

Isaacson, W. (1993), *Kissinger*, New York: Simon and Schuster.

Izard, W. (1991), *The Psychology of Emotions*, New York: Plenum.

Jackendoff, R. (1988), "Exploring the form of information in the dynamic unconscious," in M. J. Horowitz (ed.), *Psychodynamics and Cognition*, University of Chicago Press, pp. 203–20.

References

Jankowski, M. S. (1991), *Islands in the Streets: Gangs and American Urban Society*, Berkeley and Los Angeles: University of California Press.

Janoff-Bulman, R. (1979), "Characterological versus behavioral self-blame," *Journal of Personality and Social Psychology* 37, 1798–1809.

Jillson, C. C. (1988), *Constitution Making: Conflict and Consensus in the Federal Convention of 1787*, New York: Agathon Press.

Johnson-Laird, P., and Oatley, K. (1992), "Basic emotions, rationality, and folk theory," *Cognition and Emotion* 6, 201–23.

Jones, A. H. M. (1957), *Athenian Democracy*, Baltimore: Johns Hopkins University Press.

Kagan, D. (1981), *The Peace of Nicias and the Sicilian Expedition*, Ithaca, N.Y.: Cornell University Press.

Kahn, A., and Tice, T. E. (1973), "Returning a favor and retaliating harm: The effects of stated intentions and actual behavior," *Journal of Experimental Social Psychology* 9, 43–56.

Kahneman, D. (in press), "Assessments of individual well-being: A bottom-up approach," in D. Kahneman, E. Diener, and N. Schwartz (eds.), *Understanding Quality of Life: Scientific Perspectives on Enjoyment and Suffering*.

Kahneman, D., and Miller, D. T. (1986), "Norm theory: Comparing reality to its alternatives," *Psychological Review* 93, 126–53.

Kahneman, D., and Tversky, A. (1982), "The simulation heuristics," in D. Kahneman, P. Slovic, and A. Tversky (eds.), *Judgment under Uncertainty*, Cambridge University Press, pp. 201–209.

Kandel, E., and Lazear, E. P. (1992), "Peer pressure and partnerships," *Journal of Political Economy* 100, 801–17.

Kant, I. (1785), *The Metaphysics of Morals*, in *The Cambridge Edition of the Works of Immanuel Kant: Practical Philosophy*, Cambridge University Press, 1996.

Katz, J. (1988), *The Seductions of Crime*, New York: Basic Books.

Kawachi, I., et al. (1996), "A prospective study of anger and coronary heart disease," *Circulation* 94, 2090–95.

Kennedy, G. A. (ed.) (1991), *Aristotle on Rhetoric*, Oxford University Press.

Kenner, H. (1983), "Wisdom of the tribe: Why proverbs are better than aphorisms," *Harper's* (May 6), 84–86.

Kiernan, V. (1986), *The Duel in European History*, Oxford University Press.

King, G., Keohane, R. O, and Verba, S. (1994), *Designing Social Inquiry*, Princeton University Press.

Kirchsteiger, G. (1992), "The role of envy in ultimatum games," unpublished paper, Institute for Advanced Studies, Vienna.

Kishlansky, M. (1986), *Parliamentary Selection*, Cambridge University Press.

Klag, M. J., et al. (1991), "The association of skin color with blood pressure in US blacks with low socio-economic status," *Journal of the American Medical Association* 265, 599–602.

Knapp, P. H. (1988), "Steps toward a lexicon, discussion of 'Unconsciously determined defensive strategies,'" in M. J. Horowitz (ed.), *Psychodynamics and Cognition*, Chicago: University of Chicago Press, pp. 95–114.

References

Krebs, D. L., and Miller, D. T. (1985), "Altruism and aggression," in G. Lindsey and E. Aronson (eds.), *Handbook of Social Psychology*, vol. II, 3d ed., New York: Random House, pp. 1–71.

Kreech, D., and Crutchfield, R. S. (1948), *Theory and Problems of Social Psychology*, New York: MacGraw-Hill.

Kreps, D. M., and Wilson, R. (1982), "Reputation and imperfect information," *Journal of Economic Theory* 27, 253–79.

Kuran, T. (1995), *Private Truths, Public Lies: The Social Consequences of Preference Falsification*, Cambridge, Mass.: Harvard University Press.

Lacan, J. (1977), *Écrits*, New York: Norton.

Laclos, C. de (1782), *Les liaisons dangéreuses*.

Lafayette, Mme. de (1994), *The Princess of Clèves*, New York: Norton.

Lafond, J. (1986), *La Rochefoucauld: Moralisme et litérature*, Paris: Klincksieck.

Lafond, J. (ed.) (1992), *Moralistes du XVIIe Siècle*, Paris: Robert Laffont.

Laitin, D. (1995), "Marginality: A microperspective," *Rationality and Society* 7, 31–57.

Laitin, D. (1998), *Identity in Formation: The Russian-Speaking Populations in the Near Abroad*, Ithaca, N.Y.: Cornell University Press.

Lamb, S. (1996), *The Trouble with Blame*, Cambridge, Mass.: Harvard University Press.

Landman, J. (1993), *Regret*, Oxford University Press.

Lazarus, R. Z. (1991), *Emotion and Adaptation*, Oxford: Oxford University Press.

LeDoux, J. (1995), "In search of an emotional system in the brain," in M. Gazzaniga (ed.), *The Cognitive Neurosciences*, Cambridge, Mass.: M.I.T. Press, pp. 1049–61.

LeDoux, J. (1996), *The Emotional Brain*, New York: Simon and Schuster.

Le Grand, J. (1982), *The Strategy of Equality*. London: Allen and Unwin.

Leighton, S. R. (1996), "Aristotle and the emotions," in A. O. Rorty (ed.), *Essays on Aristotle's Rhetoric*, Berkeley and Los Angeles: University of California Press, pp. 206–37.

Lerner, M. (1980), *The Belief in a Just World*, New York: Plenum.

Levenson, R. W. (1992), "Autonomic nervous system differences among emotions," *Psychological Science* 3, 23–7.

Levy, R. (1973), *The Tahitians*, Chicago: University of Chicago Press.

Levy, R. (1984), "Emotion, knowing, and culture," in R. A. Shweder and R. A. LeVine (eds.), *Culture Theory: Essays on Mind, Self, and Emotion*, Cambridge University Press, pp. 214–37.

Lewis, A. (1982), *The Psychology of Taxation*, New York: St. Martin's Press.

Lewis, C. S. (1936), *The Allegory of Love*, Oxford University Press.

Lewis, D. (1973), *Counterfactuals*, Oxford: Blackwell.

Lewis, M. (1992), *Shame*, New York: The Free Press.

Lewis, M. (1995), "Embarrassment: The emotion of self-exposure and evaluation," in J. P. Tangney and K. W. Fischer (eds.), *Self-Conscious Emotions*, New York: The Guilford Press, pp. 198–218.

References

Lewis, M., and Haviland, J. (eds.) (1993), *Handbook of Emotions*, New York: The Guilford Press.

Liebermann, Y., and Syrquin, M. (1983), "On the use and abuse of rights," *Journal of Economic Behavior and Organization* 4, 25–40.

Liebowitz, M. (1983), *The Chemistry of Love*, Boston: Little, Brown.

Lincoln-Keiser, R. (1986), "Death enmity in Thull," *American Ethnologist* 13, 489–505.

Lindsay-Hartz, J., de Rivera, J., and Mascolo, M. F. (1995), "Differentiating guilt and shame and their effects on motivation," in J. P. Tangney and K. W. Fischer (eds.), *Self-Conscious Emotions*, New York: The Guilford Press, pp. 274–300.

Lodge, D. (1984), *Small World*, New York: Warner Books.

Loewenstein, G. (1996), "Out of control: Visceral influences on behavior," *Organizational Behavior and Human Decision Processes* 65, 272–92.

Loewenstein, G., Thompson, L., and Bazerman, M. (1989), "Decision making in interpersonal contexts," *Journal of Personality and Social Psychology* 57, 426–41.

Loewenstein, G., et al. (1993), "Self-serving assessments of fairness and pretrial bargaining," *Journal of Legal Studies* 22, 135–59.

Lottman, H. (1986), *L'épuration*, Paris: Fayard.

Lovejoy, A. O. (1961), *Reflections on Human Nature*, Baltimore: Johns Hopkins Press.

Loury, G. (1995), *One by One From the Inside Out*, New York: The Free Press.

Macey, J. (1986), "Promoting public-regarding legislation through statutory interpretation: An interest-group model," *Columbia Law Review* 86, 223–68.

Mackie, G. (1995), "U.S. immigration policy and local justice," in J. Elster (ed.), *Local Justice in America*, New York: Russell Sage, pp. 227–90.

Margolin, J.-L. (1997), "Chine: Une longue marche dans la nuit," in S. Courtois et al., *Le livre noir du communisme*, Paris: Robert Laffont, pp. 503–97.

Margolis, H. (1982), *Selfishness, Altruism and Rationality*, Cambridge University Press.

Markman, K. D., et al. (1993), "The mental simulation of better and worse possible worlds," *Journal of Experimental Social Psychology* 29, 87–109.

Markman, K. D., et al. (1995), "The impact of perceived control on the imagination of better and worse possible worlds," *Personality and Social Psychology Bulletin* 21, 588–95.

Mason, H. L. (1952), *The Purge of Dutch Quislings*, The Hague: Martinus Nijhoff.

Maxmen, J. S., and Ward, N. G. (1995), *Essential Psychopathology and Its Treatment*, New York: Norton.

Maynard-Smith, J. (1982), *Evolution and the Theory of Games*, Cambridge University Press.

References

McAdams, R. H. (1992), "Relative preferences," *Yale Law Journal* 102, pp. 1–104.

McAleer, K. (1994), *Dueling*, Princeton University Press.

McMullen, M. N., Markman, K. D., and Gavanski, I. (1995), "Living in neither the best nor worst of all possible worlds," in N. J. Roese and J. M. Olson (eds.), *What Might Have Been: The Social Psychology of Counterfactual Thinking*, Mahwah, N.J.: Lawrence Erlbaum, pp. 133–68.

Mele, A. (1997), "Real self-deception," *Behavioral and Brain Sciences* 20, 91–102.

Merton, R. (1957), *Social Theory and Social Structure*, Glencoe, Ill.: The Free Press.

Middleton, E. (1986), "Some testable implications of a preference for subjective novelty," *Kyklos* 39, 397–418.

Mieder, W. (1993), *Proverbs are never out of Season*, Oxford University Press.

Miller, D. T., and McFarland, C. (1986), "Counterfactual thinking and victim compensation," *Personality and Social Psychology Bulletin* 12, 513–19.

Miller, W. I. (1990), *Bloodtaking and Peacemaking*, University of Chicago Press.

Miller, W. I. (1993), *Humiliation*, Ithaca, N.Y.: Cornell University Press.

Miller, W. I. (1997), *The Anatomy of Disgust*, Cambridge, Mass.: Harvard University Press.

Miller, W. L. (1996), *Arguing about Slavery*, New York: Knopf.

Mischel, W. (1968), *Personality and Assessment*, New York: Wiley 1968.

Mittleman, M. A., et al. (1995), "Triggering of acute myocardial infarction onset by episodes of anger," *Circulation* 92, 172–75.

Montaigne, M. de (1991), *The Complete Essays*, M. A. Screech (trans.), Harmondsworth: Penguin.

Montesquieu (1721), *Lettres Persanes*.

Montesquieu (1991), *Pensées*, Paris: Robert Laffont.

Mora, G. F. de la (1987), *Egalitarian Envy*, New York: Paragon House.

Morris, H. (1987), "Nonmoral guilt," in F. Schoeman (ed.), *Responsibility, Character, and the Emotions*, Cambridge University Press, pp. 220–40.

Mui, V.-L. (1995), "The economics of envy," *Journal of Economic Behavior and Organization* 26, 311–36.

Nelson, R., and Winter, S. (1982), *An Evolutionary Theory of Economic Change*, Cambridge, Mass.: Harvard University Press.

Netanyahu, B. (1995), *The Origins of the Inquisition*, New York: Random House.

Niedenthal, P. M., Tangney, J. P., and Gavanski, I. (1994), "'If only I weren't' versus 'If only I hadn't': Distinguishing shame and guilt in counterfactual thinking," *Journal of Personality and Social Psychology* 67, 585–95.

Nietzsche, F. (1956), *The Birth of Tragedy* and *The Genealogy of Morals*, New York: Anchor Books.

Nisan, M. (1985), "Limited morality," in M. W. Berkowitz and F. Oser (eds.), *Moral Education: Theory and Practice*, Hillsdale, N.J.: Lawrence Erlbaum, pp. 403–20.

Nisard, D. (ed.) (1869–78), *Collection des auteurs latins, avec la traduction en français*, Paris: Firmin-Didot.

Nisbett, R., and Cohen, D. (1996), *Culture of Honor: The Psychology of Violence in the South*, Boulder, Colo.: Westview Press.

Nisbett, R., and Ross, L. (1980), *Human Inference*, Englewood Cliffs, N.J.: Prentice Hall.

Nussbaum, M. (1996), "Aristotle on emotions and rational persuasion," in A. O. Rorty (ed.), *Essays on Aristotle's Rhetoric*, Berkeley and Los Angeles: University of California Press, pp. 303–23.

Oatley, K. (1992), *Best Laid Schemes: The Psychology of Emotions*, Cambridge University Press.

Oatley, K., and Jenkins, J. (1996), *Understanding Emotions*, Cambridge, Mass.: Blackwell.

Ober, J. (1989), *Mass and Elite in Democratic Athens*, Princeton University Press.

O'Brien, C. C. (1992), *The Great Melody*, University of Chicago Press.

Oren, D. (1985), *Joining the Club: A History of Jews and Yale*, New Haven: Yale University Press.

Ortony, A., Clore, G. L., and Collins, A. (1988), *The Cognitive Structure of the Emotions*, Cambridge University Press.

Ostwald, M. (1986), *From Popular Sovereignty to the Rule of Law*, Berkeley: University of California Press.

Pallak, M. S., and Pittman, T. S. (1972), "General motivational effects of dissonance arousal," *Journal of Personality and Social Psychology* 7, 11–20.

Parducci, A. (1968), "The relativism of absolute judgments," *Scientific American* (December), 84–90.

Parducci, A. (1984), "Value judgments: Towards a relational theory of happiness," in J. R. Eiser (ed.), *Attitudinal Judgment*, New York: Springer, pp. 3–21.

Parducci, A. (1995), *Happiness, Pleasure and Judgment*, Mahwah, N.J.: Lawrence Erlbaum.

Pateman, C. (1970), *Participation and Democratic Theory*, Cambridge University Press.

Pavel, T. (1986), *Fictional Worlds*, Cambridge, Mass.: Harvard University Press.

Pears, D. (1985), *Motivated Irrationality*, Oxford University Press.

Perelman, C., and Olbrechts-Tyteca, L. (1969), *The New Rhetoric*, Notre Dame: University of Notre Dame Press.

Petersen, R. (1989), "Rationality, ethnicity, and military enlistment," *Social Science Information* 28, 563–98.

Petersen, R. (1997), *Fear, Hatred, Resentment: Delineating Paths to Ethnic Violence in Eastern Europe*, manuscript, Department of Political Science, Washington University, St. Louis.

Plutchik, R. (1993), "Emotions and their vicissitudes: Emotions and psychopathology," in M. Lewis and J. M. Haviland (eds.), *Handbook of Emotions*, New York: The Guilford Press, pp. 53–66.

Posner, R. (1982), "Economics, politics, and the reading of statutes and the constitution," *University of Chicago Law Review* 49, 263–91.

Prévost, J. (1951), *La création chez Stendhal*, Paris: Mercure de France.

Proust, M. (1954), *A la recherche du temps perdu*, vols. I–III, ed. de la Pléiade, Paris: Gallimard.

Rabin, M. (1993), "Incorporating fairness into game theory and economics," *American Economic Review* 83, 1281–1302.

Rabin, M. (1995), "Moral preferences, moral constraints, and self-serving biases," manuscript, Department of Economics, University of California at Berkeley.

Rakove, J. N. (1987), "The Great Compromise: Ideas, interests, and the politics of constitution making," *William and Mary Quarterly* 44, 424–57.

Ranulf, S. (1933/34), *The Jealousy of the Gods and Criminal Law at Athens*, vols. I–II, London: Williams and Norgate.

Rawls, J. (1971), *A Theory of Justice*, Cambridge, Mass.: Harvard University Press.

Réau, L. (1994), *Histoire du vandalisme*, édition augmentée, Paris: Robert Laffont.

Roberts, R. (1984), "Solomon on the control of emotions," *Philosophy and Phenomenological Research* 44, 395–403.

Roemer, J. (1985a), "Rationalizing revolutionary ideology," *Econometrica* 53, 85–108.

Roemer, J. (1985b), "Should Marxists be interested in exploitation?" *Philosophy and Public Affairs* 14, 30–65.

Roese, N. J. (1994), "The functional basis of counterfactual thinking," *Journal of Personality and Social Psychology* 66, 805–18.

Roese, N. J., and Olson, J. M. (1995), "Functions of counterfactual thinking," in N. J. Roese and J. M. Olson (eds.), *What Might Have Been: The Social Psychology of Counterfactual Thinking*, Mahwah, N.J.: Lawrence Erlbaum, pp. 169–198.

Rolls, E. T. (1995), "A theory of emotion and consciousness, and its application to understanding the neural basis of emotion," in M. Gazzaniga (ed.), *The Cognitive Neurosciences*, Cambridge, Mass.: M.I.T. Press, pp. 1091–1107.

Romilly, de J. (1996), *Alcibiade*, Paris: Editions de Fallois.

Romm, S. (1995), "Layoffs: Principles and practices," in J. Elster (ed.), *Local Justice in America*, New York: Russell Sage, pp. 153–226.

Rorty, A. (1996), "Structuring rhetoric," in A. O. Rorty (ed.), *Essays on Aristotle's Rhetoric*, Berkeley and Los Angeles: University of California Press, pp. 1–33.

Rosen, M. (1996), *On Voluntary Servitude*, Cambridge, Mass.: Harvard University Press.

Roth, A. (1995), "Bargaining experiments," in J. H. Kagel and A. E. Roth (eds.), *Handbook of Experimental Economics*, Princeton University Press, pp. 253–348.

Rougemont, D. de (1983), *Love in the Western World*, New York: Schocken Books.

Rozin, P., Haidt, J., and McCauley, C. (1993), "Disgust," in M. Lewis and J. M. Haviland (eds.), *Handbook of Emotions*, New York: The Guilford Press, pp. 575–94.

Russell, J. A. (1980), "A circumplex model of affect," *Journal of Personality and Social Psychology* 39, 1161–1178.

Ryle, G. (1971), "Jane Austen and the moralists," in S. P. Rosenbaum (ed.), *English Literature and British Philosophy*, Chicago: University of Chicago Press, pp. 168–84.

Saarni, C., and Lewis, M. (1993), "Deceit and illusion in human affairs," in M. Lewis and C. Saarni (eds.), *Lying and Deception in Everyday Life*, New York: The Guilford Press, pp. 1–29.

Sabini, J., and Silver, M. (1987), "Emotions, responsibility, and character," in F. Schoeman (ed.), *Responsibility, Character, and the Emotions*, Cambridge University Press, pp. 165–75.

Sackeim, H. A., and Gur, R. C. (1997), "Flavors of self-deception" [comment on Mele (1997)], *Behavioral and Brain Research* 20, 125–26.

Saint-Simon, C. H. de (1953–1961), *Mémoires*, vols. I–VII, Paris: Gallimard (Bibliothèque de la Pléaide).

Salovey, P., and Rodin, J. (1984), "Some antecedents and consequences of social-comparison jealousy," *Journal of Personality and Social Psychology* 50, 1100–1112.

Sankowski, E. (1977), "Responsibility of persons for their emotions," *Canadian Journal of Philosophy* 7, 829–40.

Sartre, J.-P. (1936), *Esquisse d'une théorie des émotions*, Paris: Hermann.

Sartre, J.-P. (1943), *L'être et le néant*, Paris: Gallimard.

Sass, H. (1983), "Affektdelike," *Nervenarzt* 54, 557–72.

Saulnier, V.-L. (1950), "Proverbe et paradoxe du XV\ufffd au XVI\ufffd siècle," in H. Bédarida (ed.), *Pensée humaniste et tradition chrétienne*, Paris: Boivin, pp. 87–104.

Schachter, S., and Singer, J. (1962), "Cognitive, social and physio-logical determinants of emotional state," *Psychological Review* 63, 379–99.

Schafer, R. (1976), *A New Language for Psychoanalysis*, New Haven, Conn.: Yale University Press.

Schalin, L. (1979), "On the problem of envy," *Scandinavian Psychoanalytical Review* 2, 133–58.

Scheler, M. (1972), *Ressentiment*, New York: Schocken Books.

Schelling, T. C. (1960), *The Strategy of Conflict*, Cambridge, Mass.: Harvard University Press.

References

Schlicht, E. (1985), "The emotive and cognitive view of justice," unpublished manuscript, Institute for Advanced Studies, Princeton, N.J.

Schoeck, H. (1987), *Envy*, Indianapolis: Liberty Press.

Schwartz, N., and Strack, F. (in press), "Reports of subjective well-being: Judgmental processes and their methodological implications," in D. Kahneman, E. Diener, and N. Schwartz (eds.), *Understanding Quality of Life: Scientific Perspectives on Enjoyment and Suffering*.

Scott, R. (1972), "Avarice, altruism and second party preferences," *Quarterly Journal of Economics* 86, 1–18.

Sellier, P. (ed.) (1991), *Pascal: Pensées*, Paris: Bordas.

Sen, A. (1993), "Capability and well-being," in M. Nussbaum and A. Sen (eds.), *The Quality of Life*, Oxford University Press, pp. 30–53.

Serck-Hanssen, J. (1972), "Subsidiering av kapital i utbyggingsområdene" ("Capital subsidies in development areas"), *Statsøkonomisk Tidsskrift* 86, 140–66.

Servan-Schreiber, D., and Perlstein, W. M. (1997), "Selective limbic activation and its relevance to emotional disorders," unpublished manuscript, University of Pittsburgh School of Medicine.

Shattuck, R. (1996), *Forbidden Knowledge*, New York: St. Martin's Press.

Simmel, G. (1908), *Soziologie*, Berlin: Dunker und Humblot.

Simon, H. (1954), "A behavioral theory of rational choice," *Quarterly Journal of Economics* 69, 99–118.

Simpson, G. E. (1941), "Haiti's social structure," *American Sociological Review* 6, 640–49.

Sinclair, R. K. (1988), *Democracy and Participation in Athens*, Cambridge University Press.

Smedslund, J. (1992), Review of Frijda (1986), *Cognition and Emotion* 6, 435–56.

Smedslund (1993), "How shall the concept of anger be defined?" *Theory and Psychology* 3, 5–33.

Sniderman, P., Brody, R., and Tetlock, P. E. (1991), *Political Psychology*, Cambridge University Press.

Sobel, J. (1981), "Distortion of utilities and the bargaining problem," *Econometrica* 49, 597–617.

Soble, A. (1990), *The Structure of Love*, New Haven, Conn.: Yale University Press.

Solomon, R. C. (1973), "Emotions and choice," *Review of Metaphysics* 27, 20–41.

Solomon, R. C. (1980), "Emotions and choice," in A. Rorty (ed.), *Explaining the Emotions*, Berkeley and Los Angeles: University of California Press, pp. 251–82.

Solomon, R. C. (1993), *The Passions*, Indianapolis: Hackett.

Solomon, R. L. (1980a), "The opponent-process theory of acquired motivation," *American Psychologist* 35, 691–712.

435

Solomon, R. L. (1980b), "Recent experiments testing an opponent-process theory of acquired motivation," *Acta Neurobiologiae Experimentalis (Warszawa)* 40, 271–89.

Solomon, R. L., and Corbit, J. D. (1974), "An opponent-process theory of motivation," *Psychological Review* 81, 119–45.

Sousa, R. de (1987), *The Rationality of Emotion*, Cambridge, Mass.: The M.I.T. Press.

Spacks, P. M. (1995), *Boredom*, Chicago: University of Chicago Press.

Spence, M. (1973), *Market Signaling*, Cambridge, Mass.: Harvard University Press.

Starobinski, J. (1961), "Stendhal pseudonyme," in *L'Oeil Vivant*, Paris: Gallimard, pp. 189–240.

Stendhal (1952), *Romans et Nouvelles*, vol. 1, in de la Pléiade (ed.), Paris: Gallimard.

Stendhal (1980), *De l'amour*, Del Litto, V. (ed.), Paris: Gallimard.

Striker, G. (1996), "Emotions in context: Aristotle's treatment of the passions in the *Rhetoric* and his moral psychology," in A. O. Rorty (ed.), *Essays on Aristotle's Rhetoric*, Berkeley and Los Angeles: University of California Press, pp. 286–302.

Sugden, R. (1984), "Reciprocity: The supply of public goods through voluntary contributions," *Economic Journal* 94, 772–87.

Suppes, P. (1970), *A Probabilistic Theory of Causality*, Amsterdam: North Holland.

Suppes, P., and Warren, H. (1982), "On the generation and classification of defence mechanisms," in R. Wollheim and J. Hopkins (eds.), *Philosophical Essays on Freud*, Cambridge University Press, pp. 163–79.

Sussangkarn, C., and Goldman S. (1983), "Dealing with envy," *Journal of Public Economics* 22, 103–12.

Swaan, A. de (1989), "Jealousy as a class phenomenon: The petite bourgeoisie and social security," *International Sociology* 4, 259–71.

Swenson, P. (1988), *Fair Shares*. Ithaca, N.Y.: Cornell University Press.

Tamm, D. (1984), *Retsopgøret efter besættelsen*, Copenhagen: Jurist-og Økonomforbundets Forlag.

Tangney, J. P. (1990), "Assessing individual differences in proneness to shame and guilt: Development of the self-conscious affect and attribution inventory," *Journal of Personality and Social Psychology* 59, 102–11.

Tangney, J. T., and Fischer, K. W. (eds.) (1995), *Self-Conscious Emotions*, New York: Guilford Press.

Taylor, C. (1971), "Interpretation and the science of man," *Review of Metaphysics* 3, 25–51.

Taylor, G. (1985), *Pride, Shame and Guilt*, Oxford University Press.

Telushkin, J. (1992), *Jewish Humor*, New York: Morrow.

Tennov, D. (1979), *Love and Limerence*, New York: Stein and Day.

Tesser, A. (1991), "Emotion in social comparison processes," in J. Suls and T. A. Wills (eds.), *Social Comparison*, Hillsdale, N.J.: Lawrence Erlbaum 1991, pp. 115–45.

Tesser, A., and Achee, J. (1994), "Aggression, love, conformity, and other social psychological catastrophes," in R. R. Vallacher and A. Nowak (eds.), *Dynamical Systems in Social Psychology*, New York: Academic Press, pp. 96–109.

Thaler, R. (1980), "Towards a positive theory of consumer choice," *Journal of Economic Behavior and Organization* 1, 39–60.

Thaler, R., and Johnson, E. (1990), "Gambling with the house money and trying to break even," cited after R. Thaler, *Quasi-Rational Economics*, New York: Russell Sage 1991, pp. 48–73.

Thaler, R., Kahneman, D., and Knetsch, J. (1992), "The endowment effect, loss aversion, and status quo bias," in R. Thaler, *The Winner's Curse*, New York: The Free Press, pp. 63–78.

Thompson, E. P. (1968), *The Making of the English Working Class*, Harmondsworth, U.K.: Penguin.

Thweatt, V. (1980), *La Rochefoucauld and the Seventeenth-Century Concept of the Self*, Geneva: Librairie Droz.

Titelman, G. Y. (1996), *Random House Dictionary of Popular Proverbs and Sayings*, New York: Random House.

Tocqueville, A. de (1836), "Political and social conditions of France," *The London and Westminster Review*, vols. III and XXV, 137–69.

Tocqueville, A. de (1955), *The Old Regime and the French Revolution*, New York: Anchor Books.

Tocqueville, A. de (1969), *Democracy in America*, New York: Anchor Books.

Tocqueville, A. de (1986), *"The European Revolution" and Correspondence with Gobineau*, Cloucester, Mass.: Peter Smith.

Tocqueville, A. de (1990), *Recollections: The French Revolution of 1848*, New Brunswick, N.J.: Transaction Books.

Tocqueville A. de (1998), *The old Regime and the French Revolution*, University of Chicago Press.

Todd, S. C. (1993), *The Shape of Athenian Law*, Oxford University Press.

Tomkins, S. (1992), *Affect, Imagery and Consciousness*, vols. I–IV, New York: Springer.

Truchet, J., ed. (1992): *La Rochefoucauld: Maximes*, Paris: Bordas.

Turley, K. J., Sanna, L. J., and Reiter, R. L. (1995), "Counterfactual thinking and perceptions of rape," *Basic and Applied Social Psychology* 17, 285–303.

Tversky, A., and Griffin, D. (1991), "Endowment and contrast in judgments of well-being," in R. Zeckhauser (ed.), *Strategy and Choice*, Cambridge, Mass.: M.I.T. Press, pp. 297–318.

Tversky, A., and Kahneman, D. (1974), "Judgment under uncertainty," *Science* 185, 1124–30.

437

References

Tversky, A., and Kahneman, D. (1981), "The framing of decisions and the psychology of choice," *Science* 211, 453–58.

Tversky, A., and Shafir, E. (1992), "The disjunction effect in choice under uncertainty," *Psychological Science* 3, 305–309.

Vaillant, G. (1992), *Ego Mechanisms of Defense*, Washington D.C.: American Psychiatric Association Press.

Vaillant, G. (1993), *The Wisdom of the Ego*, Cambridge, Mass.: Harvard University Press.

Vaillant, G. (1995), *The Natural History of Alcoholism Revisited*, Cambridge, Mass.: Harvard University Press.

Varian, H. (1974), "Equity, envy and efficiency," *Journal of Economic Theory* 9, 63–91.

Vasquez, C. (1987), "Judgment of contingency: Cognitive biases in depressed and nondepressed subjects," *Journal of Personality and Social Psychology* 52, 419–31.

Vauvenargues (1970), *Oeuvres Posthumes et Inédits*, Geneva: Slatkin Reprints (photographic reprint of 1857 edition).

Veblen, T. (1965), *The Theory of the Leisure Class*, New York: Augustus Kelley.

Veyne, P. (1971), *Comment on écrit l'histoire*, Paris: Seuil.

Veyne, P. (1976), *Le pain et le cirque*, Paris: Seuil.

Vigée, C. (1960), "*La Princesse de Clèves* et la tradition du refus," *Critique* 159–60, 723–54.

Vincentcassy, M. (1980), "L'envie au moyen âge," *Annales: Economies, Sociétés, Civilisations* 35, 253–71.

Waal, F. de (1996), *Good Natured*, Cambridge, Mass.: Harvard University Press.

Wagenaar, W. A. (1988), *Paradoxes of Gambling Behaviour*, Hove and London: Lawrence Erlbaum.

Walcot, P. (1978), *Envy and the Greeks*, Warminster: Aris and Phillips.

Walton, K. (1990), *Mimesis as Make-Believe*, Cambridge, Mass.: Harvard University Press.

Weber, M. (1968), *Economy and Society*, New York: Bedminster Press.

Wenzel, S. (1967), *The Sin of Sloth: Acedia in Medieval Thought and Literature*, Chapel Hill, N.C.: University of North Carolina Press.

White, M. (1987), *Philosophy, The Federalist, and the Constitution*, New York: Oxford University Press.

Whiting, B. J., et al. (1939), "The study of proverbs," *Modern Language Forum* 24, 57–83.

Wicklund, R. A., and Brehm, J. (1976), *Perspectives on Cognitive Dissonance*, Hillsbaum, N.J.: Erlbaum.

Wierzbicka, A. (1992), *Semantics, Culture, and Cognition*, Oxford University Press.

Wilensky, H. (1960), "Work, careers, and social integration," *International Social Science Journal* 12, 543–60.

References

Williams, B. A. O. (1973), *Problems of the Self*, Cambridge University Press.

Williams, B. A. O. (1981), *Moral Luck*, Cambridge University Press.

Williams, B. A. O. (1993), *Shame and Necessity*, Berkeley: University of California Press.

Wills, T. A. (1981), "Downward comparison principles in social psychology," *Psychological Bulletin* 90, 245–71.

Wilson, S. (1988), *Feuding, Conflict, and Banditry in Nineteenth-Century Corsica*, Cambridge University Press.

Winter, S. (1964), "Economic 'natural selection' and the theory of the firm," *Yale Economic Essays* 4, 225–72.

Wise, R., and Bozarth, M. (1987), "A psychomotor stimulant theory of addiction," *Psychological Review* 94, 469–92.

Xinxin, Z., and Ye, S. (1987), *Chinese Lives*, New York: Pantheon.

Yanal, R. J. (1994), "The paradox of emotion and fiction," *Pacific Philosophical Quarterly* 75, 54–75.

Zajac, E. (1995), *The Political Economy of Fairness*, Cambridge, Mass.: M.I.T. Press.

Index

Abramson, Lyn, 300
Achee, John, 42–43
action tendencies, 247, 267 n.73, 280,
     281–83, 286; *see also* equilibrium,
     emotional
   Aristotle on, 60
   inhibition of, 282
adaptive preferences, *see* preferences
addiction, 9, 40, 84, 239 n.2, 241 n.4, 249,
     257 n.43
   to reason, 290
   to violence, 210
admiration, 144, 163, 313
affirmative action, 353–54, 378, 392–93,
     396, 399–400
aggregation, 44–47
aggression, 25, 153; *see also* anger
AIDS, 354
Ailly, Abbé d', 91
Alcibiades, 162, 164, 188–89, 207, 215
Alloy, Lauren, 300
Allport, Gordon, 353
altruism, 166, 302, 322–24
amour-propre, 84 n.74, 85–95, 130, 204,
     334, 353, 398, 417
analogy, 239–40
anger, 144, 250, 251, 265, 305, 309,
     389, 404
   action tendency of, 282
   cognitive antecedents of, 250–51
   Aristotle on, 54, 58, 62–64, 104
   differs from hate, 56, 64–68
   irrational, 103–4, 250, 313–14, 353, 357
   physiological effects of, 276, 407;
     see also hypertension
anti-conformism, *see* preferences
anti-semitism, 38, 67–68, 74, 350–51, 392
anxiety, 272, 309

appraisal theory, 245, 269
approbativeness, 85, 88, 90
Aquinas, St. Thomas of, 168, 281
Aristotle, 40, 50, 52–75, 90 n.89, 134, 143,
     146, 160, 184, 192, 305, 306, 307,
     319–20, 387–88, 394
   The Rhetoric, 53–55
arousal, 30, 117, 247, 273–76, 315, 365
   Aristotle on, 55
Assemblée Constituante of 1789 (Paris),
     343, 383, 400
audience 63, 144–45, 150, 160 n.63, 204,
     227, 252, 370–71, 388–90
   inner, 93–94, 98
Austen, Jane, 121–24
   Emma, 124, 163 n.74, 259
   Mansfield Park, 122–23
   Northanger Abbey, 126 n.146
   Persuasion, 122, 245, 279
   Pride and Prejudice, 121, 325
   Sense and Sensibility, 355–56

Babcock, Linda, 346–47, 348
Bacon, Francis, 298
balance, *see* equilibrium
Balzac, Honoré de, 15, 108
Balzac, Guez de, 92
Banfield, Edward, 398–99
Barry, Brian, 337
Becker, Gary 5, 37, 301, 321–28
   on altruism, 322–24
   on envy, 322–24
   on guilt, 301, 324–25
   on love, 305, 325–27
Bedford, Gunning, 381–82,
beliefs, 336
   about emotions, 100–101, 255,
     260–62

441